KONTAKIA OF ROMANOS, BYZANTINE MELODIST

I: ON THE PERSON OF CHRIST

"The Blessed Virgin of the Veil," after a sixteenth-century icon from Novgorod. In the foreground, standing in the ambo, is St. Romanos the Melodist, who is singing the Christmas Kontakion in honor of the Mother of God.

KONTAKIA OF ROMANOS,

BYZANTINE MELODIST

I: ON THE PERSON OF CHRIST

TRANSLATED AND ANNOTATED BY
MARJORIE CARPENTER

UNIVERSITY OF MISSOURI PRESS
COLUMBIA

STANDARD BOOK NUMBER 8262–0073–7

LIBRARY OF CONGRESS CARD NUMBER 73–105267

UNIVERSITY OF MISSOURI PRESS, COLUMBIA 65201

PRINTED AND BOUND IN THE UNITED STATES OF AMERICA

COPYRIGHT © 1970 BY THE CURATORS OF THE UNIVERSITY OF MISSOURI

Photograph of frieze in Monastery Pantokrator, of which the
Kredel woodcut "Romanos the Hymn writer" is an adaptation,
has been used by permission of Hannibal Greece.

Frontispiece is reprinted from Philip Sherrard, *Constantinople:
Iconography of a Sacred City* (1965), by permission of the
publisher, Oxford University Press.

TO

PROFESSOR GEORGE LA PIANA

AND

PROFESSOR ALFRED BELLINGER

ACKNOWLEDGMENTS

To Professor George La Piana of Harvard University I owe a great debt for his direction of my first research in this field; without his knowledge of the Byzantine ritual and church history, I should have been completely lost. To Harvard University and Radcliffe College, who made available to me many rare books and a fellowship, I am grateful. Also, I wish to thank Dr. Alfred Bellinger who, in my year of study at Athens and throughout those following, encouraged my pursuit of this subject. All who have derived pleasure from Romanos' lyrics owe a debt to Trypanis and Maas for their new edition of his works.

More recently, I am indebted to Stephens College for making available the intelligent secretarial services of Mrs. Marilyn Olson, Mrs. Gladys Bradsher, and Miss Linda Hickerson in preparing this manuscript. They provided indispensable help in this exacting work, and I am happy to acknowledge their share in producing it.

FOREWORD

There are various kinds of appeal and the satisfaction of widely diversified interests in the kontakia of Romanos. The selective reader will, perhaps, not wish to pursue more than one or two.

For the student of medieval drama, the section of the Introduction that deals with that subject and the following hymns will be especially attractive:

O. 1   Nativity I (Mary and the Magi)
O. 2   Nativity II (Adam and Eve and the Nativity)
O. 3   The Massacre of the Innocents
        (The Flight into Egypt)
O. 5   The Baptism of Christ
O. 10 The Sinful Woman
O. 14 Lazarus I
O. 15 Lazarus II
O. 18 Peter's Denial
O. 19 Mary at the Cross
O. 22 The Victory of the Cross
O. 24 Resurrection I
O. 27 Resurrection IV

For one interested in theology, the following kontakia, along with the brief summary of the heresies and Romanos' beliefs as they are discussed in the Introduction, will provide some insight into the dogma of the sixth century.

O. 1   Nativity I (Mary and the Magi)
O. 4   The Presentation in the Temple
O. 6   The Epiphany

For a comparison with the sermons of the day, see the summary on p. xviii of the Introduction, where special hymns and authors of homily most closely connected with his poems are listed.

To gain some idea of the wealth of figurative language and allusions woven into the poetic sermons of Romanos, the best examples are Nativity I, Judas, Mary at the Cross, The Mission of the Apostles.

For the student of Greek, all the kontakia have value. More studies need to be made of the language and even of the meter of the poet who, more than any other, provides evidence of the state of the Greek language in the sixth century. If the reader is acquainted with the Arabic language, he will recognize the value and need for research on Ephrem and the Greek translations of Ephrem.

For the general reader, it is possible, through reading these verses, to gain a new respect for the poetic works of Romanos, the greatest of the Byzantine melodists. It is for these reasons that I have undertaken a translation into English of these beautiful Greek lyrics, although I am well aware of the inevitable inadequacies.

M.C.

COLUMBIA, MISSOURI
NOVEMBER, 1969

CONTENTS

INTRODUCTION

Although Romanos has been known to scholars of Greek literature and to some church dignitaries for centuries as the greatest of the Byzantine melodists and some have even called him the greatest of the Christian poets, few other readers have heard of him. More regrettably, they have had no opportunity to enjoy the works that support his reputation. Several reasons account for this lack. Byzantine literature has been neglected—perhaps scorned—because of the long compendia and overly contrived verbosity that characterized the works of the later centuries of the period. However, in the kontakia of Romanos and his sixth-century contemporaries, as Trypanis says, is a successful combination of "the solemnity and dignity of the sermon with the delicacy and liveliness of lyric and dramatic poetry." In his judgment, "their poetry has not been matched in subsequent centuries, and the kontakion remains the only great original achievement of Byzantine literature."[1] In spite of their excellence, most of the works of Romanos were not available in a definitive text until recently.[2] Perhaps one explanation lies in the fact that most scholars of Greek have scorned any literature later than Aristotle, while students of the Middle Ages rarely know Greek. It is to be hoped that the charm of Romanos' lyrics will establish him in his rightful place.

LIFE OF ROMANOS

We can say with assurance that Romanos belongs to the early sixth century. Internal evidence points to the fact that he was alive during the Nike

1. See Introduction, xiv, to the Oxford text.
2. The collation of manuscripts has been unusually difficult because four hundred years separated the dates of Romanos' life and those of the earliest manuscripts available. Meanwhile, the iconoclasts had destroyed many works and the language had undergone changes. The forms of the early koine were altered by some scribes in an effort to restore classical forms. At Patmos and Athos, collections of kontakia existed (kontakaria), and they contain many of the hymns of Romanos. In learned journals, Karl Krumbacher edited some of the poems, and re-edited some which Christ had included in his *Anthologia Graeca* or which Pitra had included in *Analecta Sacra* (see Basic Bibliography). Krumbacher's student Paul Maas carried on Krumbacher's investigations, and in 1963 a student of Paul Maas edited the poems that the work of the two German scholars made available to him. This Maas-Trypanis edition was published in Oxford by the Clarendon Press in 1963. Called *Romanos, Cantica Genuina*, it is the basis for the subsequent translations. It will be referred to as the Oxford Edition, or just as O. Previously, the kontakia Krumbacher had considered genuine were listed and given numbers in "Die Acrostichis der griechischen Kirchenpoesie," *Sitzungsberichte der philos.-philol. und der histor. Klasse der K. Bayer. Akad. d. Wiss.*, 1903, 551 ff. Since articles written before 1963 refer to this numbering, it will be stated also and referred to as K. Other editions of some of the kontakia will be listed in the bibliography and in the brief introduction to each kontakion.

revolution and that he saw the destruction of Hagia Sophia and its rebuilding.[3] Actually, Romanos reveals little about himself. According to the *Synaxaria*, he was born in Emesa not far from Beirut[4] and he was deacon in the Church of the Resurrection there. He came to Constantinople in the reign of Anastasius I and, probably, occupied a favored position at court.[5] He evidently flourished between A.D. 536 and 556. It seems that he was by birth a Jew but was baptized into Christianity.[6] His Christology, very closely associated with the edicts of Justinian, reflects the theological struggles against the Monophysites.[7]

3. Paul Maas documents these facts and establishes dates for several individual kontakia (*Chron.* 9). In the kontakion, On Earthquakes and Fires (O. 54, K. 62), Strophes 14–18 mention the punishment of the wicked and the rebuilding of the church. Strophe 16, line 6, may refer to the Nike revolution in the play on words ($\dot{\epsilon}\nu\dot{\iota}\kappa\alpha$); Strophe 20 explicitly mentions both Hagia Sophia and Hagia Eirene; Strophe 24 indicates that the new church is not yet ready for the celebration of the liturgy; the first dedication was in 537. The kontakion On the Presentation in the Temple (O. 4, K. 6) suggests that Romanos may have written it at the time of the introduction of the feast of the Hypapante into Constantinople in 542. Romanos mentions the earthquake that caused the seas to recede, in the poem, Ten Virgins II (O. 48, K. 62), stanza 3. The two earthquakes on July 9, 552, and August 15, 555, both occurred within his lifetime. Since Theodora died in 548, we can assume that he wrote the hymn "The Forty Martyrs II" (O. 58, K. 49) after her death, since he refers to only one ruler ($\check{\alpha}\nu\alpha\kappa\tau\iota$, Strophe 18), and he was too tactful to have left her out, had she been alive. The hymn on baptism (O. 53, K. 46) may have followed Justinian's decree, as Maas suggests, but this is not a necessary conclusion. Romanos includes references to the ritual of baptism in other kontakia. In the hymn on the Sinful Woman, #10, Strophe 5, for example, the verb $\dot{\epsilon}\mu\phi\dot{\upsilon}\omega$ reflects the baptismal liturgy, and the same kind of reference is made in Strophes 4, 10, and 15 of #5, the Epiphany kontakion. Other places in this hymn obviously refer to the rite of baptism. Also in the Oxford edition, Introduction, xv, note 5, is other evidence that Romanos must have lived in the sixth century and before Andrew of Crete (A.D. 660–740).

4. The date set aside in the *Menaion* for honoring Romanos is October 1. Petrides published an unedited office of Romanos (*B.Z.* 11 [1902], 35 ff.). This contains a canon in his honor and has the acrostic ʿΡωμανοῦ ὕμνῶ τῆς μελωδίας λύραν. It contains an invocation to Romanos to inspire others, it sings his praises, and it gives a history of Romanos, following the synaxarion. It refers to him as ἱερο κῆρυξ, and it repeats the legend of his vision.

5. Romanos usually refers to himself in the acrostic as "the humble Romanos." He was so universally acclaimed that it is hard to believe that he was not known to the rulers ($\beta\alpha\sigma\iota\lambda\epsilon\hat{\upsilon}\sigma\iota\nu$ $\dot{\epsilon}\gamma\nu\dot{\omega}\rho\iota\sigma\epsilon$). See *B.Z.* 15 (1906), 31. He may have held an official position at court, but that fact has not been established. (See Trypanis, Introduction to the Oxford edition, xvii, note 1.) Romanos admits his own need for salvation and says that he still leads a worldly life. Kontakion #10, Strophes 1 and 18.

However, he was sainted by the Greek Orthodox Church, and an icon from the sixteenth century presents him in the pulpit. Around his neck is a scroll. Did it contain words from his famous Nativity kontakion (No. 1)? Mrs. Topping refers to this icon. It is mentioned by Philip Sherrard, *Constantinople, Iconography of a Sacred City* (London, 1965), 81. The article by Eva Catafygiotu Topping, "St. Romanos: Ikon of a Poet," *Gr. Orth. Theol. Rev.*, 1966, 94–95, contains an excellent analysis of the famous Christmas kontakion. Since I am discussing the sixth-century melodist and his *literary* merits, I have not used the title "saint." *See frontispiece.*

6. Maas, in *Chron.* 30, calls attention to the second and third strophes of a hymn on Romanos by Alexander Eumorphopulos, in which the phrase "from the Hebrew race" ($\Gamma\dot{\epsilon}\nu$ος ἐξ ʿΕβραίων) was used. Several comments have been made about his use of Jewish forms of proper names and even the Semitisms. Trypanis mentions some of them. (Oxford text, Introduction, xvi, note 1.)

7. A thesis recently prepared under the direction of Trypanis at Oxford documents this characteristic in detail: R. J. Schork, "The Biblical and Patristic Sources of Christological Kontakia of Romanos the Melodist," 1957. In connection with each of my translations I shall make some allusion to theology.

THE KONTAKION

Poetic Form: English literature contains no equivalent of the kontakion. It is a poetic sermon that was sung, and many contain highly dramatic features, with dialogue strophe to strophe. The verse structure is very complicated and highly sophisticated. Usually there are about twenty-four strophes united by an acrostic. They are so structured that each strophe is like the first in the number of lines and in the number of syllables in corresponding lines. Word accent is basic; it is determined by the melody, which is announced at the beginning, along with the ēchos (ἦχος) or scheme set for the singing. A short stanza (sometimes more than one), called a koukoulion, precedes the series of strophes. The koukoulion is metrically independent of the other strophes, is not included in the acrostic, but has the same refrain. Its function is to announce the theme or the feast day. Usually the final strophe is a closing prayer.

  Actually, Romanos did not refer to his compositions as kontakia. His writings refer to "poem" (ποίημα), "song" (ἔπος), "praise" (αἰνός), "ode" (ᾠδή), "hymn" (ὕμνος), and "psalm" (ψαλμός).[8] The term *kontakion*[9] came into use in the ninth century, when the kontakion was revived after the iconoclastic controversy and became a part of the later kanon. Later, the kontakion was shortened, and it lost its homiletic character and its dialogue. From the fifth to the seventh century the genre developed into a metrical sermon, and it is in this form that Romanos brought it to perfection. The kontakia of this period were later assembled in the monasteries into kontakaria, but by that time many poems had been lost.

Music: No one knows exactly how the kontakion was sung. Until further research reveals this detail, the closest present-day scholars can come to the manner of its delivery is to suggest that it may have resembled the recitative of an oratorio. This suggestion is tentative, since one must be wary of too close an analogy with Western music for what was certainly Oriental. It may be that an individual singer, probably a priest, presented the hymn after reading the Gospels, and then double choirs chanted the refrains or, when dialogue was involved, the alternate strophes. It is known that double choirs sang the Christmas kontakion (Nativity I) every year in the palace of the emperor.

  In any case, it is important to remember that Romanos was known as a *melodist.* Interesting though the analysis of his poems as literature may be, it is probably true that one needs to hear the kontakion sung in order to appreciate its qualities fully. The melody used may be original, and in that case it is called an *idiomelon.* Otherwise, the indication πρὸς το: precedes the first strophe. It is as though the words of a hymn were headed by the direction, "Sing this to the tune of 'Rock of Ages.'" The ἦχος is not exactly a mode, although the modal

8. In the 59 genuine kontakia in the Oxford edition, there are eight called "poem"; 12 contain the word "praise" in the acrostic; 8 use "song" or "word"; 7 use "hymn"; 8 use "psalm"; 5 say "ode." Two are in the nature of prayers (δέησις and προσευχή).

9. The word probably is derived from κοντός, the shaft on which the parchment of a scroll was stretched.

indications might suggest this interpretation.[10] The authorities on Byzantine music warn present-day musicologists to think, not of scales, but of groups of melodies of a certain type built on a number of basic formulae, which characterize the ēchos.[11]

Place in the Liturgy and Source of Subjects: In 528 Justinian decreed that there be three main canonical offices: Matins (Μεσονύκτικον), Lauds ("Ορθρος), and Vespers ("Εσπερινος).[12] Kontakia for special feast days were composed for the office of the day and not the Mass. The reading of the Gospels was to be followed by a sermon and then a kontakion, or the metrical sermon might be sung in place of the homily. Romanos clearly used biblical sources for most of the kontakia in the Oxford edition. Of the fifty-nine genuine kontakia that have survived, thirty-four are on the person of Christ, and these are the ones translated for this collection. In addition, there are five drawn from other incidents in the New Testament, seven based on Old Testament characters, ten on miscellaneous subjects, and three about martyrs and saints.[13] In the last category, there are several of dubious authenticity. Trypanis plans to publish them later.

Origin of the Kontakion: In considering the origin of the kontakion as it appears in Romanos' works, account must be taken of rhythmic verse as contrasted to classical poetry, which depended on quantitative meter. Also, the unusual combination of sermon and song with elements of the dramatic should be considered. Although Romanos is credited with being the creator of the literary form, facts do not point to a sudden outpouring of this complicated verse structure.[14] According to the legend of the hagiographer,

10. There are four authentic and four plagal modes, but scholars do not agree on their equivalents in Western scales. Wellesz, *Byz. Mus.* (1961), 300.

11. Wellesz, *Byzantine Music and Hymnography* (Oxford, 1961), 349. It is not within the scope of this volume to discuss the music in detail, although Wellesz is undoubtedly right when he says that Romanos was known as a melodist, and his poems should be heard so that we realize that the stress accents fall on the highest points of the melodic curve. Reviews of the latest edition, which is rightly called the summation of all his work, mention some reservations. R. Schlötterer, *B.Z.*, 58 (1965), 379, feels that Wellesz is too inclined to consider the singer's role as resembling that of a present-day performer of a song rather than placing the music in the setting of a liturgical work. He feels that the relation of music of the troparion, kontakion, and kanon is perhaps beyond the musicologist. Kenneth Levy, reviewing the book in *Speculum* (1962), 467, feels that the material studied is too restricted. However, there is no question but that Wellesz' book is the standard reference for Byzantine music. Wellesz believes that the Byzantine chant must have been as diatonic as that of the Latin Church.

12. *Codex Justin.*

13. Other poets of the sixth century are: Dometios, who wrote a kontakion on "John the Baptist," Kyriakos, whose poem on Lazarus is compared with that of Romanos (O. 14, K. 70), and Anastasios. Beck lists others: H. G. Beck, *Kirche und theologische Literatur im byzantinischen Reich*, 429. A list of hymnographers from the fifth to the fifteenth centuries is given by Wellesz, *Byz. Mus.* (1961), 442–44.

14. Germanus, in writing the life of Romanos, credits him with introduction of the kontakion. Wellesz quotes, *Byz. Mus.* (1961), 182:

> Πρώτη καλῶν ἀπαρχὴ
> ὤφθης, σωτηρίας ἀφορμή,
> 'Ρωμανὲ πατὲρ ἡμῶν·
> ἀγγελικὴν γὰρ ὑμνῳδίαν συστησάμενος,
> θεοπρεπῶς ἐπεδείξω τὴν πολιτείαν σου.

Romanos remained in the temple of the Holy Virgin in all-night watch of the Blachernae. There he received the gift of composition of kontakia when there appeared to him in a dream the likeness of the Holy Virgin who gave him a piece of paper and commanded him to eat it. He thought best to open his mouth and eat the paper. It was the holiday of Christmas eve and straightway arousing from sleep he mounted the pulpit and began to sing Ἡ παρθένος σήμερον. Then, too, he made kontakia of other feasts and also of the official holy days so that the number of his kontakia came to about one thousand.[15]

While this legend proves nothing about the origin of the kontakion form, it does tell us that the "Greatest of the Byzantine Melodists" was considered to be inspired and that he was a prolific writer-composer.

Origin of Rhythmic Verse: Some early Christian poetry did indeed use quantitative classical meter.[16] To explain the shift to an accentual basis for rhythmic poetry, three influences must be evaluated: the tradition of the Hebrew synagogue, the sermons of the day, and some unusual Syrian hymns and homilies.[17]

First, if one tries to trace a continuous line of development of details of worship from *the synagogue* to the Christian Church of the fifth century in a search for the unusual form of the musical poetic sermon called a kontakion, some characteristics—but not all—are explicable. Christians in the apostolic age continued to worship in the temple; they sang psalms and they sang antiphons. They were, then, familiar with the parallel structure of Hebraic verse; they were accustomed to phrases that were rhythmic in their repetition of accents and phrase length.[18] Later, when they added short troparia after the psalms,

---

(Earliest first-fruit of beautiful hymns, thou wast manifested a means of salvation, Romanus our father, composing the angelic hymnody, thou hast shown thy conversation meet for God.)

One questions Wellesz' statement that "the kontakion made its appearance suddenly, without antecedents." He explains later that "antecedents of the kontakion existed in Syriac ecclesiastical poetry" and that Romanos introduced the new form of ecclesiastical poetry into the liturgy of Constantinople (*op. cit.*, 184).

15. Translated from the *Menaion* for October 1, the holy day of Saint Romanos. For a discussion of various texts of the biography, see *Analecta Bollandiana* (1894), 440. See my article in *Speculum*, 7 (January, 1932), 1–22; and see note 2, Introduction to Christmas I in the translations.

16. The "Evening Hymn," the "Ter Sanctus," and the "Lamp-Lighting Hymn" are examples of very early sacred song, which we possess. Methodius, in the fourth century "Hymn to Virginity," used a meter that is more or less classical, although it disregards strict quantitative rules. Norden reminds us that classical prose contained both parallel structure and rhyme: *Antike Kunstprosa, passim.*

17. Many of the early critical discussions of rhythmic verse in early Byzantine poetry are now outdated, but the groundwork was done by such scholars as Pitra, Christ, Krumbacher, Meyer, Grimme, Leclerq, and Norden.

Very important as evidence for early use of verse whose structure depends on accents without reference to quantity is the publication of some anonymous hymns of the fifth and sixth centuries: Maas, *Frühbyzantinische Kirchenpoesie.* Kleine Texte, Bonn (1910).

18. A. Wellesz, *A History of Byzantine Music and Hymnography*, Oxford (1949), 11. After years of research on this subject, Wellesz goes so far as to say, "an uninterrupted liturgical tradition existed from the days of the Synagogue to the Byzantine melodies of the mid seventh century, according to which the reading of the Scriptures was followed by the recitation or chanting of a poetical homily." In the 1961 edition he quotes examples of this order of scripture reading followed by a kontakion (p. 186).

these short verses depended on a heirmos, which set the pattern for the structure of the rest of the song.[19]

Second, if one examines the antitheses and paradoxes found in the *sermons* of the day, or if one extracts small units from the poetic phrases of some homilies, they can be rearranged to resemble in marked degree the sophisticated and elaborate lines in the kontakion.

Furthermore, a study of the sermons is useful in establishing not only rhythmic and forceful antitheses but also in suggesting dramatic fragments buried in the homilies. La Piana was the first to make an exhaustive study revealing this point.[20] In the introductory notes to the following set of translations are numerous references to parallel passages between Romanos and such famous preachers as Basil of Seleucia, Proclus (or Procliana),[21] Chrysostom, Gregory of Nyssa, and Theodotus of Ancyra. Some of the sermons probably postdate Romanos, but it is still instructive to see the interaction between homily and hymn. The following kontakia are especially worthy of examination in this connection:

Nativity I (O. 1, K. 1)
Massacre of the Innocents (O. 3, K. 44)
Presentation in the Temple or Hypapante (O. 4, K. 6)
The Sinful Woman (O. 11, K. 81)
The Man Possessed with Devils (O. 11, K. 81)
Lazarus I (O. 14, K. 70)
Adoration at the Cross (O. 23, K. 64)
Ascension (O. 32, K. 22)

In the Hypapante (O. 4, K. 6) there is evidence that Romanos may have borrowed directly from a letter of Basil the Great.[22]

Third, if one analyzes the *Syrian dramatic homily-hymns*, further possibilities emerge as to one source for various characteristics of the kontakion. The most famous Syrian preacher-poet was Ephrem (d. 373). Many scholars shrink from making any comparisons of the kontakia of Romanos with Ephrem's works because, admittedly, the manuscript tradition for the Syrian is very confused. Conjecture concerning the force of Ephrem's influence is certainly in order, however, since there is obviously an Ephrem tradition, his works were translated into Greek, and Romanos, who came from Syria, must have known

19. Wellesz, *Byz. Mus.* (1961), 179.
20. George La Piana, *Le Rappresentazioni sacre nelle letteratura bizantina* (Grotteferrata, 1912). The conclusions of La Piana are summarized in his article, "The Byzantine Theatre," *Speculum*, 11 (1936), 171–211, and in Brehier's review, *Le Journal des savants*, 40 (1913), 357–61. See also my article, "Romanos and the Mystery Play of the East," *University of Missouri Studies*, XI, 3 (1936). La Piana says, "It cannot be denied that the dialogue part of homilies may have produced gestures" (*op. cit.*, 157).
21. In the hymn on the Presentation (O. 4, K. 6) there are interesting parallel passages to a homily by Proclus. Migne, *P.G.*, 50, 811A, ascribes it to J. Chrysostom (Spur.); B. Marx in a study on the influence of Proclus of Constantinople ascribes it to him (*Procliana*, Münster, 1940), 85–89. Migne and Maas attribute some parallel passages to Basil of Seleucia. *P.G.*, 85, 448A, and *B.Z.*, 19 (1910), 305.
22. E. Bickersteth, "A Source of Romanos' Contakia on the Hypapante," *Actes du VI⁰ congrès international d'études byzantines* (Paris, 1950), 375–81, calls attention to the same interpretation made by Romanos and Basil of Seleucia of Simeon's prophecies. She also quotes Basil's 260th letter, *P.G.*, 32, 965–68.

his works. Further, Ephrem lived in the fourth century, so there was ample time for his famous sermons and hymns to achieve circulation in Constantinople and for them to be known by Romanos there, if he had not known them in Syria.

Three special forms of religious literature developed in Syria;[23] each had characteristics that could have influenced Romanos. The *memra*, like the kontakion, is a poetical homily that was used in the morning office after the priest had read the Gospel; it does not have strophes. The *sougitha* were sometimes written in strophes and attached to homilies; during religious festivals they were sung by choirs and often contained dialogue and an acrostic. *Madrascha* were performed by a chorus. The memra strophes, as Ephrem used them, usually have seven-syllable verses, of which two are bound together, and it is unusual for a sentence to extend through several strophes. The strophes of the madrascha represent the highest development of Ephrem's technique. They show a wide variety of meter, a refrain, an acrostic, and rhyme.

In the sougitha, which developed out of the madrascha, the acrostic begins after a few introductory strophes; twenty-two strophes are allotted to the first speaker—one for each letter of the alphabet—and then an answering strophe, headed by the same letter, is assigned to the second speaker. If we follow Grimme[24] in his conclusions that the kontakion form was borrowed from the Syrian, it must be remembered that it did not descend directly from any one of the three forms; they were combined to influence the typical Byzantine hymn of the fifth to seventh century. The short line repetition, based on an equal number of syllables, gave way to a more varied accentual rhythm; prooimia became part of the composition; and although the exterior division of Syrian strophes may well have passed over into Byzantine literature, it was in an improved form. The refrain, which seemed tagged on as an independent sentence in the Syrian expression, became, in the Byzantine kontakion, related to the content of the strophe in a way that appreciably heightened the poem's effect. The acrostics of Byzantine hymns in the best period are name and title acrostics; the richness of the Greek language made possible an advance in the use of homoioteleuton and assonance in the hands of a poet like Romanos.

Clearly, the Syrian hymns and homilies are related to the Greek homilies, for the same type of biblical allusions and the same sort of references to the Gospels appear in both. Some similarities would necessarily occur, since the purpose of each form was to follow the readings in the liturgy. The method of expanding the stories so that they become dramatic and are clothed in rhythmic phrases is, however, a characteristic that supports a theory of common origin for both Greek and Syrian expressions. The homily attributed to Proclus, "Encomium to the Virgin," contains a soliloquy of Joseph, a dialogue between Mary and Joseph, and a dialogue between Mary and the Christ child.[25] The last of the hymns assigned to

23. Trypanis, in the Introduction to the Oxford text, xii, note 4, gives a brief summary. R. Duval, *La Littérature Syriaque* (Paris, 1907), 1–45, is important.
24. H. Grimme, "Der Strophenbau in den Gedichten Ephraems des Syrers," *Collect. Friburg 20,* ii, Fribourg, 1893.
25. La Piana, *Le Rappr.*, 129–41, gives an analysis of this homily, its codices, and its connection with the apocrypha.

Ephrem (as Lamy edits the works)²⁶ is an Epiphany hymn. It is equally significant as evidence of dramatic form. Maas claims²⁷ that the Syrian influence which produced the kontakion in about A.D. 500 was at work earlier and that metrical homilies, such as the one by Proclus, were written with this inspiration. It is at least conceivable that Ephrem's predecessors Harmonius and Bardesanes²⁸ were responsible for a new literary genre that then grew into Ephrem's sougitha and in turn inspired homily and hymn of the sixth century. Especially important for a consideration of the Syrian influence on Romanos are the following:

> Nativity I (O. 1, K. 1)
> The Second Coming (O. 34, K. 7).

Perhaps the most startling evidence for the influence of Syrian homily is the publication of a homily of Melito, Bishop of Sardis. Since this is a second-century sermon and since it shows rhythmic structure similar to Byzantine song and sermon, the Syrian influence must have begun quite early.²⁹

In brief, there are many explanations of the origin of the kontakion. No sole source explains every characteristic of the form. Some of the seemingly significant linguistic echoes would undoubtedly be inevitable, since they involve phrases that were already in the public domain. Others are too unusual or too close to related poems to be ignored as evidence for the intertwining of many roots from which the kontakion grew.

DRAMA, EAST AND WEST

The kontakia are full of dramatic characteristics. The Syrian sougitha, as noted earlier, were composed in dialogue form; according to La Piana, the homilies contain very short speeches—traces of dialogue. However, La Piana also says that the use of dialogue in these works proves nothing about the existence of a sacred theatre from early days to the sixth century.³⁰

Before pursuing discussion of the liturgical drama, East and West, it is important to clarify what is meant by *drama*. Must incidents be acted out on a

---

Schork calls attention to the parallel passages in the "Christmas Hymn I" with *P.G.*, 65, col. 712, 713c, and with "The Presentation in the Temple" (O. 4, K. 6) and *P.G.*, 85, 448.

B. Marx believes that a number of the pseudo-Chrysostom homilies are by Proclus and Basil. See note 21.

26. Lamy edits, with Latin translation, various hymns and sermons of Ephrem. Many are now considered of dubious authenticity. They are, however, worthy of study for the interaction of Syriac literature and Byzantine kontakia.

Thomas Josephus Lamy, *Sancti Ephraem Syri Hymni et Sermones*, Mechliniae, I, 1882; II, 1886; III, 1889; IV, 1902 (I, xv, "Epiphany"). The "Epiphany" is appropriate for Christmas as well as for Epiphany. As he warns (p. 3), the Epiphany hymns are always directed to the baptism of the faithful; the third, fourth, and thirteenth are especially concerned with the rite of baptism. Vol. II contains several hymns on the Nativity of Christ.

27. P. Maas, *B.Z.*, 15 (1906), 290–91.

28. R. Duval, *La Littérature Syriaque*, 18.

29. Campbell Bonner, *Homily on the Passion by Melito* (London and Philadelphia, 1940).

30. La Piana, *Le Rappr.*, 33: "Dal sin qui detto possiama concludere, che tutte le prove addotte, onde affermare l'esistenza di un teatro liturgico o in altro modo sacro, dai primi tempi sino al sec. VI, non provano nulla."

stage? Must there be gestures to accompany direct speech? To what extent is the liturgy itself a drama to the priest, the singers in choirs, the congregation? Is the procession that celebrated many feast days to be considered a kind of drama?

For years the answers to these questions have been based on the assumptions of Young and Chambers[31] about the nature of drama and the normal way in which literature developed. Hardison expresses another view. He thinks that in the West, by the ninth century, the boundary between religious ritual and drama did not exist. In fact, in the early Middle Ages ritual and representational ceremonies were common, and the special celebration of Easter with the dramatization of the *Quem quaeritis* trope was a transitional phase between the sacred drama developed in the Mass and the miracle and morality plays.[32]

In the East, no evidence remains of a sacred drama performed on the stage,[33] nor is there any indication of the way in which the kontakia were delivered. There is, however, sound reason to believe that the priest chanted the passages with accompanying gestures[34] and that dialogue may well have been assigned to double choirs to increase the effects. It is reasonable to suppose that such processions as the one on Palm Sunday, described as taking place in the fourth century in Jerusalem,[35] had "essential representational elements—symbolic space, stylized

31. E. K. Chambers, *The Mediaeval Stage*, II (Oxford, 1903), 81. Dialogue by itself is not drama. "The notion of drama does not necessarily imply scenery on a regular stage, but it does imply impersonation and a distribution of roles between at least two performers."

Karl Young also emphasizes "impersonization" as essential to drama. Young's theory that literary development must move from simple to complex does not receive universal agreement. A. Williams, in *Speculum* (66), 539, agrees with Hardison, whose book he reviews.

O. B. Hardison, Jr., *Christian Rite and Christian Drama in the Middle Ages* (Johns Hopkins Press, 1965), vii and *passim*.

O. Cargill, *Drama and Liturgy* (Columbia University Press, 1930), *passim*, questions that the tropes really started the dramatic growth which would produce mystery plays.

32. Hardison, *op. cit.*, viii, and 32. Hardison insists that the Mass *was* drama to the communicant of the Western Church.

33. K. N. Sathas, *Le Théatre à Byzance* (Paris, 1931), presents interesting material on church processions and dramatic presentations in modern Greece, all related to the "Christos Paschon," which is assigned to Gregory of Nazianz. However, this work is demonstrably a late drama. Krumbacher, *Byzantinische Litteraturgeschichte* (München, 1897), 746; La Piana, *op. cit.*, 12; Magnin, *Journal des savants* (1849), 22; Paul Maas, *B.Z.*, 32 (1932), 395; La Piana, *Speculum*, 11 (1936), 171–211.

34. La Piana, *Le Rappr.*, 51: "In 580 there was recited in Constantinople a dramatic homily using more than one person." On page 58 La Piana states, "l'omelia narrativa e la culla del drama sacro; nell'omelia di drama si sviluppa gradamente, e, *aiuto dall' azione liturgica*, comincia ad assumere anche qualche *forma esteriore di azione dramatica e via via scende dall' ambone nel coro e nella nave.* Accanto alla omelia dramatica si e intanto sviluppato un genere che ha son essa delle affinita: *il canto sacro*, anch'esso di indole narrativa e dramatica e dipendente a sua volta per la forma dalle mimodie profane." He goes on to say, "Under the influence in part of Syrian literature, and even more under the impulse of natural requirements of dramatic taste, sharpened by the need to offer a Christian spectacle to replace the licentious mimes, dramatic homily and sacred song gradually formed the sacred poetry of Byzantine literature, the *prototype of all subsequent sacred representational Christian literature.*" St. John Chrysostom laments that in liturgical song not only is the rhythm and song modeled on profane music, but that the singers reproduce the movements, the gestures, the imitations of singers in the theatre. Homily Ἔπαινος τῶν ἀπαντησάντων ἐν τῇ ἐκκλησίᾳ, *P.G.*, 56, 106.

35. See the notes to the introduction of Kontakion, Lazarus I (O. 14, K. 70). The fourth-century description can be found in *Itinerarium Egeriae* (*Peregrinatio Aetheriae*), Otto Prinz, ed. (Heidelberg, 1960), 41.

costume and dialogue based on the Gospel."[36] The West later elaborated upon this ceremony, and the procession-loving Byzantines would certainly not have neglected the inherent dramatic possibilities of the event.

In the East, the kontakia and sermons that show germs of drama accompanied, not the Mass, but the special feast days. Christians were especially forbidden to attend the circus or mimes on these days.[37] The special occasions offered ample opportunity for elaborating on religious narratives that were already dramatic. The birth of Christ and the incidents connected with this event, the miracles of Christ, the death of Christ, and the cycle of the liturgical year were available as materials and the kontakia of Romanos demonstrate the extent to which poetic skill and a flair for dramatic folk touches helped to develop the narrative line and the theological point of the feast.

Evidence of the extent to which a member of the Orthodox Church feels the drama inherent in the famous Christmas kontakion can best be presented by reading the recent article by Eva Catafygiotu Topping.[38] She includes the following significant phrases: "The Incarnation, re-enacted annually in the Christmas liturgy of the Orthodox Church, is the *sacred drama* to which St. Romanos summons us. . . . Through his poetry we watch and hear the *triad of actors*, the Divine Child, Mary His human mother, and the Magi. . . . With the dramatic intensity, solemnity and concentration of ancient Greek drama they act out the Incarnation drama, the universal and eternal Christian drama. We the audience join in the affirmation of the refrain."[39] After a thorough and scholarly analysis of the dominant metaphor and symbol that is repeated in "the road" (ὅδος), she goes on to say, "Within this symbol, the *dramatis personae* play their parts. . . . The first person in the sacred drama is God Himself manifest in human form. . . . Christ in the brief eleven lines of the single *speech* which is allotted Him in the *dramatic action* of the poem explains His mission. . . . The remoteness and mystery of God are suggested by the fact that even Christ's single speech is not spoken aloud, but is communicated silently to Mary's mind." The writer then gives eloquent testimony to the moving power of the repeated references to "light" with the various Greek words that suggest the radiance and mystery of the Incarnation. Again we are brought back to drama. "Mary, the Theotokos, is the *second person* in the Incarnation drama. . . . She is the gate who has closed the old breach between God and Man. . . . In her prayer to the Magi, she echoes the petitions of the liturgy, the formula which Romanos, as deacon, must have used. . . .

36. Hardison, *op. cit.*, 112.
37. We know this from an Easter sermon of St. John Chrysostom, *P.G.*, 56, 263. Mioni makes the same point. In discussing the kontakia of Romanos, he says that after the iconoclastic controversy the Church abandoned the sumptuous superstructure of its culture and the singing of Romanos' hymns ceased. Meanwhile the West, imitating the Orientals, initiated the sacred mystery, a beginning to the modern theatre. When it lost its scenic "apparatus," the kontakion lost much of its function, which was to instruct by diverting and thus keeping members away from pagan spectacles.
   E. Mioni, "Osservazioni sulla tradizione manoscritta di Romano il Melode," *Studi Bizantini*, 5 (1939), 509.
38. Eva Catafygiotu Topping, "St. Romanos: Ikon of a Poet," *Greek Orthodox Theological Review*, 12, No. 1 (1966), 92–111.
39. Topping, 97.

The Magi, collectively the *third actor* in the poem's *sacred drama*, represent man, and re-enact his part in the encounter." The author closes her essay with the idea that Romanos, the poet and deacon, describes his liturgical service in Strophe 8, ll. 7–10. In similar fashion, the priest who chanted the hymn must have identified himself and have entered into the entire sacred drama. Basic to our understanding of this concept of drama is the statement: "St. Romanos regards the Incarnation as the genesis of a tremendous cosmic encounter of divinity and humanity. Christ, the God-Man, unites in His person the disparate worlds of heaven and earth, the eternal and the temporal, the infinite and the finite."[40]

This last statement includes an important requirement for any conclusion that the kontakia are dramatic; they were not staged; they were not presented with scenery;[41] if a degree of impersonation accompanied the dialogue, it was slight. The point is that the incidents and their theological implications were dramatic in a very real sense. The impact on the communicant was that of entering into a drama, a struggle—actually, *the one* important struggle that moved him in the sixth century.

The reader of the translations of Romanos may indeed miss the implications of this subjective aspect; in fact, those who are not familiar with the ritual of the Church, or those who are unsympathetic with the religious terminology may be put off by these theological overtones. The difference between the twentieth-century reader's taste for the dramatic and that of the sixth-century Byzantine layman is highlighted by the fact that Romanos' kontakion on the Presentation in the Temple (O. 4, K. 6) was the most popular of all of his work, if we can judge by manuscripts now available.[42] It is packed with references to the paradox existing in the two natures of Christ. This seeming contradiction enhanced the Byzantine communicant's sense of the drama of God's approach to man. Three speakers in the kontakion on the Presentation, as in the Christmas hymn, present the theological drama: Simeon representing man, Christ representing God, and Mary representing the human approach. These three characters and their speeches expressed the deepest and most vital concerns of the man of the sixth century.

If the metrical sermons for feast days are to be dramatic for the present-day reader, it is important to feel in them the liturgical cycle; thus the reader partially enters into the annual consecutive drama that the East had developed by the sixth century, although it remained undeveloped in the West.

40. Topping, 97. This point of view is supported by a Swedish theologian, Gustaf Aulen, *Christus Victor*, trans. by A. G. Herbert (New York, 1958). He discusses the difference between what he calls the "classic" idea of the Atonement, inherently dramatic, typical of the Church fathers—especially the Greek fathers—and the "subjective or humanistic view" of Anselm and the West. *Passim*, especially pp. 36–47.

41. Mioni summarizes the use of the kontakia of Romanos by saying that some of the hymns not in the ritual were lost but others continued to be sung all through the East and in various monasteries. His works exercised considerable influence on the liturgy. When the Church was finally at peace and free from dogmatic preoccupations, then the Christian basilicas revived Romanos' hymns, and during the all-night vigils the people were present *at the scenic representation of the liturgical dramas of their poet.* Translated from Mioni, "Osservazione sulla tradizione manoscritta di Romano il Melode," *Studi Bizantini*, 5 (1939), 509.

42. See introductory notes to this hymn (O. 4).

The fairest summary of the situation was made some time ago by La Piana after his thorough study of Byzantine homily:

> We can state that the principal lines of the sacred theatre and of rhythmic-dramatic Byzantine poetry are not completely unknown to us ... the dramatic homily cannot have failed to exercise a certain influence on our theatre. Not to exaggerate the matter of this influence, it is limited to reproduction of scenes, of dramatic episodes, of some traditional situations, and of some general conception; but it did not penetrate into the spirit and nature of the mediaeval theatre of the west.... The destiny of the two was different.... Byzantine liturgical drama, born in the midst of theological discussions, was suffocated by theological battles, in bloody struggles which threw Byzantium and the empire into confusion; while in the west the sacred drama became the true expression of popular art. However, the restless Byzantine monks in the midst of theological discussions, and an angry council, and perhaps a harsh condemnation wrote dialogues of which fragments remain which contributed to the dramatic genius of the west.[43]

Other conclusions of La Piana are worth recording: "The idea of reproducing in dialogue form a series of prophecies, dramatizing an apologetic motif, belongs without doubt to the Byzantine theatre." In the West the drama of religious events emerged through scenes of prophets in procession and the liberation of patriarchs from Limbo.[44]

The author of the mystery plays "Descent to Hades" and "The Annunciation" had under his eyes the Latin sermon "Vos inquam convenio, O Judaei" and also the dramatic Greek homily for elements the Latin sermon had translated. The processions of the prophets in the West undeniably had their origin in Byzantine dramatic homily.[45] Certainly the art of the Middle Ages is full of processions of prophets, and Dante found inspiration in them.

It is important to be aware of the constant cultural interchange and communication between East and West at this time. Greek monks of Sicily and Calabria founded monasteries, built churches, moved, assembled new disciples, built new churches, and were, in truth, Byzantine colonizers. The hagiographic legends give evidence of the extent and strength of their influence. Ceremonies of the Eastern Church were preserved in some of the Western rituals, and there is evidence that Greek homilies were known and read in the West during the ninth and tenth centuries—exactly the time when Latin liturgical drama was beginning. In important liturgical ceremonies of the Latin Church, choruses in Greek were sung alternately by laymen and priests, and Latin monks of the ninth century considered the Greek liturgy the more venerable.[46]

A strophe from the kontakion "Mary at the Cross" appears in Latin translation in the Ambrosian Antiphonary of the British Museum.[47] Parallel

43. Trans. from La Piana, *Le Rappr.*, 34.
44. La Piana, *Le Rappr.*, 298.
45. La Piana, *Le Rappr.*, 310: From Byzantine dramatic homily come all "the numerous series of prophetic processions entwined and attached to a great number of dramas in France, Italy, and Germany."
46. La Piana, *Le Rappr.*, 286–87.
47. *Paléographie Musicale* V (Solesmes, 1896), 6–15. In the introduction to the text, the author calls attention to the fact that this use of Greek hymnography was natural in view of the admiration

passages occur in the Roman responses for Holy Week, and the first words are in the Antiphonary of Compiègne. While it is possible that the Greek and Roman writers were drawing on a common source, the type of correspondence points to a direct borrowing in the West from the great composer of kontakia.

Certainly liturgical drama survived iconoclasm. Liutprand, Bishop of Cremona, visited Constantinople in 968. His account of the celebration of the translation of Elijah by scenic representations may simply mean that he disapproved of visiting pagan plays on saints' days; or his record may imply shock at having Hagia Sophia made into a theatre.[48] A Greek who came to Florence to attend the seventeenth Council (Basel-Ferrara-Florence) in the fifteenth century was astonished to see a representation of the Passion outside the church![49]

The cyclical play of the West, such as the Cypriot Passion cycle of the thirteenth century in which the repentant harlot speaks to the perfume merchant and to Christ, has its roots, as Mahr has indicated, in homily, kontakion, and ultimately in Ephrem.[50] Also, the Greek text of a thirteenth-century Byzantine mystery play on the Passion gives evidence of the actual scenes that were parts of

---

Charlemagne expressed for the service, which he ordered translated into Latin, and in view of the frequent embassies that went to Constantinople from the West and there heard the work of the famous melodists.

The corresponding passages follow:

Romanos' kontakion strophe γ΄	Gregorian	Ambrosian
Ὑπάγεις, ὦ τέκνον, πρὸς ἄδικον φόνον,	Vadis propitiatus ad immolandum pro omnibus	Vadis propitiator ad immolandum pro omnibus
οὐ συνέρχεταί σοι Πέτρος ὁ εἰπών σοι·	non tibi occurrit Petrus qui dicebat	non tibi occurrit Petrus qui dicebat
κἂν ἀποθνήσκω. ἔλιπέ σε Θωμᾶς, ὁ βοήσας· Μετ' αὐτοῦ θάνωμεν πάντες·	mori tecum; reliquit te Thomas qui aiebat: omnes cum eo moriamur.	pro te moriar; reliquit te Thomas qui clamabat dicens: omnes cum eo moriamur.
οὐδεὶς ἐκ τῶν πάντων, ἀλλ' εἷς ὑπὲρ πάντων θνήσκεις, τέκνον, μόνος,	Et ne ullus ex illis sed tu solus duceris, qui castam me conservasti	Et nullus de illis sed tu solus diceris, qui immaculatam me conserva
ὁ υἱὸς καὶ θεός μου.	filius et deus meus.	filius et deus meus.

It is to be noticed that this is the same kontakion that is followed in the Χριστὸς Πάσχων. The late Greek drama uses the first strophe of Romanos.

48. *Legatio, Script. Rerum Germ.*, G. H. Certz, ed. (Hanover, 1839), I, 199: "The Greeks celebrated the translation of Elijah *in ludis scenicis*."

S. Baud-Bouvy, "Sur un Sacrifice d'Abraham de Romanos et sur l'existence d'un theatre à Byzance," *Byz.*, XIII (1938), 330. To support the statement that there was never a religious theater, Baud-Bouvy suggests that Liutprand was accusing the Greeks of celebrating a sacred festival by attending pagan representations.

Fifteenth-century Byzantine liturgical drama is discussed by Milos M. Velimirovic in "Liturgical Drama in Byzantium and Russia," *Dumbarton Oaks Papers*, 16 (1962), 351–85.

49. Brehier, review of La Piana, *Le Journal des savants*, 11 (1913), 361.

50. August C. Mahr, *Relations of Passion Plays to St. Ephrem the Syrian* (Columbus, 1942), discussed in connection with Romanos, "The Sinful Woman" (O. 10, K. 15).

a fully developed performance of the events connected with Christ's death and resurrection.[51]

INFLUENCE OF ROMANOS

Mioni[52] lists as imitators of Romanos: Gregory of Syracuse, Eulogius, Orestes Arseniis, Simeon Metaphrastes, Joseph the Hymnographer, Stephen Gabriel, Theodore Studites, and others. At times their imitations amount to plagiarism; for example, Joseph the Hymnographer, in his "Song on Vigil of the Nativity" fairly pillaged Romanos' Christmas Kontakion I; Patriarch Eulogius, in his homily on Palm Sunday, quoted Romanos at the beginning of his sermon; Eusebius of Alexandria used much of Victory of the Cross (Kontakion 22), and the unknown author of "Christus Patiens" inserted in his late drama lines from Mary at the Cross. Anonymous hymns imitating Romanos abound in the literature.

LITURGICAL CYCLE

Since the kontakia of Romanos were composed for the office and for feast days, it is important to observe how thoroughly he covered the liturgical year. The Easter cycle was determined in the fourth century, and the different contemporary liturgical books of the Church make the divisions clear.

The dates and the offices for important movable feasts of the liturgical year depend on the dating of Easter. As early as 325, the forty fast days before Easter were part of the Church calendar. The *Triodion* covers the ten weeks preceding Easter Sunday and then gives way to the *Pentekostarion*; this office sequence continues through Whitsunday, the seventh Sunday (and fiftieth day) after Easter; then the *Oktoechos* is the basis for the office until two Sundays before Christmas. Special gospels were assigned for special days in this series, and in the period from the fifth to the seventh century, when Romanos flourished, there were hymns (kontakia, usually) to follow or supplant sermons on the event to be celebrated. The details of liturgical practice have not survived, but it is clear that practices varied from one religious center to another. Where special information about procedures has become available, this is indicated in notes to the translated kontakia in this collection.

Of the edited kontakia in the Oxford edition, those for the pre-Easter season consist of sixteen for the Lenten season, including Palm Sunday, and

51. M. Carpenter, "Romanos and the Mystery Play of the East," in Rodney P. Robinson, ed., *Philological Studies in Honor of Walter Miller*, University of Missouri Studies, XI, 3 (1937), 21–51. In later Byzantium there was a sacred drama; see J. J. Tierney, "Romano il Melode," *Studi Bizantini*, 7 (1953), 208–13: "In Besanzio c'era anche un teatro sacro almeno nella tarda epoca bizantina."

Baud-Bouvy, *op. cit.*, 333, contends that this one scenario proves nothing about religious drama in Greece; it merely indicates that Cyprus tried to have mystery plays like those in the West.

52. E. Mioni, "Osservazioni sulla tradizione manoscritta di Romano il Melode," *Studi Bizantini*, 5 (1939), 509.

seventeen for Holy Week. For Easter Sunday, Romanos wrote four Resurrection kontakia, followed by ten kontakia for the seven weeks after Easter. A grouping of kontakia according to the liturgical year follows; it will be observed that only a few feast days were not celebrated by one of his kontakia,[53] and this observation does not take into account the number of poems that were lost.

Kontakia of Romanos for Special Days of Liturgical Year

> The Lenten Season (*Triodion*)
> > On Life in the Monasteries (for Sabbath of Cheese-Eating Week)
> > On the Victory of the Cross (may be used in mid Lent)
> > On the Adoration at the Cross (may be used in mid Lent)
> > On the Prodigal Son
> > On Fasting
> > On Noah
> > On Earthquakes and Fires
> > On Abraham and Isaac
> > On Repentance
> > On Jacob and Esau
> > On the Crucifixion
> > A Prayer
> > On the Raising of Lazarus I
> > On the Raising of Lazarus II
> > On Dives and Lazarus
>
> Palm Sunday
> > On the Entry into Jerusalem
>
> Holy Week
> > On Joseph I
> > On Joseph II
> > On the Ten Virgins I
> > On the Ten Virgins II
> > On the Sinful Woman
> > On Judas
> > On Peter's Denial
> > On Mary at the Cross
> > On the Passion of Christ
> > On the Resurrection I (occasionally)
> > On the Victory of the Cross (occasionally)
> > On the Healing of the Lame Man by Peter and John
>
> Easter Sunday
> > On the Resurrection (II, or III, or V, or VI)
> > On Doubting Thomas (occasionally)
>
> Post Easter (seven weeks or fifty days to Whitsuntide) *Pentekostarion*
> > On Doubting Thomas

53. All feast days of the *Triodion* contain kontakia of Romanos, with the exception of the first Sunday in Lent and the Sunday of Cheese-Eating Week. There is, however, a kontakion for the Sabbath of that week.

On the Marriage at Cana
On the Healing of the Leper
On the Resurrection IV
On the Multiplication of the Loaves
On the Woman of Samaria
On the Man Possessed with Devils
On the Ascension (forty days after Easter)
On the Woman with an Issue of Blood
On Pentecost (fifty days after Easter)
Whitsunday (until two weeks before Christmas) *Oktoechos*
March 20, On the Forty Martyrs of Sebasteia I and II
March 25, On the Annunciation I
June 30, On the Mission of the Apostles
July 20, On Elijah
August 29, On the Beheading of John the Baptist
September 8, On the Nativity of the Virgin Mary
All Saints' Day, On All Martyrs
Christmas
December 17, On the Three Children
December 25, On the Nativity I
December 26, On the Nativity II
On the Annunciation II
December 29, On the Massacre of the Innocents
January 6, On Baptism
On the Baptism of Christ
January 7, On the Epiphany
February 2, On the Presentation in the Temple

This listing cannot be established as the calendar of the sixth century. If it is compared with the list of kontakia as arranged by topics in the index to the Oxford text, the versatility of Romanos will be apparent.

THEOLOGY

It is both important and unimportant to summarize the theology with which the kontakia of Romanos abound. It is important because of the frequent references to the controversies of the day—at times the allusions are implicit, but more often they provide the point of departure for the poet's special emphasis; it is unimportant because Romanos was not himself either a theologian or a philosopher. His work reflects, however, the preoccupation of the sixth-century Greek Christian with theological disputes. Often the struggle was over a single word, so that the contemporary ministerial student who said that he had decided that theology was a "victory of language over thought" might well find support for his statement in the poems of the Great Melodist. Romanos was especially careful to support the edicts of Justinian and what was considered the orthodox point of view.

With this in mind, a brief statement of the various Church councils that had by the sixth century established the dogma, might be helpful:

1. *Nicaea* in 325 established the Creed, with particular emphasis on the true divinity of the Son of God (ὁμοούσιος).
2. *Constantinople* in 381 refuted Macedonius and established the divinity of the Holy Spirit.
3. *Ephesus* in 431 proclaimed Mary as the Mother of God and refuted Nestorius.
4. *Chalcedon* in 451 defined the two natures of Christ in an attempt to refute the Monophysites.
5. *Constantinople* in 553 under Justinian condemned the errors of Origen and confirmed Chalcedon.

The last two councils influenced most strongly the emphases in Romanos. Especially in such a kontakion as the "Presentation in the Temple" (O. 4, K. 6) is this point about the two natures of Christ belabored.

It is significant that this particular poem was very popular, judged by the number of manuscripts that survive. Constantly in the translations and introductions to individual kontakia, Romanos' preoccupation with the divine-human natures of Christ emerges. The Holy Ghost receives little attention; apparently the controversies over this member of the Trinity had died down. Against the Jews—in fact against all adversaries of the Christian dogma as he heard it proclaimed—Romanos is unattractively dogmatic and at times violently opposed.

The heresies that Romanos subtly or openly attempted to refute in his works may be summarized:

Arianism: Condemned at Nicaea; in brief, it denies Christ's divinity. Romanos refers to this heresy in Resurrection V (O. 28, K. 74), where he calls it by name, and again in the kontakion The Healing of the Leper (O. 8, K. 78), Strophe 16. Less open references occur in The Presentation in the Temple (O. 4, K. 6), Strophe 7, in Resurrection V (O. 28, K. 74), Strophe 2, and in The Marriage at Cana (O. 7, K. 77), Strophe 15. The last mentioned passage is one of many outbursts against the Jews. The kontakion on Judas is especially violent and vituperative about them.

Docetism: According to this heresy, Christ's human body only seemed real. Romanos, in both the Epiphany hymn (O. 6, K. 5), Strophe 9, and in Resurrection V (O. 28, K. 74), Strophe 16, takes pains to refer to the "heavenly body" of Christ.

Nestorianism: Nestorius, a Syrian monk of the fifth century, argued against the union of the two natures in Christ and also refused to give Mary the title "Mother of God." Romanos proclaims the union of God and man in Presentation in the Temple (O. 4, K. 6), Strophe 8, in Passion of Christ (O. 20, K. 19), Strophe 19, and again in Resurrection V (O. 28, K. 74), Strophe 18.

Novatianism:	This older heresy would exclude all apostates from communion. Romanos in the reassurance given Peter refutes it. Peter (O. 18, K. 18), Strophe 22. His theological dogma in Resurrection V bears on this heresy as well as on Nestorianism.
Monophysitism:	Christ is like God and like man. Theodora supported this belief. Romanos emphasizes it in the Epiphany (O.6, K. 5), Strophe 12, and in The Marriage at Cana (O. 7, K. 77), Strophe 21, which also refers to "Theotokos."

Romanos' expressions give rise to the thought that he understood so little the philosophical implications of the various theological disputes he found it necessary to be repetitively arbitrary. Even so, or perhaps all the more, one must admire the manner in which a point of theology is woven into a dramatic situation and given poetic flavor by the use of antithesis and figure of speech.

It might be useful to summarize here the theology of Romanos as reflected in his works. Frequently repeated is the assurance that it was of His own will that Christ took human form and died in order to redeem Adam and all mankind. Romanos repeats the word οἰκονομία and uses it to include the idea of God's dispensation both in regard to the incarnation and to the entire plan of redemption.[54] As for Mary, she is "the wall and powerful support of all who trust her"; her "virginity is unsullied"; she has special "power of intercession with Christ for mortals." She is at times called "Theotokos," as in Presentation in the Temple, Strophe 9, but the *idea* of her being mother of Christ who is both man and God is more frequently expressed than the rather infrequent use of the epithet. God the Father and the Holy Spirit are the matter for Romanos' lyrics less frequently than Christ and Mary.[55] The devil is of real concern,[56] and so is Antichrist.[57]

The importance Romanos attaches to God's grace in offering repentance to the sinner is unquestionable.[58] He repeatedly exhorts the people to have faith and to accept, in faith, such knowledge as is beyond their understanding.[59] Baptism is a

54. For example, see The Ascension (O. 32, K. 22), both the prooimion and Strophe 15. Also, Resurrection VI (O. 29, K. 20), Strophe 6. Without the use of the technical word for the "plan of salvation" the idea is often expressed figuratively: "To open Eden, He dwelt in Nazareth." It is stated directly: "He became flesh sanctifying the whole race of men, . . . He who was sinless willed to be crucified." Throughout the kontakion The Victory of the Cross (O. 22, K. 9), we find references to the power of the cross to redeem Adam and overthrow the devil.
55. Naturally, the kontakion Pentecost does treat of the Holy Spirit (O. 33, K. 23).
56. The devil is given many names. He is *the devil* (ὁ διάβολος) in sixteen kontakia; he is referred to as *the enemy* (ὁ ἐχθρός) in eleven, as *Satan* in six, as *Belial* in seven, as *the snake* in five, and *the deceiver* (ὁ πλάνος) in five. The kontakia that introduce the devil at some length are: Resurrection V and the two kontakia on the forty martyrs. In addition to the dramatic dialogue between Hades and Death, there is a touch of the poet's insight into human nature when Romanos has the devil ask the monks why they should work for no pay!
57. Antichrist is directly mentioned in The Second Coming (O. 34, K. 7), Strophes 7–11.
58. The assurance of forgiveness is emphasized in Peter's Denial (O. 18, K. 18), Strophe 22, and in many kontakia the refrain repeats this idea. The debt motif is particularly stressed in The Sinful Woman (O. 10, K. 15), Strophes 2 and 16. The Mission of the Apostles (O. 31, K. 25) repeats the idea in Christ's commission to His disciples.
59. Notice especially Strophe 10 in The Epiphany (O. 6, K. 5); also Doubting Thomas (O. 30, K. 21), Strophe 3, and Pentecost (O. 33, K. 23), Strophe 7.

second birth and cure for sin; it brings incorruptibility and it confounds the enemy.[60] While monastic life is honored, the monks are reminded that not everyone is suited for that life.[61] Romanos deplores heathen practices, sacrifices, and worship of idols.[62] He reviles the Jews,[63] and he discounts the classic authors,[64] on the grounds that they were pagans.

In brief, Romanos the poet-preacher presents a very simple theology in his kontakia. It is not surprising that his songs pleased people who supported orthodoxy in a day when theological issues were of general interest and dispute. It was reassuring to these people to be told that mercy, chastity, and repentance were sure passports to salvation—especially when this reassurance was put in dramatic form and set to beautiful music.

MANUSCRIPTS AND EDITIONS

Manuscripts: The painstaking work that Krumbacher and then Paul Maas did in collating the manuscripts of Romanos is used as the basis for the Maas-Trypanis text, which is followed almost without exception in the following translations. Critical analysis of variant readings is not one of the purposes of this book,[65] nor is the clear grouping of families of manuscripts—there is no one from which the others are derived.[66] Actually, the collection of poems into kontakaria was not made until

60. There is direct reference to the liturgy of baptism in The Forty Martyrs I (O. 57, K. 48), Strophe 16:

$$\beta\acute{\alpha}\pi\tau\iota\sigma\mu\alpha \; \dot{\alpha}\pi o\lambda\hat{\upsilon}\nu o\nu \; \tau\grave{o} \; \pi\tau\alpha\acute{\iota}\sigma\mu\alpha\tau\alpha.$$

The word 'ἐμφύω, used in the liturgy when the priest breathes on the candidate for baptism, is used in The Sinful Woman (O. 10, K. 15), Strophe 5, and also in The Epiphany (O. 5, K. 4), and On Baptism (O. 53, K. 46). The Mission of the Apostles (O. 31, K. 25) reminds the disciples of their obligation to baptize the repentant.
61. The kontakion On Life in the Monastery (O. 55, K. 8), Strophes 10–13.
62. Especially is this true in the kontakion The Three Children (O. 46, K. 27), Strophes 4 and 13.
63. The second prooimion to the kontakion On the Entry into Jerusalem (O. 16, K. 10) makes direct references to the Jews; later he terms them "the lawless" and hits out against them. They are shown in Lazarus II as in need of a demonstration of Christ's power. The Massacre (O. 3, K. 44), Strophe 12, is typical of Romanos' violent attacks. Judas (O. 17, K. 16) is full of this kind of vituperation. It is picked up again in Mission of the Apostles (O. 31, K. 25), in which Thomas is told to do what he longed to do against the Jews (Strophe 11).
64. In Pentecost (O. 33, K. 23), Strophe 17. It is not at all clear that he really knows Plato, Demosthenes, Homer, Pythagoras. Since Justinian had closed the School at Athens in 529, Romanos would speak against the classical philosophers. In Lazarus II, Strophe 18, there is an echo of classical terminology in the phrase, ὕλην ῥευστὴν; and in The Sinful Woman, Strophe 11, we find the Platonic "idea" in the harlot's nourishment by her concept of Christ.
65. Reviewers of the Oxford text do not always agree with the method of making decisions on the basis that "the majority reading of manuscripts must be assumed to be the probable reading of the archetype." Trypanis states this principle in his introduction, xxviii. Objections are raised by G. Zuntz, "Probleme des Romanos-Textes," Byz., 34 (1964), 469–534, and by H. Hunger in his review, *ibid.*, 437. The criticism stems from the fact that the reviewers would have preferred a complete critical apparatus, and from their objection to the basis for determining metrical laws.
66. The French edition presents stemmata for each of four kontakia in Vol. I, 38–39. Mioni gives details of the way in which, in later centuries, the liturgical use of the kontakia was limited so that only the prooimion and initial strophe of some survive. He concludes that Patmiacus 213 is the superior manuscript, and he agrees that no direct connection between manuscripts can be established.

at least four centuries after Romanos lived. These kontakaria are not, strictly speaking, liturgical books; they are, rather, anthologies.[67] They contain copies of hymns, and some employ similarity of subject as the unifying principle, others authorship by one writer. The earliest manuscripts date from the tenth and eleventh centuries and are to be found in the two monasteries at Mount Athos and Mount Patmos. The latter collection provides the main source for the readings used in the Oxford text of Maas-Trypanis.

Editions: In the early nineteenth century, Cardinal J. B. Pitra edited many of the works of Romanos.[68] In spite of the fact that the texts were known to be faulty because he did not have access to a large number of manuscripts, he at least introduced Romanos to scholars of the West. W. Christ and M. Paranikas repeated some of these poems in a subsequent edition.[69] Karl Krumbacher, who died in 1909, made a detailed study of several kontakia; his listing and numbering of the works of Romanos is now accepted as the standard for other scholars. His numbering appears with the numbering of the Oxford text throughout the translations in this book.[70] The many valuable analyses and texts published by Krumbacher and Maas[71] appeared in journals not readily available to students of Romanos, and a definitive text is, therefore, most welcome.

Two other centers for careful work on editions of Romanos have made use of a team of scholars working under one editor. Such is the series edited at the University of Athens under N. B. Tomadakis.[72] The French edition was edited by José Grosdidier de Matons and his associates at the Sorbonne.[73] The latter is useful for its introductory material to each kontakion. A few hymns have been edited by Cammelli[74] and by Mioni.[75]

He maintains that the differences of the codices are in direct proportion to the distance from the place of origin. E. Mioni, "Osservazioni sulla tradizione manoscritta di Romano il Melode," *Studi Bizantini*, 5 (1939), 507–13.

67. Mioni also comments on the wide diffusion of the kontakia in Greece, Asia Minor, Palestine, Egypt, and in scattered monasteries of the Byzantine type. He maintains that by the end of the sixth century Romanos' kontakia were sung in all of the Oriental world, even though it cannot be asserted that the widest dispersion came while Romanos was alive. It must certainly be true of the areas close to the rule of Constantinople (*op. cit.*, 508).

68. His work has been superseded by that of more recent editors, but it is still important. The exact titles are in the Basic Bibliography for this book.

69. W. Christ and M. Paranikas, *Anthologia Graeca Carminum Christianorum*, Leipzig, 1871.

70. This number, stated as *K.*, is given in "Die Akrostichis in der griechischen Kirchenpoesie," *Sitzungsberichte der philos.-philol. und der histor. Klasse der K. Bayer. Akad. d. Wiss.* (1903), 551–618. When references are made to the article accompanying the list, it is referred to as *Acros.* See the Basic Bibliography.

71. See the list in the Basic Bibliography.

72. N. B. Tomadakis, Ῥωμανοῦ τοῦ Μελῳδοῦ ὕμνοι ἐκδιδόμενοι ἐκ πατμιακῶν κωδίκων Athens, I, 1952; II, 1954; III, 1957; IV, 1961. For the sake of brevity, individual scholars are not identified in the references.

73. José Grosdidier de Matons, *Romanos le mélode: Hymnes*, Paris, I, 1964; II, 1965; III, 1965; IV, 1967. Again, no reference is made to individual contributing editors. The notes are thorough and helpful.

74. G. Cammelli, *Romano il Melode*, Florence, 1930. Along with translations into Italian and a good introduction, he has edited the following: O. 1, O. 4, O. 17, O. 19, O. 25, O. 34, and O. 48.

75. E. Mioni, *Romano il Melode*, Turin, 1937. He edited ten kontakia, some of which are of dubious authenticity.

In the following list of abbreviations for the critical apparatus, it should be noted that the Oxford edition groups all of the Patmos manuscripts under P, and a group of Western manuscripts under Δ; this coding has not been used by the other editors.

STYLE of ROMANOS

Frustration is intrinsic in any attempt to translate poetry. The difficulties are magnified in the case of Romanos. The rhythms that were designed to fit the now-vanished music cannot be recaptured, although the echoes from strophe to strophe of both accents and thought might partially be illustrated by parallel translations of two strophes of Nativity I, the famous Christmas kontakion.

Delta strophe	Epsilon strophe
While saying secret	To us quite clearly
Thoughts such as these to herself,	Balaam revealed all the sense
Entreating Him who	Of words prophetic;
Knows all the secrets there are,	When in advance they foretold
She hears the Magi	A star to rise up;
Who ask to see Him;	This thing they foresaw
Then straightway the maiden called out:	In saying this star would o'erthrow
"Who are ye?"	Prophecies,
To her query,	Divinations;
An answering question replied,	And saying that it would destroy
"Who art thou?	Parables,
That produced such an One?	And wise teachings of old,
Who thy sire?	Enigmas—
And who could have given thee birth	A star as much brighter than this—
For thou, strange it is, hast become	This one which just now clearly shines
Both the mother and nurse of a son	As the maker of stars is more bright
Who has no genealogical line,	Than all others that shine in the sky;
'Twas His star	And they wrote
That we saw when we came and saw here	That this star forth from Jacob would flash,

A new-born babe,
The God before time.

Even in this attempt to keep roughly to the repeated fall of accents and number of syllables in corresponding lines,[76] there is certainly no remnant of the poetic effect the similar endings in Greek give to the sound. Assonance and homoioteleuton necessarily abound wherever there is parallel structure, even though there is no rhyme in the strict sense of the word.

Usually, groups of similarly accented phrases are tied together so that antithesis in idea is underlined. For example, in the kontakion on Judas (O. 17,

76. The translation does not retain exactly the same series of accents as the original, but it does repeat the units in the same manner. The Greek text of Maas-Trypanis provides the heirmos, or syllabic pattern, for both the introductory strophe (prooimion) and for the subsequent strophes. This is placed at the beginning of each kontakion. In addition, Maas includes a diagram of the special metrical scheme for each poem. The last item in the introduction to the translation of each poem gives the exact reference to this material. It is, of course, important only to the one who wishes to read the Greek.

K. 16) the triads match the refrain (ἵλεως, ἵλεως, ἵλεως) and the opening of the last strophe (ἅγιε, ἅγιε, ἅγιε). The first strophe reads:

Who on hearing this did not grow numb?
Who on seeing this did not tremble?
Jesus, kissed in treachery,
Christ, sold through jealousy,
God, overpowered through His own will?
What kind of earth bore this outrage?
What kind of sea endured the sight of the unholy deed?
How did Heaven submit?
How did air permit?
How did the world exist
When He, the judge, was bargained for, sold, betrayed?
Have mercy, have mercy, have mercy on us.

Romanos especially liked to present in a series participial phrases, rhetorical questions, and word epithets. Tragic fear and horror are intensified by a series of hyperboles in such poems as Peter's Denial (O. 18, K. 18), Strophes 10 and 11, and The Beheading of John the Baptist (O. 38, K. 26), Strophe 16, ll. 7–10.

Examples of antitheses are numerous, but the most common occur in connection with Christ's humility as contrasted with His divinity. "They recline while He stands; they are fed while He serves; they are washed while He wipes their feet" (Judas, Strophe 8). "Christ who wouldn't answer His accusers speaks to the robber; He who did not deem Pilate worthy of a word, speaks to the murderer" (Triumph of the Cross, Strophe 10). The emphasis on the two natures of Christ makes this use of antithesis especially effective in The Presentation at the Temple; for example, "The One at whom the powers of Heaven tremble . . . [is held] in the arms of the Elder" (Prooimion), and especially Strophe 1: "He who is the creator of Adam, is being baptized as a child./ He who is not to be contained in space is held in the arms of the Elder./ He who exists in the infinite arms of His Father,/ Of His own will is limited in His flesh, and not in His divinity."

Plays on words are, of course, untranslatable; at times, they are indicated in notes to the translations. The most noteworthy are repeated plays on the *Word*. Mary begs Christ to give her some reassurance as He goes to the cross, and she says, "Give me word, O Word, some word. . . ."[77] In the Nativity kontakion Mary is the gate and the door in an involved play on those words.[78]

Figures of speech fare somewhat better in translation. At times, we have metaphors that juxtapose strongly contrasting ideas or materials. "He who [appeared as] a pillar . . . is attached to a pillar, rock upon [wood]."[79] References to light and fire are abundant. Christ is, of course, *the* light to illumine all the earth and all mankind.[80] Blindness results when man is out of touch with Christ. Adam was blind until God sent light to him.[81] John the Baptist fears to touch the

77. Mary at the Cross (O. 19, K. 17), Strophe 1.
78. Nativity I (O. 1, K. 1), Strophe 9. Compare this with Mary as the opened gate protected by Christ, Presentation (O. 4, K. 6), Strophe 9.
79. The Passion of Christ (O. 20, K. 19), Strophe 14.
80. Especially is this effective in the refrain to Epiphany (O. 6, K. 5).
81. Adam has to grope as he reaches for his clothes! Epiphany (O. 6, K. 5), Strophes 1 and 2.

"unapproachable light" and hesitates to put his hand in the fire.[82] Fire is commanded to fast when the three children are in the fiery furnace. The Nativity kontakion, as Mrs. Topping has suggested, is brilliant with the imagery of fire and light.[83]

Christ quenches thirst and is called the "spring of salvation,"[84] or even compared to rain.[85] Seas and rivers, mountains and valleys are frequently used in similes, as are other natural phenomena. Especially effective are some extended comparisons. The "echo of those who weep for the young children/ Makes a crash like thunder on earth,/ For the hills and ravines and deep valleys of the mountains cried aloud in answer./ As though imitating the wailing,/ They practised beats of lamentation [in antiphony]."[86]

Allusions to agriculture abound. Thomas prays that his doubt be lifted as one would lighten a load of hay. Peter's instability makes him like stubble blown in the wind. Naturally, many farming comparisons center on allusions to the vine and the tree.[87] In Judas, the tree is called the executioner,[88] and in Victory of the Cross, the devil brags that the wood cast in the ground has become sweet, in that Christ is being crucified. His attitude changes as he realizes what the cross is bringing to pass, and the tree becomes a place for nests to protect robbers and harlots. The figures then become hopelessly involved when the sinners cling to the tree as they swim to safety in a calm harbor![89]

Nautical comparisons are rather frequent, and one extended metaphor is effective in Ten Virgins when the ship is represented as being kept from its course when the cargo does not include mercy.[90] The good shepherd provides many comparisons, and so does the arena for contests and games. One effective short allusion to military life is the rather naïve conclusion that the Lord must have risen, otherwise the angel would not be seated in the presence of the general![91]

The figure of Christ as the Great Physician is developed with involved additions to the comparison when Christ tells Mary that He will throw off His cloak and use His spear to cut the callousness of the wicked, and then He will use

82. Theophany (Epiphany) or Baptism of Christ (O. 5, K. 4). It is to be expected that Epiphany and Theophany would be full of the imagery of light.
83. See Introduction, page xxii.
84. See All Saints (O. 59, K. 24), Strophe 11; also, Joseph I (O. 12, K. 43), Strophe 1; Passion (O. 10, K. 19), Strophes 18 and 22; Thomas (O. 30, K. 21), Strophe 14; Forty Martyrs II (O. 58, K. 49), Strophe 4; Apostles (O. 31, K. 25), Strophe 8.
85. Baptism of Christ (O. 5, K. 4), Strophe 4; Joseph II (O. 44, K. 11), Strophe 2; Resurrection VI (O. 29, K. 20), Strophe 18. The powerful paradox in the fire plus refreshing dew (φρέαρ ἀνόρυκτον), Nativity I, 1, is suggested also in the phrase, τὴν κάμιναν ἐδρόσισεν (bedewed the furnace), Three Boys in the Fiery Furnace (O. 46, K. 27), Strophe 26.
86. The Massacre of the Innocents (O. 3, K. 44), Strophe 10.
87. Victory of the Cross (O. 22, K. 9), Strophes 12 and 15; Adoration at the Cross (O. 23, K. 64), Strophe 3; Resurrection V (O. 28, K. 74), Strophe 30; Nativity I (O. 1, K. 1), Strophe 1; Nativity II (O. 2, K. 42), Strophe 1; Ten Virgins II (O. 48, K. 14), Strophe 6; Judas (O. 17, K. 16), Strophe 22; Forty Martyrs (O. 58, K. 49), Strophe 4; Joseph I (O. 43, K. 12), Strophe 24.
88. Judas (O. 17, K. 16), Strophe 22.
89. Victory of the Cross (O. 22, K. 9), Strophe 16.
90. Ten Virgins I (O. 47, K. 13), Strophe 4.
91. Resurrection VI (O. 29, K. 20), Strophe 21.

the vinegar as an astringent and His cross as a healing remedy.[92] Many comparisons allude to the Bible: "They plug up their ears like the adder" is said of those who plot the death of Christ in the second Lazarus hymn.[93] In Psalm 58 the poison of the wicked is compared to "the adder which stoppeth her ear." Effective short comparisons abound; their aptness can be judged fairly well from the translations, although they do not do full justice to the lyrical and dramatic power in the kontakia.

No one is more aware of these faults than the translator. I present these translations in the hope that they will serve as an introduction to an experience with early Greek ecclesiastical poetry and will stimulate further investigation of a richly rewarding literature.

Of the fifty-nine genuine kontakia edited by Maas-Trypanis in the Oxford edition, the following translations include only the thirty-four concerned with the life of Christ. A later volume should contain those poems that deal with episodes from the New Testament and the Old Testament, with martyrs, and with a miscellaneous group of Romanos' works.

92. Mary at the Cross (O. 19, K. 17), Strophe 13.
93. Lazarus II (O. 15, K. 71), Strophe 11.

BASIC BIBLIOGRAPHY AND ABBREVIATIONS

Beck, H. G., *Kirche und theologische Literatur im byzantinischen Reich.* München, 1959.   *K. Lit.*

Cammelli, G., *Romano il Melode.* Firenze, 1930.   *R.M.*

Carpenter, M., "The Paper that Romanos Swallowed." *Speculum*, 7 (January, 1932), 1–22.   *Christmas*

———, "Romanos and the Mystery Play of the East," in Rodney P. Robinson, ed., *Philological Studies in Honor of Walter Miller.* University of Missouri Studies, XI, 3 (1937), 21–51.   *Myst.*

Krumbacher, K., *Geschichte der byzantinischen Literatur.* Leipzig, 1897 (2).   *G.B.L.*

———, "Studien zu Romanos." *Sitzungsberichte der philos.- philol. und der histor. Klasse der K. Bayer. Akad. d. Wiss.*, II, München, 1898, 69.   *Stud.*

———, "Umarbeitungen bei Romanos." *Ibid.*, II (1899), 1.   *Umarb.*

———, "Romanos und Kyriakos." *Ibid.* (1901), 693.   *R.u.K.*

———, "Die Akrostichis in der griechischen Kirchenpoesie." *Ibid.* (1903), 551.   *Acros.*

———, The numbering of kontakia is referred to as K.   *K.*

———, "Miscellen zu Romanos." *Abhandlungen der philos.- philol. und der histor. Klasse der K. Bayer. Akad. d. Wiss.*, XXIV (München, 1907), iii, 1.   *Misc.*

———, "Der heilige Georg." *Ibid.*, XXV (1911), iii, 261.   *h.G.*

Lamy, Thomas Josephus, *Sancti Ephraem Syri Hymni et Sermones.* Mechliniae, 1882, 1886, 1889, 1902. 4 vols.

La Piana, George, *Le Rappresentazioni sacre nella letteratura bizantina.* Grottaferrata, 1912.   *Le Rappr.*

Maas, P., "Die Chronologie der Hymnen des Romanos." *Byz. Zeitschrift*, 15 (1906), 1.   *Chron.*

———, "Grammatische und metrische Umarbeitungen in der Ueberlieferung des Romanos." *Byz. Zeitschrift*, 16 (1907), 565.   *Gram.*

———, "Das Kontakion." *Byz. Zeitschrift*, 19 (1910), 285.   *Kont.*

——, "Das Weihnachtslied des Romanos." *Byz. Zeitschrift*, 24 (1923–1924), 1.   *Weihn.*

——, *Frühbyzantinische Kirchenpoesie: Anonyme Hymnen des V.-VI. Jahrhunderts.* Kleine Texte für Vorlesungen und Übungen herausg. von H. Lietzmann (Berlin, 1931), 52–53.   *Frühbyz.*

——, "Romanos auf Papyrus." *Byzantion*, XIV (1939), 381.   *R. Pap.*

—— and C. A. Trypanis, *Sancti Romani Melodi Cantica Genuina.* Oxford, Clarendon Press, 1963.*   O.*

Mahr, August C., *Relations of Passion Plays to St. Ephrem, the Syrian.* Columbus, Wartburg Press, 1942.   *Pass. Pl.*

Matons, J. Grosdidier de, *Romanos le mélode: Hymnes* (French edition). Paris, 1964–1965. 4 vols.   *Fr. ed.*

Meyer, W., "Anfang und Ursprung der lateinischen and griechischen rythmischen Dichtung." *Abhandlungen der philos.-philol. und der histor. Klasse der K. Bayer. Akad. d. Wiss.*, XVII (München, 1885), ii, 370.   *A.u.U.*

——, *Gesammelte Abhandlungen zur mittellateinischen Rythmik.*, II (Berlin, 1905), 1.

Mioni, E., *Romano il Melode.* Turin, 1937.   *Mioni*

Pitra, J. B., *Analecta sacra spicilegio Solesmensi parata.* Paris, 1876, I.   *A.S.*

——, *Sanctus Romanus Veterum melodorum princeps.* Roma, 1888.

——, *Hymnographie de l'église grecque.* Rome, 1867.   *Hymn.*

Schork, R. J., "The Biblical and Patristic Sources of the Christological Hymns of Romanos the Melodist." Unpublished doctoral thesis, Oxford, 1957.   *Schork*

Tomadakis, N. B., Ῥωμανοῦ τοῦ Μελωδοῦ Ὕμνοι. Athens, 1952, 1954, 1957, 1961. 4 vols.   *Tom.*

Topping, Eva Catafygiotu, "St. Romanos: Ikon of a Poet." *Greek Orthodox Theological Review*, 12 (1966), 92–111.

——, "The Poet-Priest in Byzantium." *Ibid.* (1969), 31–41.

——, "A Byzantine Song for Simeon." *Traditio* (1968), 409–20.

Trypanis, C. A., "The Meters of Romanos." *Byzantion*, 36 (1966), 560–627.

Wellesz, E., *Byzantine Music and Hymnography*, 2d ed. Oxford, 1961.   *Byz. Mus.*

    * This is the edition used for the translations. It is referred to as the Oxford text, and the corresponding numbering of Krumbacher, "Die Akrostichis in der griechischen Kirchenpoesie," (*Acros.*) is indicated by K.

Abbreviations of Reference Material Frequently Cited

B.Z.   *Byzantinische Zeitschrift*
Byz.   *Byzantion*
E.O.   *Echos d'Orient*
O.C.   *Oriens Christianus*
P.G.   Migne, *Patrologia Graeca*
P.L.   Migne, *Patrologia Latina*
Sp.   *Speculum*

Texts Used for Bible and Apocrypha

The Holy Bible, Authorized Version with Encyclopedia. International Bible Press, Philadelphia, Pa.
Novum Testamentum Graece, A. F. C. Tischendorf. Leipzig, 1865.
Vetus Testamentum Graecum, L. Van Ess. Lipsiae, 1894.
O.T. Apocrypha, English, Goodspeed. Chicago, 1938.
The Apocryphal New Testament, English, M. R. James. Oxford, 1926.
Evangelia Apocrypha, Constantinus Tischendorf, ed. Lipsiae, 1853.

Manuscripts Used in Oxford Edition

A   *Athous Batopediou* 1041, X–XI century
B   *Athous Laurae* I 27, X–XI century
D   *Athous Laurae* I 28, XI century
G   *Sinaiticus* 925, X century
J   *Sinaiticus* 927, XIII century
K   *Sinaiticus* 928, XIV century
M   *Mosquensis Synod*, 437, XII century
P   { *Patmiacus* 212, XI century
      { *Patmiacus* 213, XI century
S   *Vaticanus gr.* 2008, XII century
T   *Taurinensis* B. iv. 34, XI century
Δ   { C *Corsinianus* 366, X–XI century
      { V *Vindobonensis*, suppl. gr. 96, XII century
      { c *Cryptoferratensis* Δa. 5, XII century

a   Cryptoferratensis Δa. 6, XII century
b   Cryptoferratensis Δa. 1, XI–XII century
k   Mosquensis synod. 153, XII century
m   Vaticanus gr. 1212, XII century
p   Vaticanus gr. 1829, XI century
y   Parisinus gr. 1571, XIII century

TABLE OF KONTAKIA AS NUMBERED IN DIFFERENT EDITIONS

Articles on the kontakia that appeared before recent editions were published refer to them by the numbering used in Krumbacher's *Acros.* (see Bibliography). In recent years the work of French scholars has been presented in four volumes edited by José Grosdidier de Matons, and that of Greek scholars in four volumes edited by N. B. Tomadakis. The different numberings are at times confusing; the following table shows by each title the main editions for each kontakion. Other editors, such as Pitra, Mioni, and Cammelli, are mentioned in the introductory comments for individual hymns, but they are not included here because each has edited only a few of Romanos' poems.

Title	Number in Maas-Trypanis (Oxford edition) (*Ox. ed.*)	Number in Krumbacher (*Acros.*)	Volume and Number in French edition (*Fr. Ed.*)	Volume and Number in Edition by Tomadakis (*Tom.*)
Nativity I	1	1	II, x	
Nativity II	2	42	II, xi	III, #36
Massacre of Innocents	3	44	II, xv	I, #6
Presentation	4	6	II, xiv	II, #27
Baptism of Christ	5	4	II, xvi	
Epiphany	6	5	II, xvii	IV, #40
Marriage at Cana	7	77	II, xviii	
Healing Leper	8	78	II, xx	
Woman of Samaria	9	80	II, xix	II, #26
Sinful Woman	10	15	III, xxi	
Man with Devils	11	81	III, xxii	
Woman with Issue of Blood	12	82	III, xxiii	IV, #41
Miracle of the Loaves	13	83	III, xxiv	IV, #45
Lazarus I	14	70	III, xxvi	I, #7
Lazarus II	15	71	III, xxvii	I, #8
Entry to Jerusalem	16	10	IV, xxxii	III, #33
Judas	17	16	IV, xxxiii	II, #24
Peter's Denial	18	18	IV, xxxiv	
Mary at the Cross	19	17	IV, xxxv	II, #21
Passion	20	19	IV, xxxvi	II, #22
Crucifixion	21	67	IV, xxxvii	I, #2
Victory of the Cross	22	9	IV, xxxviii	IV, #44
Adoration at the Cross	23	64	IV, xxxix	IV, #49
Resurrection I	24	72	IV, xli (R.2)	
Resurrection II	25	73	IV, xlii (R.3)	III, #29
Resurrection III	26	75	IV, xliv (R.5)	IV, #42
Resurrection IV	27	79	IV, xlv (R.6)	

DEFINITIONS OF TECHNICAL TERMS

Acrostic:	The use of the initial letters of the troparia or theotakia to spell the author's name, form a verse, or give the alphabet.
Ainoi:	Praises or Lauds.
Antiphony:	Method of responsive singing; three odes preceding the Introit; psalms interspersed with invocations as a refrain.
Apodeipnon:	The service following dinner.
Apostolon:	Book containing the epistles.
Automelon:	A kind of stichera that has its own modulation and is the prototype for stichera prosomoia.
Didache:	Ecclesiastical homilies.
Dogmatikoi:	Kanons concerned with theological dogma.
Encomia:	Hymns of praise.
Eisodos:	The entrance or Introit. *The great entrance* and *the less entrance* refer to the processions that convey the sacred offerings and the gospel book to the altar.
Eisodikon:	Verse sung at the Introit.
Ephymnium:	Refrain or conclusion of the troparion.
Euchologion:	Book containing prayers and important occasional offices of church.
Evangelion:	Collection of the gospels.
Ἐωθινά:	Troparia sung after Lauds.
ἦχος:	The indication of tone or mood.
Introit:	See Eisodos, above.
Heirmos:	Troparion on which the harmonic song, syllabic meter, and sequence of tone accents of all the troparia in the ode depend.
Heirmologion:	Book containing the heirmoi.
Horologion:	Book containing prayers of the daily hours and a collection of troparia, kontakia, and kanons.
Hymnologion:	Book containing hymns for the year, with musical notes.
Idiomela:	Stichera sung in an impressive manner, containing their own modulation.
Kanon:	A form of hymn composed of odes and troparia.
Kantica:	Odes modeled on biblical odes.
Katabasia:	Repetition of the heirmos at the end of the ode, when the two choruses descend from the choir loft and unite in the center of the church.
Kathismata:	Sections of the psalter; troparia sung in the morning office after the third, sixth, and ninth odes of the kanon.

Kontakia:	After ninth century, hymns sung after the sixth ode of the kanon. Fifth to seventh centuries: poems consisting of metrically responsive strophes, written for feast days. Metrical sermons, often dramatic. See Introduction.
Kontakarion:	Book containing kontakia.
Koukoulion:	Prooimion to the kontakia.
Lectiones:	Readings from the lives of saints, *cf. Synaxaria.*
Menaion:	Book including songs according to feast days. It is arranged by months, and it includes commemoration of saints on appropriate days.
Odes:	Division of the kanon, composed of troparia.
Oikoi:	Short poems following the kontakia, composed especially for the saint.
Oktoechos:	Book arranged according to eight modes (after Whitsuntide).
Panegyricus:	Book containing appropriate speeches for saints' days.
Paracletice:	Book containing the troparia, stichera, and hymns for particular tone of each day.
Pentekostarion:	Book containing the offices from Passover to the eighth day of Pentecost.
Prooimion:	Short poem preceding the heirmos of the kontakia.
Psalterion:	Book of Psalms.
Staseis:	Divisions of the *Psalterion.*
Stauroanastasimon:	Kanon on the Cross and the Resurrection.
Stichera:	Troparia added to the verses of psalms.
Stichera prosomoia:	Stichera connected by an equal number of syllables.
Sticherarion:	Book in manuscript that contains words and musical notes of verses when their own modulation is to be used.
Stichoi:	Verses of psalms; verses celebrating a saint's life and deeds. They precede the readings from the *Synaxaria.*
Synaxaria:	Readings from the lives of the saints, following the sixth ode of the kanon.
Theotokarion:	Book containing theotokia, honoring the Virgin Mary.
Triodia:	Series of three odes.
Triodion:	Book containing offices for ten weeks before Easter.
Trisagion:	Sung after the lesser entrance; threefold incantation of Agios (Sanctus) refrain.
Troparion:	Generic word for church songs; special term for hymn whose rhythm depends on a heirmos.
Tropologion:	Ancient book containing troparia.

KONTAKIA OF ROMANOS, BYZANTINE MELODIST

I: ON THE PERSON OF CHRIST

ON THE NATIVITY I (MARY AND THE MAGI)

O. 1 (K. 1)

Title: Τῆς ἁγίας καὶ πανσέπτου γεννήσεως τοῦ κυρίου ἡμῶν Ἰησοῦ Χριστοῦ

Manuscripts and editions: The prooimion and all the strophes except 19 are in all manuscripts. A has them in slightly different order, with a different acrostic. Maas in general follows P.

> This kontakion occurs in the *Menaion*, Prooimion and Strophe 1 for December 25.
> Pitra edited Nativity I in *A.S.*, I, 1.
> Maas, *Weihn.*, 1 ff.
> Cammelli, *R.M.*, 88 ff.
> French edition, II, 50–77.

Tone: ἦχος γ′

Acrostic: τοῦ ταπεινοῦ Ῥωμανοῦ [ὁ] ὕμνος (ʽΟ is omitted in B, D, and Δ).[1]

Refrain: παιδίον νέον, ὁ πρὸ αἰώνων θεός

Biblical source and place in the liturgy: The birth of Christ as told in Matthew ii.1–2, and Luke ii.1–15, is the basis of the narrative. The refrain echoes Psalm lxxiv.12 and I Corinthians ii.7.

> This kontakion has an uncontested place in the services for Christmas. According to tradition, it was composed with the aid of the Virgin.[2] The style, however, does not indicate that it was one of the earliest of the works of Romanos. The date of 518 for its composition is in line with the general content. It was for years sung on Christmas Day at the table of the emperors,[3] and for years sung by the double choir in Hagia Sophia in celebration of the birth of Christ.

Analysis of content: The prooimion states the theme for the feast day and the setting for the Nativity. Strophe 1 and the beginning of the second strophe give the narrative,

---

1. Probably Strophe 19 is not genuine. *Fr. ed.*, II, 45, agrees with Maas.
2. See my article, *Speculum*, 7 (January, 1932), 1 ff. The legend was, of course, not used in this article as a literary commentary of the writer of the *Menaion*; it was simply a departure for a consideration of the possible dual sources of this kontakion. This should clear up the misinterpretation in the note by L. A. Paton in *Speculum*, 7 (1932), 553. Actually, my purpose was explicitly stated on page 4 in the phrase, "a possible *poetic* truth."
3. Codini, *De Offic.* (Bonn, 1839), VII, C.

with allusions to David and Adam. The dialogue begins in Strophe 2, in which Mary's questions about the marvel of the virgin birth present the theology that continues into Strophe 3, with Mary presenting the paradox of king and manger.

The central section of the kontakion is the dialogue between Mary and the Magi; they question her about her parentage, and we have the antithesis of father, mother, fatherless. Strophe 5 allows the Magi to tell about the star; Strophes 6 and 7 include Mary's prayer to the Christ child to admit the Magi, and Christ answers in Strophes 8 and 9 that they should be allowed to enter. In Strophe 10, the Magi question Mary about Joseph; she answers them in Strophes 11 and 12 and inquires about their journey. For three strophes they tell of Babylon and Jerusalem. Mary, in Strophes 16 and 17, expresses astonishment that they eluded Herod and asks how they succeeded in doing so. They answer her in the next two strophes. Strophe 20 provides a transition, Strophe 21 states the prayer of the Magi as they offer their gifts, and the concluding three strophes include Mary's prayer to the Christ child to save the world.

Connection with homily: My article in *Speculum*, *Christmas*, 9, lists the sermons of interest in this connection. One has to be aware constantly (see Introduction, page xx) of the fact that certain phrases were common in the framework of early Christian writers. Some combinations of parallel phrases become significant. For example, if Basil's prose account[4] is arranged to emphasize the end rhymes, the following parallels with the prooimion emerge:

Basil (1472)
Μετὰ μάγων προσκυνήσωμεν,
μετὰ ποιμένων δοξάσωμεν,
μετὰ ἀγγέλων χορεύσωμεν,
ὅτι ἐτέχθη ἡμῖν σήμερον Σωτὴρ - - -ός

Romanos prooimion, 3–6
ἄγγελοι μετὰ ποιμένων δοξολογοῦσι,
μάγοι δὲ μετὰ ἀστέρος ὁδοιποροῦσι,
δἰ ἡμᾶς γὰρ ἐγεννήθη

However, they become typically nonsignificant when the many similar passages are considered.[5]

Certainly the play in Strophe 9 on the word θύρα, or *door*—which is used repeatedly by Romanos—is very common in Greek homily. The wording of the idea of the birth restoring Adam and Eve becomes significant when the phrase "Bethlehem opens up Eden" is followed by "Come let us enjoy the pleasures of Paradise," for this idea is to be found also in Theodotus of Ancyra (*P.G.*, lxxvii, 1949) in which the refrain of Romanos is also echoed. See the parallel passages as printed in *Speculum*.[6]

4. *P.G.*, xxxi, 1457–76.
5. *Christmas*, 14n2.
6. *Christmas*, 18n3.

The theological impact is made vivid in the brochure by Mrs. Topping that was discussed in the Introduction, pages xxii–xxiii. Comparisons of this kontakion with the Akathistos support the belief held by many that it, too, was by Romanos.[7]

Style of Romanos: For good dialogue with interesting folk touches, this hymn is perhaps unsurpassed. For example, Mary says that she will have need for these beautiful gifts when she takes that trip to Egypt. The Magi tell her that they answered Herod by telling him only the things he could understand! Mary shows a bit of jealousy of Sarah, and she is clever in explaining away the presence of Joseph, who can refute all doubts about her virginity! The emphasis on the divine and the human Christ is pervasive, as are the many antitheses between the all-powerful Christ and the small babe in the manger. Also, the statement that this event has been willed by Christ is of theological importance. Many references to the Old Testament are woven into the sermon-hymn-song. "The newborn babe, the God before all time," as used in the refrain, is both biblical and a part of homily tradition. The opening three words of the prooimion were evidently much loved for their melodious rhythm and for their appropriateness.

Meter: The metrical scheme is given in the Oxford edition, 517, I.

7. The best summary of the arguments about the authorship is included by Wellesz, *Byz. Mus.*, 191–97. He has made a careful study of the manuscripts of the hymn in *Dumbarton Oaks Papers*, ix, x (1956), 141–74, and in his book, *The Akathistos Hymn*, M.M.B. Transcripta, IX (1957). Combining as it does the features of the kontakion and of the litany, the style is much like that of Romanos. The various attributions to the Patriarch Sergius, George Pisides, and the Patriarch Germanus, as well as to Photius are due chiefly to the second prooimion, which clearly indicates a hymn celebrating a victory. However, the existence of a Latin ninth-century St. Gall manuscript clinches the fact that the hymn must have been written earlier and that it probably belongs to Romanos. The style is his; the Christology fits his approach to theological dogma.

ON THE NATIVITY I (MARY AND THE MAGI)

O. 1

Prooimion: The Virgin today gives birth to the superessential One,
        And the earth proffers the cave to the unapproachable One.
    Angels with the shepherds sing songs of praise;
        The Magi, with the star to guide pursue their way.
    For us there has been born,
        A newborn babe, the God before time.

Strophe 1:   Bethlehem opened Eden, come let us behold;
        We have found joy[1] in this hidden place, come let us seize
        The pleasures of Paradise within the cave;
    There appeared an unwatered root which sprouted forgiveness;
        There was found an undug well
        From which David once yearned to drink;[2]
    And there the Virgin brought forth an infant
        Who at once quenched their thirst, that of Adam and of David.
    Come, then, let us hasten to this place where there has been born
        A newborn babe, the God before time.

Strophe 2:   The father became of His own will the son of His mother,
        The Savior of children lay as a child in the manger.
        His mother looked down at Him and said:
MARY   "Tell me, my child, how the seed was planted in me and how
        it grew in me?
        I behold Thee, merciful One, and I am amazed
        That I, who am unwed, nurse Thee;
    And though I see Thee in swaddling clothes, still I behold
        My virginity untouched,
    For Thou hast preserved it, and yet consented to be born
        A newborn babe, the God before time.

1. According to *Fr. ed.*, II, 50n1, Greek commentators interpret the Hebrew *Eden* by τρυφή.
2. I Chron. xi.17–20.

4

Strophe 3: "Exalted King, what hast Thou to do with lowly ones?
MARY   Creator of Heaven, why hast Thou come to men on earth?
                Didst Thou long for the cave, or joy in the manger?
        Lo, there is no place, for Thy handmaiden at the inn;
                There is no place, not even a cave,
                Since that, too, belongs to another.
        On Sarah, as she was to bring forth a child,
        Was bestowed a great inheritance of land, but to me,
                Not even a den.
        I made use of the cave in which Thou dids't will to dwell as
                A newborn babe, the God before time."

Strophe 4: While she was pondering these things in secret,
                And entreating Him who has knowledge of all secret things,
                She hears the Magi who are seeking the child.
        Straightway, the maiden called out to them: "Who are you?"
MAGI   And they to her: "Who art thou
                Who hast produced and brought forth such an One?
        Who, thy father? Who, thy mother?
                For thou hast become the mother and nurse of a fatherless son.
        It was His star that we saw when we came to behold
                A newborn babe, the God before time.

Strophe 5: "Clearly did Balaam reveal to us
MAGI   The meaning of the words which were prophesied,
                Saying that a star would rise up,
        A star which would dim all prophecies and divinations,
                A star to destroy the parables of the wise,
                Their teachings and their enigmas,
        A star much brighter than this star which just appeared,
                For He is the maker of stars
        About whom it was written: 'From Jacob shall rise up
                A newborn babe, the God before time'." [3]

Strophe 6: When Mary heard the words of wonder,
                She knelt in obeisance to the One from her womb,
MARY   And crying out, she said: "Great things, my child,
        Great are all the things which Thou hast done for

3. Num. xxiv.17.

My humble station;
    For lo, the Magi without are seeking Thee;
Those who are kings of the east
    Seek Thy presence,
And the wealthy of Thy people beg to behold Thee;
For truly the people are Thine. They are the ones for
        whom Thou wast known as
    A newborn babe, the God before time.

Strophe 7:   "Since the people are Thine, my child, bid them
MARY   To come beneath this roof that they may see
            A poverty full of plenty, and beggary which is honored.
    I consider Thee a glory and cause for boast, so that I am not ashamed.
            Thou, thyself, art the grace and the comeliness
        Of my dwelling. Bid them enter.
    To me the want is no concern,
        For I consider Thee as a treasure which the kings came to see;
    For the kings and the Magi know that Thou hast appeared as
            A newborn babe, the God before time."

Strophe 8:   Jesus Christ, who is truly our God,
                Secretly suggested to His mother:
CHRIST   "Admit them, for my word led them,
    And shone on those who were seeking me.
            To all appearances, it is a star;
            But in reality, it is a power.
    It went with the Magi in service to me;
            And still it stands outside fulfilling its ministry,[4]
    And revealing with its beams the place where there has been born,
            A newborn babe, the God before time.

Strophe 9:   "Now receive, revered one, receive those who received me;
CHRIST   For I am in them as I am in thy arms,
                Nor was I away from thee when I accompanied them."

---

4. διακονίαν would probably allude to the liturgy for the point in the service when the deacon shows the priest the plate and the chalice. ὡς λειτουργῶν μοι is quoted by Mrs. Topping in this connection as a prophetic description of the poet himself in the ecclesiastical imagery of the star. E. C. Topping, "St. Romanos: Ikon of a Poet," *Gr. Orth. Theol. Rev.*, 12 (1966), 95, 111.

She, then, opens the door and receives the group of Magi.
>> She opens the door, she who is the unopened gate
>> Through which Christ alone passed;
> She opens the door, she who was opened
>> And yet never gave up the treasure of her virginity;
> She opened the door, she, from whom was born the door,
>> A newborn babe, the God before time.

Strophe 10: Straightway, the Magi hastened into the room,
>> And seeing Christ there they trembled because they knew
>> His mother, and her husband.
MAGI   So they spoke in fear: "This, thy son, is without genealogy.[5]
>> How is it then, Virgin, that we actually see
>> Within thy dwelling
> One who wooed thee? Was thy conception without taint?
>> Is not thy dwelling to be blamed since Joseph is with thee?
> There are a host of envious ones who seek where has been born
>> A newborn babe, the God before time."

Strophe 11: "I shall remind you," Mary said to the Magi,
MARY   "For what reason I have Joseph in my dwelling.
>> It is for the refutation of all who doubt.
> He himself will tell what he heard about my child,
>> For in his sleep he saw a holy angel
>> Who told him whence I conceived.[6]
> A goddess, shining like fire, reassured him
>> In the night and settled his thorny doubts.
> Therefore Joseph is with me to reveal that here is
>> A newborn babe, the God before time.

Strophe 12: "Clearly he will explain all the things that he heard.
MARY   Clearly he will report the things that he himself saw
>> Among the heavenly beings and mortals on earth—
> How the shepherds sang songs, and the shining ones sang with men of clay,
>> How the star ran ahead of you Magi to light your way and
>> To guide you.
> Then, passing by things foreordained,
>> Tell us the things which have happened to you.

5. Heb. vii.3.
6. Matt. i.20.

7

Whence have you come? How have ye gathered to see
A newborn babe, the God before time?"

Strophe 13:   When the radiant Virgin spake unto them with these words,
The lights of the East in answer replied:
MAGI   "Dost thou wish to know whence we have come here?
From the land of the Chaldeans where they do not say:
'Lord, God of Gods';[7]
From Babylon, where they do not know
Who is the maker of things which they worship;
From this place there came and started us on our way
Thy Son's spark from the Persian fire.
Having left behind the fire which is all-consuming, we shall
Behold the fire which refreshes,
A newborn babe, the God before time.

Strophe 14:   "All is vanity of vanities;[8]
MAGI   But no one is found among us who knows these things.
Some stray, and others are led astray.
Therefore, Virgin, all thanks to thy child through whose aid we
have been redeemed
Not only from error but also from the tribulation
Of all the countries through which we passed.
The races are godless; their tongues, unknown;[9]
But we have wandered over the earth, we have searched it out
By the light of the star, as we sought where has been born
A newborn babe, the God before time.

Strophe 15:   "So, while still we had Him as Light,
MAGI   We journeyed through all Jerusalem, duly fulfilling the
Words of the prophecy;
For we had heard that God threatened to search her;[10]
And by the star we went around
Desiring to see a great judgment;

7. Deut. x.17.
8. Eccles. i.14.
9. Zeph. i.12.
10. Zeph. i.12.

But it was not found, because the Ark had been taken away,
    The Ark with the beautiful things of old it contained.[11]
Ancient things were set aside,[12] and all things were renewed by
    A newborn babe, the God before time."

Strophe 16: "What!" said Mary to the faithful Magi,
MARY   "Did you pass through all Jerusalem,
          That city which slays prophets?[13]
    How did you come without harm through a city which mistreats all?
          And how did you elude Herod
          The godless one, who inspires murders not laws?"
MAGI   They answer her: "Virgin,
          We did not elude him, but we mocked him,
    And we conversed with all as we sought where was born
          A newborn babe, the God before time."

Strophe 17: When the Virgin heard their experiences,
MARY   She said to them: "What did Herod,
          The King, and the Pharisees ask you?"
MAGI   "First Herod, and then the chiefs of thy nation, as thou didst say,
          Inquired in detail about the time of the appearance of
          This star;[14]
    But the result was that they did not learn.
          They were not eager to see the One about whom they asked;
    For those who search are bound to behold
          A newborn babe, the God before time.

Strophe 18: "Foolish people suspected us of being senseless,
MAGI   And they asked us, 'Whence and when have you come?'
          'How did you follow hidden paths?'
    But we answered by referring to things which they understood:
          'How did *you* travel through
          The great desert which you traversed?'
    The One who led them out of Egypt
          Is the One who has just guided the men from Chaldea to Him.

11. II Kings xxiv.13.
12. II Cor. v.17.
13. Luke xiii.34.
14. Matt. ii.7.

Formerly, it was with a pillar of fire;[15] now with a star to reveal
    A newborn babe, the God before time.

Strophe 19: "The star was everywhere guiding our way,
MAGI   Just as Moses brought his wand for you,
          And the light of the knowledge of God shone round about.
Long ago manna fed you and the rock gave you to drink;[16]
          Hope of seeing Him satisfied us.
          So, nourished by His grace,
We intended to travel the pathless road
          And not to turn back in Persia;
For we yearn to behold, to worship, and to praise
          A newborn babe, the God before time."

Strophe 20: Such were the words of the Magi who did not stray.
          Their words were confirmed by the Virgin
          While the child approved both of her who after childbirth
Remained a mother without stain, and of the Magi who after
          Their journey show no fatigue of mind nor body;
          For none of them felt weariness
Just as Habakkuk did not weary when he went to Daniel.[17]
He who appeared to the prophets also appeared to the Magi
          A newborn babe, the God before time.

Strophe 21: After all the explanations were made,
          The Magi picked up their gifts and knelt
          Before the gift of gifts and the myrrh of myrrh.
Then they offered to Christ gold, frankincense, and myrrh,
MAGI   Saying: "Receive the triple gift
          Like the thrice-holy hymn of the Seraphim.
Do not reject it as the offerings of Cain;
          But accept it as the offering of Abel[18]
For the sake of her who produced Thee and from whom Thou hast
          been born for us as
          A newborn babe, the God before time."

15. Ex. xiii.21.
16. Ex. xvi.31, and xvii.5–6.
17. The editor of the *Fr. ed.* (II, 73*n*1) calls attention to a Syriac version of *The Gospel of Infancy*. Translated from the French: "The angel brought his food to the prophet Daniel who had been cast in the furnace to the lions at Babylon. This same angel by the aid of the Holy Spirit, guided the Kings of Persia to Jerusalem." The Greek name is Abakoum (Bel and Dragon, 33).
18. Gen. iv.4–6.

Strophe 22: When the blameless virgin saw the Magi
        Carrying in their hands the new and shining gifts, and
          kneeling before Him,
        And when she saw the shepherds singing hymns and the star
          clearly revealing Him,
    She entreated the One who is creator and Lord of all saying:
MARY   "Receive the three gifts, my child,
        And grant three prayers for her who gave Thee birth.
    I beg Thee in behalf of the heavens above
        And the fruits of the earth, and those who dwell thereon,
    Be reconciled to all for my sake, since Thou hast been born
        A newborn babe, the God before time.

Strophe 23: "For I am not simply Thy mother, O merciful savior,
MARY   Nor is it without prearranged plan that I give milk to Thee,
          the giver of milk;
        But I supplicate Thee in behalf of all men.
    Thou hast made me the pride and boast of all my race;[19]
        For Thy universe considers me as a powerful protection,
        Rampart, and stay.
    May those who were cast from the joys of Paradise
        Look to me that I may direct them
    To a perception of all things. Grant this for me who gave birth to Thee,
        A newborn babe, the God before time.

Strophe 24: "Save the world, Savior. For its sake Thou didst come.
MARY   Establish Thy kingdom. For its sake Thou hast let Thy light shine
        On me and the Magi, and all creation.
    Lo, the Magi, on whom Thou hast allowed the light of Thy
        Countenance to shine
        Are falling down before Thee, and they bring Thee gifts
    Of gold, beautiful things, much sought after.
        I have need of them, since I am about to go
    To Egypt, and flee with Thee, for Thee, my Guide, my Son, my Maker,
        my Redeemer, and
        Newborn babe, the God before time."

19. Compare Judith xv.9–11.

ON THE NATIVITY II
(ADAM AND EVE AND THE NATIVITY)

O. 2 (K. 42)

Title: Εἰς τὴν ἁγίαν γέννησιν τοῦ κυρίου ἡμῶν Ἰσοῦ Χριστοῦ
Τῆς ὑπεραγίας Θεοτόκου

Manuscripts and editions: The kontakion exists complete in A and P. The prooimion and some
strophes are given in B, T, J, and some "In another hand"[1] in G and M.

It was edited by Pitra, *A.S.*, I, 514–15.

It appears in the *Menaion* for December 26 (prooimion and first strophe).

It was edited by S. Eustratiadis, Ἀπόστολος βαρναβᾶς, III (1931),
901 f., and by E. Mioni, *Bolletino della Badia greca di Grottaferrata* (new
series XII, 1958), 5–12.

Tomadakis has it in Vol. III, #36, 357–86.

The French edition includes it, II, 86–111.

Maas edited a revision or recasting of the kontakion in *Gram.*, 565–87.

Tone: πλάγιος β′

Acrostic: Τοῦ ταπεινοῦ Ῥωμανοῦ

Refrain: ἡ κεχαριτωμένη

Biblical source and place in the liturgy: This kontakion is usually placed on December 26. The
prooimion and the first strophe are used as the kontakion in a kanon of Matins on
that date. The festival consecrated to the Virgin on December 26 is very old. The
refrain "Mary full of grace" should be compared to the Akathistos.[2]

Analysis of content: The theme is the redemption of man, and the hymn is centered on Mary as
the mediator between man and Christ. The prooimion contains many echoes of
Nativity I; it announces the theme of the birth of Christ and the emphasis on the

1. *Fr. ed.*, II, 87.
2. The best summary of the scholarship that has assigned various dates to the famous Akathistos is
to be found in Wellesz, *Byzantine Music and Hymnography* (2d ed., 1961), 191–97. The form of this
hymn is unusual in that it combines a series of salutations with the combination of narrative and dia-
logue that is peculiar to the kontakion. Once the idea that it must have been composed on the
occasion of a victory in time of siege was discarded, and once the Latin version was published, an
early date for the Akathistos seems more probable. My own opinion is that Romanos was the
author. Its refrain is identical with that of Kontakion #36. Wellesz included a detailed bibli-
ography in his discussion. See note 7 to Kontakion 1.

Virgin. The first two strophes focus on the marvel of Mary's virginity and her wonder at her present status and power. Strophes 3 through 7 contain the dialogue between Adam and Eve in which she tells him to rise up and hear the pleasant news and he replies that the voice he hears is pleasant, but he does not trust women! Eve reassures him and he admits that he senses a fragrance like that in Paradise. Strophes 8 and 9 contain the pleading, first of Adam and then of Eve, to Mary. Adam says that he represents the human race and he begs for mercy; Eve says that she suffers more than he does because she has to put up with his blaming her and wishing she had never been created. Mary is touched by their condition, and for three strophes she is presented as the merciful tender-hearted mother of a merciful son; she then appeals to Christ. In Strophes 13 and 14 Christ answers Mary; He restates that He came to live on earth only to save Adam and Eve and all mankind, and He reviews the reason for His birth. Strophes 15 through 18 are a dialogue between Christ and Mary, in which she asks for knowledge of His future plans. He tells her of His crucifixion and reassures her. The last strophe ends the kontakion rather abruptly: Christ tells of His resurrection and then, in about four lines, Mary returns to tell Adam and Eve that she has been successful as a mediator. The emphasis throughout the poem is clearly on Mary as the mediator and Christ as the Redeemer of the human race.

Connection with homily: I know of no specific parallels in homily, but sermons and hymns honoring Mary abound.

Style of Romanos: The dialogue is vivid. The insights into human nature are particularly exemplified in Adam's distrust of all women, after his painful experience, and in Eve's feeling that she has had to listen to a lot of complaints since their expulsion from Paradise. It is Eve who takes the initiative in rousing Adam to hear the good news, just as she is supposed to have taken the initiative in eating the apple! Again, in the dialogue between Mary and Christ, she will not let well enough alone, and although she is told that Christ will listen to her, she presses on (womanlike?) to know more about Christ's plans. Of course, the poet uses Eve's insistence to make Christ's death and resurrection explicit in its purpose. The ending is very abrupt; it lacks the usual finesse of Romanos in unifying a kontakion.

Meter: The metrical scheme is given in the Oxford edition, 517, II.

ON THE NATIVITY II
(ADAM AND EVE AND THE NATIVITY)

O. 2

Prooimion: He who was engendered before the Morning Star, without mother,
       from the Father,
       Has today, on earth, been born without father from thee.
Whereupon a star announces the good tidings to the Magi,
       And angels with shepherds sing songs of praise to
       Thy miraculous Son,
           Mary, full of grace.[1]

Strophe 1: The vine which produced the unfertilized fruit carried
       It as though in the encircling arms of the branches, and said:
MARY   "Thou, my fruit, my life,
       By whom I am known as I am and was. Thou art my God.
As I behold the seal of my virginity unbroken,
       I proclaim Thee the immutable Word become flesh.
I know no seed; I know Thee as one who delivers from corruption;
       For I am pure after having Thee as issue from me;
For Thou hast left my womb as Thou hast found it;
       Thou hast kept it safe.
For this reason the whole creation rejoices with me, crying:
           'Mary, full of grace.'

Strophe 2: "I do not disregard the grace which I receive from Thee, Master,
MARY   I do not discount the value which I attained when I gave birth to Thee;
For I rule over the world,
       Since, bearing Thy power in my womb, I am sovereign of all.
Thou hast transformed my worthlessness by Thy condescension;
       Thou hast humbled Thyself and exalted my race.
Now rejoice with me Heaven and earth,
       For I carry your creator in my arms.

---

1. The refrain becomes ambiguous in some strophes unless the name *Mary* is inserted. The Greek reads merely "full of grace."

Earthborn, lay aside sadness as you behold the joy
        Which I brought forth from my immaculate womb as
                I heard myself called:
                    'Mary, full of grace'."

Strophe 3:   While Mary hymned praise to the One whom she bore,
                        And caressed the babe whom she alone brought forth,
                Eve, who had given birth in pain,
                        Heard her, and rejoicing, said to Adam:
EVE   "A virgin has given birth to the Redemption of the curse;
                        Who has caused this hoped-for news to ring out in my ears?
                Her voice alone has released me from my torment.
                        Her childbirth has wounded the one who wounded me.
                She is the one whom the son of Amos prophesied as the rod of Jesse.[2]
                        It has brought forth a branch on which I shall feed and not die,
                                Mary, full of grace."

Strophe 4:   On hearing the swallow which sings at dawn,
                        Adam arose, freed from his deathlike sleep.
EVE   "Hear me, your wife,
                        Who long ago caused the fall of mortals; now I rise again.
                Consider the miracles; behold the woman who knew no man
                        Is healing you through her offspring.
                The serpent hitherto saw me and leaped for joy;
                        But now seeing those who are descended from us,
                            he flees creeping away.
                He did raise his head against me; but now, humbled,
                        He fawns; he does not mock, for he fears the One
                            whom she brought forth,
                                Mary, full of grace."

Strophe 5:   Adam, hearing the word which his wife contrived,
                        Immediately shook off the weight from his eyelids,
                Threw back his head as though from sleep,
                        And opening the ears which he had blocked through disobedience,
                            he spoke as follows:

2. This, of course, refers to the prophecy of Isaiah who was the son of Amoz. Amoz was not the prophet Amos.

16

ADAM   "I hear a clear warbling, a pleasant humming;
         But the voice of the singer does not charm me now;
For it is a woman whose voice I fear.
         I have had experience; from it, I distrust a female.[3]
The sound pleases me for it is sweet; but the musical
         instrument disturbs me
         For fear that a woman again lead me astray and bring disgrace on me,
             Mary, full of grace."

Strophe 6:   "Be fully reassured, my husband, by the words of your wife;
EVE   For you will not find me again giving you bitter advice.
The ancient things have passed away,
         And Christ, the son of Mary, brings to light all things new.
Catch the scent of this fresh smell, and at once burst into new life.
         Stand erect like an ear of corn, for spring has overtaken you.
Jesus Christ breathes forth a fresh breeze.
         Escaping from the burning heat where you were,
Come, follow me to Mary and with me cling to
         Her immaculate feet, and she will at once be moved to pity,
             Mary, full of grace."

Strophe 7:   "I recognize, wife, the spring, and I sense the luxury
ADAM   Which we enjoyed in the past; for indeed I see
A new, another paradise, the virgin,
         Bearing in her arms the tree of life itself, which once
The Cherubim kept sacred, kept me from touching.
         And I, watching the untouched tree grow,
Am aware, wife, of a new breath-bringing life
         To me, who was formerly dust and lifeless clay,
Making me come alive. And now, strengthened by this fragrance,
         I advance to her who causes the fruit of our life to grow,
             Mary, full of grace.

Strophe 8:   "Here am I at thy feet, O mother, virgin immaculate,
ADAM   And through me, the whole human race clings to thy feet.

3. In the poet's treatment of Eve, and in Adam's comments about her, I agree with Paul Maas that there is no belittling of women. Maas, *B.Z.*, 46 (1953), 140: "Dass Romanos bei dieser Gelegenheit das weibliche geschlecht verlästert, lässt tief blicken." Certainly, Romanos was no hater of women. The touches of humor of this type may be evidence of some influence of the mimes.

Do not disregard thy children
    Since thy Son has regenerated those who are in a state of corruption.
Take pity on me, Adam, the first created man, grown old in Hades;
    Pity thy father in his pleading, daughter;
Seeing my tears, have mercy on me,
    And lend a favoring ear to my lamentations.
Beholding the rags which I wear, which the serpent has woven for me,
    Alter my poverty by the power of Him to whom thou
      hast given birth,
        Mary, full of grace."

Strophe 9:   "Now, hope of my spirit, hear me, Eve,
EVE   And drive away the shame of one who bore her children in pain.
As thou dost know, I suffer more in my heart
    As I endure the complaining of Adam,
For he, as he remembers past joy turns against me,
    Railing at me as follows: 'If only you had not come
      forth from my side.
It was not good to take you as my helpmate;
    For I should not then have fallen into this abyss.'
Then I, not able to bear the reproaches and insults,
    Bend my head until thou dost restore me,
      Mary, full of grace."

Strophe 10:   The eyes of Mary as she beheld Eve
    And as she looked on Adam, quickly filled with tears;
However she held them back, and tried earnestly
    To conquer her nature, though she had given birth to her son,
      Christ, in a manner beyond nature.
But, sympathizing with her parents, her heart was troubled.
    A tender mother was only fitting for the Merciful One.
MARY   Hence she said to them: "Cease your lamentations,
    I shall become mediator for you in the presence of my son.
Dispel your sense of misfortune, since I have produced joy;
    For I have come now to pillage all kinds of grief.
      I, Mary, full of grace.

Strophe 11:   "I have a son who is merciful, even too compassionate,
MARY   As I know from what I experienced; I observe how He spares:

Although He is fire, he inhabited
    My womb and did not consume me, humble as I am.
Just as a father pities his children, my child pities
    Those who fear Him, as David prophesied.
Restraining your tears, then, accept me
    As your mediator in the presence of my son.
For, as a source of grace, the God before all time has been born.
    Be at peace, without sorrow, for I go to Him,
        I, Mary, full of grace.''

Strophe 12: With these words, Mary as lover of mankind [4]
    Cheers Eve and her husband.
Going to the crib,
    She bows her head and entreats her son as she says:
MARY "My son, since Thou hast exalted me through Thy condescension,
    My poor race, through me, now beseeches Thee.
For Adam, lamenting bitterly, came to me,
    And Eve joined him in his complaints.
The serpent is the cause of this, since he despoiled them of their honor.
    Therefore, they are begging to be covered, as they cry to me:
        'Mary, full of grace'.''

Strophe 13: As soon as the immaculate one brought these petitions
    To the God lying in the cradle, at once He received them
        and subscribed to
The writings of the prophets; [5]
CHRIST He says: "O mother, I save them because of thee and through thee.
Had I not willed to save them, I should not have dwelt in thee,
    I should not have allowed my light to shine from thee, and thou
        wouldst not have heard thyself called my mother.
It is for thy race that I lie in the crib;
    At my will I now give milk to thy breasts.

4. If τυγχάνουσα is to be supplied rather than the reading in A, then the meaning added is that she has "attained at this time" the role of lover of man. The French edition uses A καὶ ἄλλοις δὲ τοῖς πλείοσι, and this, the editors believe, is Romanos' typical prelude to a long speech. *Fr. ed.*, II, 103n2.
5. This could mean "of matters hidden"; it could refer to the interpreters or prophets. A uses ἐσχάτως, which would introduce the idea of the last days.

Thou dost bear me in thy arms for their sake. The Cherubim
    do not see me,
      But thou dost behold me, and carry me and cherish me as son.
        Mary, full of grace.

Strophe 14: "I, the creator of the universe, have taken thee as mother;
CHRIST   And, as a child, I grow—I, perfect, from thee, without stain.
I am swathed in swaddling clothes
    For the sake of those who long ago wore covering of skin;
The cave is beloved by me for the sake of those who hated
    The pleasure of paradise, and loved corruption,
And transgressed my life-bearing command.
    I came down to earth in order that they might have
      incorruptible life.
But if thou dost learn, holy one, that I am crucified, and died for them,
    Thou, along with all creation, wilt be disturbed and mourn,
      Mary, full of grace."

Strophe 15: When He, who created all languages, said these things,
    And quickly answered the prayers of His mother,
MARY   Mary said, "If yet again
    I speak, do not, O Molder of clay, be angry with me, mere clay;
For, as the one who gave Thee birth, I take courage to
    speak freely to my child,
    For Thou hast given all reason to boast to me, Thy child.
Now I wish to know what it is that Thou art going to accomplish.
    Do not conceal from me Thy plan for eternity.
Thee have I produced, complete; tell me now the purpose which
    Thou hast for us
    So that I may learn from this what kind of grace I have received,
      Mary, full of grace."

Strophe 16: "I am conquered by the loving concern which I have for man,"
CHRIST   The Maker answered. "To thee, my mother and my servant,
I shall not cause pain, but I shall let thee know,
    O Mary, what I intend to do; and I shall care for thy soul.
You will see me, the babe whom thou dost carry in thy hands,
    With his hands nailed to the cross in a short while, because

I love thy race.

    The one to whom thou dost give milk, others will cause to drink gall.
The one whom thou dost call life, thou shalt see hanging on a cross,
    And thou shalt weep for him as dead; but thou shalt greet me risen,
        Mary, full of grace.

Strophe 17: "Of my own will shall I experience these things,
CHRIST   And the cause of all these things will be my own dispensation,
The plan which long ago, from the beginning until now
    I have shown for men. As God, I live to save."
Mary, when she heard what He said, sighed from the depths
MARY   Of her heart, and said: "O fruit of my womb, do not let
        the lawless crush Thee;
I caused Thee to burst into life, let me not see Thy destruction."
    He answered her with these words:
CHRIST "Cease, mother, lamenting for things which thou dost not understand;
        for unless these things are brought to pass,
    All of those people for whom thou dost intercede will be destroyed,
        Mary, full of grace.

Strophe 18: "Consider my death as a sleep, mother;
CHRIST   After I have passed three days in the tomb, of my own free will,
After this, thou shalt see me
    Risen both for the renewal of the earth, and those on earth,
Announce these things to all, mother; in these things
        thou shalt be enriched.
    Because of them, thou art queen; for them, thou shalt rejoice."
At once Mary went to Adam,
    And bringing the good news to Eve, she said:
MARY "Be patient a while longer, for you heard from Him
    The future which He said was waiting for you who cry out to me,
        'Mary, full of grace'."

ON THE MASSACRE OF THE INNOCENTS
(THE FLIGHT INTO EGYPT)

O. 3 (K. 44)

Titles: Εἰς τὰ ἅγια νήπια. B, G
  Τῶν ἁγίων νηπίων. D, P

Manuscripts and editions: B has only one strophe, D has 3; P is the chief source. It has been edited by C. Rhikakis in the edition of Tomadakis, I, 117–45.
  It appears also in the French edition, II, 119–225. The latter expresses some doubt as to its authorship by Romanos because of the lack of consistency in the answers of the soldiers to Herod and in the occasional lapse of relevance in the refrain.
  Certainly frequent metrical irregularities occur, but Maas-Trypanis have included it among the genuine kontakia in the Oxford edition.

Tone: ἦχος πλάγιος β′

Acrostic: τοῦ ταπεινοῦ ‘Ρωμανοῦ

Refrain: ὅτι ὁ κράτος αὐτοῦ καθαιρεῖται ταχύ

Biblical source and place in the liturgy: The twenty-eighth of December is set aside for the "Feast of the Holy Innocents." Duchesne dates the origin of this ritual in the fifth century.[1] This ritual would not then be later than Romanos.[2]
  Matthew ii.13–18 provides the biblical narrative.

Analysis of content: The prooimion introduces the topic of the slaughtering of innocents by Herod's decree. Strophe 1 connects the incident with the Old Testament, and the next two strophes tell of Herod's growing fear even though he boasts that the Magi's prophecy has not really bothered him. Strophes 4 through 6 give his dialogue with the army. At first the soldiers refuse to obey an order against children, but then they suddenly urge the attack as they recall the sins of the Jews against characters of the Old Testament. The next three strophes describe the growing anger and fury of the King and its results on the people. Strophes 9 through 11 relate the mourning of the people; following more invectives against the Jews and additional descriptions of Herod's fury, Strophe 14 presents details of

---

1. In Constantinople it was on December 29. L. Duchesne, *Origines du culte chrétien* (Paris, 1920), 268.
2. The editor of the *Fr. ed.*, II, 199, suggests that it would be later.

the slaughter. Strophes 15 through 17 give us the figure of the tree planted in Egypt, the assurance of the great power of God as evidenced in the overthrow of idols, and His ministry to those in flight. The usual closing prayer includes the poet's personal prayer for forgiveness.

Connection with homily: Romanos' additions and amplifications may well have been influenced by some of the many homilies on this subject, especially those by Basil of Seleucia, "De Infantibus in Bethlehem ab Herode Sublatis" (*P.G.*, 85, 387–400), and Gregory of Nyssa, "In Diem Natalem Christi" (*P.G.* dubia, 46, 1128–50). Basil of Seleucia, in his homily, gives Herod's direct commands, describes the killings, and tells of the flight into Egypt. There are many verbal similarities, such as the references to women becoming daring, the sharp blows of the swords, mothers who struck in defense of their children, and the horrible details of cutting in two the nursing infants (Romanos, Strophes 11 and 14).

     Migne lists the homily of Gregory of Nyssa as *dubia*, but both Bardenhewer and Mercati consider it as genuine and a reflection of the influence of Ephrem.[3] The references that parallel Romanos are very frequent in this homily: the bare sword, the nursing mothers, the necks bared to the slayer.[4] Aside from the vivid realism of these passages, there are other parallels to the earlier strophes of Romanos' kontakion. For example, the lamb and the lion are introduced by Basil of Seleucia[5] and the fathers who mourned with the mothers.[6] The references to the return to Abraham's bosom,[7] the pursuit into mountains and valleys,[8] have parallels in Pseudo-Chrysostom,[9] who refers to Abraham's bosom and to Herod's mad rage. The latter are perhaps purely coincidental.

Style of Romanos: Certainly this kontakion is not one of the most pleasing of the poet's works. Metrical flaws and the fact that the refrain does not always make sense leave one with the feeling that he may have been condensing some well-known homily. This feeling is especially strong when the soldiers object to Herod's order to make war on babes (Strophe 5, 1–5) and then at once change to urging Herod to make a good job of it (Strophe 5, 5–12). Objections to the horrors of the gory details of the slaughter itself could hardly be considered valid, since realistic detail, pleasant or unpleasant, is a characteristic of Romanos. Modern taste may also reject his tirade against the Jews in Strophe 12, but, again, this attitude is expressed strongly by Romanos in other poems.

     There are many indications of his characteristic play on words and rhetorical antithesis: Those who exult at the news of Christ's birth are balanced by

3. Otto Bardenhewer, *Geschichte der Altkirchlichen Literatur* (Freiburg, 1924), III, 207; S. J. Mercati, *S. Ephraem Syri Opera* (Rome, 1915), I, 36–41.
4. See especially *P.G.*, 46, 1145A: πῶς ἄν τις διαγράψει - - - χερσὶ τοῦ δημία διαφθειρόμενον; and 1145B, τίς ἄν τὸ πολυειδὲς through τέκνον τοῖς κόλποις ἐδέχετο.
5. *P.G.*, 85, 393C.
6. *P.G.*, 85, 396B.
7. *P.G.*, 85, 397C.
8. *P.G.*, 85, 393A.
9. *P.G.*, 61, 702C and 699D.

those who mourn at the slaughter of the innocents; passages contrast the power of Jesus as God on a throne and His humble birth in a manger; Herod laughs at himself as ruler of land and sea who falls into terror over the existence of a babe; the fruit to be planted is contrasted with the desert's arid sterility; and the faithful are urged to offer up their weeping and not sweet hymns.

The kontakion alludes to many characters in the Old Testament: Ramah, Jacob, Rachel, Benjamin, Isaiah, Abel, Zacharias, David and Goliath, and Moses.

It is chiefly in wealth of figurative language that one sees the imagination of the poet at work on more than the gory details of the slaughter. The prooimion states that Herod will mow the children down like wheat. Other agricultural comparisons appear in mention of the young branches, the flowers that fall after their first bloom, the premature harvest of the green vineyard. Chiefly, however, the motif is one of the hunt, quite appropriately. Wolf, dogs, lamb, and lion, vultures and the eagle, nets and snares are details of the references to Herod the hunter, and we have the darts of his anger used, not for burning away the brambles, but for murder. One of the most effective details occurs when the poet develops the idea of the weeping of bereft parents echoing from the hills with a sound like thunder and introduces vivid reference to practise beats that sound back and forth antiphonally. In Strophe 10, 3–5, the pertinence of the words ἀντηχοῦντες ὠλόλυζον· τὴν οἰμωγὴν - - - ἀφομοιοῦντες συνέπασχον ἀλλήλοις defy translation, which necessarily loses the onomatopoeia.

The touches of human nature in Herod's assuring the soldiers that this is an easy war and in their first rejection of his orders for fear of ridicule are worthy of Romanos, even though the condensed end to the fifth strophe is not clear.

Meter: The metrical scheme is given in the Oxford edition, 518, III.

ON THE MASSACRE OF THE INNOCENTS
(THE FLIGHT INTO EGYPT)

O. 3

Prooimion: At the time when the King was born in Bethlehem,
  The Magi left the land of the Persians[1] with gifts,
   Guided by a star from on high;
 But Herod is stirring up trouble and mowing down the children
   like wheat, lamenting
    That his power will soon be destroyed.

Strophe 1: While those on high and those on earth are rejoicing,
  What is there at Ramah to cause
  Endless lamentation there? Jacob is exulting; but why
   is Rachel mourning?[2]
 Joseph has been recognized; but why does Rachel groan?
  Benjamin has been exalted;[3] why, then does Rachel weep?
 Come, then, let us see the lamentation and mourning;
  For she does not mourn for the first children,
  But those who were betrayed and redeemed,
 Those whom the most savage Herod has now slaughtered.
  For he matched the very time at which the star shone forth,
 And sent to Bethlehem to deprive Rachel of her children because of
   the child of Mary.
  But she found them again with joy,
  While Herod laments
   That his power will soon be destroyed.

Strophe 2: The anxiety which he had always feared
  Now came to him when he did not wish it;

---

1. *L'Évangile arabe de l'enfance*, trans. by Peeters, *Évangiles apocryphes*, II (Paris, 1914), 3. See Romanos O. 1.
2. Jer. xxxi.15; Matt. ii.18.
3. Benjamin was blessed by Moses (Deut. xxxiii.12); Saul was of the tribe of Benjamin (I Sam. ix.1), and David succeeded him. Christ's being "the root and offspring of David" (Rev. xxii.16) explains Romanos' statement that "Benjamin has become exalted." Rachel was buried near Ephrath or Bethlehem (Gen. xlviii.7).

For what he had not expected he learned on studying the
    sayings of the prophet,
For Isaiah says: "Unto us a child is born, and unto us a son is given,
    And the government shall be upon his shoulders,
And his name shall be called,
    Messenger of great wisdom." He is a strong God
    Upon His throne, and in the manger; and He is everywhere,
      and infinite.
Herod, frightened, deeply feared Him, and investigated carefully to learn
    Where had been born, where appeared the King of the universe.
    And he learned for a certainty
      That his power will soon be destroyed.

Strophe 3:   He was suddenly aroused from peaceful slumber,
    And he was thrown into confusion through fear,
    For he was constrained by fear, and he trembled at the name
      of the one who was born.
When he learned from the Magi the power of the child,
    He uttered cries of suffering mixed with laughter:

HEROD   "O, of all unexpected evils, that a babe should make me afraid!
    O, miserable idea that
    I should tremble before a child whom I have not seen!
I rule over sea and land,[4] and an infant terrifies me!
    What shall I do today? What shall I plan for tomorrow?
Suddenly a star has shone upon the whole earth, and has heralded Him
    As mighty King who will destroy
    My kingdom, and I mourn
      That my power will soon be destroyed."

Strophe 4:   These words he uttered in his confusion,
    And mulling over these thoughts, he pondered
    How he could most quickly destroy the infant whom
      the Magi proclaimed.
Calling his army, he gave them license
    As he spoke to all of them in a rough voice as follows:

HEROD   "Go quickly into cities and the countryside

---

4. *Cf.* Romanos, On the Three Children (O. 46). There Nebuchadnezzar is "lord of land and sea," Strophe 6.

In full armor, and bearing yourselves proudly,

    Assuming a garb of mercilessness,

And slay all the sons of Bethlehem.

    This war has no difficulty, no cause for timidity,

I send you against babes, tender two-year-olds; no one opposes

    A royal order. All people tremble,

    And they do not say

        'His power will soon be destroyed'."

Strophe 5:   When they heard this, the army

        At once answered the speech of Herod:

ARMY   "We are afraid to bring about what you have commanded,

        for fear that we be ridiculed.

For who of foolish men will not laugh

    That we make war on babes?

If it is Bethlehem where the babe is born,

    Command us and we shall soon destroy it all,

    Palaces and homes.

Then no one will say to you, 'King, do not bother with this matter,'

    No one will blame you for finding out what you learned.

Attack, attack the one who comes on earth from Heaven.

    It was a tradition in Bethlehem to produce kings;

    Do not give offense to Bethlehem

        Lest your power will soon be destroyed.

Strophe 6:   "Hitherto Bethlehem produced David,

ARMY   The great king; Goliath, a foreigner,

    Feared David after he was born with a terror as great as we

        now feel for the one just born

Therefore, if it seems best to you, O King,

    Let all Bethlehem and its boundary spots be searched

So that among the infants slaughtered there

    We may find this babe who has been born[5]

    And destroy him with the others.

The birth was revealed to you and the place was made known to you;

    The Magi mocked you and the prophets terrified you.

---

5. Two lines here are obviously corrupt. The French edition uses τὸ γεννηθέντα to modify βρέφος, and this makes sense better than τῷ γεννηθέντι in the Oxford text. The neuter accusative of the participle is used elsewhere by Romanos: Kontakion 26, Strophe 1, λυθέντα; and Kontakion 43, Strophe 11, ὁρῶντα. *Fr. ed.,* II, 213n1.

Command your followers, then, and we shall wipe from the earth
    The one who wants to overthrow your kingdom
    And do not be fearful
        That your power will soon be destroyed."

Strophe 7:   Immediately after he had hearkened to the words
    Of his soldiers, the slayer of infants
    Became as a fire, and sent forth as javelins the darts of his anger,
Not for burning thorns, but for murdering babes,
    And defacing the earth with blood.
For his mind was unhinged and his reason darkened,
    Not by drunkenness but by envy.
    He himself became a grape of bitterness
As the unjust man cut down young branches for the sake of one;
    The former he did cut off;
But he did not overtake the latter.
For this reason he was filled with savage anger as he heard the report;
    And he remained in mourning
        That his power would soon be destroyed.

Strophe 8:   The wolf, having tracked down the great whelp,
    Arouses the wicked dogs against him;
    They run in and outside Bethlehem seeking their prey.
But he mangles the lambs, and not the lion,
    For he cannot with his glance meet him face to face.
The vultures hunted the eagle on the mountains,
    But He was in hiding,
    Covering and warming with His wings
The nest which He had just built with His own hands,
    Although it was just a short time ago that the virgin, without husband,
      had given birth to Him;
For He is His father and maker of the world and creator of peace.
    And if Herod makes war, toiling uselessly,
    He will in truth sing a dirge
        That his power will soon be destroyed.

Strophe 9:   When a shining cloud spread over
    All Judaea and cast its shadow,
    Herod introduced darkest night and covered all men with gloom.

At once he revealed the children, who by nature
    Are joyous and laughter loving, weeping bitterly.
Those who a short time ago were rejoicing in the
    Childbirth of the immaculate and pure Mary
    Are now wailing with lamentations.
Just as though a flower on the very day of its bloom fell to the ground,
    And everyone seeing it mourned and declared to Rachel:
"Come, weep, Rachel, join in mourning with us, a song of distress
    In place of a joyous ode, in place of a sweet hymn,
    Let us offer weeping."
        (His power will soon be destroyed.)[6]

Strophe 10: The echo of those who weep for the young children
    Makes a crash like thunder on the earth,
    For the hills and ravines and deep valleys of the mountains
        cried aloud in answer.
As though imitating the wailing,
    They practised beats of lamentation with one another.
It was necessary to see the earth full of blood,
    And the desert and the uninhabited places,
    For this lawless and very arrogant man extended
His anger right up to these places.
    For he pursued the mothers and when he caught up with them
He snatched the children[7] from their very arms, like the fledgling
    of a sparrow singing a sweet song.
    And he slaughtered them, not understanding, the wicked fellow,
    That in spite of doing these things,
        His power will soon be destroyed.

Strophe 11: With bared swords, the soldiers met
    The mothers carrying their children in their arms.
    Overcome with fear, the mothers cast down their children whom
        they had nursed with love,
For women are by nature fearful—
    Perhaps also they become impulsive and rash.

6. The text here shows a lacuna that is probably to be explained by the fact that the refrain does not, in this strophe, fit the sense.
7. The reading τέκνα, which Trypanis marked *dub*, would make better sense than ταύτας.

It was in this spirit that some of them importunately
      begged their murderers,
      And they laid bare their necks to them
      Since they desired to die before
Their children rather than see them slaughtered.
      Each mother became a reliable witness of this.
So that each cried bitterly: "Kill them, but the bosom of Abraham
      Will receive them like the faithful Abel."
      But Herod mourns
         That his power will soon be destroyed.

Strophe 12: As the lawless ones shed the innocent blood
      Of the blameless children, it is necessary to recall
      Abel, as he offered to God his sacrifice, pure and undefiled,
And then be reassured. For he was slain.
      Also, one must consider Zacharias
As he brings his accusation there before God
      Against those who murdered him.
      For always the Jews and those who govern them
Were insolent and lawless,
      Murderers, and stupid, and transgressors of the law.[8]
They rejected Moses; they cut Isaiah in pieces,[9]
      And now they are slaughtering the children of Rachel.
      Hence, indeed, they mourn
         (That his power will soon be destroyed.)[10]

Strophe 13: O depravity, O madness of the King,
      O pitiless temper which made war
      On babes and showed no mercy to his own people;
He was not mindful of his own children
      Nor of the fact that there is the same nature for all.
He did not pity his family; but maddened with rage
      He at first ignored even himself[11]
      And then all of his brothers,

8. Romanos, a Christianized Jew, is especially violent against them.
9. An old tradition, referred to in "The Ascension of Isaiah." See Heb. xi.37.
10. Obviously, this is another place where the manuscript is faulty and where the refrain does not fit the meaning of the strophe.
11. That is to say: He paid no attention to his own paternal instinct. According to tradition, Herod did destroy some of his own family. *Golden Legend*, trans. by Ryan and Ripperger (New York, 1941), 66–67.

As he attacked all people like a wild beast
　　When it flees from its pursuers who lay snares for it.
Fathers mourned for their sons and mothers with them;
　　　but the shameless man
　　Did not care about them; but one thing alone
　　He considered as he wept
　　　That his power would soon be destroyed.

Strophe 14: With daggers they are slain mercilessly
　　These blameless infants as though in a massacre;
　　Some were transfixed and breathed their last horribly;
Others were cut in two
　　Still others had their heads cut off as they suckled
And drew milk from the breasts of their mothers.
　　Then, as a result of this the cherished heads of the babes hung
　　From the breasts, and the nipples were still held
Within their mouths by their delicate teeth.
　　Then the distress of the women who were nursing the infants
Redoubled and became intolerable as they were physically torn from
　　　their two-year-old infants,
　　And as they were robbed of their babes by order of the King.
　　Because of this order, he weeps
　　　That his power will soon be destroyed.

Strophe 15: Herod was seeking an unripe grape by which he would make
　　An unseasonable harvest.
　　Winter was settling in when Mary produced the unfertilized grape,
And he did not find a ripened fruit but reaped a green harvest.
　　For the fruit of the only pure virgin
Is going to flee to Egypt along with the vine
　　To be planted there and bring forth fruit—
　　Flee to the land of the Jews,
Arid and barren of anything beautiful,
　　And arrive at the Nile, which is fertile—
Not as Moses on the river, thrown in the marsh, protected
　　　by a wicker basket,
　　But rather as one to overthrow all their idols there.[12]

12. This reference to Isa. xix.1 is used several times by Romanos and was included in the Gospels of
the Infancy.

As Herod is a friend of these idols, he sees
  That his power will soon be destroyed.

Strophe 16: Nets and snares were fashioned, then,
  For the young fawn of the Virgin and mother of God,
  But the trap was broken and the fawn escaped, tearing the snare.[13]
With his mother, like a blameless deer, he fled
  Into Egypt, as Micah once said.[14]
O Thou who art everywhere and who rulest over all,
    where dost Thou flee?
  Where dost Thou lead? In what city
  Shalt Thou make Thy dwelling?
What house will contain Thee, what place will support Thee?
  No part of creation anywhere is invisible to Thy sight,
But all things are laid bare to Thee, Thou art the maker of all, O Christ.
  Why, then, dost Thou flee, Holy One?
  Because of Thee, Herod mourns as he weeps
    That his power will soon be destroyed.

Strophe 17: The one who flees, flees absolutely, in order that He may escape
    Being recognized by those who seek Him.
But the only merciful Jesus, our Savior, fled in His visible form,
    But by all of His deeds was made known to all.
    At the very time when He arrived in Egypt,
Straightway all of the statues fashioned by man were shaken down.
    For the one who caused the trembling in Herod
Also brought on the quaking of the idols.
    He was hidden in the arms of His mother, and He acted as God.
    He proceeded into Egypt and an angel from on high
Ministered to His flight. Of His own will was He banished as a
    poor little babe,
    And as wealthy, He announced to all
    Why Herod mourns
        That his power will soon be destroyed.

Strophe 18: You, then, my brothers, grant me pardon
    For my heedlessness; and let us rise
    To worship the One who came to save the whole human race,

13. Ps. cxxiv.7.
14. Mic. vii.15.

As we cry out from contrite heart to the Master
  To be delivered from the slayer of men
And quickly released from our sins
  To find the road of virtue.
  And I am the first to say this
For I have sinned greatly, both knowingly and in ignorance;
  And I have angered God by my impure deeds.
For this reason, I beg you to rise with me and cry out sincerely,
  "By the intercession of Thy holy mother, O God,
  And of Thy holy Innocent Babe,
    Do not separate me from Thy kingdom, Christ."

ON THE PRESENTATION IN THE TEMPLE

O. 4 (K. 6)

Title: Εἰς τὴν ὑπαπαντὴν τοῦ κυρίου ἡμῶν Ἰησοῦ Χριστοῦ

Manuscripts and editions: Pitra, *A.S.*, I, 5.

            Krumbacher, *Stud.*, 184–201.

            Cammelli, *R.M.*, 121–54.

            Tomadakis, II, 305–32.

            French edition, II, 172–225.

            Menaion, February 2, Prooimion I and Strophe 1.

            The French edition, in its introduction to this hymn, points out (II, 163*n*2) that there are, in all, thirty manuscripts for this kontakion and that its popularity is attested also by the fact that it is the only kontakion for this feast—at least, we suppose that it was written for the Epiphany, which in 542 was transferred to February 2. The Western or Italian family of manuscripts use *Δ*; the French edition relies chiefly on A, while Maas puts the emphasis on A and P, although he does include a larger number of manuscripts than usual in the critical apparatus.

            The third prooimion shows evidence of much revision. It must have been composed at the time of some danger to the city or to the rulers. This circumstance would certainly not give it any exact date. The word $βασιλεῖς$ would point to the fact that Theodora was alive. Perhaps, then, it would be dated between A.D. 542 and 548, but such dating is very dubious.

Tone: ἦχος ά

Acrostic: τοῦ ταπεινοῦ Ῥωμανοῦ τὸ ἔπος

Refrain: Ὁ μόνος φιλάνθρωπος

Biblical source and place in the liturgy: Luke ii.21–38, tells of the presentation of the Christ child in the Temple, eight days after His birth, and of the elder, Simeon, who had prayed to see the Christ and then to be released from life.

            The festival of the Hypapante (late form of ὑπάντησις, or "coming to meet") was celebrated in Jerusalem, according to Etheria;[1] but at that time, since the East did not celebrate the birth of Christ on December 25, the festival occurred

---

1. *Itinerarium Etheriae*, Otto Prinz, ed. (Heidelberg, 1960), 36.

on February 14, or forty days after Epiphany. The settling upon February 2 for the celebration probably dates from A.D. 542.[2]

Analysis of content: The incident of Simeon and the Christ child becomes the vehicle for an emphasis on the two natures of Christ. The formula used against the Monophysites reflects in Strophe 16 the Justinian law after the Council of Chalcedon. "Thou hast at the same time remained on high and come here below." Simeon uses the exact phrases from controversies: "The perfect image of the incomprehensible nature [hypostasis] of the Father" (Strophe 6), and "One, visible and invisible, finite and infinite" (Strophe 8). The paradox of the two natures is first expressed by the angels in the series of antitheses in Strophes 1 and 2. Then Mary advances with the child and ponders on the miracle by way of wondering what to call Him—man or God—and she wonders whether to give Him milk or worship Him. Simeon in three strophes expresses his joy and fear as he enunciates a series of epithets of adoration with the antithetical reminders that Christ is both finite and infinite and beyond natural laws. One strophe is directed to Mary, with the figure of Mary as the closed gate, opened, protected by Christ; then Simeon prophesies how all men are to be saved, in Strophes 10 and 11, and this passage leads to the central statement of theology in Strophe 12, in which the heresies are answered by way of comments on the questions that will be raised by Christ's death on the cross. "Some [will] surmise that His body is divine (οὐράνιον σῶμα); others, that it is mere phantasy (ἄλλοι φαντασίαν); . . ." Simeon then foretells that Mary's anxieties will be as a sword that will pierce her, and the poet devotes three strophes to Simeon's prayer that he may now be released from the earth. Christ replies in one strophe, in which He states that He has fulfilled all the prophecies. The closing prayer in Strophe 18 asks that violence and oppression be kept from the faithful, and the last phrase reiterates that Christ became man without undergoing change[3] (ἄνθρωπος ἀτρέπτως γενόμενος).

Connection with homily: Before the day of Romanos there were very few sermons or poems for this festival.[4] There is, however, a letter of St. Basil to Bishop Optimus that contains striking parallels to Strophes 10 through 13, to which E. Bickersteth has called attention.[5] Bickersteth notes that scholars have known that Romanos borrowed ideas and words from two sources: the hymns of Ephrem the Syrian and the dramatic sermons of Basil of Seleucia; on one occasion he took as model for four successive strophes the final paragraphs of an exegetical letter of Basil the Great.

---

2. Paul Maas, *Chron.*, 9. Maas suggests that the date of the transfer may well have been the occasion of this poem.

3. The last strophe with the reference to violence is one that appears in different forms in different manuscripts.

4. That of Cyril of Alexandria, *P.G.*, 77, 1039D–49C and one of Pseudo-Chrysostom, *P.G.*, 50, 807–12, are mentioned in the French edition, II, 165n1, as having some relation to phrasing in the kontakion. The one attributed to Athanasius of Alexandria is clearly apocryphal; it is by George of Nicomedia in the ninth century.

5. E. Bickersteth, "A Source of Romanos' Hypapante Contakion," *Actes du VI Congr. Intern. Études Byz.* (Paris, 1950), 375–81. Basil's 260th letter, Migne, *P.G.*, 32, 953D.

In Romanos' Presentation kontakion, he has Simeon, when speaking to the Virgin, use direct speech and thereby reduces Basil's version by about one half. Romanos omits Anna and the prophets; he adds speeches by the angels, the Virgin, and God. Also, Romanos places the *Nunc dimittis* after and not before Simeon's prophecy. One interesting detail is his treatment of the idea of what happens to a sinner. Basil says that the believer who sins falls, dies, then rises and lives in righteousness. Romanos adds another idea in Strophe 11.[6] Also, note that Basil speaks of the various heresies in phrases reminiscent of Romanos.[7] Again worthy of comparison is the idea expressed in the thirteenth strophe of Romanos when Simeon tells the Virgin that after the doubts and contradictions that will occur to her at the time of the crucifixion, Christ will send healing to her heart.[8] Paul Maas calls attention to parallels to be found in the homilies of Basil of Seleucia,[9] and the French edition mentions similar passages in Cyril of Jerusalem, Cyril of Alexandria, and St. John Chrysostom.[10] Quite clearly the authors of both hymns and homilies were intent on references to the terminology of the controversies of the day, and it becomes almost impossible to say who, other than Justinian, was the originator of the special terminology.[11]

Style of Romanos: This kontakion is not to modern taste, since the emphasis is not on the drama of the situation but on answers to heretics. It is, therefore, difficult for us to realize that it was the most popular of all of the kontakia of Romanos, even more popular than the Mary–Magi Christmas kontakion.[12] In spite of the theological emphasis, there is evidence of the happy turn of phrase typical of Romanos. The antitheses seem to flow, the figures of speech he loved are frequent: the fire of divinity, the seal of divinity, Christ held as a lamp, frequent references to light, the gate of chastity, the healing power of Christ. Mary's wonder at what to call

6. Bickersteth, 377–78:
Compare Romanos, Strophe 11:   Basil, 965A:

τῇ μὲν ἁμαρτίᾳ   τὸν στήκοντα
---τῇ δὲ τῇ χάριτι   ----χαριζομένης

A recently published article calls attention to these images of engraving, which alternate with light-fire metaphors. Mrs. Eva Topping had also noted the abundance of the latter metaphors in Kontakion 1. She is aware of the theological appeal of both of these poems, and she writes vividly of their power. Eva C. Topping, "A Byzantine Song for Simeon," *Traditio*, XXIV (1968), 409–40.

7. Romanos, Strophe 12, 6–8:   Basil, 965B:

καὶ οὐράνιον-- τίνες--   --ἀλλὰ δὲ ἐπουράνιον σῶμα--.

8. Romanos, Strophe 13:   Basil, 968A:

Ἀλλὰ μετὰ----   μετὰ τὸν σκανδαλίσμου
Φιλάνθρωπος   ---καρδίαν·

9. *B.Z.*, XIX, 305. He refers to Basil, *P.G.*, 85, 425–51, where there are parallels with the speech of the Virgin. Also, *B.Z.*, XV, 15; Maas calls attention to the fact that Justinian in 553 cited Cyril in the question of "οὐράνιον σῶμα."

10. *Fr. ed.*, II, notes on pages 167, 191, 197.

11. The edict of Justinian against heretics was pronounced in 532.

12. We would have to except the Akathistos, *if* it is also the work of Romanos.

Christ and whether to give Him milk or to worship Him is another evidence of the personal focus that lends reality to the situation.[13]

Meter: The metrical scheme is given in the Oxford edition, 518, IV. It is noteworthy that it follows the scheme of Kontakia 34 and 57. The French edition even comments that the kontakaria show about 35 prooimia that indicate the use of the meter of the first strophe (*Τῇ Θεοτόκῳ προσδράμωμεν*).

13. Basil of Seleucia, *P.G.*, 85, 448A, has a similar passage ending:
Τί οὖν ἐπὶ σοῦ διαπράξομαι;
Γαλακτροφήσω ἢ δοξολογήσω;
(Maas, *Kont.*, 305).

ON THE PRESENTATION IN THE TEMPLE

O. 4

Prooimion I: Let the chorus of angels be amazed at the marvel,
    And let us mortals lift up our voices in a hymn,
    As we see the ineffable condescension of God;
For the hands of an old man embrace
    The One at whom the powers of Heaven tremble.
    The only friend of man.

Prooimion II: Thou who for us didst assume flesh from the Virgin,
    Thou who wast lifted up as an infant in the arms of an old man,
    Magnify the power of our faithful rulers;[1]
Strengthen them in Thy power, O Word,
    Make joyous their righteous kingdom,
    Thou, the only friend of man.[2]

Prooimion III: Thou who didst sanctify the Virgin's womb by Thy birth,
    Thou who hast blest the hands of Simeon, as was fitting,
    Thou, who dost hasten to save us, O Christ, God,
Bring peace to the state in the midst of wars,
    And strengthen the rulers whom Thou dost love,
    Thou, the only friend of man.

Strophe 1: Let us hasten to the mother of God, if we wish to see her
    Son presented to Simeon.
    The angels, beholding from on high, were amazed, saying:
ANGELS   "We behold now marvelous and remarkable things,
        incomprehensible, ineffable.
    He who is the Creator of Adam, is being baptized as a child.
    He who is not to be contained in space is held in the arms
        of the Elder.[3]

1. Ps. lxxv.10: "The horns of the righteous shall be exalted." Romanos frequently uses the phrase "exalt your horn" meaning "increase your power." The horn throughout the O.T. was used metaphorically to signify honor, strength, power, because horns were considered important to animals both as weapons and ornamentation; they are even symbols of victory.
2. Most strophes need *Thou* or *He* to complete the sentence in English. The gender of the Greek makes the meaning clear.
3. Similar to Cyril of Jerusalem, *P.G.*, 33, 1196.

He who exists in the infinite arms of His Father,
    Of His own will is limited in His flesh and not in His divinity,
        The only friend of man."

Strophe 2:   When they pronounced these words, invisibly they adored the Lord,
    And they called men happy
      Because the One borne on the wings of the Cherubim
        lived among them,
Because He appeared accessible to men on earth,
    But inaccessible to the angels.
      He who fashions children in the wombs of their mothers[4]
Became, without change, the child of the Virgin,
    and remained inseparable
      From the Father and Holy Spirit, coeternal with them,
        The only friend of man.

Strophe 3:   While the angels sang hymns to the lover of men, Mary advanced,
    Holding Him in her arms;
      And she pondered on how she became mother and remained a virgin,
For she realized that the birth was supernatural; she was
    awed and she trembled.
    Meditating on these things, she said to herself:
MARY   "How shall I find a name for Thee, my son?
For if I call Thee the man I see Thou art, yet Thou art more than man.
    Thou hast kept my virginity unsullied,
      Thou, the only friend of man.

Strophe 4:   "Shall I call Thee perfect man? But I know that Thy
MARY   conception was divine,
    For no mortal man
    Was ever conceived without intercourse and seed as Thou,
      O blameless One.
And if I call Thee God, I am amazed at seeing Thee in
    every respect like me,
    For Thou hast no traits which differ from those of man,
    Yet Thou wast conceived and born without sin.

4. Isa. xliv.24.

Shall I give Thee milk, or worship Thee, for Thy deeds [5]
    Proclaim Thee God beyond time, even after Thou didst become man?
        Thou, the only friend of man."

Strophe 5:   Thus the Lord was brought in and carried along with
        the burnt offerings
    In the temple, as was written.
    The blessed Simeon received Him from the arms of His mother.
Joy and fear constrained the righteous man, for with the eyes of the spirit
    He saw the ranks of archangels and of angels
    Standing erect with reverence and glorifying Christ;
SIMEON   And praying earnestly to himself, he cried: "Guard
    Me, and do not let the fire of Thy divinity harm me,
        Thou, the only friend of man.

Strophe 6:   "Miserable a short time ago, I am now made strong, since I have seen
SIMEON   Thy salvation, O Lord,
    Thou art the perfect image
    Of the incomprehensible nature of the Father,
        the inaccessible luminary,
The unchangeable seal of divinity, the radiance of glory [6]
    Which in truth illumines the spirits of men, [7]
    Thou, existing before time and Creator of the universe.
For Thou art the light shining from afar, inviolate, infinite,
    And incomprehensible, although Thou hast become man,
        Thou, the only friend of man.

Strophe 7:   "O Thou, good, and lover of man, Thou who hast of old received
SIMEON   the offerings of Abel
    And of other righteous men, [8]
    To whom, all-holy One wilt Thou present the sacrifices
    and burnt offerings?

5. See note 13 of the introduction to this poem.
6. Wisd. of Sol. vii.26; Heb. i.3.
7. Again, parallels are found in Cyril of Jerusalem, *P.G.*, 33, 1196B.
8. This corresponds to the old liturgical formula: Ἐπίβλεψον ἡμᾶς, ὁ Θεός---- καὶ πρόσδεξαι αὐτήν, ὡς προσδέξω Ἄβελ τὰ δῶρα. See *Fr. ed.*, II, 183n1.

Since I know that there is no greater one, O Lord, not to be
    apprehended with mere reason,
    For Thy Father in no way surpasses Thee in substance,
    Thou art cosubstantial and coeternal.
But in order that Thou mayst reveal that Thou art in truth what
    Thou hast become,
    As protector of Thy own law, Thou hast presented the sacrifice,
    Thou, the only friend of man.

Strophe 8:
SIMEON

"Thou art great and glorious, Thou whom the Almighty
    miraculously produced,
    O all-holy child of Mary;
    For I call Thee one, visible and invisible, finite and infinite.
I believe and know Thee to be the eternal Son of God in
    accordance with nature;
    Yet I confess Thee, as son of the Virgin, to be beyond natural law;
    Therefore indeed it is with daring that I hold Thee as a lamp,
For every man who holds up the light among men is illumined
    and not consumed.
    And so, shine down on me, O inextinguishable lamp,
    Thou, the only friend of man."

Strophe 9:

SIMEON

Hearing these things, the immaculate virgin stood amazed.
    The old man addressed her:
    "All the prophets heralded thy son whom thou hast
    produced without seed;
Also, a prophet has announced these events and proclaimed the miracle:[9]
    That thou, Mother of God, art the closed gate,
    For through thee the Lord has entered and come forth,
And the gate of thy chastity was not opened nor disturbed;
    He traveled through it and kept it intact.
    He, the only friend of man.

Strophe 10:
SIMEON

"Now, all-holy, blameless one, I shall prophesy and explain
    to thee everything
    About the downfall and the resurrection
    Thy son has in store for Him: the life, redemption, and
    resurrection of all;

9. Ezek. xliv.2.

The Lord has not come that some might fall and others be resurrected,
  Nor does the All-merciful One rejoice in the fall of man,[10]
  Nor has He become manifest under the pretext of causing to fall
    those who are upright,
But rather He zealously draws near those who have fallen to
    raise them up again,
  Redeeming from death His own creature,
    He, the only friend of man.

Strophe 11: "The manner of the fall and resurrection has been established
SIMEON   for the upright
    In the light of grace.
    The upright fall in sin, and lie as though dead;[11]
But they are raised up through righteousness and faith and are
        saved through grace;
    Passions of the flesh are destroyed and subside;
    The soul is aflame with virtues leading to the divine.
For whenever fornication finally subsides, chastity is established;
    He then checks what is worse, and restores what is better,
        He, the only friend of man.

Strophe 12: "Inspired by Christ, I prophesy to thee that from this source will come
SIMEON   The sign to be disputed:
    The cross will be the sign which the lawless will erect for Christ.
Some will proclaim Him God crucified; but others will call Him man,
    The opinions of pious and impious thus set in opposition.
    Some surmise that His body is divine;
Others, that it is mere phantasy; still others say that He assumed
        from thee body without soul.
    While others say, with soul.
        He, the only friend of man.[12]

Strophe 13: "This mystery offers such contradiction that in thy mind
SIMEON   There will be uncertainty;
    For, O blameless one, whenever thou dost see thy son
        nailed to the cross,

10. See introduction to this kontakion for the theology of this strophe as compared with the letter of Basil of Cesarea, *P.G.,* 32, 964C–65A. See also Ezek. xviii.32.
11. Rom. vi.10–11.
12. Maas discusses the way in which the theology of Romanos adheres in the entire kontakion to edicts of Justinian. See *Chron., B.Z.* 15 (1906), 1–44. Also see note 10 for similarities.

And art mindful of the words which the angel spake and of
  the divine conception,
  And of the ineffable miracles, at once thou wilt doubt;[13]

The anxiety of thy suffering will be a sword for thee;
But after this He will send quick healing for thy heart,
  And unshaken peace to His disciples,
   He, the only friend of man."

Strophe 14: When he had spoken these words to the blameless one, the
    righteous old man
    Spoke to the Infant:
SIMEON   "Now let Thy servant depart in peace for I have seen Thee, O Lord.
 Let me depart to life everlasting, O Life incomparable,
   Since Thou hast promised me this before Thou didst come
    into the world,
   Observe carefully the limit in time of Thy word, O Word.[14]
 Dismiss me, O Holy One, into the presence of Abraham
   and the patriarchs,
   Release me soon from the perishable world,
    Thou, the only friend of man.

Strophe 15: "Miserable and wretched are the present circumstances, since
SIMEON   they are transitory
    And always have an end.
   For this reason Thou hast separated all the righteous from
    the world here;
 Lord, Thou hast made provision that Enoch and Elias should
   not taste death,[15]
   Thou hast seen fit that they be mysteriously translated from here
   In order that they may be in regions shining with light and
    free from tears.
 And now, O Creator, separate me from the transient world,
   receive my spirit,

13. The editor of the *Fr. ed.*, II, 191n2, calls attention to the fact that Origen, in his seventeenth homily on St. Luke, mentions Mary's doubts. The concept also occurs in St. John Chrysostom's homily on Ps. xiii and the Pseudo-Chrys. homily, *P.G.*, 50, 811.

14. Pseudo Matt. xvi (Tischendorf, ed.) "Simeon was 112 years old" (Annorum centum duodecim). Luke ii.25–29 does not state that Simeon was old but merely that he was "waiting for the consolation of Israel" and that he had been promised not "to see death before he had seen the Lord's Christ."

15. Gen. v.24; Heb. xi.5; Ecclus. xliv.16.

44

And number me among Thy holy ones
Thou, the only friend of man.

Strophe 16:   "Since Thou hast become life and resurrection for all men
SIMEON   through Thy goodness,
    Release me from this life.
    Thou who art immortal, send me away from this life,
        which is mortal:
Give my body over to mortal death, as with all Thy friends,
    But grant me, Merciful One, life spiritual and eternal.
    Since I have seen Thee in the flesh, and have been deemed
        worthy to hold Thee,
I behold Thy glory along with Thy Father and the Holy Spirit,
    For Thou hast at the same time, remained on high, and
        come here below,
            Thou, the only friend of man."

Strophe 17:   The King of Heavenly Powers received the prayer of the righteous man,
    And unseen by others addressed him:
CHRIST   "Now, O my friend, I release you from the temporal world
        for an eternal home.
To Moses and the other prophets I send you. Tell them
    That, as they foretold in their prophecies, lo, I have come,
    And have been born of a virgin as they announced.
I have been seen by men in the world and have dwelt among them
        as they foretold.[16]
    Soon, I shall appear, redeeming all of you
        I, the only friend of man."

Strophe 18:   O Thou, all-holy, long-suffering, source of life and restoration,
    Source of goodness,
    Look down from Heaven and behold all those who trust Thee.
Redeem our life, Lord, from all violence and oppression
    And guide all men in the faith of truth
    Through the intercessions of the holy Virgin, Mother of God.
Save Thy world and protect all those in the world,
    Thou, who, without undergoing change, became man for us,
        Thou, the only friend of man.

16. Bar. iii.38.

ON THE BAPTISM OF CHRIST (EPIPHANY)

O. 5 (K. 4)

Title: Εἰς τὰ ἄγια θεοφάνια (φῶτα, CP)

Manuscripts and editions: All of the manuscripts except K and J (Sinai) contain this kontakion complete. This is true of only three others, Nativity I, Presentation, and Resurrection VI. The kontakaria have preserved many hymns for the Epiphany: two are by Romanos, six are preortia, five are later and written with his heirmos.[1]

The prooimion and first strophe are in the *Menaion*, January 6.

The kontakion was edited by Pitra, *A.S.*, I, iii.

It appears in the French edition, II, 236–57.

Tone: ἦχος δ′

Acrostic: τοῦ ταπεινοῦ ʿΡωμανοῦ

Refrain: τὸ φῶς τὸ ἀπρόσιτον

Biblical source and place in the liturgy: Matthew iii.13–17.

This hymn was clearly intended for the Epiphany, which, for the Eastern church, combined a celebration of the visit of the Magi to the newborn Christ and also the baptism of Christ; it included even the Marriage at Cana. The visit of the Magi was assigned to December 25, the Marriage at Cana (Kontakion 7) to the Wednesday of the second week after Easter, with the Baptism the only feast to be celebrated on January 6. The liturgy focuses attention on the baptism of Christ as the demonstration of His human nature and on the need for all believers to be baptized. The blessing of the waters still takes place on this day.

Analysis of content: The prooimion announces the theme and specifies the appearance of light (Theophany). The first strophe elaborates on the birth of Christ as light to the world and introduces Adam, to whom Christ is represented as speaking in Strophes 2 and 3. Here Adam's nakedness is treated with reference to the importance of the coming of Christ for him and all men. Strophe 4 introduces John the Baptist and his hesitancy to baptize "the unapproachable Light." Strophes 6 and 7 expand the idea of John's fear of being presumptuous. Strophes 8 through 12 give Christ's answers and provide the poet with an opportunity to expound on the nature of Christ. Strophe 10 contains an answer to the Nestorians; Strophe 17 has an

---

1. *Fr. ed.*, II, 229.

allusion to the Blessing of the Waters. John voices one more objection in Strophe 12 and is called "a wrangler" and asked to proceed with the baptism in Strophe 13. Strophes 14, 15, and 16 present the actual baptism, with John's recognition of the tremendous implications of his act. Strophe 18 includes not only a brief closing prayer, but also the climax of the event when the voice from on high cries, "This is my beloved Son." The Holy Spirit is mentioned in this kontakion, although Romanos does not make many references to any but Father and Son.

Connection with homily: Most homilies on the Epiphany have more phrases in common with Romanos' On the Epiphany than with this hymn. A sermon of Pseudo-Chrysostom (*P.G.*, 50, 801–6) contains a very long dialogue between Christ and John the Baptist, with extensive lists of Christ's reasons for this baptism and with one touch very like Romanos' manner. In Strophe 10, Chrysostom has Christ remind John the Baptist that He is not asking for the kind of sermon appropriate for sinners, and in the sermon also Christ suggests that He does not need to be preached to. The date of the homily is uncertain, but it seems more likely that Romanos inspired the preacher than that the poet relied on the homily. Notes from the French edition date this kontakion before 527.[2]

This homily should be compared with Kontakion 53 On Baptism. In it the various rites connected with baptism are mentioned: "I believe" (Strophe 3,1), "clothed in white" (Strophe 11,3) and the recitation of a psalm (Strophe 11,8). See Maas, *B.Z.*, XV, 26.

It is also worthy of note that in Strophes 4, 10, and 15 Romanos uses the verb ἐμφύω, which is associated with a confession. He also used it in the kontakion On the Sinful Woman.

Romanos often mentions the nudity of Adam. He refers to it in the kontakion On the Nativity II, where Mary pleads for Adam whom the serpent despoiled, and in Strophe 2 of the kontakion On the Epiphany, in which Hades laughs at the blinded Adam as he gropes for his clothes. St. John Chrysostom, in his fifth homily on Genesis, *P.G.*, 53, 103, and 126, has a similar reference.

Ephrem's works suggest relationships with this kontakion. There is in the British Museum a codex, edited by Lamy,[3] entitled "Hymn of Our Lord and John." It has many points of similarity to this kontakion of Romanos. Strophes are arranged in alphabetical order, each strophe with four verses, and each verse in seven syllables. The poet says that he was mentally transported to the Jordan, where he joined the crowd, who were amazed at Christ's baptism. Christ calls Himself the Bridegroom and then begins the dialogue with John in which John speaks of his hesitation in daring to baptize Christ and Christ reiterates that He wills John's act. The figure of speech about light and touching fire occurs. Christ explains that His baptism brings freedom to men. Adam is specifically mentioned, and the theological point is made in Strophe 40 that Christ's baptism is intended to prevent error on the part of those who say, "If He were not away from the Father, why does He avoid baptism?"

2. *Fr. ed.*, II, 232n1.
3. Thomas Josephus Lamy, *Sancti Ephraem Syri Hymni et Sermones*, I, XIV, 114–30.

Granted that this answer to a heresy that caused discussion later than Ephrem probably indicates that the hymn is merely one of the pseudo-Ephrem group, it is still important to notice that rhythmic verse of the kind known in the fourth century was composed in a manner that bears many connections with Romanos.

Style of Romanos: The various theological points are woven into the dialogue between John the Baptist and Christ, which expands upon John the Baptist's hesitation as it is reported in Matthew. The reality of the dialogue is given several touches in Christ's answers when He says, "You will say in the case of Gabriel I willed it" (Strophe 9), and also when He interrupts the objections of John in Strophe 13. The various references to Old Testament characters and to Mary's obedience as contrasted with John's hesitation are, of course, typical of Romanos' style. Antitheses abound in the reaction of angels on high and of John on the bank of the river; Christ, who could use the clouds as cloak, stands naked in the Jordan.

Meter: The French edition points out that the heirmos is very popular and that the prooimion Ἐπεφάνης σήμερον was followed in some hundred hymns.[4]

The metrical scheme is given in the Oxford edition, 519, V.

4. *Fr. ed.*, II, 232.

ON THE BAPTISM OF CHRIST (EPIPHANY)

O. 5

Prooimion: Today Thou hast appeared to the world
        And Thy light, O Lord, has been a sign to us
        With the full knowledge of those who sing hymns to Thee
          Thou hast come, Thou hast appeared,
          O light unapproachable.

Strophe 1:   In the Galilee of nations, in the country of Zebulun and in the
        land of the Naphthali,
        Christ, a great light, has shone forth, as the prophet said.[1]
        For those in darkness, a shining light has been seen, sending
        its beams from Bethlehem;
      Or rather, Christ, born of Mary, the sun of righteousness,
        Sends forth rays of light to the world.
      Hither, then, all naked sons of Adam,[2]
        Let us clothe him again that we may be warmed.
      As covering for the naked, as light for those in darkness,
          Thou hast come, Thou hast appeared,
          O light unapproachable.

Strophe 2:   God did not despise the one who, in Paradise, was tricked by guile
        And despoiled of the robe which God had woven for him.
        Again He has come to him, calling with holy voice the one
        who was misled:

CHRIST   "Where art thou, Adam? This time do not hide from me; I wish
        to see you.
        Even if you are naked and poor, do not be ashamed, for I am
        fashioned like you.
      Even though you desired it, you did not become God;
        But I now have willed it and become flesh.

---

1. Isa. ix.1–6; Matt. iv.15–16; *Protevangelium*, xix, 2.
2. *Cf.* On the Nativity II, Strophe 12. St. John Chrysostom (*P.G.*, 53, 103, and 126) in his homily on Genesis elaborates on the theme, "and they knew that they were naked" (Gen. iii.7).

Draw near to me and recognize me so that you may say:
> 'Thou hast come, Thou hast appeared,
> O light unapproachable.'

Strophe 3:
CHRIST

"Overcome by feelings of pity, I, the merciful, have come
> to my creature,
> Holding out my hands that I may embrace you.
> Do not feel shame before me; it is for you who are naked that I
> became naked and came to be baptized.
Now the Jordan is opened for me,[3] and John
> Prepares the way for me in the water and in the hearts of men."
Having thus addressed the man—in deed, not in words—
> The Savior came, as he had said,
Directing His footsteps near the river, He appeared
> To the Forerunner
> As the unapproachable light.[3]

Strophe 4:

Seeing the river in the desert, and the dew in the furnace,
> and the rain shower in the Virgin,[4]
> John, seeing Christ in the Jordan,
> Was struck with fear, just as his father trembled before Gabriel.
But now things were more momentous than ever before,
> For the Lord of the angels was coming to a servant,
> wishing to be baptized.
So the Baptist, recognizing the Creator,
> And taking measure of himself, spoke as he trembled:

JOHN

"Stop, Redeemer, let it be enough up to this point;
> For I know who Thou art,
> The unapproachable light."

Strophe 5:
JOHN

"If I bring to pass, Savior, what Thou hast ordered, I shall raise
> my horn aloft;
> However, I shall not hastily seize what is beyond my power.
> I know who Thou art, and I am not unaware of what Thou wert,
> for I recognized Thee from Thy mother's womb.

---

3. Ps. cxiv.5: "The Jordan is driven back"; John i.33: "Thou shalt see the Spirit descending";
John v.35: "He was a burning and shining light."
4. Three miracles: Moses obtains water from the rock, Num. xx.2–13; three boys in the fiery
furnace, Dan. iii.23–27; dew on the fleece of Gideon, Judg. vi.37.

How, then, should I not recognize Thy appearance now, the One
Whom I observed hidden in Thy mother's womb, as I
skipped with joy?
Stop, then, Savior, and do not overwhelm me.
It is sufficient that I am deemed worthy to see Thee.
It is wonderful for me if Thou dost call me Forerunner,
For Thou art
The unapproachable light.

Strophe 6:

JOHN

"I ask to hand over to Thee the role of baptizing, for it is fitting for Thee;
For I have need of being baptized by Thee.
Thou dost come to me and anticipate me in asking what I
would ask Thee.
What dost Thou seek from a man, Lover of man? Why dost Thou
Incline Thy head beneath my hand? For it is not its custom
to hold fire.[5]
This hand is poor and does not know how to lend to the rich;
This hand is weak and cannot resist pressure from the strong;
It will be of service to the sinners as they have need;
For Thou art
The unapproachable light.

Strophe 7:

JOHN

"Why didst Thou come to this water? What dost Thou wish to
wash away, or what sin,
Thou who wast conceived and born without sin?
Thou dost come to me; but Heaven and earth keep watch to see
if I shall be rash.
Thou dost say to me, 'Baptize me'; but angels will look down
from on high
And then say, 'Know thyself; to what lengths will this go?'
As Moses said, 'Choose another,
O Savior, for this which Thou dost ask of me
Is too much, and I am afraid.'[6] I beseech Thee
How shall I baptize
The unapproachable light?'"

5. On Doubting Thomas (Strophes 1, 2, and 14) makes frequent use of the idea of fear at touching fire. Origen on Jeremiah quotes the Savior as saying, "He that is near me is near the fire." *Agrapha,* B8, James, *Apoc. N.T.* (Oxford, 1926), 35.
6. Ex. iv.10–13.

Strophe 8:   He who knows all in advance, seeing the fear of the
                    Forerunner, answered him:

CHRIST   "O John, rightly, rightly you fear me;
                    Nevertheless, now permit this, for it is fitting to bring to pass
                        what was foreordained;
                And now shake off this fear.
                    You owe me your ministry,[7] and it is necessary now to fulfill it.
                I once sent Gabriel on a mission,
                    And he accomplished it well at the time of your birth.
                Then do you send your hand to me as messenger,
                        In order that it may baptize
                        The unapproachable light.

Strophe 9:   "Now you are terrified, Baptist, and tremble before this great deed,
CHRIST   for it is great;
                    But your parent observed greater than this;
                    Consider Mary and consider well how she bore me.
                Of course you will say to me, 'In that case you willed it.'
                    Well, now, I will this.
                    Do not hesitate, baptize me; merely lend me your right hand.
                I dwell in your spirit and possess you entirely;
                    Why then, do you not lend me your hand?
                I am within you and outside you; why do you flee me?
                        Stand and hold
                        The unapproachable light.

Strophe 10:   "I do not ask you, Baptist, to step out of bounds. I do not say to you,
CHRIST   'Tell me the things you would say to the lawless, and what
                            you suggest to sinners.'
                    Only baptize me in silence[8] and in expectation of what
                        follows the baptism.
                For you will achieve honor from this such as did not
                    Fall to the lot of the angels; for I shall make you greater than
                        all the prophets.[9]
                No one of them saw me clearly,
                    But rather in images, shadows, and dreams.

7. See the use of λειτουργίαν in On the Nativity I, note 4.
8. *Cf.* Pseud.-Chrysostom (*P.G.*, 50, 803). Especially close are the words: Στῆσον τὴν γλῶτταν,
καὶ κίνησον πρὸς τὸ ἔργον τὴν δεξίαν.
9. Matt. xi.9–11.

But you, according to my will, see me standing at your side;
>> You touch
>> The unapproachable light.

Strophe 11: "Discontinue what you are saying, and do what you hear.
CHRIST
>> Do not bear witness for me;[10]
>> For always there is a faithful witness in Heaven.
>> The people, standing here, do not rightly receive your witness;
> Then let them learn from Heaven who I am and of whom I was born,
>> And what grace I am about to bestow on my well-beloved.
> I shall open up the Heavens and have the Holy Spirit descend;
>> I shall give them this as a pledge.
> Come, then, draw near so that you may learn
>> From what source flashes forth
>> The unapproachable light."

Strophe 12: When he heard the mysterious and awesome words, the one born
>> of the barren woman spoke to the One born of a virgin,
JOHN
>> "If I speak again, do not be angry with me, Redeemer,
>> For necessity impels me to speak very freely.
> Why, O Savior, just so that they may know Thee, shall
>> I endanger my poor hand by casting it in the furnace?
> Formerly Uzzah[11] stretched forth his hand
>> To grasp the Ark and it was broken off.
> Now, if I hold the head of my God,
>> How shall I not be burned by
>> The unapproachable light?"

Strophe 13: "O Baptist, and wrangler, prepare quickly, not for an argument,
CHRIST
>> But for ministry; for lo, you will see what I shall bring to pass.
>> So, I shall represent for you the pleasing and splendid
>> form of my church
> As I grant to your right hand the power which after this
>> I shall furnish abundantly to the hands of my
>> disciples and priests.

---

10. *This moment* is not the time for your witness, nor is it necessary.
11. II Sam. vi.6–8, *not* II Kings, as in *Fr. ed.*, II, 253n3.

Clearly shall I show you the Holy Spirit;
    I shall cause you to hear the voice of my Father
Declaring me His true Son and proclaiming,
      'This is He,
      The unapproachable light'."

Strophe 14: After these awesome words, the son of Zacharias said to the Creator:
JOHN   "I do not strive against Thee; I do what Thou dost command."
      Saying this, he then approached the Savior, and as a humble
        servant, he gazed earnestly
As he reverently beheld the naked limbs of the One
      Who commands the clouds to cover the Heavens as a cloak,
And as he again saw the One in the middle of the river
      Who appeared in the midst of the three children,
The dew in the fire and the flaming fire in the Jordan,[12]
      Springing forth
      As the unapproachable light.

Strophe 15: Seeing these marvels, the son of the priest, in his role as priest,
      Holds out his hand and takes Christ by the hand
      As he cried out to the beholders:
JOHN   "You see in the Jordan the voluntary rain,
      The torrents of delights, as was written in the Scripture;
        in the passage of the waters
You see a great sea in the river.
      Let no one consider me rash;
I do not do this as a reckless person, but as a servant;
      For this is the Lord and He told me to do this.
      Hence I baptize
      The unapproachable light.

Strophe 16: "He as God of all gave strength to me, weak as a mortal, as He said:
JOHN   'Hold out your hand and I shall give you strength.'
      For how would I have had the power unless the very thing
      happened which He said would take place?

12. The story of On the Three Children [in the Fiery Furnace], Strophe 21, combines πνεῦμα δρόσου and ἡ φλόξ. Matt. iii.11 refers to baptism with water and with fire. The Old Testament is full of the image of fire for the power of God, and the references to fire in the Jordan may well call to mind the Israelites passing over the Jordan through the power of God (Josh. iii).

How would I have had the ability to baptize the abyss,
Since I am mortal,
Had I not first received and claimed power from on high?
For I realize now that He is standing by me
That I am greater than I was formerly.
I am something different, I am changed, glorified,
As I behold and baptize
The unapproachable light.

Strophe 17: "I no longer speak as I did before, 'I do not unlace the thongs

JOHN   of Thy sandals,'[13]
For lo, I advance from His feet to His head;
I no longer tread on the earth, but Heaven itself; for what I bring
to pass is heavenly.
Nay, rather, I surpass the Heavens for they support
But they do not see whom they support; but I see and baptize Him.
Rejoice, O Heaven, and earth proclaim the news.[14]
Be blest, springs of water;[15]
For in appearing, He has filled all with blessing
He illumines all men,
The unapproachable light."

Strophe 18: At divine command, then, the son of Zacharias exalted his spirit
And stretching out his hand he placed it on the King;
He immersed Him in the water, and then led back to the land
the Lord of earth and of the firmament.
From on high a voice pointed Him out as though by a finger, crying out:
"This is my beloved Son."
To this Father, and to the baptized Son
And to His Spirit, I cry:[16]
"Destroy, O Redeemer, those who oppress my soul;
Put an end to my errors,
O unapproachable light."

13. John i.27.
14. Ps. xcvi.11.
15. A reference to the blessing of the water.
16. Ps. cxliii.12. Usually, all of the closing prayer is personal.

ON THE EPIPHANY

O. 6 (K. 5)

Title: Τοῦ ἁγίου Ἰωάννου τοῦ Προδρόμου A
Εἰς τὰ ἅγια Θεοφάνια: εἰς τὰ ἀπόλυτρα D
εἰς τὴν σύναξιν τοῦ Προδρόμου M
Εἰς τὸν Πρόδρομον καὶ εἰς τὸ βάπτισμα καὶ εἰς Ἀδάμ Δ

Manuscripts and editions: Maas uses chiefly P, T, and Δ.
This kontakion appears in the French edition, II, 270–83, and the
Tomadakis edition, IV, 103–83.
Pitra had published parts of it, *A.S.*, #4, 23–27.
The *Menaion* for January 7 includes the prooimion and the first strophe.

Tone: ἦχος πλάγιος β'

Acrostic: Τοῦ ταπεινοῦ Ῥωμανοῦ

Refrain: τὸν φανέντα καὶ φωτίσαντα πάντα

Biblical source and place in the liturgy: The kontakion is sung on January 6, although the *Menaion*
includes parts of it on January 7, and the French edition follows that date. The
festival is that which is now celebrated as the Epiphany. The hymn appears in all
of the kontakaria and has passed into the liturgy. It is hard to draw any con-
clusions about the intentions of early authors, but internal evidence points to the
hymn's having been composed for January 6. Western and Eastern celebration of
this day differed. There are many variant readings for the end of Strophe 5, which
might be the result of differences between the Eastern and Western texts. In
general, P follows the Eastern tradition and D the Western. *Itinerarium Aetheriae*
describes the ritual in Jerusalem.[1]

Analysis of content: The content is decidedly didactic and theological: The prooimion gives the
setting, with the reference to the Jordan's turning back and a supernatural light
appearing at the time of Christ's baptism. The poem tells of the light that appeared
for Adam and for Abraham, of God's appearance to Jacob and to Moses, and of the
visions of Isaiah and of Daniel. Strophes 9 and 10 are strictly theological and a bit
arbitrary in that Romanos asserts his lack of need to know or understand those
who are confused about the union of the two natures of Christ. The confession of

---

1. *Itinerarium Aetheriae*, Otto Prinz, ed. (Heidelberg, 1960), xxv, 12.

faith in Strophe 11 and the allusions to the baptismal rite in Strophe 12 place the hymn in its liturgical setting. Strophes 13, 14, 15, and 16 are repetitions of wonder at the mystery of Christ, and Strophe 18 is the closing prayer.

Style of Romanos: This kontakion is clearly of the type intended to teach the dogma of the two natures of Christ and combat the Monophysites. It contains frequent allusions to biblical characters of the Old Testament who have in one way or another been privileged to see God as a light or in other forms. Intended for the celebration of the Epiphany, the refrain, "Thou hast appeared and illumined all things," is appropriate. In fact, Romanos as a theologian becomes, not convincing but disagreeable, when he insists there is no point in trying to understand the position of those who do not believe as he does. However, he develops figures of speech with his usual facility; for example, the light that shone on Adam, Strophe 1, the elaboration of the symbol of the salt and the food in Strophe 14, the typical use of the motif of the spring of fresh water in Strophe 16, and the closing reference to Christ the Physician are characteristic not only of Romanos but of the period in which he wrote. The hymn is not dramatic, but it does have some touches of insight into character, as when Adam gropes for his clothes after he was blinded, in Strophe 2. Again, in Strophe 6, the poet exclaims with some humor on the impossibility of seeing anything through a crevice as Moses was forced to do.

Meter: The heirmos is a very well known one, as the French edition points out.[2]
The metrical scheme is given in the Oxford edition, 519, VI.

2. *Fr. ed.*, II, 265n1.

ON THE EPIPHANY

O. 6

Prooimion: The Jordan turned back in fear,[1] terrified by Thy physical presence;
    John, accomplishing his prophetic ministry, shrank back,
        trembling with fear.
Ranks of angels were struck with amazement
      To see Thee physically baptized in the river waters,
      And all who dwell in darkness were illumined as they sang to Thee
        Who hast appeared and illumined all things.[1]

Strophe 1: To Adam, blinded in Eden, appeared a sun from Bethlehem,
      And he opened his eyes, washing them in the waters of the Jordan.
An unquenchable light shone upon him who had been covered
        with darkness and shadows.
    No more will there be night for him; but all is day.
    The dawn before daybreak has been born for him.[2]
    For in the twilight[3] he was covered over, as it was written.
He who fell in the evening found light shining upon him;
      He escaped from darkness and advanced towards dawn,
        Which has appeared and illumined all things.

Strophe 2: When Adam was willfully disabled, as he tasted of the fruit
        which produces blindness,
    Immediately against his will he was made naked, for as he
        found himself blind,
               the one who disabled him unclothed him.[4]

---

1. The editor of the *Fr. ed.*, II, 271n2, cites various sources for the statement that a supernatural light shone on Christ at the time of His baptism. Also, see Isa. ix.2, and Luke i.79.

    The story of the Jordan's turning back in fear is recorded in Ps. cxiv.5; it occurs also in *Chronique d'Alexandrie* (Bonn), I, 422, 1. This postdates Romanos; he knew of the story from other sources. It occurs in the liturgy of January 6, *Fr. ed.*, II, 271n2.

2. Ps. xlvi.5: τὸ πρὸς πρωῒ πρωΐ.

3. Gen. iii.8: "In the cool of the day." Greek translation: "τῷ πνεύματι τῆς ημέρας." *Fr. ed.*, II, 273n1, refers to the translation as τὸ δειλινόν.

4. Romanos often alludes to Adam's nudity and the sense he had of being despoiled, for example, On the Nativity II, Strophe 12; also, St. John Chrysostom, *P.G.*, 53, 103, and 126. The biblical account of the fig leaf (Gen. iii.7) is omitted.

He was, then, naked and maimed and groping; he tried to seize

                         the one who had disrobed him;

    But the latter, seeing him, laughed at

    How he stretched out his hands everywhere and demanded

    His cloak—even after having been made naked.

And so, the One whose nature is merciful seeing this, came to him saying:

    "Though you are naked and maimed, I receive you. Come to me

        Who has appeared and illumined all things."

Strophe 3:   Adam, sing praise, sing praise to Him;

                    fall down before Him who comes to you;

    For He has appeared for you as you come forward to see Him,

               to grope after Him, and to greet Him.

He whom you feared when you were deceived, for your sake has

        been made like you.

    He descended to earth in order that He might take you up on high.

    He became mortal that you might be divine,

    And that you might put on the first beauty.[5]

Wishing to reopen Eden, He dwelt in Nazareth.

    For this, then, sing, O man, and singing, charm the One

        Who has appeared and illumined all things.

Strophe 4:   When God was seen by Abraham as he sat beneath the

        oak tree in Mamre[6]

    He was seen as a man, but Abraham did not recognize Him

        for what He was,

                       for he could not have endured it.

Today He has not appeared in this way to us, but in His own person,

                  for the Word was made flesh.

    From this, the enigma is clear:

    To our ancestors, darkness; to patriarchs, images;

    But to the children, Truth itself.

For God appeared to Abraham,[7] but he did not know Him as God.

    But we behold Him because He wills it, and we hold fast to Him

        Who has appeared and illumined all things.

5. Bar., v.2.
6. Gen. xviii.1.
7. Gen. xvii.1.

Strophe 5:   Jacob saw God at the top of a ladder, but in a dream;[8]
        The one who struggled with him in the night was not God
          in his nature,
                                  but in the form of a man.
     Now it is not images but veritable deeds which have constructed
                              a figure for the human race.
      Now the wisdom of the Father has appeared,
      The power and strength and Word of knowledge,
      Cleansing the transgression of the world.
   For Thou hast come in the flesh, the sanctification of everyone;
      For this reason it is appropriate for each to extol, glorify, and
        magnify the One[9]
        Who has appeared and illumined all things.

Strophe 6:   Although Moses was very confident of being loved, he asked to see
        the One whom he loved
      And he said with the prayer of a suppliant: "If Thou dost
                    love me, show Thyself to me."
     But he was not considered worthy of a view of the face,
              but of the back—and that not complete.[10]
      But what is it possible for one looking through a crevice to see
      Except a mere part of what he wishes to behold?
      Praise be to Thee, since Thou hast revealed all of Thyself to all of us.
   We look not from a partial view;
      We behold not a part but the whole of the One
        Who has appeared and illumined all things.

Strophe 7:   Once Isaiah, son of Amos, said that he had seen God,
      Raised on high on a throne, His dwelling filled with His glory;[11]
   He saw Him as a prophet in the "slumber of the spirit,"[12]
        not with physical eyes.
      But we behold with the eyes of our bodies
      The Lord of hosts, and we send up to Him
      The song of the six-winged angels:

---

8. Gen. xxviii.12, and xxxii.24–26.
9. The latter half of this strophe is very difficult in some manuscripts. See the introduction to this kontakion.
10. Ex. xxxiii.18–23.
11. Isa. vi.1–4.
12. Paul, in Rom. xi.8.

> "Holy, Holy, Holy, Thou art God incarnate;
>> We hallow the Three in One, the Holy of holy Ones,
>> Who has appeared and illumined all things."

Strophe 8: The eyes of earth-born have strength to see the celestial figure.
>> The eyes of men of clay have beheld the insufferable beam
>>> of the immaterial light.
> This the prophets and kings did not see, although they wished to.
>> The great Daniel was called "a man of desire" [13]
>> Because he wished to gaze at
>> The One who beholds us.
> We are not imagining things, for we live soberly, [14] we are
>>> not of the night;
>> But we see in the light of day the One made flesh,
>>> Who has appeared and illumined all things.

Strophe 9: A new Heaven has appeared for us, and on it the God of all descends.
>> The prophet has called the body of the Incorporeal One
>>> "Heaven of Heaven," [15]
> For even if He was born and wrapped in swaddling clothes, He is
>>> the blameless Heaven;
>> For He is Heaven and not a celestial body [16]
>> For He was born of Mary, the Virgin,
>> And united to God, we know not how.
> He is not outside the bosom of His Father but coexistent with Him.
>> The One whom we adore is the Holy of holy ones,
>>> Who has appeared and illumined all things.

Strophe 10: If only we understood the points of the opposition! We have
>> nothing to do with what is beyond us.
>> The word [17] is near us; and why should we seek to go
>>> far off to learn?
> In the faith we have what we desire; where are we to put the boundaries?
>> The road is straight lest anyone lead us astray;
>> Mary has shown us the path
>> For she called her son Lord;

13. Dan. ix.23. Really a play on words; he was beloved of the king, "ἐπιθυμιῶν." See also Luke x.24; Matt. xiii.17.
14. I Thess. v.6.
15. Ps. lxviii.33: "To Him that rideth upon the heaven of heavens which were of old."
16. Repeated emphasis on the two natures of Christ.
17. See Deut. xxx.14. The "word" of the creed or the slogan of the edicts is probably meant.

Her son was not really her son, as we have been taught,[18]
  But He was incarnated from her and from the Holy Spirit, He
    Who has appeared and illumined all things.

Strophe 11: Exalt our horn, O Jesus,[19] for we hold fast Thy uncontaminated truths,
  Proclaiming them in confidence: "God is with us, nations,
    know and understand."
Indeed, as the prophet said: "The people shall see Thee and
    be in labor."[20]
  Lo, we were in labor and we gave birth—[21]
  We have made available for all the spirit of Thy salvation,
  For on earth we talk of heavenly matters.
All flesh has seen Thee, and still has flourished as before.
  Creation on seeing the Creator has been brightened.
    He appeared and illumined all things.

Strophe 12: Now the garment of mourning is rent; we have put on the white robe[22]
  Which the spirit has woven for us from the lamb's fleece of our
    Lamb and our God;
Sin is taken away, and immortality is given us,[23]
    our restoration is clear.
  The Forerunner has proclaimed it when he said:
  "Lo now, the Lamb of God
  Who takes away the sins of all the world."[24]
He has shown the instrument of the gift[25] for all those who are
    much in debt.
  He who leaped in his mother's womb[26] has now heralded and
    made known the One
    Who appeared and illumined all things.

Strophe 13: O, the message of the Baptist, and the mystery in it!
  He calls the shepherd lamb, and not only a lamb, but one to
    free from mistakes.

---

18. Can he really mean that the Virgin is not to be called the "Mother of God"?
19. The phrase *exalt our horn* is used frequently by Romanos and also in the Bible to mean *increase our power*. See, for example, Ps. lxxxix.17.
20. Hab. iii.10.
21. Isa. xxvi.18.
22. Baptismal rite.
23. I Cor. xv.53.
24. John i.29.
25. Really, the paper or document, metaphor for Christ.
26. Luke i.41.

He showed the lawless that the goat which they sent into the
      desert was ineffective.[27]
    "Lo," he said, "the lamb; there is no longer need of the goat;[28]
    Put your hands on Him,
    All of you who confess your sins,
For He has come to take them away, those of the people
      and of the whole world.
    For lo, the One whom the Father has sent to us is the One
      who carries away evil,
        Who appeared and illumined all things."

Strophe 14: Great mystery for Christians; there is no lack of witness in you.
      On all sides you have confirmation; you are made secure by
        all inspired scripture,
    All things witness to you: the law and the prophets, and
        especially the fathers.[29]
    You are the salt of each generation,[30]
    Seasoning for the faithful the food which is incorruptible.
    If we eat it, we shall not die.
    You seasoned a dish for Isaac[31] from which he loved to eat,
      And he blessed his son, symbolizing in his blessings
        The One who appeared and illumined all things.

Strophe 15: Let us all raise our eyes to God in the Heavens,
      Crying as Jeremiah did:[32] Our God is the One seen on earth;
    He voluntarily lived among men, and did not suffer change;
      He revealed Himself to the prophets in changed forms.
      Ezekiel observed Him
      In the form of man on a fiery chariot;[33]
    And Daniel saw Him as Son of God and ancient of days,[34]
      Old and young, as he proclaimed Him the Lord
        Who appeared and illumined all things.

27. τράγος, like the scapegoat in Lev. xvi.8.
28. *Cf.* Aaron in Lev. xvi.21.
29. Patriarchs of the Old Testament.
30. The New Testament speaks of Christians as "the salt of the earth"; in the Old Testament, sacrifices were salted to show the alliance of God and His people. See Lev. ii.13. The *Fr. ed.*, II, 289n1, calls attention to the fact that St. Ignatius, in his *Letter to the Magnesians*, 10, calls Christ the salt that preserves from corruption.
31. Gen. xxvii; Romanos, O. 42 (K. 68), On Jacob and Esau.
32. Really from Bar. iii.35–38; *Fr. ed.*, II, 289n 3.
33. Ezek. i.26.
34. Dan. vii.9, 13.

Strophe 16: He has caused gloomy night to disappear and revealed all as noon;
   Jesus, our Savior, has illumined the world with His light
    which knows no evening.
  The land of Zebulun [35] in its abundance even imitates Eden,
   For the torrent of luxury waters it.
   And causes an ever-flowing spring to well up. [36]
   The men of old did not find it
  When they dug the well of the oath, the well of Shebah, [35]
    it was not a source of eternal life; [37]
   In Galilee we behold the living water
    Who appeared and illumined all things.

Strophe 17: I shall look to Thee, Jesus, to enlighten my thinking
   And to speak to my reasoning, "Come unto me and drink,
    ye who always thirst." [38]
  Water your humility which your wandering has crushed.
   It has caused it to disappear through hunger and thirst,
   Not hunger from a lack of food, nor thirst from a lack of water,
   But of hearing the words of the Spirit, [39]
  For the Spirit does not find its master for either teaching or learning.
   Therefore it groans, concealing the judge who will reveal the
    One who has appeared and illumined all things. [40]

Strophe 18: I glorified in Thy epiphany; grant me a clear sign;
   Cleanse me from hidden sins, [41] for my hidden wounds destroy me.
  In a way which cannot be discerned, send Thy invisible salve for
   my hidden wound.
   I fall before Thee, Savior, as did the woman with the issue of blood, [42]
   And touching the hem of Thy garment, I say:
   "If only I touch Thee, I shall be saved."
  O Physician of souls, do not make my faith vain.
   As I uncover my suffering, I shall find for my salvation the One
    Who appeared and illumined all things.

35. The land of Zebulun is referred to in Matt. iv.13, 15. The well of the oath refers to the one Abraham dug, Gen. xxi.33. Isaac dug it again and called it "Shebah," Gen. xxvi.18 and 33. Nazareth is in the part of Galilee where the tribe of Zebulun lived.
36. Ps. xxxvi.8–9.
37. Jer. ii.13.
38. John vii.37.
39. Isa. v.13.
40. This whole strophe is not clear. The root meaning is, I suppose, that man has sinned and never finds his master until Christ appears.
41. Ps. xix.13.
42. Mark v.25–28; Matt. ix.20; Romanos, O. 12 (K. 82), On the Woman with an Issue of Blood.

ON THE MARRIAGE AT CANA

O. 7 (K. 77)

Title: Εἰς τὸν ἐν κανᾷ γάμον

Manuscripts and editions: The kontakion occurs only in the Patmos manuscript P.
Aside from the Oxford edition, it appears only in the French edition, II, 300–322. The editor of the latter edition thinks that this poem was little utilized.

Tone: ἦχος πλάγιος β'

Acrostic: τὸ ἔπος ʽΡωμανοῦ ταπεινοῦ

Refrain: ὁ τὰ πάντα ἐν σοφίᾳ ποιήσας

Biblical source and place in the liturgy: This kontakion is marked for the second week after Easter. The French edition places it on Wednesday of the second week after Easter. The narrative comes from John ii.1–11.

Analysis of content: The prooimion states the occasion and includes a prayer for forgiveness. The first three strophes justify marriage and reveal Romanos' dislike of extremes of celibacy and monasticism. Strophe 4 recalls the parting of the waters for the Israelites and moves on to the events in Cana, as told in the Gospel of John.
The central part of the poem is taken up with answers to theological questions. For three strophes Mary explains how she knew Christ could perform miracles, since this was supposed to be the first; the emphasis is, of course, on the miracle of her virginity. Then, in three strophes Christ answers the criticism that He was subject to special times or seasons, and in three strophes He assures the faithful that He is living within a divine plan. Strophe 16 provides a transition through Christ's saying that "children must obey their parents," and the narrative of the miracle concludes in four strophes, with the last strophe a closing prayer. The last strophes contain a rare but rather direct allusion to the Eucharist.

Connections with homily: There are no known connections with homily, nor with drama. The style is particularly lacking in freshness of imagery or in dialogue, which reveals human nature. In fact, Christ is presented in a rather displeasing manner as one who wanted angels to applaud each act of creation.

Meter: The metrical scheme is given in the Oxford edition, 519, VI.

ON THE MARRIAGE AT CANA

O. 7

Prooimion: Thou who hast by Thy power changed water into wine,
       Change into joy the affliction of the sins which oppress me,
       Through the mediation of the Virgin, O Christ, God,
       Who hast created all things in Thy wisdom.

Strophe 1: God, honoring virginity, inhabited a virgin's womb,
       He was born of her without seed;
                      He did not break the seals of her purity;
He himself has espoused the church, virgin and without stain.
       The mother of Christ, then, is both virgin and bride.
       He is also a virgin; but the bridal couch is sacred,
       For He has made of the bridal chamber a heaven.[1]
Even though He was born of a virginal and holy womb,
       He does not feel disgust at the unions of wedlock,
       He who has in wisdom created all things.

Strophe 2: Hence, He who had no mortal marriage, He who alone is
       holy and awesome,
       Was present in the bridal chamber, as the divine John taught.[2]
He who experienced childbirth without wedding came
       to the marriage.
       He who alone is borne upon the wings of the Cherubim,
       He who exists in the bosom of the Father, inseparable from Him,
       Reclined in a mortal home;
He who knew no sin, dined with sinners,[3]
       In order that He might by His presence show that marriage
       is to be honored.
       He who has in wisdom created all things.

1. The womb contains God and is therefore a heaven.
2. John ii.2.
3. Matt. xi.19; Luke vii.34.

Strophe 3:   It is from this point that the great Paul reasonably took
his point of departure and wrote, saying
That marriage is honorable and that the marriage couch is pure;[4]
For virgins are radiant because of marriage, since they were
    born in marriage;
Indeed the mother of God, the holy Virgin,
Even though she remained a pure virgin after childbirth,
Still it was marriage which brought her forth;
Just so, the multitude of those who remain virgins for Christ,
Were born in wedlock, which sanctified from the womb
The One who has in wisdom created all things.

Strophe 4:   Now we propose to tell of a miracle,
the one which He performed in Cana,
He who first revealed to the Egyptians
and to the Hebrews themselves the power of miracles;
For at that time, the nature of the waters
was miraculously changed to blood.
He vented His anger on the Egyptians in ten plagues;[5]
He made the sea passable for the Hebrews;
They traveled through it as though it were dry land.
In the arid land He furnished for them water from a rock;
And now at the marriage feast, again He transforms nature,
He who has in wisdom created all things.

Strophe 5:   When Christ was present at the marriage feast,[6]
and the crowd of guests were faring sumptuously,
The supply of wine failed them,
and their joy was turned into distress;
The bridegroom was upset; the cupbearers muttered unceasingly;
There was this one sad display of penury,
And there was no small clamor in the room.
Recognizing it, the all-holy Mary
Came at once and said to her son: "They have no wine,
But I beg you, my son, show that you can do all things,
Thou who has in wisdom created all things."

4. Heb. xiii.4.
5. The word *anger* is in opposition with *ten plagues*, and it might be better to translate this as *ten-plague anger*.
6. John ii.3.

Strophe 6: We beg of you, holy Virgin, from what sort of miracles did you know
How your son would be able to offer wine
when He had not harvested the grapes
And had never before worked wonders, as John, inspired of God wrote?[7]
Teach us, how, when you had never gazed upon
And never made trial of His miracles,
How did you summon Him to this miracle?
For the question now posed to us in this matter is not simple,
As to how you said to your son: "Give them wine,"
He who has in wisdom created all things.

Strophe 7: Let us learn the word which the mother of the God of all said to us:
MARY
"Listen," she said, "my friends, instruct yourselves
and know the mystery;
I have seen my son working miracles even before this miracle;
John was not yet His disciple,
John was not yet discipled to Christ
At the time when He did those miracles.[8]
The first, the very beginning of His miracles, is this one
Which John beheld in Cana, as my son knew,
He who has in wisdom created all things.

Strophe 8: "Seeing that no one among men clearly has faith
MARY
In things written in books by those
who were not eyewitnesses of His grace,
I shall omit these things; but I shall touch
on more important matters of which I have knowledge.
For I know that I did not know a husband,
And I bore a son—beyond natural law and reason,
And I know that I remained a virgin as I had been.
Do you, O man, ask for a miracle greater than this birth?
Gabriel came to me saying how this one would be born,
He who has in wisdom created all things.

Strophe 9: "After my conception, I myself saw Elizabeth call me
MARY
Mother of God before the actual birth;[9]
after the birth, Simeon praised me in song;[10]

7. John ii.11.
8. If Cana is the first public miracle, then Mary might refer to some of the stories about the infant
Christ in the Apocryphal gospels.
9. Luke i.42.
10. Luke ii.25.

70

Anna greeted me with joy;[11] the Magi from Persia
$$\text{hastened to the manger,}$$
For a heavenly star proclaimed the birth in advance;
Shepherds with angels heralded joy,[12]
And creation rejoiced with them.
What would I be able to ask for greater than these miracles?
Indeed from them I have faith that it is my son
Who has in wisdom created all things."

Strophe 10: But Christ, seeing His mother saying, "Grant me this request,"
CHRIST   At once said to her:
"What do you wish, woman, my hour has not come."[13]
Certain men made use of this saying as a pretext for impiety;
They said that Christ submitted to necessity,
They said that He was a slave to periods of time;[14]
But they do not understand the meaning of His phrase.
However, the mouth of the impious who practice evil has been stopped,[15]
Since straightway He performed the miracle,
He who has in wisdom created all things.

Strophe 11: "Now answer, my child," said the all-holy mother of Christ,
MARY   "Thou who dost control with measurement the periods of time,
how, my son and Lord, dost Thou await *a* time?
Thou who hast regulated the division of the seasons,
how dost Thou await *a* season?
Thou who art the creator of the visible and the invisible,
Thou who, as master, dost day and night regulate
The ceaseless revolutions, as Thou dost will them—
Thou who hast defined the years in beautifully ordered cycles—
How, then, dost Thou await a time for the miracle which I ask of Thee
Who hast in wisdom created all things?"

Strophe 12: "I knew before you told me, revered Virgin, that the wine was just
CHRIST   beginning to give out for them,"
The Ineffable and Merciful straightway
answered His holy mother.

11. Luke ii.36–38.
12. Compare with the prooimion of Nativity I.
13. John ii.4.
14. This same idea is taken up by St. John of Damascus, *P.G.*, 59, 134.
15. Ps. lxiii.11.

"I know all the concerns of your heart

                                  which you set in motion in this matter;

    For within yourself you reasoned as follows:

      'Necessity now summons my son to a miracle,

      And He puts it off under the pretext of "the time".'

Holy mother, learn now the meaning of the delay,

    For when you know it, I shall grant you this favor,

      I, who in wisdom have created all things.

Strophe 13: "Lift up your heart at these words, and know, chaste one,

CHRIST

                                    what I am saying.

    At the time when I brought forward Heaven and earth

                  and all things from a state of nonexistence,

I would have been quite able at that time to arrange in order

                      at once all that I had produced;

    But I introduced a certain well-regulated order.

    Creation was accomplished in six days—

    Not that I did not have the power,

But in order that the chorus of angels, seeing what I did, each deed in turn,

    Would deify me, singing a hymn: 'Glory to Thee, Powerful One,

      Who hast in wisdom created all things.'

Strophe 14: "Listen carefully, holy one, how I was able in another way

CHRIST

    To ransom the fallen and not take on the form of a poor slave;

However, I did allow being conceived and born as a man,

    And taking milk at your breasts, O Virgin,

    And everything in me progressed in order;

    For as far as I am concerned nothing is without order.

And so now I am willing to accomplish the miracle in a

      well-regulated order,

    A thing which I consent to do for the salvation of man,

      I, who have in wisdom created all things.

Strophe 15: "Mark what I say, holy one; for at this time I was willing first

CHRIST

    To announce to the Israelites

                          and to teach them the hope of faith,

In order that in the presence of miracles they might learn

                    thoroughly who has sent me

    And that they might know with certainty the glory of my Father,

And His will, for He desires that in every way
I be glorified along with Him by all men.
For what He who engendered me has done, these things I also do,
Since I am cosubstantial with Him and His spirit,
I, who have in wisdom created all things.

Strophe 16: "For if they had understood all these things at the time
CHRIST   when they saw the awesome miracles,
They would understand that I am God before time,
even though I have become man.
But now, contrary to order, before the teaching,
you have asked for miracles;
And it is for this reason that I delayed a short time in answer to you:
If I was waiting for the time to perform miracles,
It was for this reason alone.
But, since it is necessary that parents be honored by their children,
I shall pay observance to you, Mother, for I am able to do all things,
I, who have in wisdom created all things.

Strophe 17: "Quickly then, tell the members of the household that they are to
CHRIST   serve under my directions,
And they will thereafter be the witnesses of a miracle
for themselves and for others.
For I do not now wish Peter to serve me, nor yet John, nor Andrew,
Nor any one of my disciples,
So that no suspicion of lack of accomplishment
Come to men because of them.
But now I want these servants to assist me
So that they themselves may be witnesses that I can do all things,
I, who have in wisdom created all things."

Strophe 18: Yielding to these words, the mother of Christ at once spoke out
With earnestness to the servants of the wedding feast:
MARY   "Whatever my son says to you, do it."
There were at the time six urns in the house, as the Gospel says,[16]
Then Christ ordered the servants:
CHRIST   "Fill up the urns with water,"
And straightway the work was done;

16. John ii.5–6.

They filled up all the urns with fresh water,
  And they stood there to know what He wished to do about it,
    He who has in wisdom created all things.

Strophe 19: Now I shall praise the urns, telling how they were shown to be
    full of wine
      How suddenly and quickly the change took place.[17]
  Then the Master spoke out clearly to the servants,

                                                    as it is written:

CHRIST   "Draw the wine which was not harvested,
      And after that, offer drink to the guests;
        Replenish the dry cups;
  Let all the crowd and the bridegroom himself enjoy it;
      For I have in marvelous fashion given pleasure to all,
        I who have in wisdom created all things."

Strophe 20: When Christ, as sign of His power, clearly changed the water into wine,
      All the crowd rejoiced, for they considered the taste marvelous.
  Now we all partake at the banquet in the church
      For Christ's blood is changed into wine [18]
      And we drink it with holy joy,
        Praising the great bridegroom,
  For He is the true bridegroom, the Son of Mary,
      The Word before all time who took the form of a servant,
        He who has in wisdom created all things.

Strophe 21: O Thou dwelling on high, Holy, Savior of all, guard the wine in us,
      Thou, all-surveying, keep it unadulterated.
                      Drive off from here all who are of ill repute,[19]
  The villains who dilute Thy holy wine with water.
      The ones who always water down Thy dogma
      Are condemned to Hell fire.
      But deliver us, O Sinless One
  From the lamentations of Thy judgment, O Merciful God,
      By the prayers of the holy Virgin and mother of God,
        Thou who hast in wisdom created all things.

17. Maas is responsible for the reading μεταχώνευσις, which literally means a welding together, remolding.
18. One of the few allusions to the Eucharist.
19. κακοδόξους, the Greek word, may well mean those who have the wrong doctrine, although its usual meaning is those of ill repute. Probably Romanos desired both levels of meaning.

74

ON THE HEALING OF THE LEPER

O. 8 (K. 78)

Title: Εἰς τὸν λεπρόν

Manuscripts and editions: This kontakion is only in P.

Some strophes were previously edited by Maas, *Chron.*, 18–19.

The complete poem is edited in the French edition, II, 360–80.

It seems clear that the refrain was changed when a new prooimion was added. The Oxford edition keeps the shorter refrain throughout all the strophes. The text is not in good condition.

Tone: ἦχος δ′

Acrostic: τοῦ ταπεινοῦ Ῥωμανοῦ

Refrain: ˆ ὁ φιλάνθρωπος

Biblical source and place in the liturgy: On Wednesday of the third week of Easter, the story of the leper (Matt. viii.1–4; Mark i.40–45; Luke v.12–15) is read. The poet altered the story to suit his purpose.

Analysis of content: Although words are put in the mouth of the leper and of Christ, the poem is not dramatic; it is clearly theological and pedagogical. If repetition makes people learn, they would certainly get the point that is emphasized here about the two natures of Christ. The first two strophes contain the usual epithets of praise and glorification of Christ, with reference to the divine-human natures in Him. The third strophe especially refers to His healing power, and, along with the fourth strophe, it introduces the narrative of the leper.

The narrative fills Strophes 4 through 12. The leper is, in the version of Romanos, in the midst of a crowd. After a general description of the horrors of leprosy, the leper speaks of his distress and reassures himself by recalling other miracles of Christ. The healing of the paralytic and the woman with the issue of blood had really not yet taken place, but Romanos' leper mentions them. The essential point, *if Thou wilt*, is repeated, and, as the narrative is concluded in Strophes 13 through 16, the power of Christ is emphasized. Romanos mentions the Arians directly in Strophe 16, and Strophe 17 deals with the theology of the "Three-in-One." The closing prayer, with the request for the forgiveness of sins, mentions the Virgin, as did the dubious prooimion. It is possible that the allusions to the Virgin are later additions.

Connection with homily: The theme or story of Lazarus is used in Greek homily, but there are no special passages on which Romanos seems to have drawn.

Style of Romanos: This is one of the kontakia that is least pleasing to modern taste. It does not sparkle with any originality nor with any of the touches of dramatic realism that are frequent in Romanos' works. The one possible exception is the comparison the leper makes between the effectiveness of his inarticulate faith and of a request an expert might word. The whole poem drones on, with pedagogical reiteration of the two natures of Christ—His power, His mercy, and His share in the Trinity. The story does, of course, suit the season, for repentance and the assurance of forgiveness would be appropriate for the Easter season.

Meter: The metrical scheme is given in the Oxford edition, 520, VII.

ON THE HEALING OF THE LEPER

O. 8

Prooimion: As Thou hast cured the leper of his affliction, O All-powerful,
        Heal, as Merciful One, the sickness of our souls
    Through the intercession of the mother of God,
        O Physician of our souls, Lover of man,
            Savior, and the only Sinless One.

Strophe 1:   Let us sing a hymn to the God and Benefactor of the race,
                                                Christ, the Savior,
        The root of blessings who rejoices our spirits,
    Since He is comfort and security for men,
        As One who is full of mercy and pity and a physician of faith.
    He who by His unspeakable wisdom orders all things,
        And by His divine will, as God, heals the illness of the soul,
    He who alone as All-powerful and Indivisible controls all,
        He who possesses and dispenses to all grace and glory
        And forgiveness of sins,
            The Lover of man.

Strophe 2:   The Master and Creator of time has arrived in the world at a fixed time;
        The Creator has voluntarily come among His own to save us;[1]
    He who fashioned Adam has become Adam mysteriously
        And the mystery eludes words and mind
    For the Word became flesh without submitting to change[2]
        And remained Word, which existed before,[3]
                                        inseparable from the Father;
    He who is the father of the centuries lived among us
        in mysterious fashion.
        For He had no shame Himself in the fallen
        Nature of man,
            The Lover of man.

1. John i.11.
2. All of Strophes 1 and 2 are directly aimed at the Nestorians.
3. John i.14.

Strophe 3:   He doctors the miserable nature, which is subject to many ills;
   Feeling pity for it, He has come and examined all things,
      for He is good.
   He takes care of those in distress; He saves those in dire straits;
      He heals those who are ill, like a good physician.[4]
   He drives all demons from men;
      And as God He orders the blind to see again

                                    and the paralytic to walk;
   He cleanses lepers by His divine will alone;
      Since Thou[5] art Thyself the Creator
      Of all the visible and the invisible
         O Lover of man.

Strophe 4:   Let us observe carefully what Christ said

                                    to the leper who came up to Him,
      And how the sick man showed his illness to the all-wise Physician.
   The Gospels of the God-inspired Matthew, and Mark, and Luke
      tell of this clearly—[6]
      How in the great and countless crowd of many people
   Who followed near Christ, he came up by Him;
      But he was not ashamed to show to all of them

                                    the defilement of his disease,
   And so, he fell on the ground in front of all, crying:
      "O Lover of man."

Strophe 5:   This disease is hated and shameful among all men;
      Those who have experienced the dread disease

                                    hasten to conceal it;
   More than all other diseases among men, it is deforming,
      Since the flesh is fed on by it as though by fodder;
   It extends over all the limbs
      As though desirous of representing man as a complete degradation;
   The vile sickness is of the same family as the *lobe*,[7]

4. Matt. xi.5; Luke vii.22.
5. The shift to second person certainly must be the result of adjusting to a different refrain in the prooimion. This prooimion may not be the first one written by Romanos. The French edition uses a different refrain throughout to correspond with that in the prooimion.
6. Matt. viii.1–2; Mark i.40; Luke v.12.
7. In the Byzantine period the term λώβη was in current use in Byzantium; the word λέπρα was explained by Ducange as a disease. See under λώβη in Ducange, and see French edition, II, 367n3.

Which the skill of the doctor cannot entirely cure;
But Christ banished it,
    The Lover of man.

Strophe 6:   The leper in fighting by reason of the disease, lamented in a
        flood of tears;
    Every hour he would notice that he took on some additional pain,
LEPER   And he says words such as these: "Woe is me, my flesh has
        been dipped repeatedly
    In a terrible dye against all nature because of this illness
Like a stain which passes through my whole body; [8]
    My flesh is changed and has become for me a terrible sight
Like a scar from a burn, a putrefaction horrible to behold;
    I haven't a single hope of health
    Unless He will give it to me,
        The Lover of man.

Strophe 7:   "In haste, then, my soul, go to Christ, the Son of the virgin,
LEPER   In order that He may give the healing which, in the hands of man,
        it was not possible to receive.
Christ gave the man who was blind [9] and in darkness from birth
    The sight of which nature had deprived him.
He snatched from death the son of the widow;
    He strengthened the ancient limbs of the paralytic, which had
        been enervated through disease;
Nothing stands out against Him as God and Creator;
    Therefore I have faith that He
    Is not merely son of man,
        The Lover of man.

Strophe 8:   "A doctor does not have the power to complete the nature
LEPER   which has come to him defective; [10]
    Christ did this for the man born blind from his mother's womb;
And hence it is clear that He is Himself the Creator
    Of the first man, that He made him from the earth;

8. The priest is told to look for "flesh that burneth with a white bright spot." Lev. xiii.24–28.
9. The poet has not observed the chronological order of the various miracles mentioned in this strophe.
10. John ix.32.

For it is from the earth that He has just now brought forth the one
  of whom I spoke;
  And He is the Creator, the Master, and the eternal God
  of the nature.
In me the strength of the flesh rebels against nature;
  But He voluntarily was brought into the world beyond all nature
  From virgin mother,
  The Lover of man.

Strophe 9: "Fortified by faith, the woman with the issue of blood was healed
LEPER   by touching the hem of His garment,[11]
  And I, too, shall hasten to importune the eternal Master's goodness."
As he said this, he ran with his prayer
  And bowing down to the earth on his knees he entreated Christ,
And with two words he wrote his prayer,
  As he said: "If it is Thy will, Thou art able
                    to cure me completely, O Lord."[12]
For it was not a flow of words, but faith that the Merciful One seeks,
  He who knows every thought, the Guide
  And Creator of men,
  The Lover of man.

Strophe 10: Whenever anyone constrained by necessity lacks assistance and words
  And has no ability to phrase a request so that
                    it may come before the ruler,
At once he resorts to wise men who are able
  To phrase the prayer of the suppliant concisely, not in many words,
And as these very wise people, skilled in words,
  Compose in a few phrases the unskilled expression of the thought,
And write these words on pages of measured length,
  The king, taking this prayer
  Understands the sense of the words,
  The Lover of man.

Strophe 11: "It is by faith that I,[13] an ordinary person, present my petition
LEPER   to the wise,

---

11. Matt. ix.20; Mark v.25; Luke viii.43; Romanos, O. 12 (K. 82).
12. Matt. viii.2; Mark i.40; Luke v.12.
13. *Cf.* Lazarus I, Strophe 2 (O. 14; K. 70).

For I hastened and reached for this very holy
and comprehensible faith;
I summoned its aid, and it dictated concisely
In my behalf my prayer to King, Jesus.
In two words, like a very clever orator,
It expressed all the thoughts of my prayer.
I have my request written on the paper of my soul;
I present it to you. Hasten, have pity on me,
O Benefactor of all men,
Lover of man.

Strophe 12: "Suppose, then, Thou dost not wish to purify me, befouled, unworthy;
LEPER   I am mindful of this; before all else I said this:
'If Thou art willing, Thou hast the power.'
For I know Thy power, that no one opposes Thee;
But I fear that purifying me be neglected,[14]
Merely confirm it by a nod, Merciful One,
And the leprosy will vanish.
Even if Thou wert born man from the Virgin Mary, without seed,
Still through the centuries, Thou art the Word of God,
God and Creator of all men,
Lover of man."

Strophe 13: "Because of your faith, I shall relieve you of your disease,"
CHRIST   Christ answered the leper,
"Since this prayer which was offered by you to me gave me pleasure;
Because of its power, indeed, my decision will follow;
When you said, 'If it is Thy will, my Lord, Thou canst.'
Indeed I am Lord and Master, and I wish to save;
For this reason I issue commands, and I have power, and I say:
'If I will it, be purified.'
And as Merciful, I will it, and I command as One with absolute power,
For I have power coming to the assistance of my will,
As Lord and Creator,
Lover of man."

Strophe 14: As the One Merciful God, He stretched out His hand
and touched him,

14. The word ὑπέρθη is difficult to bring into this context. The French edition would prefer ἀπείπῃς. The general meaning is clear.

And the leper straightway was purified in his whole body;
He was relieved of the leprosy, which fled immediately.
The color of his flesh regained its natural beauty;
All who were present there were astounded;

LEPER   The leper cried out: "Thou art the only God, all powerful,
And Thou hast come into the world to recall an erring world;
For these deeds are not at all the work of man;
Thou art God of the whole universe,
Lover of man."

Strophe 15: But when the Merciful One heard this,

He commanded the leper in front of all:

CHRIST   "Go, fulfill the law, and hasten to show yourself to the priest,
And present the gift which Moses, my servant, has ordered
That those purified of leprosy in the nation present.
The Jews call me an enemy of the law,
And say that I am an implacable enemy of Moses;
Become a witness for me before them that I fulfill all points of the law.[15]
As pay for your cure, give me your witness,
For I am Guardian of the law,
The Lover of man."

Strophe 16: Put to death by the command of the Lord,

the disease of the leper fled,

For the sickness trembled on seeing the Creator and Redeemer
No more indeed than the Arians trembled before the absolute power,
The authority of the Word, the Son of God;
For He is before the centuries,
Eternal, born from a Father eternal, His Son,

independent of time,

He remains through the centuries as He was through all time,
For He of His own will assumed flesh, born of the Virgin,
Not leaving the Father,
The Lover of man.

Strophe 17: We who love the sacred dogma of our God and Creator, Christ,
We all revere in faith the Deity, truly unique,[16]

---

15. Matt. v.17–18.
16. He may mean, instead, a deity organized in units, when he says μοναδικόν.

Really in three persons, consubstantial, coeternal,

    In order that we may turn away from the error of Godless men:

Against the Hebrews, three hypostases,

    Avoiding the plague of polytheism: one essence.

Of one essence, the Father, the Son, the Spirit;[17]

    From them, He was made flesh from the Virgin, of His own will,

    One of the Trinity,

        The Lover of man.

Strophe 18:   Son of God, Thou who dost rule before the centuries and

        through the centuries,

    As Thou didst show pity on the leper, driving away his disease

                with a word, by Thy power,

Save us, too, as we approach Thy kindness,

    And grant us pardon for our sins.

For Thou, alone, as Creator of all men, hast power

    To set us free from sins; we entreat Thee, then, grant us help,

Through the revered mother of God, the Virgin Mary,

    By whom we all come in Thy presence invoking aid,

    Crying, "Have mercy,

        O Lover of man."

17. That is, the three persons of the Trinity have a common origin. This opposes the Arians' view.

ON THE WOMAN OF SAMARIA

O. 9 (K. 80)

Title: Εἰς τὴν Σαμαρεῖτιδα

Manuscripts and editions: The manuscript that contains this hymn is P.
It is edited by Tom. II, 283–304, and it is in *Fr. ed.*, II, 329–53.
There are many dubious readings and lacunae.

Tone: ἦχος β′

Acrostic: Τοῦ ταπεινοῦ Ῥωμανοῦ αἶνος

Refrain: Ἀγαλλίασιν καὶ ἀπολύτρωσιν

Biblical source and place in the liturgy: This kontakion is marked for the fourth Sunday of Easter. The story is in John iv.

Analysis of content: Like all of the kontakia on miracles, this poem places emphasis on the evidence of the divinity of Christ. Along with this emphasis and appropriate to the Easter season is the assurance of redemption for those who have sinned.

   The prooimion announces the theme with specific mention of Christ at the well and the woman of Samaria. The refrain carries the message of redemption.

   The first three strophes are introductory, with references to the parable of the talents and an introduction to the exegesis that is to follow on the narrative.

   The allegory throughout is threefold: The town of Sichara is the pagan world; the woman of Samaria is the symbol for the non-Jewish Church; her five husbands are forms of idolatry, which the Church must leave behind in order to claim redemption. The narrative follows that of the Gospel of John, iv, with Strophes 4, 8, and 11 relating the specific incidents. References to Mary, the baptismal font, Jacob's well, and the various analogies with the Church, idolatry, and the power of living water to bring redemption are worked in, bit by bit. The central three strophes deal with the two natures of Christ and this passage introduces His promise to all men. The poem ends with two strophes in which Christ promises eternal life to those who are willing to give up for Him all they hold dear. Christ's promise takes the place of the usual closing prayer.

Connections with homily: Origen's commentary on the Gospel of John includes the same
analogies as those in this kontakion.[1] However, the symbolism may well have
been in general use. No direct influence can be traced in parallel phrases, nor do
the commentaries on St. John Chrysostom have any obvious connection.[2]

Meter: The metrical scheme is given in the Oxford edition, 520, VIII.

1. Origen, *Commentarii in Evangelium Ioannis*, XIII, Chaps. 1–52; *P.G.*, 14, 400–500.
2. *Fr. ed.*, II, 325*n*1,2.

ON THE WOMAN OF SAMARIA

O. 9

Prooimion: When the Lord came to the well,
> The woman of Samaria asked the All-merciful One:
"Give me the water of faith,
> And I shall receive the flowing streams of the font:
> > Exceeding great joy and redemption."

Strophe 1: Do not, my soul, hide the talent which was given you,
> So as not to endure the shame of negligence
> On the day when the Lord will come to judge the world.[1]
For when He comes, He will exact judgment of you immediately.[2]
> Not just what you took, but what you procured for yourself
> > > will He manage to calculate.[3]
> For from each one He takes the money borrowed with interest.
My soul, do not be careless; my soul, be a merchant;
> > > my soul, give and receive,
> In order that, when your King comes, He may give you
> > in return for your diligence
> > Exceeding great joy and redemption.

Strophe 2: You were not worthy of having what you possess and what you keep
> Through[4] the grace of the giver. Do not hesitate, then, to distribute
> To those who ask, just as the woman of Samaria once shared.
For having drawn from the well by herself, she shared with others
> what she received.
> No one asked her, and yet she gave to all ungrudgingly
> > of her free gift.

---

1. Ps. ix.8; Rom. ii.16.
2. The editor of the French edition adopts χρῆμα instead of κρῖμα. However, the latter is used both in the Oxford edition and by *Tom.* There is no good reason for the substitution of the French edition, it seems.
3. μεθοδεύω not only means *to calculate* but implies that the calculation is crafty or clever.
4. Instead of σύ, which the Oxford edition uses, I adopted διά, which was the conjecture of Maas, even though a slight metrical difficulty is caused by that reading.

She thirsts, yet gives lavishly,[5] not drinking,

               she gives to drink.

When she has not yet tasted, still as one who is drunk, she cries out
   to those of her race:

WOMAN   "Come, I have found a spring; is not this the
       One who furnishes
         Exceeding great joy and redemption?"

Strophe 3: Since we have just drunk of the immortal waters of which
       The woman of Samaria became a discoverer,
      Let us examine carefully all the springs;
    Let us take into our hands for a bit the readings of the Gospel,
       As we see the light of Christ,[6] the water that
               the woman of Samaria drank long ago,
       And as we see how she furnished from that water, other water,
    And for what reason she did not drink although thirsty, let us
        see also what kept her from it;
       For all of these things the Book of miracles[7] tells us,
      And furnishes
         Exceeding great joy and redemption.

Strophe 4: What, then, does the Bible teach? Christ, it says, the source
       Of the breath of life for all men, when He was
       Weary from a journey, sat down near a spring of Samaria.
    And it was the season of burning heat. It was the sixth hour,
        as the Scripture says,[8]
       It was the middle of the day when the Messiah came
               to illumine those in darkness.
      The Spring came upon the spring, not to drink but to cleanse.
    The fountain of immortality was near the stream of the wretched woman
               as though it were in need.
      He is tired from walking, He who tirelessly walked on the sea,[9]

5. It would be beyond my powers as translator to convey the effect in the assonance and antithesis in the two verbs, διψᾷ and δαψιλεύεται.

6. The editor of the French edition thinks that τὸ φῶς is an error for σοφῶς. The latter could be more easily translated, but Christ is "the light" so often in the poems of Romanos that it would seem better to keep that metonymy.

7. The word μεγαλεῖον meaning *Holy Book* is authenticated by Ducange, *Glossarium ad scriptores mediae et infimae graecitatis* (Lyons, 1688).

8. John iv.5–6.

9. Matt. xiv.25; Mark vi.48; John vi.19.

He who furnishes
    Exceeding great joy and redemption.

Strophe 5:   But when the Merciful One was near the spring, as I said,
    Then the woman of Samaria, coming from her native village, Sichar,
    Arrived, and she had her urn on her shoulders; [10]
And who would not call blessed the arrival and departure of this woman?
    For she departed in filth; she entered into the figure
                          of the church as blameless;
    She departed, and she drew out life like a sponge.
She departed bearing water; she became a bearer of God;
    and who does not bless
    This woman; or rather who does not revere her, the type
    of the nations
    As she brings
        Exceeding great joy and redemption?

Strophe 6:   The holy woman arrived then, and prudently drew up the water;
    As she saw the Master tired and thirsty, saying:
CHRIST   "Woman give me to drink," she was not annoyed,
WOMAN   But she said with some censure: "And how is it that you, a Jew, ask me?"
    She reminded him of the law, but then,
                        sensibly she offered the drink.
    She did not say: "I do not offer a drink to someone of another race,"
But she said: "How is it that you ask?" Just as once the
                  Mother of God said to the angel:
    "How can this thing be? How can He who has no mother take
    me as mother? [11]
    He who offers
        Exceeding great joy and redemption."

Strophe 7:   Lo, it seems to me that she is the painter of two images, the
    Woman of Samaria from Sichar: an image of the Church
    and of Mary.
    Therefore, let us not slight her, for she has charm.
WOMAN   Again, let the woman speak to the Creator:
                "How is it that you ask me?

10. John iv.7–9.
11. Luke i.34.

If I give you to drink, and you drink,

                                                   you will transgress the Jewish law,

And I shall from the water receive you as espoused husband."

How beautiful are the words of the woman of Samaria,

                                               they roughly sketch for me

The baptismal font at the spring from which he took her as servant,

He who furnishes

        Exceeding great joy and redemption.

Strophe 8:   "Now hear me, woman," Jesus answered her:

JESUS

        "If you had known my gift, and who it is speaking to you, saying,

    'Give me water,' you would ask Him for living water;

For He offers living water."

                        In answer to this she said, perplexed:

WOMAN

        "You do not have a vessel for drawing water; the well is deep,

                    and from whence will the water come?

Are you better or finer than Joseph our sire?

For he once gave us this spring; and how then is it possible

                          for you to say now:

'I am able to give you living water which does not fail to provide [12]

For the one who seeks

        Exceeding great joy and redemption'?"

Strophe 9:   "Woman, you do not know what you say; you have not arrived

CHRIST   where I wish;

    Therefore, pay attention and open your heart to me,

    So that I may enter in and dwell in it; for this I wish.

For the one who drinks this water, will again

                        on each occasion be thirsty;

    But the water which I give to those who are on fire with faith

                  will be refreshing after the thirst;

    For within those who drink it, there will be a stream,

A spring of immortality which bursts forth and swells with eternal life.

    This is what formerly the Hebrew children found in the desert; [13]

    But they did not find

        Exceeding great joy and redemption."

12. John iv.10–12.
13. Ex. xv.23; Ex. xvii.6; Num. xx.8; I Cor. x.4.

Strophe 10:   By these words the thirst of the Samaritan woman was abated,
         And the situation was reversed. For she who at first was drinking,
         Now was drunk; and He who from the first was filled, now drinks.

WOMAN   The woman then bows down before Him: "Give me, Lord," she says,
                                          "give me this water,
         So that I shall not ever run to this well which Jacob gave me.
         Let the things which are old be fruitless; and let the new flourish.
         Let the things which are of the moment be passed over;
                           for this is the time for the water which you have;
         Let it spring forth and refresh me and those in the faith
         Who ask for
            Exceeding great joy and redemption."

Strophe 11:   "If you wish that I give you the streams of pure water,
CHRIST   Go, and call your husband; I shall not imitate your reproach;
         I shall not say: 'You are a woman of Samaria, and how is it
            that you ask for water?'
       I do not increase your thirst; for I have brought you
                             to thirst through thirst.
         I exaggerated being thirsty and I was tormented by thirst
                    in order that I might reveal you as thirsty.
         Go, then, and call your husband and return."
WOMAN   The woman said, "I think that I have no husband,"
                          and the Creator said to her:
CHRIST   "Truly do you have none? You have five,
                     the sixth you do not possess,[14]
         So that you may receive
            Exceeding great joy and redemption."

Strophe 12:   O wise enigmas! O wise characteristics!
         In the faith of the holy woman is pictured
         All the features of the church in true colors which
           do not grow old;
     For the way in which the woman denied a husband when she had many,
         Is just the way the church denied many gods, like husbands,
         And left them and became betrothed to one Master in coming
           forth from the water.
     She had five husbands and the sixth she did not have;
                           and leaving the five

14. Christ is, of course, the sixth. The Church is His bride.

Husbands of impiety, she now takes Thee, as the sixth,
   as she comes
From the water,
    Exceeding great joy and redemption.

Strophe 13: Let us hate the forms of idolatry;
    The woman from the nations who was given in marriage rejects
    And denies what is the sweet and seemingly better root[15] as bitter.
But perhaps someone will ask, "How do these five forms
    of idolatry begin?"
There are manifold errors and forms of idolatry;
                 but there are five horns:[16]
    Impiety, licentiousness, intercourse,
And in addition to these: lack of mercy, and murder of children,
                as David taught, saying:
    "They sacrificed to the demons their sons and daughters,
    And they have not found
       Exceeding great joy and redemption."

Strophe 14: The espoused church of the nations,[17] then, left these things,
    And she hurries here to the well of the baptismal font
    And denies the things of the past, just as the woman
    of Samaria did;
For she did not conceal what had formerly been true from Him who
    knows all in advance,
But she said, "I do not have . . . ." She did not say, "I have not had,"
                meaning, I think, this:
    "Even if I formerly had husbands, I do not now wish to have
These husbands which I did have; for I now possess Thee
          who hast now taken me in Thy net;

15. The reading Ἀμείνην is marked *non intellegitur* in the notes to the Oxford edition. The editor of the French edition connects it with ἀμοινῆς, as used by St. Basil, and judges that it may be connected with the Hebrew word for faith. (*Fr. ed.*, II, 342n1). Could it not rather be an error for or a peculiar form of the feminine accusative of ἀμείνων? However, the New Testament does not use this comparative of ἀγαθός. Blass, DeBrunner, *Greek Grammar of the New Testament* (University of Chicago Press, 1962), 33. In any case, the idea of the poet is that what would have seemed the better root because it was sweeter, actually would prove bitter.

16. The Apocalypse refers to paganism as a beast with many horns (Rev. v). Origen mentions the five senses, which control man before he meets Christ. Idolatry as a form of adultery is a common figure of speech. *Fr. ed.*, II, 343n2.

17. "The woman of the nations" is the Church, which reaches out beyond Jews to Samaria!

And I am by faith rescued[18] from the filth of my sins
      That I may receive
            Exceeding great joy and redemption."

Strophe 15: The holy woman, when she discerned the quality of the Savior
            From the things revealed, yearned still more
            To know what the situation was and who was the one at the well.
      And no doubt she was busy with thoughts such as these:
WOMAN   "Is he a god or is it a man whom I see?
                              Of Heaven, or of earth?
            For lo, He reveals both in one to me;
      He thirsts and gives to drink, He teaches and prophesies,
                              and again He challenges me,[19]
            As He reveals to me, a sinner, all my trespasses
            In order that I may receive
                  Exceeding great joy and redemption.

Strophe 16: "Is He not, then, from Heaven, and yet He wears earthly form?
WOMAN   If, then, being God and mortal, He was revealed to me as man,
            And thirsted; as God, He gave me to drink and prophesied.
      It was not in the guise of an angel,[20] since He knew my life
                              and was concerned about it,
            But it was as an Invisible One who was visible today
                        in order to appear and to accuse me.
            It was in His province to know me and to proclaim what I am.
      I shall draw upon His spirit; I shall drink His wisdom;
                        I shall wash clean in His words,
            Cleansing all the filth of my sins so that with pure will,
            I may receive
                  Exceeding great joy and redemption.

Strophe 17: "Son of a mortal as I see Thee, Son of God as I know Thee,
WOMAN   Enlighten my heart, O Lord, teach me
            Who Thou art." Good was the prayer of the woman of Samaria:

18. The verb means literally "to bail out" and points up the act of drawing water from the well. It also connotes "to be exhausted from." All levels of meaning defy translation into one English word.
19. προσκαλῶν means both that Christ calls her to Him and that He challenges her.
20. γὰρ ἐν οὐρανῷ is marked as a dubious reading. It would seem to say that no mere angel from Heaven could do what Christ has done. The French edition substituted γὰρ ἐν ἀθρώπῳ, which would mean that no mere man could do what Christ did. There are metrical difficulties with both readings.

"Behold, I see Thee clearly; by faith I understand Thee;
do not conceal Thyself from me;
Art Thou not the Christ whom the prophets
prophesied would come?
If Thou art He, as they say, tell me frankly;
For in truth I see that Thou dost know what I have done,[21] and
All the secrets of my heart; and therefore, I entreat Thee
with my free will
That I may receive
Exceeding great joy and redemption."

Strophe 18: When He who sees [all] observed the reasoning of the wise woman
And the faith of her heart, straightway He answered
CHRIST The woman: "The One whom you call 'Messiah,' whom the prophets
Prophesied would come at this time, you see and even hear His voice.
I am the One, I whom you see, and
whom you hold in the center of your heart.
Loving you, I have come to attract you to me and to save you.
Now announce this to all those who wish to be saved
in the city of Sichar,
To your relatives and fellow citizens; and all come together
Who are filled with
Exceeding great joy and redemption.[22]

Strophe 19: "Lo, woman, you are drawn up from the deep well of misery;
CHRIST I who had no vessel to draw water with have purified your heart
Without water, and I have cleansed your spirit without streams
of water,
And voluntarily I dwelt in you and showed you what I am; and I
did not drink."
While these words were said and these things came to pass,
the disciples arrived;
According to the Scripture, they were not near the spring at the time
[of the incident];
But after this, they arrived, and when they learned all these things,
they marveled and said:

21. John iv.19, 25.
22. Strophes 18, 19, 20, 21, and 22 depend on John iv.26–30.

DISCIPLES   "O ineffable love of man! He has condescended to a woman!
          He who offers
             Exceeding great joy and redemption."

Strophe 20: The woman of Samaria is full of courage, and she runs to the
            people of Samaria
       Leaving behind her urn, and taking on the shoulders
       Of her heart the One who tests the heart and reins; [23]
  And she arrived at the city and trumpeted to all these words:
WOMAN   "Old people and children, young men and virgins, [24]
                    hurry to the spring.
       The water is overflowing and pours out for all.
     There I saw a man; and I should not say 'a man,'
               for His deeds were those of a God
       As He prophesied and told me everything. He wills to save all
       And offer
          Exceeding great joy and redemption."

Strophe 21: The heralds of the Savior said nothing at all
       When they found Him in conversation with a woman—
       He was born of a virgin on earth in His plan of redemption.
  When they departed to find food they found a nourishment which
          had not been cultivated:
       The One who gave to all who asked the food of immortality.
                   He replied to them:
CHRIST   "My food is the will of my Father.
  I eat food about which you are ignorant; if any one eat of this,
       He will pour forth on all the breath of perfection
        and unfailing faith
       Which gives
          Great and exceeding joy and redemption."

Strophe 22: Crowds of Samaritans came to the Creator,
       Leaving their houses; and they were shown in their faith to be
       Like the homes of the one who speaks in the inspired Scriptures:

23. Ps. vii.9.
24. Ps. cxlviii.12.

95

They say: "As is written, I shall dwell in and tarry among [25]
    The homes of those who abandon all:
                                fields, parents, and all that is held dear, [26]
    And I shall be their God and Savior from snares;
And they will be my people, sanctified, and making their dwelling
    In the Trinity, eternal, indivisible, which bounteously
    Pours forth
        Exceeding great joy and redemption."

25. This passage may, possibly, refer to Lev. xxvi.11–12.
26. The reference to those who leave all for Christ is from Matt. xix.29. It was quite usual to refer to a Christian as a temple of God. Paul, in II Cor. vi.16, uses the words, "I shall live in them, etc."

ON THE SINFUL WOMAN

O. 10 (K. 15)

Title: Εἰς τὴν πόρνην

Manuscripts and editions: There are three hymns on this subject. One is anonymous; it has a refrain very similar to this kontakion. Another survives only in a fragment.[1] The manuscripts used by Maas-Trypanis are P and Δ.

Krumbacher had edited this kontakion, *Acros.*, #15.

Other editions: *Fr. ed.*, III, xxi; Pitra, *A.S.*, I, xii, 85–92.

Tone: ἦχος πλάγιος δ′

Acrostic: τοῦ ταπ(ε)ινοῦ ʽΡωμανοῦ

Refrain: τοῦ βαρβόρου τῶν ἔργων μου

Biblical source and place in the liturgy: Luke's account of the dinner at the house of Simon (Luke vii.36–50), is followed closely by Romanos in Strophes 11 through 18.

In the course of Holy Week, on Wednesday, the Bishop of Jerusalem is conducted to the accompaniment of hymn singing to the church of Anastasis,[2] where the sections of the Gospel dealing with Judas as he negotiates for the betrayal of Jesus are read. Both Matthew and Mark make a close connection between the plot of Judas and the anointing *at Bethany*. The anointing by Mary at the house of Simon in Bethany belongs, then, to Holy Week, but Romanos takes as his subject the story of another anointing.

The harlot goes to the house of Simon the Pharisee to anoint Jesus, early in His ministry. This is the story Luke tells with the parable of the debtors and is the one upon which Romanos elaborates.

In the light of the liturgical use of this kontakion in Holy Week, it may seem odd that Romanos chose this incident, but it is very much in line with his desire to sermonize upon the forgiveness of Christ; it also serves his poetic purpose by permitting a significant dialogue between the harlot and the perfume merchant. The poem would be useful as a penitential meditation.

In choosing this topic, Romanos may well have been influenced, as a reader suggested to me, by the fact that Theodora had established a monastic foundation called μετάνοια, *repentance*. It is likely that her own past would incline

1. *Fr. ed.*, III, 13–17.
2. *Itinerarium Aetheriae*, 34, Otto Prinz, ed. (Heidelberg, 1960), 43.

her to this kind of welfare program. The word *repentance* would naturally occur in a poem on the topic of the harlot, whether or not the poet had in mind the project of Theodora. Details about her Convent of Repentance are to be found in Procopius, *Buildings*, I, ix, and his *Anekdota*, xvii, 5. See also Fr. D. J. Constantelos, *Byzantine Philanthropy and Social Welfare* (New Brunswick, N.J., 1968), 272.

Analysis of content: The first prooimion contains the prayer of the poet for forgiveness, and the second, the prayer of the harlot. The first three strophes relate the narrative, and Strophes 4 through 8 present the harlot's thoughts, hopes, and plans. A dialogue between the harlot and the perfume merchant occurs in Strophes 9 through 12; Simon and Christ carry on a conversation in the next five strophes. Christ continues His rebuke of Simon in the last strophe, before a short closing prayer.

Connection with homily: A sermon by Pseudo-Chrysostom that emphasizes Christ's forgiveness of sinners is entitled: Εἰς τὴν πόρνην καὶ τὸν φαρισαῖον.[3] Not only does this homily bear the same title as Romanos' poem, but there are many parallels between the two works. The sermon is, however, briefer than the kontakion. The similarities might mean that Romanos took the idea for his work from the rhetorical sermon and elaborated upon it, or it might just as logically be that the poetic ideas of the kontakion provided the inspiration for the homily.

  Some of the homilies Migne included under the group called *Pseudo-Chrysostom* may well postdate Romanos. The French edition of Romanos' kontakion claims that his is, clearly, the prior work.[4] Schork, on the other hand, insists that the homily was the direct source for Romanos.[5] He gives as his reasons the fact that no phrases in the homily are in the metrical form of the hymn, whereas Romanos alters phrases to suit the meter. He also notes that the author of the homily quotes directly from the Bible, while Romanos uses poetical expressions. Both reasons are a bit inconclusive, since the nature of the two literary forms would demand those changes in any case. Also, the fact that Romanos elaborates upon the comparison between the Anna-Elias episode and the harlot-Simon incident by adding references to Emmanuel and Samuel could work either way. In short, parallels are clear; the comparative dates cannot be established with certainty. Mahr goes so far as to state that the homily is a corruption of the kontakion of Romanos.[6]

Connections with drama of the East and the West

Ephrem and the Orient
St. Ephrem, who died A.D. 373,[7] wrote a homily about the harlot and the purchase

---

3. Migne, *P.G.*, 59, 531–36. Also notice Pseudo-Amphilochius, Migne, *P.G.*, 39–66.
4. *Fr. ed.*, III, 16.
5. R. J. Schork, "The Biblical and Patristic Sources of the Christological Hymns of Romanos the Melodist," Ph.D. thesis, Oxford, 1957 (unpublished), 184.
6. August C. Mahr, *Relations of Passion Plays to St. Ephrem, the Syrian* (Columbus, Wartburg Press, 1942), 4–6.
7. Mahr, 27.

of ointment. He wrote in Syriac and not in Greek, but his works were translated into Greek. Romanos, himself a Syrian, must have known them. Mahr discusses this relationship in detail; the particular dialogue between the harlot and the perfume merchant occurs only three times after Ephrem, up until the thirteenth century: Romanos' version, that of the Pseudo-Chrysostom homily,[8] and the Cypriot Passion Cycle of the thirteenth century or earlier. No allusion to it occurs in the works of either the Greek or Latin Fathers, aside from the two sixth-century authors. It is certainly a peculiarly Oriental motif, and Mahr seems justified in claiming that Ephrem provided a common source for both Romanos and Pseudo-Chrysostom.

The Western Passion plays

La Piana stresses the fact that, between the fifth and the tenth centuries, political and liturgical influences from East to West are demonstrable. He points out that the monks in the period between the ninth and eleventh centuries were responsible for a real Byzantine religious colonization of the West.[9] There is a thirteenth-century cyclical Greek Passion play in which the repentant harlot speaks to Christ. Mahr presents this play, with translations, and concludes that the purchase of ointment and the figurative use of Christ as the Great Physician occur both in the Syriac and the Greek–Latin versions of Ephrem. The scenario of the thirteenth century seems to indicate that the homily of Pseudo-Chrysostom is a direct source; its relationship to the kontakion of Romanos has just been discussed.

Style of Romanos: The very choice of biblical source shows the freedom with which Romanos treated the New Testament story, since he chose a story not immediately connected with Holy Week. The inclusion of his personal testimony about his need of repentance is a bit unusual. In other kontakia he refers to the fact that he led a worldly life and held a high position at court. The final prayer is usually one of general intercession, with an emphasis on the moral lesson of the kontakion, but this kontakion ends with six lines of a personal prayer.

The elaborations of biblical stories that frequently enrich his poems are evidenced here in the allusions to the Canaanite, Rahab, Anna, and Michal.

The figures of speech and plays on words are typically pervasive in this kontakion. Some may seem to modern taste to be forced. The debt motif is, of course, in Luke, but the elaboration of what constitutes interest and principal on the debt to Christ is Romanos' addition. The poem contains more than the usual number of comparisons to food and to odor. The details of crumbs vs. bread and use of the adjective *greedy* add to reality; the contrast of spice and perfume with the bad odor of her deeds makes her action more vivid. The use, in the refrain, of *slime* or *filth* introduces a disagreeably powerful sense image. The antitheses in Strophe 3 between slave and daughter, harlot and chaste woman, dog and lamb are characteristic rhetorical devices. So are plays on words that are, unfortunately

8. Mahr puts the Pseudo-Amphilochius homily and others in a diagram; their web of inter-relationships makes clear the fact that relationships are present but difficult to clarify if one wants to hold to a position of only one direct line of influence. Mahr, 34.
9. George La Piana, *Le Rappresentazioni sacre nella letteratura bizantina* (Grottoferrata, 1912), 284–85.

in many instances, impossible to reproduce in a translation. For example, in Strophe 11, the harlot says that she is nourished by the "vision" of the One who is "invisible." Actually, she is nourished by ἰδέαν, which connotes the "idea" in a Platonic sense, the picture, the model. And Christ has no φύσιν or nature. The theological point of Christ's divinity and humanity, of the physical and the spiritual, is thus brought out in the Greek. Again, in Strophe 4, she "rushes [to fulfill] her plan about repentance." This is a very weak statement of the power in the Greek which has her push (ὠθήσουσα) what is in her mind (ἔννοιαν) toward her change of heart (μετάνοιαν).

Above all, the dialogue is characteristic of Romanos, especially because he states the thoughts as well as the words of the harlot as she hurries to the seller of perfume (τὴν φρένα δὲ τῆς σοφῆς). The actual dialogue with the perfume merchant allows her to expand on the worth of her lover. The conversation between Christ and Simon is a repetition of the report in Luke. It is significant, however, that this passage in the Gospel exhibits a flair for insight into human nature that seems to have interested Romanos. Its connection with Ephrem and the homily and Western liturgical drama has been discussed, and the exact parallels can be seen in the publication by Mahr.[10]

Meter: The metrical scheme is given in the Oxford edition, 521, IX.

10. Mahr, 3.

ON THE SINFUL WOMAN

O. 10

Prooimion I: O Christ, God, Thou who didst call a sinner Thy daughter,[1]
        Thou who dost declare me a son of repentance,[2]
        I beg Thee deliver me
            From the slime of my deeds.

Prooimion II: Staying close to Thy footsteps, the sinful woman
        With broken heart called out in her repentance to Thee,
                O Christ, God, who knowest secrets:
HARLOT   "How shall I gaze on Thee, for I have beguiled all men
                      with my glances?
        How shall I importune Thee, Merciful One, for I have provoked Thee,
                     my Creator, to anger?
      Nonetheless, receive, O Lord, this perfume as pleader,
        And grant me pardon
            For the slime of my deeds."

Strophe 1: When she saw the words of Christ spreading everywhere
        like aromatic spice
      As they dispensed the breath of life to all the faithful,
The harlot hated the bad odor of her deeds;
      And she pondered upon her shame, and considered the pain
        brought about by these acts.
For there is much affliction there among the dissolute—[3]
      Of whom I am one; and I am ready for the lashes
That the harlot feared. She did not remain in sin,
      While I, though terrified, persist
        In the slime of my deeds.

---

1. Christ did not call the harlot "daughter." He did call the woman healed of the issue of blood by that name. Matt. ix.22; Mark v.34; Luke viii.48.
2. The phrase *son of repentance* is a Semitism. It means, of course, one who, when repentant, can be pardoned.
3. *Cf.* Pseudo-Chrysostom: Εἰς τὴν πόρνην καὶ τὸν φαρισαῖα; P.G., 59, 531: πολλὴ γὰρ θλῖψις καὶ ὀδύνη γίνεται τοῖς πόρνοις ἐκεῖ.

Strophe 2:   For I am never ready to be separated from evil,
                    Nor do I remember the terrible things which I am going to
                       behold there [in Hell].
                 Nor do I consider the mercy of Christ,
                    How it seeks me and surrounds me as I deliberately wander astray.
                 For it is for my sake that He seeks me everywhere;
                    It is for me that He dines with the Pharisee,[4] He who
                       nourishes all men.
                 He sets up a table as an altar on which He is laid as votive offering,
                    Remitting their debt to the debtors
                 So that each of them, taking courage,
                    Comes to Him, saying, "Deliver me, O Lord,
                       From the slime of my deeds."

Strophe 3:   The odor of the table of Christ attracted the woman
                    Who a short time ago was lost, but who now was firmly established.
                 She was at first a dog, and in the end a ewe lamb.
                    She is a slave and a daughter; a harlot and a chaste woman.
                 Hence, in greedy haste she comes first to the table,
                    Leaving the crumbs, she seized the bread on it.
                 More famished than the Canaanite of old,[5]
                    She satisfied her empty spirit, for she had much faith.
                 She was not redeemed by her cry, but she was saved by her silence,
                    For with weeping she said to herself: "O Lord, deliver me
                       From the slime of my deeds."

Strophe 4:   I should like to search the heart of the wise woman
                    And to know how there shone forth in her the Lord
                 Who is the bloom of youthful beauty and the creator of beauty.
                    The sinful woman loved Him before she saw Him,
                 As the Gospel reports:
                    As Christ was seated in the house of the Pharisee,
                 A certain woman heard of it and at once hastened there
                    Rushing to fulfill her plan of repentance.

4. The account of the dinner with Simon, the Pharisee, is in Luke vii.36–50.

5. Romanos does not observe strict chronological order. πάλαι would seem to indicate that the Canaanite woman had asked Christ to help her daughter before—long before—the dinner at the house of Simon. Matthew tells of the Canaanite woman in xv.21–28. Most authorities put the incident at Simon's house between the second and third Passover and that of the woman from Canaan after the third Passover. Since πάλαι suggests more ancient times, this might be a reference to the woman of Zarephath, a city of the Sidonians. Elijah had raised up her son (I Kings xvii. 17–24).

HARLOT "Come my soul," she said to herself, "behold the opportunity
   you were seeking;
  The One to purify you is at hand; why remain
   In the slime of your deeds?

Strophe 5: "I am going to Him for it is for me that He has come.
HARLOT   I leave my former friends, for now I earnestly yearn for Him;
And I bring perfume to the One who loves me, and I caress Him;
  I weep, I groan, and I try to win Him over to love me.
I am changed by my love of the Loved One,
  And I love my lover as He wishes to be loved.
I kneel as I groan, for this He wishes.
  I am silent and maintain my silence, for He is delighted with that.
I break with the past that I may please the new.
  In short, as I breathe, I renounce[6]
   The slime of my deeds.

Strophe 6: "I shall, then, go to Him; I shall be enlightened, as
HARLOT   the Scripture records.
  I shall draw nigh God and not feel shame before Him.
He does not upbraid me; He does not say,
  'Hitherto you were in darkness; now you have come to see
   me, the Sun.'
Therefore, I take the perfume and go forward.
  I shall make the house of the Pharisee a baptistery,
For there I shall be cleansed of my sin
  And purified of my lawlessness.
I shall mix the bath with weeping, with oil and with perfume;
  I shall cleanse myself and escape
   From the slime of my deeds.

Strophe 7: "Formerly Rahab[7] received spies;
HARLOT   And since she was faithful she received life as a reward
   for their entertainment.
The One who had sent them was the model of life
  For He bears the name of Jesus.[8]

6. Strophes 5, 17: ἐμφύω, the verb *to breathe upon*, reflects the baptismal liturgy when the priest breathes upon the candidate as he asks, "Do you renounce Satan?" Also, in John xx.22, Christ breathes upon the apostles as he bestows upon them the Holy Spirit.
7. The story of Rahab who hid the spies and was granted her life is told in Josh. ii.1–24.
8. In the Septuagint, the name of Josua or Yehosua is transcribed Ἰησοῦς.

At that time a courtesan received in hospitality the upright;
    Now, a harlot seeks the chaste son of a virgin to anoint
      Him with perfume.
The former woman released the men she had concealed;
    But I cling to Him whom I love—
Not as a spy of the land but as a guardian of all men;[9]
    And I am strong as I am raised up
      From the slime of my deeds.

Strophe 8:   "Lo, the day has dawned which I longed to see,
HARLOT   A time favorable for me.[10]
My God is lodged in the house of Simon.
    I shall hasten to Him and weep, just as Anna did about her sterility.[11]
Simon may consider me drunk,
    Just as Elias then considered Anna. I shall keep on praying
And saying, 'Lord, I do not ask for a child.
    I seek my very own soul which I have lost!
O Emmanuel, born of a virgin, just as Thou hast removed the stigma
      of sterility when Samuel was born[12]
    Of the childless woman, so deliver me, a harlot,
      From the slime of my deeds'."

Strophe 9:   The faithful woman is heartened by these thoughts,
    And she hastens to the purchase of the myrrh;
She approaches the perfume dealer, saying to him:
HARLOT   "Give me, if you have it, a perfume worthy of my friend
Whom I love purely and with good reason.
    He has completely won my heart and soul.[13]
Do not bother me with any question of price.
    If necessary, I am ready to give even my skin and bones
That I may have something to give
    The One who hastens to purify me
      From the slime of my deeds."

9. ἐπίσκοπον πάντων, "guardian of all," "the bishop of all." The phrase *all seeing* is used in Wisd. of Sol. vii.23.
10. *The acceptable year of the Lord* is a phrase used in Isa. lxi.2.
11. I Sam. i.13–15.
12. Said of Elizabeth: Luke i.25.
13. Ps. xxvi.2.

Strophe 10:	As he saw the fervor and zeal of the holy woman
PERFUME	He said to her: "Tell me who is the one whom you love so much
MERCHANT	That he has charmed you to [purchase] this love potion?
	Does he really have something worthy of the gift of my perfume?"
	The devout woman at once raised her voice
	And cried with assurance in answer to the perfume merchant:
HARLOT	"What are you saying to me, fellow, 'Does he have something worthy?'
	Nothing is of enough worth for the worth of the One most
	worthy of all.
	Not Heaven, nor earth, nor the whole world
	Is to be compared to the One who hastens to free me
	From the slime of my deeds.

Strophe 11:	"He is the Son of David and for this reason beautiful to behold;
HARLOT	Son of God and God, and hence the source of my delight.
	I have not seen Him, but I have heard of Him, and I
	have been nourished
	By the vision of Him who is by nature invisible.
	Michal having seen David loved him;[14]
	And I, having beheld the Son of David, yearn for Him and love Him.
	She renounced all the rights of royalty
	And at that time followed David who was poor as a beggar.
	As for me, I scorn sinful wealth, and I purchase perfume
	For the One who cleanses my spirit
	From the slime of my deeds."

Strophe 12:	Joyfully she cut off his flow of words,
	And in silence took the fine perfume
	And entered the house of the Pharisee,
	Hastening as though she had been invited to perfume the banquet.
	But Simon, when he saw this,
	Began to blame the Lord, the harlot, and himself;
	The former, because He did not recognize her as she drew near;
	The woman, because she showed no shame in falling down before Him;
	And himself for having inconsiderately received such people,
	Especially her, as she cried out: "Release me
	From the slime of my deeds."

14. The story of Michal's marriage to David is told in I Sam. xviii.20.

Strophe 13: O Ignorance! What does he say?

SIMON   "This have I done; I considered Jesus as one of the prophets,
And He did not know her whom each of us recognized;
         He did not discern who she was, and He would have if He
           had been a prophet."
He who tests hearts and souls,[15]
         Observing the troubled thoughts of the Pharisee,
At once became for Him a rod of justice,

CHRIST   And He said: "O Simon, hear the blessing
Which has come to you and to her whom you behold
         Crying with tears, 'Master, release me
           From the slime of my deeds.'

Strophe 14: "I seem to you blameworthy because I did not reproach her

CHRIST   As she hastened to flee from her iniquity,
But your reproof of me is not just, Simon.
         Consider what I am going to say to you and judge:
A moneylender had two debtors,
         One for five hundred and one for only fifty dollars.[16]
Since they were without means of payment,
         The moneylender forgave what was owed.
Tell me, which of them would love him more?
         Who would feel under obligations to cry to him, 'Release me
           From the slime of my deeds'?"

Strophe 15: Hearing this, the wise Pharisee said:

SIMON   "Master, it is clear to all
That there would be more obligation to love him
         On the part of the one for whom the moneylender forgave
           the larger debt."
The Lord answered him:

CHRIST   "You answered correctly, Simon; it is just as you say;
For the One whom you have not anointed with oil,
         She has anointed with perfume;
The One whom you did not lovingly embrace, she has embraced
           tenderly as she called to me,
         'I have grasped Thy feet lest I fall
           In the slime of my deeds.'

15. Ps. vii.9; Jer. xvii.10.
16. Luke vii.41–44.

106

Strophe 16: "Now that I have shown you who loves me with tenderness,
CHRIST   I shall show you, my good fellow, who is the creditor
And give you to understand who are his debtors.
       You are one of them as is the woman whom you see in tears.
I am the creditor of both—
       Not only of both of you, but of all men—
For I have loaned to all men the things they possess:
       Spirit, breath, perception, body, and movement.
Then, O Simon, pray and cry out as much as you can
       To the creditor of the world: 'Release me
              From the slime of my deeds.'

Strophe 17: "You are not able to give back to me what you owe me;
CHRIST   And if I am silent so that the debt may be forgiven you,
Then do not judge the woman who has judged herself;
       Do not scorn the one who has scorned herself.
I exact no payment of your debts nor hers.
       As one who releases you both from debt, I have come for all men.
Simon, you have lived within the law; but you are in debt;
       Come then in the presence of my free gift that you
              may reimburse me.
Behold the harlot whom you see; consider her like the church
       Crying out: 'I breathe[17]
              On the slime of my deeds.'

Strophe 18: "Withdraw; from henceforth you are freed of your debt;
CHRIST   Be on your way. You are without obligation;
You are freed; do not again be under the yoke of slavery.
       Since the record of debt has been torn up, do not create another."[18]
In the same way, my Jesus, speak to me also,
       Since I am not able to repay with interest what I owe,
For I have used up the capital.
       Hence, do not ask back from me
The interest from the capital of my spirit and my body.
       In mercy relieve me, let me go free, and loose me
              From the slime of my deeds.

17. The verb *to breathe upon* reflects the Baptismal liturgy, when the priest breathes upon the candidate as he asks, "Do you renounce Satan?" See note 6, above.
18. St. Paul, in Col. ii.14, refers to the condemnation of men as being nailed to the cross.

ON THE MAN POSSESSED WITH DEVILS

O. 11 (K. 81)

Title: Εἰς τὸν ἐσχηκότα τὸν λεγεῶνα τῶν δαιμόνων

Manuscripts and editions: The only manuscript is P.
>   Other editions are that by Paul Maas, "Das Kontakion," *B.Z.*, 19 (1910), 285–306, and the French edition, III, 55–77.
>   The Oxford edition questions the genuineness of Strophe 24 because the upsilon in the acrostic is doubled and because of the meter and the style of the contents. The editor of the French edition sees no reason to question it.

Tone: ἦχος α΄

Acrostic: ὁ ψαλμὸς οὗτος ἐστὶν ῾Ρωμανοῦ

Refrain: ὁ πάντων δεσπότης

Biblical source and place in the liturgy: The manuscript states that the kontakion is intended for the Wednesday of the fifth week after Easter. The poem itself explicitly indicates the office of a vigil in which a psalm is followed by reading from the Gospels; possibly there was one reading from the Old Testament, one Epistle and one of the Gospels.[1] Then the kontakion was sung, its subject based on the material read.
>   The story of the man possessed by devils is told by three of the Gospels: Matthew viii.28–34; Mark v.2–17; Luke viii.26–37. The theological point about the ignorance of the demon as to the divine nature is, perhaps, the poet's explanation of I Corinthians ii.7–8.

Analysis of content: The prooimion announces the dual theme of this particular miracle and the special role of the Enemy, *the* demon. At times, "demons" are referred to, but the emphasis is on the devil. Strophes 1 and 2 give the setting of the vigil and the purpose of holding the devil up to ridicule, while 3 and 4 touch on Christ's relation to demons. Strophe 5 introduces the narrative of the man possessed by demons; Strophes 6 and 7 exclaim about the horror of his condition, and 8 and 9

---

1. The French edition records that in the fourth-century monasteries the all-night vigils did use the three readings. Etheria (*Itinerarium Egeriae*, Otto Prinz, ed., Heidelberg, 1960, xxiv, 33) describes only one reading in connection with the vigil of the Resurrection, and Basil in his letter (#107, *P.G.*, 32, 764) mentions no reading, but he does write of songs sung by an officiating priest, to which the congregation sang a response. The exact festival for which this was intended and the exact form of the office is really not known.

relate specifically what the demons were doing to him. The man comes to Christ in Strophe 10; the disciples ask Christ to help him and He replies that He will, gladly; He had come for this purpose. This occupies the central strophes, 10 to 14. Then an important theological point is made in the next four strophes, in which the poet explains that the devil cannot hear Christ and is ignorant of His actual identity as Son of God. After an odd parenthesis on the use of the term, "sons of God," Christ secretly disciplines the demon. Strophes 22 and 23 complete the story, with the devil asking permission to go into the swine. This passage leads to the last two strophes, which reiterate the power of God and pray to the "Master of all" for salvation. The departure from the Gospel is chiefly that of having the disciples ask Christ to help the man possessed of devils.

Connection with homily: Paul Maas called attention to the close connection between this kontakion and a homily of Basil of Seleucia,[2] and the editor of the French edition cites some of the passages. Maas felt that the imitation by Romanos was not to his credit, but the editor of the French edition is of the opinion that, on a matter of dogma such as the relation of Christ to a devil who does not know His divinity, the poet is prudent.[3] The parallel passages are most striking in the following strophes: In Strophe 7, Romanos compares the fate of a dead body in a tomb to that of the man possessed of devils; Basil makes the same contrast, but the poet adds a few details. In Strophe 17, in which the question is raised by the devil as to the right of Christ to interfere in his kingdom, the question, "What have you to do with us?" is treated in similar fashion by both poet and preacher, with parallel references to the Magi and the harlot. Basil mentions the blind man, the paralytic, and the miracle of raising from death as evidence of Christ's interference. The explanations in Strophe 19 for the devil's not recognizing Christ include the contrast between the divinity of Christ and His human appearance. The divinity-humanity of Christ is such a constant theme of Romanos that the dependence on Basil of Seleucia is less obvious, although the reference to the temptation of Christ to prove His divinity by casting Himself down from the pinnacle is significant. The rather odd explanations of who can be called sons of God in Strophe 20 can be laid at Basil's door. The need to know the number of demons (Strophe 21) and the destructive nature of the demons (Strophe 22) or the eternal enmity of the devil are emphasized by both poet and preacher.

Style of Romanos: It is perhaps because of Romanos' prudence theologically that the poem shows few of his strong features. The dialogue is not very convincing as compared with that between Christ and the devil in the Resurrection hymns, and the imagery lacks the usual freshness.

Meter: The metrical scheme is presented in the Oxford edition, 521, X.

2. Maas, "Das Kontakion," *B.Z.,* 19, 300–302; Basil of Seleucia, *P.G.,* 85, 269B–277C.
3. *Fr. ed.,* III, 49–51.

ON THE MAN POSSESSED WITH DEVILS

O. 11

Prooimion: Mindful of Thy miracles, Lord,
        We beseech Thee to be delivered
                        from the Evil One and from his harm,
    For only Thou art
    Master of all.

Strophe 1:   The faithful people in love of Christ
        Coming together keep nightly vigil with psalms and odes,
        Unceasingly singing hymns to God.
    After a psalm was sung,[1]
        We were gladdened by a well-ordered reading of the Scriptures.
    Again we sang hymns to Christ and publicly pilloried the enemy;
        For this is the kithara of wisdom,
        And the Guide and Teacher of this wisdom is Christ,
           Master of all.[2]

Strophe 2:   It is fine to sing psalms and to hymn God,
        And to wound the devils with our reproaches;
        They have always been our enemies.
    But how do we know the way to wound them?
        Whenever we rejoice in making a comedy of their fall,
    Whenever in the churches we represent the dramatic
        Triumph over the demons,[3] the devil really suffers.
        For he has no power against man unless God assents,
           The Master of all.

---

1. See Introduction to this poem and its note 1.
2. The refrain may reflect Wisd. of Sol. vi.7, but the idea is common. Romanos makes use of it in his kontakion On the Second Coming.
3. It is very tempting to see in the verbs κωμῳδοῦμεν and τραγῳδῶμεν a reference to an actual presentation in the church of the comedy of the devil's fall and the dramatic tragedy of the triumph over the devils. The conclusion would seem even more justified when later, in Strophe 4, the verb ἐκπομπεύσωμεν occurs—used technically of the processions in which ribald jests were made. These processions were so closely connected with Greek drama that Romanos is to be applauded for the sustained figure of speech, but there seems no justification for assuming that the scene as it appears in the kontakion was actually presented dramatically in the church.

Strophe 3:   Christ, always helping those who are unworthy,
              On seeing those who cast Him aside grows angry;
              And immediately the enemies come forward;
       But the Friend of man does not permit them
              To be punished by the demons too much, beyond measure;
       For in an invisible form the demons rise up against
              Those who were deprived of God's providence,
              But invisibly He delivers them from their error,
                     He, the Master of all.

Strophe 4:   These are not bits of trivialities which we are talking about,
              But deeds of light are being discussed,
              Clearly revealing the downfall of the demons.
       Let us abuse with ribald jests their strength
              Which weakens whenever the Creator arrives.
       Christ has come and they weakened. They fled from Him as from
              a just man.[4]
              Seeing His body, they were led astray,
              Not knowing that He is truly God and the Son of God,
                     The Master of all.

Strophe 5:   As a true witness is the evangelist[5]
              Who described their weakness.
              Let us read the Scripture.
       When Christ came up to the land from the sea,
              A certain man, possessed of demons, came from the city.[6]
       He had been taken prisoner and was enslaved by the demon
              Who confined him with very many chains;
              But after a long time Christ came loosening the chains,
                     The Master of all.

Strophe 6:   The wicked murderer who had become his master
              For many years kept him from hiding
              The shameful parts of his body;

---

4. They did not recognize Him as Christ; they thought he was merely a saint.
5. The story is told in three of the Gospels: Matt. viii.28; Mark v.2; Luke viii.27.
6. The editor of the French edition considers it absurd to say that he came "from the city." Luke says, τις ἐκ τῆς πόλεως. "A man out of the city met him" certainly seems to mean that he came from the city.

He was not covered with any clothing;
    He did not live in a house but in tombs.
O indescribable misfortune! O ineffable tragedy!
    A living man in tombs!
Truly, he would have been more wretched than the dead, unless
      there had appeared
        The Master of all.

Strophe 7:   A dead body lies with the honor of funeral shrouds,
    Concealed within the tomb;
    The earth covers its lack of form.
For if the tomb holds the one who has died, as he lies there
    He feels neither what is painful nor what is pleasant.
But the wretched man possessed by devils is not comparable to the dead,
    For he was brought down into the tomb while he was alive,
    And he would have been without funeral shroud and without
      life unless there had appeared
        The Master of all.

Strophe 8:   For the demon put him to torture among the dead
    And also bitterly tortured him among the living,
    Heaping upon him twofold evils;
Among the living, he laid chains upon him;
    Among the dead, he shut him off in prison for his destruction.[7]
He pursued him in the deserts, in the hills he threw
      him down precipices;
    He threw him down in pits and trenches
    Hastening everywhere to put him to death,
    Had He not saved him,
      He, the Master of all.

Strophe 9:   The murderer, howling terribly, like a dog,
    Prepared the murder of the wretched man;
    In truth, he opposed him like the Evil One.
The demon was always trying to cast him down
    From beetling crags, or to drown him in the water,

7. The construction is not clear. Why the genitive φυλακῆς? Also, εἰς φθορὰν might indicate the purpose, or it might be a reference to time "until his decay."

Or to pierce him with swords, or to kill him in the mountains,
    Or to consume him with fire;[8]
    But he was not able to, because He guarded him,
        He, Master of all.

Strophe 10: These things then the man possessed of demons endured,
    Deprived of his sense and of his reason,
    Driven from place to place,
At the time when he met Christ,
    And saw the King, Master and All-merciful.
He took assurance; he stirred up his reason,
    He announced the injustice,
    Crying out: "Deliver me from the unjust enemy and have mercy,[9]
        O Master of all."

Strophe 11: The group of the disciples of Christ were filled with compassion,
    And going up to Him, they prayed on his behalf,
DISCIPLES   Saying, "Look, O Christ, and have pity.
See how the nature which Thou hast created is wantonly insulted,
    How the enemy dishonors the image of Thy glory,[10]
How the man is tyrannized whom Thou hast honored with Thy hands,
    How he is punished because of jealousy,[11]
    The age-old jealousy of the Enemy. Save him, All-powerful,
        Master of all.

Strophe 12: "O Christ, save, O save, Thy suppliant
DISCIPLES   Who has been treated unjustly by the demon;
    And as the Merciful One, heal him
O Savior, lest our Enemy laugh in mockery,
    And in his wickedness, say, 'I have gained strength.'
We know, O Lover of man, that he is weak if it is Thy will.
    He will be destroyed if Thou dost merely nod Thy head.
    For at Thy nod, all the universe was created and will always endure,
        O Master of all."

8. Is this a detail from the Gospel account of another man possessed of a "dumb spirit"? Mark ix.17–22. Lake, mountains, fire are all somewhere in one of the Gospels. The poet adds the "piercing with swords."
9. The appeal of the man is another detail added by the poet. In fact, according to Luke, the man begged that Christ not torment him.
10. The disciples, in alluding to the worth of any one of God's created creatures, add another appeal that is not given in the Gospel accounts.
11. Ps. xii.5.

Strophe 13: Christ, on hearing His disciples,
       Rejoiced at their words,
       And immediately answered them:
CHRIST   "I approve of your zeal
         Since I wish you to become compassionate;
    But before you entreated me, my heart was open to this man;
      Indeed, it was for his sake
      That I, knowing all in advance, came up from the sea,
        I, Master of all.

Strophe 14: "I have come from Heaven to save all men,
CHRIST   Unsolicited aid for all.
      For this reason I became man
    That I might redeem from the curse
      The race of my flesh. Hence, I became incarnate,
  I, the Merciful, took on living flesh; for I wish to save man
      On whom I took pity and willed to come
      In a virgin's womb without leaving Heaven, I, indivisible,
       Master of all."

Strophe 15: Christ was instructing His disciples;
      The demon was deaf to these words,[12]
      And turned away from the reproach.
    The condemned blames the judge,
      The unjust finds fault with the good dispenser of justice.
DEMON   He said: "What do you have to do with us, Jesus?[13]
                              You are man to all appearances;
      We do not submit to a man;
      But if you are God, I beg you do not put me to torture,
        O Master of all.

Strophe 16: "To what end have you come to torment us
DEMON   Before the allotted time, believing that you have power
      Which God alone can have?
    To be sure, we know clearly that we lie under judgment
      From Heaven, and that a terrible judgment

---

12. Christ made him deaf to words that proclaimed His divinity; He did not at this time want it known. So, too, in Mark iii.11–12 and Luke iv.41, the demons were ordered not to make Christ known as Son of God although in this case they recognized Him.
13. Matt. viii.29; Mark v.7; Luke viii.28.

Is set as penalty for us on the day of judgment.
    But you advance the time against us
    As though you were God and had invincible power,
        As Master of all.

Strophe 17: "For I now recognize you as the son of Mary,
DEMON   Claiming Nazareth as your native land;
    And yet you give us orders as though from on high.
You have come to us as a troublesome enemy,
    You are revealed as a formidable hunter of us.
We lord it over the whole world, we hold all things as booty;
    But you come as absolute dictator,
    Driving us from our possessions,
        As Master of all.

Strophe 18: "Easily I recall that at the time of your birth you drew away
DEMON   From us the Magi out of Persia,[14]
        And that you won over the harlots to recover their senses.[15]
You have taken captive the greedy tax gatherers;[16]
    And the dead, seized by us, you have snatched away;
You have set free those possessed of demons; you have deprived
        us of everything—
    Things which no one descended from Adam could ever do;
    But I beg you not to beat me,
        O Master of all."

Strophe 19: Since he was only a terrible murderer, he did not clearly
        Recognize Christ as the Creator Himself,
        Because he was deceived by His appearance.
For if he had known that He was Lord,
    He would not have dared say to Him: "What do you have
        to do with us?"
These are not words of one who understands; just as formerly
    He tempted Christ on the pinnacle, when he said,
    "If Thou art the Son of God"[17]—Then, too, he doubted that He is
        Master of all.

14. Matt. ii.1.
15. Luke vii.36–50; John viii.3–11. See Romanos' kontakion On the Sinful Woman, #10.
16. Matt. xxi.32; Luke v.27, vii.29, xv.1, xix.2–9.
17. Matt. iv.5–6; Luke iv.9.

Strophe 20:   Let us not be amazed that he did not recognize the Lord
              Even though he called Him "Son of God";
              For "the sons of God" long ago was said of
          Those who love God the Almighty.[18]
              Israel was called "first-born son,"[19]
       And in the account of the Creation, we find that sons of God
              Were those born of union with women;
              And this is what he considered Christ to be, though He now appeared
                Master of all.[20]

Strophe 21:   Jesus, Himself, as powerful God,
              Secretly punished the demon,
              Bringing an end to his boldness;
CHRIST   And He said to him: "What is your name?"
              As a judge to be feared, He questions the abominable one,
       And not as one who does not know what he asks; but that we may know
              By how many demons man has been tried.
DEMON   The demon says: "Legion is my name as Thou dost know,[21]
                Master of all."

Strophe 22:   Now, when commanded to come forth from the man,
              He rebelled and yet earnestly entreated Christ.
              (To all appearances, boldness;
         But secretly it was a supplication;
              A fear of a beating moved his prayer.)
        But a herd of swine was at the time feeding on the mountain.
              The demon saw the straits he was in
DEMON   And he cried out to Christ: "If you cast me out, grant what I ask,
                Master of all.

18. "Sons of God" as a term to be explained is discussed by the poet in a way that echoes Basil of Seleucia, as indicated in the introduction to this hymn. Paul, in Rom. viii, wrote that the sons of God are those who love God. Those who love the all-powerful God, Pantokrator, are called sons of God in the Old Testament in the case of Job; and in Psalm 89 the all-powerful God makes a covenant with David, who is to be His son.
19. Ex. iv.22; Ps. lxxxix.27.
20. The book of Genesis is by metonymy referred to simply as "The Creation." The passage referred to is Genesis vi.1–4. An explanation of the queer practice mentioned here certainly has a basis in Oriental and polytheistic concepts. How did it get into the Bible? No satisfactory explanation is made. Romanos got his idea from Basil of Seleucia. In the Old Testament, "sons of God" does refer to fallen angels, and by the time of Romanos, it seems to have meant simply all men as descendants of Seth.
21. Mark v.9; Luke viii.30.

Strophe 23: "Christ Jesus, if Thou dost drive me out,

DEMON   At least satisfy the request which I ask:

             Allow me to enter into the swine."

And then, at the command of Christ, the Lord,

          The demons immediately departed from the man;

They entered into the swine, and they were drowned in the steep

             trenches of the river.[22]

          Truly great are Thy works,[23]

          Thou who hast snatched us from the hands of the Enemy, O our God,

             Master of all.

Strophe 24 [probably spurious]:[24] For the demons are not more powerful

          Than any swine, or animal, or bird

          Unless God allows them to be.

And consider how the bold ones did not dare

          Even to stop in the swine without a command.

But when they received permission, they did not spare the swine.

          Just so they would like to dispose

          Of all things were it not that He forcibly keeps watch,

             He, Master of all.

Strophe 25: Servants of Christ who love always

          To keep vigil and to sing to His glory,

          Who have just now abused the devil with ribald jests,

Let us pray to our Pilot

          That we may safely pass through the billows of life.

We know that he has a sleepless eye[25] in order to guard us,

          And through the prayers of the mother of God,

          He brings us through to a harbor which is calm and good,

             He, the Master of all.

22. Matt. viii.32; Mark v.13; Luke viii.33.

23. Ps. cxi.2.

24. The editor of the French edition sees no reason to question this strophe. The Oxford edition notes "Stropham spuriam arguunt materia, metrum, acrostichis."

25. *The eye which knows no sleep* is a phrase used also by Romanos in the refrain for On Joseph II, #44 (K. 11).

ON THE WOMAN WITH AN ISSUE OF BLOOD

O. 12 (K. 82)

Title: Εἰς τὴν αἱμόρρουν

Manuscripts and editions: The only manuscript is P.
The hymn is edited by Tomadakis, IV, 183–205, and it is in the French edition, III, 86–101.

Tone: ἦχος πλάγιος δ'

Acrostic: ψαλμὸς τοῦ κύρου Ῥωμανοῦ

Refrain: " Σῶτερ, σῶσον με."

Biblical source and place in the liturgy: The miracle of the healing of the ailing woman is told in Matt. ix.20–23, Mark v.24–35, and in Luke viii.43–49. The poet amplifies the short narrative to include the reflections of the woman, presented as though in actual speech, her reproof of the followers, and an apparent distinction between the crowd and the apostles. There are changes: the Gospels state that Jesus did not know who had touched Him, the poet has Christ know who had done it; the poet adds the woman's fears of being ill treated by the crowd.

This kontakion was intended for use on the Wednesday of the sixth week after Easter.

Analysis of content: The prooimion states the subject of the narrative and makes it clear that the poet wishes to consider the woman's physical ailment as a symbol of spiritual ills that need the healing of Christ.

Certain inconsistencies are apparent or at least a lack of clarity in the poet's organization of ideas. In Strophes 1 and 2 the poet first expresses his personal need of salvation and then explains that the woman was silent in words, but let her hand speak for her. The next two strophes work into the story and explain her reasons for silence. It is necessary to understand that her silence is to be only towards Christ, for in Strophes 6 through 12, she enters into a verbal dialogue with the crowd and accuses them of jealousy in trying to keep her from the healing that Christ *wanted* for her. The next two strophes underline the fact that Christ's power comes from His divine will, and the poet insists, as the Gospels did not, that Christ knew who had touched Him, evidenced by His taunting the disciples with their ignorance and their pretext of blaming His loss of power on the pressure of the crowds. Strophes 14 and 15 are full of reiteration of the woman's faith, which Christ knows, and this faith led to her freedom from fear of allowing herself to be

119

seen. In Strophes 19 and 20 Christ promises her continued health and explains that He allowed the crowd to witness the miracle in order to make it clear that He wants to heal everyone. The closing prayer brings us back to the personal need for spiritual healing.

Connection with homily: A sermon attributed to St. John Chrysostom mentions the fear of the woman that the crowd would chase her away if they knew she had come for healing (*P.G.*, 59, 576–78). As is suggested by the editor of the French edition, the preacher and the poet may have known a common source (*Fr. ed.*, III, 81*n*1).

Style of Romanos: From any viewpoint, this is not one of the better poems. The dialogue is not vivid, not even quite clear. The amplifications do not add to the effect of the narrative in the Gospel; the theology, which emphasizes the two natures of Christ and His foreknowledge, is weak, and even the allusions to the Old Testament and the figures of speech are rare and unimpressive.

Meter: The metrical scheme is given in the Oxford edition, 522, XI.

ON THE WOMAN WITH AN ISSUE OF BLOOD

O. 12

Prooimion: Like the woman with the issue of blood, I fall down before Thee, Lord,
> So that Thou wilt deliver me from distress, O Lover of man,
> And grant to me forgiveness for my failures,
> In order that I may cry out to Thee with contrition of heart,
> > "Savior, save me."

Strophe 1:   I hymn Thee in odes, O exalted King,
> > since Thou dost not deprive me of Thy glory;
> For Thou dost overlook my sins, wishing to find me repentant,
> Thou who art in Thy nature sinless; hence I beg that Thy long suffering
> Produce in me conversion
> And not presumption, for I cry:
> > "Savior, save me."

Strophe 2:   Now Thou didst walk upon the earth with feet of incorruption,
> > dispensing healing to all;
> For Thou didst give sight to the blind,
> > muscular control to the weakened
> By the touch of Thy hand, and by a word, by Thy will alone;[1]
> > and this the woman with the issue of blood had heard.
> She came to Thee to be saved, silent in speech,
> But crying out earnestly to Thee with her hand:
> > "Savior, save me."

Strophe 3:   Unnoticed she came to Thee, Savior,
> > for indeed she considered Thee only a man,[2]
> But when she was cured, she was taught that Thou art God and man;
> Secretly she touched the hem of Thy garment,
> > laying hold on it with her hand, fearful in spirit.

---

1. For metrical reasons, the editor of the French text does not keep the reading μόνῳ θελήματι, but Maas notes the similarity to the third strophe of Kontakion #8, On the Healing of the Leper. There we have ἐν τῷ θείῳ βουλήματι μόνῳ, and the phrase occurs along with references to healing of the blind, the paralytic, the man possessed of demons, *and* the leper.
2. Matt. ix.20–23; Mark v.25–35; Luke viii.43–49.

She thought that she would rob Thee with her hand;
By Thee she was robbed as she cried to Thee:
"Savior, save me."

Strophe 4: Listener, do you wish to know clearly how
the Savior was robbed and also robbed?
The woman knew what she had to do, and because of the
theft kept silence;
For if she had made herself known, the enemy would have found out
about the deliverance of the young woman [3]
And cast her into despair;
Hence Christ heard her say silently:
"Savior, save me."

Strophe 5: The woman with the issue of blood, it seems to me,
not only reasoned in this way, but said to herself:
WOMAN "How shall I be seen by the All-seeing One,
as I come bearing the shame of my sins?
If the blameless One sees the issue of blood, He will cast me
away as impure,
And this will be more terrible than my disease,
If He turns away from me as I cry to Him:
'Savior, save me.'

Strophe 6: "On seeing me, all the people pushed me away,
WOMAN 'Now where are you going?' they cried to me;
'Just consider, woman, your shame,
know who you are and whom you now wish to approach,
The impure to the pure! Go away and purify yourself of your filth,
And when you have rubbed off your stain,
Then you will run to Him crying out:
"Savior, save me".'

Strophe 7: "Do you men, perhaps, wish to be harder on me
WOMAN than my misfortune?
Am I, then acting as though ruled by ignorance? I know that He is pure,

3. Young? She had suffered from the ailment for twelve years, according to the three accounts, and is referred to as a woman (γυνή) and not a girl (κόρη).

122

It is for this reason that I have come to Him
                  in order to be relieved of the shame of the stain,
Do not then prevent me from gathering strength for myself.
I beg you allow me to cry out:
      'Savior, save me'."

Strophe 8: "You do not know what you ask, woman, go away
CROWD   so that we shall not all come under blame;
If we allow you to go, we shall all be considered guilty of His dishonor;
If the ones who accompany Him see you again going near Him,
They will blame us as scorning Him,
And they will consider us foolish, when you cry out:
      'Savior, save me'."

Strophe 9: "It is you, wretches, who have been ruled by jealousy;
WOMAN   and that is why you do not wish me to be saved,
The spring gushes forth for all;
                  for what reason do you block it?
See, I go to my Creator,
          and if He is made angry, He will not be under reproach;
But if He saves me from my disease,
You will feel shame when I cry out:
      'Savior, save me.'

Strophe 10: "You are witnesses of His healings; and why do you forbid those
WOMAN   who approach?
Each day He calls out and begs:
              'Come unto me all who are weary and heavy laden
For I shall give you rest.'[4] He rejoices in giving the gift of health to all,
And why do you bully me, preventing me,
As though under pretext of respect, from crying out to Him:
      'Savior, save me.'

Strophe 11: "Why did I appear before you?
WOMAN   Because I shall receive healing, as you know not.
Are you[5] the initiated followers of Christ?
             Why do you follow Him gloomily?

4. Matt. xi.28.

5. She is speaking to the crowd of Jews, reminding them that they are not the disciples, "the initiated." The verb she uses for this group of people carries the idea of their being sullen observers.

You tread on the heels of the Immaculate One;[6] hence, withdraw, and
even then He is not alone.[7]
You breathe forth a breath of jealousy, of murder;
That is why you prevent me from crying out:
'Savior, save me'."

Strophe 12: These, I think, were the words of the woman with the issue of blood
to those who wanted to scare her away.
Secretly she touched the hem of His garment;
she tried to rob Him as though He were a man,
He who in His divinity knows no sleep. However, Christ bore being
robbed—
He who of old stole the side of Adam in Eden,[8]
He who formed the woman now crying out to Him,
"Savior, save me."

Strophe 13: He who knows all things before their origin,
who was not unaware before this of what she suffered,
Turning to His disciples, said:

CHRIST "Who has just now touched the hem of my garment?
Who has taken whatever she desired? How, then, do you
guard my treasure?[9]
While you, my disciples, were watchful
Lest I be robbed, despoiled by a hand crying out
'Savior, save me.'

Strophe 14: "By whom was this done? You ought to know, my friends;
CHRIST I just now revealed to you the dramatic act,
and now I shall disclose how the one who stole
Made use of my power; without words she came to me crying,
And clinging to my robe like a message,
She took possession of healing as she cried to me,
'Savior, save me.'

6. A double meaning is, of course, implied. The crowd follows Christ around and they would
overthrow or supplant Him. πτερνίζω has the latter meaning in the Old Testament.
7. The idea seems to be that Christ will be protected well enough by the apostles. He does not
need the crowd to send her away.
8. Gen. ii.21–22.
9. The editor of the French edition points out an interesting parallel in the irony of the question
Mary puts to Joseph in the Annunciation Kontakion, #36, Strophe 12, l. 4:

πῶς οὐκ ἐφύλαξας τὴν παρθενίαν μου;

Strophe 15: "She who came near me received the healing,
CHRIST
  for she plundered the power from me.
Why do you say to me, Simon Bar-Jonah,
  that crowds of people were pressing me?
They do not touch my divinity,
  but she, in touching my visible robe,
Clearly grasped my divine nature,
And took possession of health as she cried to me,
  'Savior, save me'."

Strophe 16: When she saw that she was not unobserved, the woman
  reasoned as follows
WOMAN
And said: "Now that I am purified of my stain,
  I shall be seen by my Savior, Jesus,
For I am no longer afraid,
  for it is by His will that I have accomplished this.
What He willed, this I did;
For, in faith I came crying out to Him,
  'Savior, save me.'

Strophe 17: "Surely the Creator was not ignorant of what I did,
WOMAN
  for He supported me, as He is indeed merciful,
Merely by touching Him, I reaped healing, since really He
  was gladly despoiled.
Therefore I am not afraid now of being seen as I announce to my God
That He is the Healer of the sick and the Savior of souls,
And the Master of nature to whom I cry,
  'Savior, save me.'

Strophe 18: "I fled for refuge to Thee, a good physician,
WOMAN
  casting aside my shame.
Do not stir up Thy anger against me,
  and do not be annoyed by Thy servant,
For I have accomplished what Thou didst will;
  for before I considered doing this deed,
Thou wert there preparing me for it.
Thou didst know my heart as I cried to Thee:
  'Savior, save me'."

Strophe 19: "Now, O woman, be strengthened in your faith;

CHRIST   since you despoiled me of my own will, henceforth take courage;

For it was not for the sake of shaming you

                that I brought you into the midst of all these people,

But in order that I might assure them

                that I rejoice in being despoiled; I did not reproach you.

Henceforth, then, be in good health,

You who up until the end of your malady cried out to me,

        'Savior, save me.'

Strophe 20: "This is not the work of my hand,

CHRIST   but the accomplishment of your faith;

For many have touched my garment,

                        but they did not gain the power,

Since they did not bring faith;

                but you, when you touched me with much faith,

Gained for yourself health; and hence I have brought you

Before all, that you might cry out,

        'Savior, save me'."

Strophe 21: O incomprehensible Son of God, incarnate for us as Lover of man,

As Thou hast delivered her just now from the issue of blood,[10]

                do deliver me from my sins,

Thou who alone art free from sin.

                By prayers and intercessions of the saints,

O Thou who alone art powerful, incline my heart[11]

Always to meditate on Thy words

        In order to save me.

10. Ps. li.17.
11. Ps. cxix.36, 148.

126

ON THE MULTIPLICATION OF LOAVES

O. 13 (K. 83)

Title: Εἰς τοὺς πέντε ἄρτους

Manuscripts and editions: P is the only manuscript that contains this kontakion.
In addition to the Oxford edition, there are two others: Tomadakis, IV, 333–74, and the French edition, III, 110–31.

Tone: ἦχος πλάγιος δ´

Acrostic: Ποίημα Ῥωμανοῦ τοῦ ταπεινοῦ

Refrain: ἄρτος ἀφθαρσίας ἐπουράνιος

Biblical source and place in the liturgy: The kontakion is marked for Wednesday of the seventh week after Easter.

The miracle of the feeding of the five thousand is told in each of the Gospels: Matthew xiv.15–22; Mark vi.35–45; Luke ix.10–18; John vi.5–15.

It is chiefly Mark's version the poet seems to use. In John's account, Christ asks Philip how to feed the multitude, in order to try his faith, but this question would not suit the purposes of Romanos, as is clear in the following analysis.

The Lord's Supper is presented as in Matthew xxvi.26; Mark xiv.22; and Luke xxii.19.

Analysis of content: The prooimion gives the setting as the Lord's Supper or Communion. The first three strophes amplify the account of the occasion with an emphasis on the sharing of bread, which the refrain carries consistently throughout. Strophes 4, 5, and 6 introduce the miracle and emphasize the ability of Christ to see the needs of people and to preach and teach. Strophe 7 introduces the disciples, who are powerless to foresee events, as distinct from Christ's powers. Three strophes (8, 9, and 10) contain the words of the disciples, who tell Christ of their concern for the people in the crowd—especially the women and little children who cannot endure fasting and cannot buy food unless they are sent away. Christ, in Strophe 11, taunts them for their human worries. They point out to Him the size of the multitude, and for five strophes He reminds them just who He is, and He compares their lack of power with His foreknowledge. Strophe 18 is the center of the story; the disciples are sent to bring the five loaves and Christ promises to feed the crowd. Strophes 19 and 20 contain the blessing of the loaves and Christ's command that they multiply. The last three strophes are the poet's statement that only through faith can one comprehend that such a miracle took place, just as only through faith can one understand the virgin birth. His closing prayer is that this faith be strengthened.

Obviously, the kontakion is appropriate for the series after Easter that commemorates miracles. The series of miracles began with On the Marriage at Cana (#7), in which the turning of water into wine also symbolizes the Eucharist. Kontakion #13 summarizes the attitude toward miracles that Romanos wished his listeners to have: to approach them with faith and not with reason or logic. The contrast between the divine power of Christ and that of mere mortals is here emphasized, as it is elsewhere in the poet's works.

Connection with homily: There are, of course, sermons on this topic. The one by Basil of Seleucia (*P.G.*, 85, 360B–365C) contains the same treatment of the prayer of blessing, but there are no real evidences of parallel passages.

Style of Romanos: The amplifications on the Gospel narrative are fairly typical of Romanos. He expands dialogues with some touches of human nature in the attitude of the disciples. Christ, in His answers to them, seems less attractive than usual, in that He is made to scorn their lack of power rather excessively even for the poet's usual device of antithesis to create a central point. The use of the barren land as a symbol of a people who lack the spiritual power they might have seems a bit forced.

Meter: The metrical scheme is given in the Oxford edition, 522, XII.

ON THE MULTIPLICATION OF LOAVES

O. 13

Prooimion: O Christ, our God, Merciful One,
      Deliver us who feed on Thy flesh from famine,
                  and from all distress;
     Consider us worthy of Thy eternal blessings,
            through the prayers of the Mother of God;
      For, O Savior, Thou art
       The heavenly bread of immortality.[1]

Strophe 1:   All the angels on high marvel at the affairs of earth
      For earth-born men dwelling here below
   Are exalted in spirit and reach what is on high
      As they share in Christ, crucified.[2]
   For all together partake of His body,
      As they eagerly come to the bread of life,
      They hope for eternal salvation from it.
   Even though visibly, to all appearances, it is bread
      It sanctifies them spiritually because it is
       The heavenly bread of immortality.

Strophe 2:   That the bread which we take is the flesh of the Immanuel,
      The Master Himself was the first to teach us;
   For when He voluntarily went to His Passion,
      Christ broke the bread of salvation,[3]
   And said to His apostles, as it is written:
CHRIST   "Now draw near; eat of this,
      And eating, you will receive eternal life,
   For this is my flesh, this food,
      Since really, I whom you behold, am
       The heavenly bread of immortality.

1. John vi.58.
2. Heb. iii.14.
3. Matt. xxvi.26–28; Mark xiv.22–24; Luke xxii.19–20; I Cor. xi.23–25.

Strophe 3: We all know, we who possess complete faith in Christ,
  That as we approach, eager for the mystic bread
And in addition take the cup of salvation,
  If we are of pure heart and without dissimulation
We are all participants of the flesh and blood
  Of Christ with faith in Him, and we hope
    From this a life like that of the angels;
For, in very truth, the body of the One who suffered,
  The very holy body of Jesus Christ is
    The heavenly bread of immortality.

Strophe 4: We have all come now to listen to the way the Gospels
    proclaim the story,
  And to admire Jesus, for He mysteriously
Once fed five thousand people in a desolate place,
  Awesome miracle and filled with every kind of wonder!
For the Savior, taking five loaves of bread, as is written,
  From them fed these thousands,
    And all were filled to satiety by His ineffable wisdom;
For they had no need of a quantity of bread
  Since indeed Christ was present,
    The heavenly bread of immortality.

Strophe 5: I wish now to make a record of how the multitude was fed
  When the farmer and the doctor were in the desert:
The land which had been weakened and produced only brambles
  Hastened at once to the presence of its benefactor.[4]
Christ saw them and took pity on all.
  First of all He wisely gave them healing,
    And graciously gave power to their weakness.
They, then, profiting from the healing,
  Knew, all of them, that He was[5]
    The heavenly bread of immortality.

4. The editor of the French edition makes note of a similar reference in Romanos' kontakion On the Beheading of John the Baptist, #38, Strophe 17. In it, Romanos mentions that the daughter of Herodias was born in a land ἀκανθοφόρος. The bramble-bearing, sterile land is used figuratively to refer to people who were deprived of divine teaching and who let the tares choke out the good wheat, as in the parable of the sower. See also Heb. vi.8.
5. Grammatically, the subject of the verb may be the *healing* that has just been referred to, but the poet in other strophes uses Christ as "the heavenly bread," and hence it seemed best to translate in this way.

Strophe 6:   The God of all, healed all of those who were in distress,
                    Administering, as Lord, to the ills of the spirit.
                He, the wealthy heir[6] took all the poor
                    As co-heirs, if only they wished it.
                While the good news was being told them,
                    The close of the day, sunset,[7] drew near,
                    And the whole assembly of people,
                Replete with teaching, were completely without food;
                    And they realized that for men Christ is
                        The heavenly bread of immortality.

Strophe 7:   Easily can we understand what the apostles said to Christ,
                    And what the Savior immediately answered,
                For He, as One who knows the future, foresaw what would happen;
                    But they were unable to know any of this,
                For He is God and Creator of all;
                    But they were weak, since they were merely the created;
                    He is powerful; but they are without power.
                However, He gave power to them,
                    Nourishing them in divine manner, since He is
                        The heavenly bread of immortality.

Strophe 8:   When the disciples of the Redeemer saw
                    That the day was drawing to a close, they hastened to go to Him,[8]
DISCIPLES   Crying out: "Master, the day has declined;
                    And all these people are wasting away from hunger.
                This place is a desert, as Thou dost know;
                    Dismiss them before evening comes
                    So that they may go to the villages and buy bread.
                For they are not strong enough to endure fasting
                    As we are to whom Thou dost give strength since Thou art
                        The heavenly bread of immortality.

Strophe 9:   "Thou art, by Thy very nature, the great Savior of the world,
DISCIPLES   and Thou hast taught all people wisdom;
                    Thou hast nourished the people with words of truth;

---

6. Matt. xxi.38; Rom. viii.17; Heb. i.2.
7. Literally, "the measure of the day moved towards the setting of the sun."
8. Matt. xiv.15–19; Mark vi.35–37; Luke ix.12–14.

Thou hast guided men in the paths of salvation
    Giving them a knowledge of justice.
They have nourished their souls spiritually;
    But now they have need of providing for their bodies—
    Especially the little children and their mothers.
Worrying about this, we beg of Thee
    Nourish them, Redeemer, since Thou art
      The heavenly bread of immortality.

Strophe 10: "Now, indeed, O Lord, we see how all men love Thee;
DISCIPLES   They love Thy words in preference to all other pleasure;
But if evening comes, indeed they must turn back,
    For there is no means of obtaining bread here in the desert,
And they would likely fall, since they could not endure lack of food.
    Dismiss them, for we are indeed worried;
    Let them go away, that they may enjoy nourishment before evening.
Thou hast taught Thy disciples and apostles
    Compassion for all, for Thou art
      The heavenly bread of immortality."

Strophe 11: Listen carefully now to what the Lord said to the disciples:
CHRIST   "Since you are worried, give nourishment and bread
      to the hungry.
    They have no need for buying supplies from others.
    Nourish them all and hurry!"[9]
At once they answered Him and said,
DISCIPLES   "The crowd assembled here is immense,
    And if we wish to buy bread, O merciful One,
Two hundred denaria will not be enough
    For them; but Thou alone art by nature
      The heavenly bread of immortality.

Strophe 12: "As far as we can learn,[10] and we shall not conceal the truth from you,
DISCIPLES   Master, we can find only five barley loaves;

9. In this phrase Christ rebukes the disciples, who seemed to be giving Him a lesson in compassion. They needed to be reminded of their own helplessness.
10. Trypanis has marked the initial two words with asterisks as being dubious; the editor of the French edition changes μάθωμεν to ἐμάθομεν, and it makes sense to translate it freely as meaning "to the best of our knowledge."

No one of us brought anything into the desert,
   But a child is here who has them.[11]
O Lover of man, no other resource is possible for us.
   For an enormous and boundless number of people, O Man of pity,
   How can these five loaves be sufficient?
In addition, he has two fishes.
   But hasten, and nourish them, since Thou art
      The heavenly bread of immortality."

Strophe 13: When Christ heard these words of His disciples,
CHRIST   He answered them in this way: "You are mistaken if you
            do not know
That I am the Creator of the universe; I provide for the world;
   I now know clearly what these people need;
I see the desert and that the sun is setting;
   Indeed I arranged the setting of the sun;[12]
   I understand the distress of the crowd which is here;
I know what I have in mind to do for them.
   I myself shall cure their hunger, for I am
      The heavenly bread of immortality.

Strophe 14: "Sometimes you suppose that I think as a man;
CHRIST   You do not recognize that I know all things before they happen,
Because of my power to foresee hidden things,
   I knew before you that you had no bread;
However, I am in agreement with your desire when you say:
   'Give nourishment to all who are gathered here.'
   You think as human beings when your worries are absurd.
Why are you worried, my disciples?
   Do you not know that I provide bounteously for all? I am
      The heavenly bread of immortality.

Strophe 15: "Do you not remember how my virgin mother begged me
CHRIST   At the time of the wedding in Cana,[13] saying, 'My son,

---

11. John vi.9.
12. Compare St. John Chrysostom, "εἰ δὲ καὶ ἡ ὥρα παρῆλθεν, ἀλλ' ὁ μὴ ὑποκείμενος ὥρα
ὑμῖν διαλέγεται," P.G., 57–58, 497.
13. Romanos, O. 7; John ii.3.

133

Those who are being entertained here at the wedding do not have wine'?
    Or do you not remember how, obedient to her, for she
      is my mother,
As God, I changed the nature of the water
    And without the vine, I gave them wine?[14]
    Just so, I have the power now to nourish[15]
With a mere nod the entire multitude,
    For I am the vine, and for those who hunger, I am
      The heavenly bread of immortality.

Strophe 16: "Even though you consider carefully, can you as mere
CHRIST   men secure nourishment,
    Or can you, though you are worried, feed the people?
Or, then, if you cannot feed them, have you the power to keep silent?
    I, alone, as Creator take thought for all.
I exist as good, God before the centuries.
    And I provide every kind of food for all people;[16]
    But you, on beholding the multitude, are worried,
And you do not consider the One who provides abundantly,
    As I am set before all, offering
      The heavenly bread of immortality.

Strophe 17: "I know in advance what you are thinking and what you are saying
CHRIST   to each other,
    As you see the people, the means of provision,[17] and the hour.
You are reasoning, 'Who will feed the entire crowd in the desert?'
    Well, know clearly, friends, who I am.
I fed Israel in the desert;[18]
    I gave them bread from Heaven;
    In a region without water, I made water to flow from a rock;[19]
And in addition, I furnished them quail[20]
    In abundance, since I am
      The heavenly bread of immortality.

14. John ii.1–12.
15. The reading ἄρτι (now) as given in ms. P seems to me better than the emendation Trypanis adopts: ἄρτῳ. This would, of course, mean "nourish with bread."
16. Ps. cxxxvi.25.
17. The editor of the French edition uses τόπου, which would make a simple sequence of ideas—the people, the *place*, the hour. Trypanis gives no variant reading for τρόπου.
18. Ex. xvi.4.
19. Ps. lxxviii.16; Ex. xvii.6–7.
20. Num. xi.31–33; Ps. cv.40.

Strophe 18: "At once my word and my nod are able to save the universe.

CHRIST
         In order that you may know my power right now,
Have all the men, and the women, and the little children
         Be seated in good order,[21]
And I, as God, will make the desert fruit-bearing.
         While I harvest the fruit at my nod,
         You will become the workers and the servants,
And I shall feed the whole multitude,
         Since I, alone, am set before all,
            The heavenly bread of immortality."

Strophe 19: In response to what they heard from Christ, the apostles acted with speed.
         At His command, they immediately had the crowd
Recline in set order and in suitable fashion.
         The ground served them both as tables and beds.
Christ had brought to Him the five loaves of bread,
         And straightway, lifting His eyes to the Father, He said:[22]

CHRIST
         "I am doing Thy deeds; for I am Thy Son;
For in the beginning, I created the whole world
         Together with Thee and the Holy Spirit; for I am
            The heavenly bread of immortality."

Strophe 20: Behold how the masters, the servants of Christ, were
            arranged and attended
         The Servant, Jesus; and they found Him at once.
For the Lord blessed the five loaves of bread,
         Speaking to them as follows in spiritual fashion:[23]

CHRIST
         "Grow and multiply perceptibly,[24]
         And nourish now all who are assembled here."
         And immediately the loaves obeyed the Lord;
They multiplied invisibly
         As Christ spoke to them, for He is
            The heavenly bread of immortality.

21. Matt. xiv.19; Mark vi.39; Luke ix.14; John vi.10.
22. No prayer for power is intended, but Christ does acknowledge His relationship to God and the Holy Spirit. In a homily on this same topic, Basil of Seleucia uses the same approach. See P.G., 85, 360B–365C.
23. Literally, He speaks "invisibly," but surely they are meant to hear. The idea must be that this is no ordinary speech.
24. By recalling God's promises to Adam and Noah, "Grow and multiply," the power of God to generate life is underlined.

Strophe 21: The mind of man is not entirely able to reason out this miracle.
How did the invisible loaves merge into the visible?
Where did their inexplicable increase become active—
In the hands of the disciples or on the tables?
Since I do not know the manner in which the ineffable sight took place,
I shall keep silence about the miracle; but by faith I shall
Correct my mind, as I cannot exactly fathom the depths of the mystery,
When I see twelve baskets of bread
Filled with pieces, as He alone knew, He,
The heavenly bread of immortality.

Strophe 22: So increase for all of us the magnitude of Thy mercy,
And just as Thou didst then satisfy the multitude
In wisdom and didst nourish them by Thy power,
So now satisfy all of us with justice,
Strengthen us in our faith in Thee, Lord;
As the Merciful, nourish us all,
And grant us Thy grace and forgiveness of sins,
Through the intercessory prayers of the mother of God,
Since Thou alone art kind and merciful,
The heavenly bread of immortality.

Strophe 23: O Christ, Savior without stain, all of us owe Thee a hymn,
And we have faith that Thou, as God before all time,
Wast born of the virgin and that Thou dost remain what Thou art.
Only Thou dost know the miracle of Thy birth.
For we do not know how the loaves produced loaves;
How can we understand in our human hearts, O Savior,
Thy birth from one who knew no husband?
So, all of us sing hymns praising Thee,
Because Thou art God of all, as Thou art
The heavenly bread of immortality.

ON THE RAISING OF LAZARUS I

O. 14 (K. 70)

Title: Εἰς τὸν δίκαιον καὶ τετραήμερον Λάζαρον

Manuscripts and editions: E. Mioni, *Romano il Melode*, edited this, 199–212, using P as his
manuscript.

It is in Tomadakis, edited by J.-Th. Papadimitrious, 157–76.

The French edition edits it, III, 154–79.

The Oxford edition also uses P, as do all of the other editors.

There are several very peculiar readings and an organization of the
narrative, which will be discussed in connection with the liturgy and possible
sources. That the kontakion is genuinely by Romanos is not doubted.

Tone: ἦχος πλάγιος β′

Acrostic: τοῦ ταπεινοῦ ῾Ρωμανοῦ

Refrain: ἀναστήσεται καὶ στήσεται λέγων· ῾σὺ εἶ ζωὴ καὶ ἀνάστασιν᾽.

Biblical source and place in the liturgy: From the end of the fourth century on, the Resurrection
of Lazarus was a part of Holy Week. A description of the ceremonies in Jerusalem
is available,[1] and they were probably typical of the other churches in the East. On
the Sabbath of the seventh week of Lent, in the afternoon, the bishop says,
"Omnes hodie hora septima in Lazario parati sumus." The procession then goes
toward Bethany (near Lazarion) and stops at the church built on the spot where
Mary is supposed to have met Christ. Bishop, monks, and worshippers then
chant one hymn and one antiphon, and the Gospel is read from John xi. After the
blessing by the bishop and a prayer, the procession moves on to the church at
Lazarion, high above Bethany. Here a crowd gathers, not only at the church, but
in the adjoining fields, and again there are hymns and an antiphon appropriate for
the day, as John xii is read. The third part of the ritual is the actual visit to the
tomb of Lazarus in Bethany; the announcement of Easter comes with the words,
"Cum venisset Iesus in Bethana ante sex dies paschae."

The Roman Church celebrates the resurrection of Lazarus on Friday of
of the fourth week of Lent.

In the *Acta Pilati*, Part II, xx–xxiii, there is a dialogue between Satan and
Hades on the subject of Lazarus, but Romanos is original in having Death and
Hades converse. Compare with the Resurrection kontakia.

---

1. *Itinerarium Egeriae (Peregrinatio Aetheriae)*, Otto Prinz, ed. (Heidelberg, 1960), 41.

Analysis of content: If the kontakion of Romanos, Lazarus I, was written only for the first part of this procession, it is not surprising that we have the otherwise strange omission of the meeting of Christ and Mary and the resurrection of Lazarus. Actually, in Lazarus I, after the moral about the victory of faith and love is pointed out and after the mention of the sisters is introduced, along with a statement of Christ to the disciples that they should go to the home of Lazarus, who is ill, there are some brief digressions on the Pauline teaching that death is but a sleep and some theological underlining of the two natures of Christ. This introductory material requires seven strophes. Eight strophes, the heart of the hymn, are devoted to a sprightly dialogue between Hades and Death, who complain that they are being despoiled. Rather abruptly the poem turns back to Christ and the disciples as He asks where Lazarus is buried. This episode ends suddenly, and the closing prayer fills the final strophe. Was this poem, then, intended only for the first part of the day's ritual?

It is noteworthy that only part of John xi is used as a source. Lazarus II may well have been intended to be a companion piece, for it contains the actual resurrection of Lazarus. It has left some trace in the ritual, although its text is very confused.

Connections with homily: Only one other Byzantine hymn on the resurrection of Lazarus survives; it is by Kyriakos. Krumbacher published it,[2] and he concludes that it was probably earlier than the kontakion of Romanos.[3] The poem by Kyriakos refers to Hades and Death, but it contains no dialogue between them.[4] In spite of the popularity of the subject of the resurrection of Lazarus, only a few kontakia on the subject remain as evidence.

There are, however, many sermons on the subject. The parallels with Romanos are most obvious in the sermons by St. John Chrysostom, for example, St. John Chrysostom, spuria, "In Quatriduanum," *P.G.*, 62, 771. After the words, "If you had been here . . .," the sermon asks where Christ really was, and the words correspond very closely to those of Romanos' Strophe 8, 1–3.

τῷ μὲν σώματι οὐκ ἦν ἐκεῖ, τῇ δὲ θεότητι - - -	νῦν σώματι τῇ γὰρ θεότητι
Also in his sermon, "In Lazarum I," the miracle of the resurrection is described as	Compare with Romanos, Strophe 7, 5.
καὶ πρὸ θαυμάτων θαύματα	θαῦμα πρὸ θαύματος

Similar references to the resurrection of Elijah as a payment of debt (πρὸς χάριν γυναικὸς)[5] occur, as Romanos develops the idea in Strophe 15. Later in the same

2. Krumbacher, *R.u.K.*, 726, 735.
3. Krumbacher, *R.u.K.*, 722, 723. He points out that the heirmos in the poem of Kyriakos is used by only one other poet, namely, Romanos in his Judas hymn. Other considerations favor this decision, although it is not absolutely established.
4. Krumbacher, *R.u.K.*, 733, lines 180–85.
5. *P.G.*, 62, 778B.

sermon the danger of losing the kingdom of the dead parallels Strophe 14, 1–3, of Romanos.

Both homily and hymn explain that Christ really knew where Lazarus was buried and reiterate His two natures. Amphilochius takes pains to give us anatomical details of Lazarus' resurrection.[6]

Meter: The meter is given in the Oxford edition, 523, XIII.

6. *P.G.*, 39, 65A.

ON THE RAISING OF LAZARUS I

O. 14

Prooimion: Thou hast come, O Lord, to the tomb of Lazarus
        And Thou hast raised him up after four days among the dead,
        After Thou hast conquered Hades, O Powerful One.
    Taking pity on the tears of Mary and Martha,[1]
        Thou hast said to them:
            "He will be resurrected[2] and he will rise up
            Saying, 'Thou art the Life and Resurrection'."

Strophe 1:   In considering the tomb and those in the tomb, we weep,
        But we should not; for we do not know whence they have come,
        And where they are now, and who has them.
    They have come from temporal life, released from its sorrows;
        They are at peace, waiting for the receiving of divine light.[3]
        The Lover of man has them in His charge, and He has divested
           them of their temporal clothing
        In order that He may clothe them with an eternal body.
    Why, then, do we weep in vain? Why do we not trust Christ,
          as He cries:
CHRIST   "He who believes on me shall not perish,[4]
        For even if he knows corruption, after that corruption,
           He will be resurrected and he will rise up
           Saying, 'Thou art the Life and the Resurrection'"?

Strophe 2:   The man of faith always has power for whatever he wishes,
        Since he possesses a faith which lends strength to all things;
        From it, he gains power from Christ for whatever he asks.

1. John xi.21–25.
2. ἀναστήσεται, when it refers to Lazarus, at times seems to mean "He will be given life again," and at times "He will be put together again and restored to his former condition." The latter is true in Strophe 13.
3. Wisd. of Sol. iv.7: "An upright man will be at rest." φαῦσιν (root φαω-φαινω) as divine light occurs in Gen. i.15: καὶ ἔστωσαν εἰς φαῦσιν ἐν τῷ στερεώματι τοῦ οὐρανοῦ.
4. John xi.25.

This faith is a great possession; if a man have it,

he has control of everything.

Mary and Martha had it and were renowned for it.

When they saw that their brother Lazarus,

a man of faith, had become ill,

They sent word to the Creator:

MARY Saying, "Hasten Master, for the one whom Thou lovest is ill;

and But show Thyself in time and he will be saved;

MARTHA For if the light of Thy face appears,[5]

He will be resurrected and he will rise up

Saying, 'Thou art the Life and Resurrection'."

Strophe 3: Summoned by the faith of the women, He came,

He who of His own free will became physician of soul and body,[6]

And immediately He spoke to His friends:

CHRIST "Arise; let us go into Judaea where we were once;

For I have received a letter[7] which I read with pleasure

For faith has dictated it and infallible hope wrote it,

And love sealed it.

Why should I keep from you what has happened? Mary and Martha

With faith pray to me on behalf of Lazarus,

Since he is now ill. If I go to him now

He will be resurrected, and he will rise up

Saying, 'Thou art the Life and the Resurrection'."

Strophe 4: After He said this, the One who knows

All thoughts remained for two days

In the place where He was, as the Scripture says.

He waited in order that the will of those who loved Him

might be made clear;

For Martha, Mary, and Lazarus loved the Master—

Not just for one time or another time, but constantly, consistently,

In times of relaxation and in times of anxiety.

---

5. The connection between the "light of Thy face" and salvation is made in Ps. lxxx, 3 and 19. Num. vi.25–26 has the famous prayer of dismissal: "The Lord make His face shine upon thee, the Lord lift up His countenance upon thee and give thee peace."
6. Christ refers to Himself as a physician. Matt. ix.12; Mark ii.17; Luke v.31. The homily of the day referred to Him in this way. Ps. Chrys., *P.G.*, 62, 773: Ἰησοῦν, ἀληθινὸν ἰατρόν.
7. In the account in John xi.6, he had simply "heard" that Lazarus was sick.

So it happened that Christ, seeing that this disposition was
    growing even greater,
    Saved one [of the sisters] and honored the other;
    And as for Lazarus, He told them:
        "He will be resurrected and he will rise up
        Saying, 'Thou art the Life and the Resurrection'."

Strophe 5:   But probably you are saying: "Make it clear to us: which
        one did He honor,
    And which one did He save? For we know that as far as
        Lazarus is concerned,
    Christ snatched him from the hands of Hades."
Mary was, as the Scripture says, the one whom He saved
    from seven devils,[8]
    And also the one who anointed with myrrh the Giver of perfumes,
    And with her hair dried the feet of the One who
    cleansed all mankind
    From stain of the wily one.
Martha He honored, since she served them with love;[9]
    He inspired her with confidence[10] when she was weeping
    About her brother, and He said to her:
        "He will be resurrected and he will rise up
        Saying, 'Thou art the Life and the Resurrection'."

Strophe 6:   Again the Lord spoke to the disciples;
CHRIST   "See now Lazarus, our friend, has fallen asleep,
    And I wish to go and awaken him."
But they did not understand that the Redeemer referred to
    death as sleep,[11]
    Indeed if Paul had been there,[12] he would have known the
    word of the Word,
    For, instructed by Him, he sent to his churches epistles
    Calling the dead those who have fallen asleep.

8. Romanos confuses the three Marys. Mary the sister of Lazarus is, of course, not Mary Magdalene, nor Mary of Bethany. Here he might refer to the harlot (see Kontakion #10) or to the anointing at Bethany. Probably Romanos was at the moment using some contemporary source, some homily he knew.
9. Luke x.38–42.
10. John xi.24.
11. In the O.T., "sleep" in the sense of death occurs: Gen. xlvii.30. Ps. xiii.3 refers to the sleep of death, as does Dan. xii.2.
12. Paul makes the connection, I Cor. xv.20; I Thess. iv.13.

For who can die if he loves Christ?
How can he fall if he eats the living bread?[13]
He has in his heart the miracle
As a phylactery,[14] so that even if he perish,
He will be resurrected and he will rise up
Saying, "Thou art the Life and the Resurrection."

Strophe 7:   When they understood that the Lord said sleep
Meaning death, for He told them plainly:
"I go now to resurrect him,"
They nodded to one another, probably communicating with
head and hands;
DISCIPLES   "We see a miracle before a miracle,[15] and so we are afraid.
For He did not learn that Lazarus was dead, which is what
He had said; but that he was ill,
And He predicts what we are going to see;
Fear! Astonishment! Amazement! Some[16] have said that He is mere man!
They have not felt awe before His power
When He says a word and immediately the one who was dead,
Will be resurrected and he will rise up
Saying, 'Thou art the Life and the Resurrection'."

Strophe 8:   Now Jesus goes into Judaea, in His body;
For in His divinity He cares for and occupies
The whole world and even those from out of the earth like
the miserable locusts.[17]
He who fills the universe arrived, then, arrived
in Bethany to accomplish His divine work.
When Hades heard the sound of His footsteps,

13. John vi.51.
14. A phylactery was used to ward off illness and accidents, and μυστήριον refers to the Eucharist as a measure of safety.
15. In referring to the miracle of Lazarus' resurrection as before the miracle of Christ's own resurrection, the poet uses words parallel to those of Ps. Chrys., P.G., 62, 771: πρὸ θαυμάτων θαύματα γυμνάζοντος. Also, the poet wishes to make clear that Christ knew in advance the death and resurrection of Lazarus. This strophe and Strophe 17 both make this point clear.
16. The Nestorians made this claim. Romanos refutes it implicitly and explicitly. Kontakion #20, Strophe 19, l. 2.
17. Isa. xl.22. The locusts came in swarms and symbolize the multitude. Also, they are insignificant (Num. xiii.33). Grasshoppers and locusts are not identical, but they are of the same group. Goethe, in his prelude to *Faust*, has Satan allude to man as a grasshopper!

HADES   He whispered to Death: "What are those feet, O Death,
Which march over my head?
Probably Jesus is coming; and again He has come to exact
payment from us.
Just as formerly the son of the widow escaped us,
So now it is Lazarus.
He will be resurrected and he will rise up
Saying, 'Thou art the Life and the Resurrection.'

Strophe 9:   "Victorious Death, unconquerable, listen

HADES   To Hades, your friend, and be freed from your toil.
Do not bring me nourishment for I cannot digest it.
You bring me the bound dead,[18] and when I swallow them,

I vomit.

When they are buried, I seize them and rejoice;

but when they are spoiled I cannot hold them.

Those who are within me, I exact for myself,

and those whom I cause to be prepared I claim for myself;

Why, then, are you disturbed?
Stop, make ready, and take possession of the friend

of the Nazarene, O Death,

Be obedient, bearing in mind
That he after a short time of four days
Will be resurrected and he will rise up
Saying, 'Thou art the Life and the Resurrection'."

Strophe 10:   When he heard these words, Death bellowed
And, crying out with anger, he said to Hades:

DEATH   "You give me good advice as though you were free from evils;
Give advice to your stomach which you have never fed up until now,
For indeed I grew weary of bringing food to you; yet you have
never said, 'That is enough.'[19]
But you were as insatiable as the sea in receiving the
rivers of the dead
Never reaching satiety.

18. The dead Lazarus is represented in art in a shroud and the Byzantine Greek word that means *to lay out for burial* is λαζορόω (Liddell and Scott).
19. *Acta Pilati*, II, xxi.

Why, then, do you talk to me like this?

                               First learn what you are teaching me,

    Be calm and make ready.

    For the one whom you have in you, after a brief critical moment

        Will be resurrected and he will rise up

        Saying, 'Thou art the Life and the Resurrection.'

Strophe 11: "The life of mortals has always seemed as water to you;

DEATH   That is why you open wide and never cease to swallow them.[20]

      Then let this be enough and do not become more full;

For the feet which you hear, and I see they are threatening,

      Are footsteps of one who is raging, and who is angered at you.

      As He draws near the tomb, He kicks at your gates,[21]

      And searches for the contents of your belly.

He has come, He who will purge you; and you have need of Him,

                             for you are all distended.

    You will then be lightened if Lazarus,

    Emptied from your entrails,

        Will be resurrected and will rise up

        Saying, 'Thou art the Life and the Resurrection'."

Strophe 12: "These are foul and shameful remarks you address to me,

HADES   Hades, your friend. Seeing my misfortunes, you rejoice;

      But I because of these things weep over myself

For I see the limbs of Lazarus, already disintegrating

        before putrefaction

      As though they seem to rise again, they work at reassembling,

      For they are crawling like ants when the worms withdraw,

      And the bad odor has disappeared.

Alas, Jesus has really come; and He, sending

                         His fragrance towards us,

    Has perfumed the ill-smelling corpse.

    And now the man who perished and was reduced to ashes

        Will be resurrected and will rise up

        Saying, 'Thou art the Life and the Resurrection'."

20. Isa. v.14.

21. I adopt σοῦ for οὐ, as does the Greek edition (*Tom.* I, #7); the sense is better than the reading in O., and iconography supports it, as the editor of the French edition agrees (II, 169*n*1).

Strophe 13: When he heard this, Death cried out;

          And then he ran and seized Hades by the hand.

          And they both beheld the terrifying and awesome sight.

    The fragrance of the Son of God permeated His friend,

          And made ready his body for the call of the Giver of Life,

          It reordered his hair and reconstructed his skin,

          And put together his inner organs,

    And stretched out his veins so that the blood could again

                                  flow through them,

          And repaired his arteries,

          So that Lazarus be made ready when called.[22]

            He will be resurrected and will rise up

            Saying, "Thou art the Life and the Resurrection."

Strophe 14: Hades and Death had barely seen all the things

          Which took place, than they spoke to one another with sorrow:

HADES   "Never will our empire be prominent and victorious.

and   The tomb has become like a dye which changes corruption into life.

DEATH   The funeral monument is considered as a thread,

                     and whoever wishes cuts it without any trouble,

          And it redeems whomever it wishes, brother, son, daughter,[23]

          And those who dwell on earth laugh at us.

    Whether a man be slave or free, if he wishes, he despoils us.

          And whether a heavenly or earthly being,

          One has only to say a word, and immediately the dead

            Will be resurrected and will rise up

            Saying, 'Thou art the Life and the Resurrection.'

Strophe 15: "Formerly Elijah was a man on earth,

HADES   And when he wished to raise up the son of a widow,

and   It was through us that he offered pay for what he consumed.

DEATH   He consumed the nourishment of the poor woman;

                          but we set the evaluation.

          The prophet was supported; Death was turned aside

          Along with Hades when the young child was demanded back.

---

22. Ps. Chrysos. (P.G., 62, 777) in his third homily has the reconstitution follow a different order: eye and nose; cheeks, neck attached to shoulders, hands prepared to move; arteries fitted in; fingers arranged.

23. Resurrection of Lazarus, *brother* of Mary and Martha; the *son* of the widow of Nain (Luke vii.11–17); the *daughter* of Jairus (Mark v.22–24; Matt. ix.18–20; Luke viii.41–42).

The tears and prayers of the famished sent it to death.[24]
All the earth was ravaged by hunger and by thirst, for there was no rain
But the Prophet said with rejoicing
To the widow: 'You ask for your son,
He will be resurrected and will rise up
Saying, "Thou art the Life and the Resurrection".'

Strophe 16: "The recent defeat has made us forgetful
HADES   Of our former fall; and henceforth Elijah
and   And Elisha shall pass out of our minds as though they were nothing;
DEATH   But even now the wounds of their blows are to be found on us,
Especially of Elisha who performed miracles,
For while he was alive he resurrected a corpse, and when
he was dead, he snatched from death
A dead body which had been thrown on him.[25]
This completely guarantees that no one
of the faithful will die,
But he will live, especially whenever
He is connected with the bodies of the saints,
He will be resurrected and will rise up
Saying, 'Thou art the Life and the Resurrection'."

Strophe 17: All these things, then, they said as they groaned
And as they lamented about the resurrection from the dead,
Bemoaning themselves and all that was theirs.
But the Creator arrived at the tomb of the dead man
for whom He had come
After asking, it seems, where Lazarus was buried.
He asked, through irony, He who made man with His own hand.
As He says, "Where does Lazarus lie?"
He wishes to know what He already knew; just as He
formerly asked: "Where are you Adam?"[26]

---

24. I Kings xvii. Compare, too, with Romanos' kontakion on Elijah (#45). The source of Romanos' kontakion on Elijah seems to be Syrian. Elijah is represented as being very hard-hearted. The child of the widow dies in order to teach Elijah compassion. He felt none for the famished people and is not as noble a character as the Greek concept of the prophet who was present at the Second Coming.
25. II Kings xiii.20–22; Ecclus. xlviii.13–14.
26. Gen. iii.9.

Just so, He said: "Where is Lazarus?"
Just a short time ago, He said to Martha:
   "He will be resurrected and will rise up
   Saying, 'Thou art the Life and the Resurrection'."

Strophe 18:   Almighty Lord, merciful father of the humble,
      Thou who hast saved Lazarus
    Just now by the sound of Thy voice,
  Just so, from Thy throne, allow those who have gone before us
                      to see Thy joyous countenance.
    And grant that we may live out our present span of life in peace,
    And that we come to the end pleasing to Thee,
                  so that, living or dying,
    We may be governed by Thy will.
  Give us a sign, an order, tell us Thy purpose to save us,[27]
    For Thou shalt not destroy the one who loves Thee,
    But Thou dost control him in life and summon him in death
      And he will be resurrected and will rise up
      Saying, "Thou art the Life and the Resurrection."

27. Very peculiar constructions, and the text is seemingly suspect.

ON THE RAISING OF LAZARUS II

O. 15 (K. 71)

Title: Εἰς τὸν ὅσιον καὶ δίκαιον Λάζαρον τὸν τετραήμερον

Manuscripts and editions: The manuscript transmission is very faulty. P has strophes of the entire kontakion; some strophes are in M and T, others in A, B, D, M, T, and V. The introduction to this kontakion in the French edition includes an analysis of the differences in the prooimia and the refrain in the various manuscripts, and Krumbacher mentions the various revisions (*Acros.*, 582). It may well be that we are dealing with two different hymns, but there is a rough unity to the ideas, more than the editor of the French edition seems to grant.

> E. Mioni, *Romano il Melode*, 211–23.
> Pitra, *A.S.*, I, 473–75.
> French edition, III, 182–219.
> Tomadakis, I, 8, 185–94.

Tone: ἦχος β′

Acrostic: τοῦ ταπεινοῦ ʿΡωμανοῦ

Refrain: Μαρίας καὶ Μάρθας τὰ δάκρυα

Biblical source and place in the liturgy: The liturgical customs connected with this poem were discussed under Lazarus I. It is clear that this kontakion begins and ends at Bethany and follows the narrative in John xii rather than John xi. As is indicated in the analysis, much of this hymn is devoted to the effect on Hades, Adam, and all mankind, with more definite references to Palm Sunday. Christ's desire to use the miracle to convince the Jews is emphasized. In having Abraham and the other "just" call out to Christ, the poet moves to the theme of the coming resurrection of Christ.

Analysis of content: The poet begins with the events in Bethany and the first eight strophes concern Mary and Martha. The effect of these events on Hades and the wicked is discussed in three strophes; four strophes devoted to wonder at Christ follow and connect the raising of Lazarus with Palm Sunday, which is only natural for this hymn. The three closing strophes contain prayers and a return to Bethany. The shift of the refrain from the tears of Mary and Martha to the tears of Adam is unexpected, but it does have a point, in the light of the theology that is to be emphasized.

Any lack of smoothness in the transitions is probably due to the many occasions on which the poem was recast. Does this recasting point to local celebrations, which must have adapted existing material to the uses of local groups?

Connection with homily: The parallels in homily are not outstanding.

Meter: The meter is given in the Oxford edition, 523, XIV.

ON THE RAISING OF LAZARUS II

O. 15

Prooimion: O Christ, Thou who knowest all things,
   Thou hast asked to learn where the tomb of Lazarus is,[1]
 And arriving there, Thou hast raised him up on the fourth day,
   O All-powerful One,
  Taking pity, Merciful One,
   On the tears of Mary and Martha.

Strophe 1: The Master, checking the lamentations of Mary and Martha,
      immediately stilled them when He raised up their brother.
 It was possible, then, to see marvel of marvels,
      how the lifeless suddenly was seen to be alive.
 For when His voice descended, it caused
       the bolts of the gate of Hades
 To shake; and it broke down the bars of the door of Death;[2]
 And on the fourth day, He raised up the dead; as the Merciful One,
   He took pity on
    The tears of Mary and Martha.

Strophe 2: Let us all, with love, hurry to Bethany to see
      Christ there, weeping for His friend.
 For wishing all things to be ordained by law,
      He controls all things in His dual nature.
 He suffers as son of David;[3] as Son of God,
 He redeems the whole world from all the evil of the serpent,
 And on the fourth day, He raised up Lazarus, taking pity on
    The tears of Mary and Martha.

---

1. This poem seems a continuation of Lazarus I and bears out the hypothesis that this kontakion was sung after the procession reached Bethany.
2. Ps. cvii.16; Isa. xlv.2; *Acta Pilati*, xxi.3.
3. Rom. i.3–4; II Tim. ii.8, and Rev. v.5; *passim* in the N.T. "His dual nature" is seen in His sorrow over Lazarus *and* His power to resurrect him.

Strophe 3:   Together sustained by faith, the two

                                          announced to Christ and God the death

            Of their brother, saying,

MARY   "Hasten, come, Thou who art always present in all places,[4]

and   For Lazarus whom Thou dost love is ill; if Thou come near,

MARTHA   Death will vanish, and Thy friend will be saved from corruption,

            And the Jews will see that Thou, the Merciful One, hast taken pity on

                  The tears of Mary and Martha."

Strophe 4:   The Creator of all spoke on behalf of the disciples, saying:

CHRIST   "Friends and companions, our friend has fallen asleep."

            He was secretly teaching them in advance,

                              because He knows and cares for all things—

            "Let us go, then, let us advance and see the unusual tomb,[5]

            And let us cause the mourning of Mary and Martha to cease

            As I raise up Lazarus from the tomb,

                        and as Merciful One take pity on

                The tears of Mary and Martha."

Strophe 5:   When they heard these words, the apostles

                            as with one voice cried out to the Lord,

APOSTLES   "Sleep exists for man for his safety

                       and not at all for his destruction."

CHRIST   And so He spoke to them openly: "He is dead.

            As mortal I am away from him; but as God, I know all things.

            If we truly arrive in time,[6]

                    I shall resurrect the dead, and cause to cease

                The tears of Mary and Martha."

Strophe 6:   They all, then, arrived together,

                    when Mary and her sister came to meet them, crying bitterly,

MARY   "Lord, where wert Thou? For he whom Thou lovest has departed,

and   and lo, he is not here."

MARTHA   As they cried out these words, He, himself, wept.

---

4. John xi.3.
5. The son of the widow of Nain and the daughter of Jairus had been raised from the dead, but they had not been buried. Hence, the raising of Lazarus is strange and unusual.
6. Christ is supposed (John xi.6) to have waited two days. Does He mean, then, "If we arrive before the body has decomposed?"

CHRIST   But He asked: "Where is the tomb of my friend? Now
I am going to release him from the chains of Hades,
                since as the only lover of man, I take pity on
     The tears of Mary and Martha."

Strophe 7:   When they arrived at the tomb, He who is in the bosom
            of His Father, His Sire, called out:

CHRIST   "Thou hast sent me into the world
            that I might bring life to the dead.
I have come, then, to raise up Lazarus
And to reveal to the Jews that I am going to arise from the tomb
On the third day, I who after the fourth day resurrect my friend and
     now take pity on
       The tears of Mary and Martha."

Strophe 8:   In order that He might bring an end to the mourning of Martha,
     the Savior of all spoke to her and addressed these divine words to her:

CHRIST   "I exist as the light of the world
            and the resurrection of all from the dead;
He who believes on me shall never die;
It was for this end that I appeared to resurrect Adam
            and the descendants of Adam
And on the fourth day to resurrect Lazarus
         taking pity, as a Merciful One, on
     The tears of Mary and Martha."

Strophe 9:   When the command was given with a nod of His head, Hades was
     made to totter,
       and also the power of Death and the arrogance of the Devil.
With the sound of His voice, He raised up from the bowels of the earth
       the one who was four days dead.
When they saw this, Abraham and all the righteous cried out:
"Now, take courage, since the resurrection of all has come.
He has delivered from the bonds of death
     the one whom He loves, as He, the Merciful One, takes pity on
     The tears of Mary and Martha."

Strophe 10:   Hades, now a prisoner, sees himself despoiled of this Lazarus,
     whom a short time ago he held enchained below;

For when the King of the angels came against him,

                        the strength of demons was destroyed;

And the serpent who trails over the earth on his stomach,

Now, pierced in the mouth by the wooden spear,[7] appears as dead.

But Adam rejoices when he sees Christ

                             in His goodness take pity on

      The tears of Mary and Martha.

Strophe 11: Rising from the tomb, the friend reveals his eyes

                        and hands bound by a cloth;

They release him—those who have their hearts

                       bound by the ill will of slander,

Those who, as they plug up their ears like the adder,[8]

Prepare their hands for most wicked slaughter, that they may pour out

The harmless and innocent blood[9] of the One who raises up the

      dead and checks

        The tears of Mary and Martha.

Strophe 12: Having heard the words of the children, which came from pure hearts

          and innocent lips,

                       they were all filled with fear

Saying to one another: "Who is this man?"[10]

                  O madness and complete stupidity!

A short time ago they saw raised from the dead

A corpse who had become fetid, and they do not know

      who resurrected him,

And who destroyed with His voice the power of Hades,

              and in accord with His merciful nature checked

      The tears of Mary and Martha!

Strophe 13: O Thy unspeakable compassion, all merciful Jesus,

                who didst consent to come for me and to me,

7. The cross on which Christ was crucified.

8. The reference is to Ps. 58.4, in which the poison of the wicked is compared to "the adder which stoppeth her ear." There are metrical difficulties in the line, and a grammatical question raised by the use of the dative, τοῖς ὠσίν, after βοοῦντες. (I presume from βοέω instead of βόω.)

9. Ps. cvi.38; Prov. vi.17.

10. Matt. xxi.10 and 15. The cries of the children and the questions of the crowd are put close together in Matthew.

...[11] how didst Thou calmly ride upon the ass
           and advance into the city of God-slayers?
Foreseeing their terrible lack of faith, Thou didst command
Them to release the bonds of Lazarus, that they might see
The One whom in a short time they wish to put to death [12] with
     no pity for
         The tears of Mary and Martha.

Strophe 14: O Savior, all came with palms on the occasion of Thy arrival,
               crying out "Hosanna" to Thee; [13]
Now all of us bring hymns to Thee out of piteous mouths,
As we wave the branches of our spirit [14] and cry out:
"O Thou, truly among those on high, save the world which Thou
     hast created, Lord,
And blot out our sins, just as formerly Thou hast dried
     The tears of Mary and Martha."

Strophe 15: O Lover of man, the holy church holds a high festival,
               faithfully calling together her children;
It meets Thee with palms and spreads out garments of joy
So that with Thy disciples and Thy friend,
Thou mayst advance and legislate a deep peace [15] for Thy servants,
And release them from oppression, as formerly Thou hast checked
     The tears of Mary and Martha.

Strophe 16: Incline Thy ear, O God of the universe, and hear our prayers,
               and snatch us from the bonds of death,
For our enemies who always surround us, [16] visibly and invisibly,
Threaten to have us put to death and besides to deprive us of our faith.
Arise, and quickly let all be destroyed and let them know
That Thou art our God [17] and dost pity us as Thou didst have pity on
     The tears of Mary and Martha.

11. Some verb must be supplied: *Maas:* προβλέπων.
12. John xii.10.
13. Matt. xxi.8–9; Mark xi.8–10.
14. In the liturgy for Palm Sunday there are stichera that read, "Let us offer, my brothers, the psalms of our virtue to Christ."
15. The ass on which Christ rode is a symbol of peace. Zech. ix.9.
16. Ps. xvii.9, 11.
17. Ps. lxxxiii.17–18. Is this a biblical allusion, or does it refer to some particular siege of Byzantium? Since there is no specific event in Justinian's reign that would seem to be appropriate, the reference to Psalms is probably what the poet had in mind.

Strophe 17:   Let us who are dead because of our sins and who dwell in the tomb
                                     because of our knowledge of evil imitate [18]
            The sisters of faithful Lazarus as we cry to Christ
                                        with tears, in faith and in love:
            "Save us, Thou who didst will to become man,
            And resurrect us from the tomb of our sins, Thou, alone immortal,
            Through the prayers of Thy friend, Lazarus, whom Thou didst raise up,
                    O Lord, in checking
                        The tears of Mary and Martha."

Strophe 18:   Let us hate matter, which is in a state of flux, [19]
                                        and hasten to meet Christ the Savior in Bethany [20]
            Let us then dine with Him and with his friend Lazarus and the apostles
            So that we may by their prayers be delivered from our past sins.
            If we cleanse every stain from our hearts, we shall see perfectly
            His divine resurrection, which He offered us when He took away
                        The tears of Adam and Eve.

18. Peculiar structure, probably due to faulty text. The reference is probably to Gen. ii.9.
19. An interesting phrase of classical philosophy in the midst of the theology. Heraclitus "$\pi\acute{\alpha}\nu\tau\alpha$ $\rho\epsilon\hat{\iota}$"
20. Again, notice that Romanos places the dinner at Bethany, even though he does follow the Gospel of John in general. See also notes for On the Sinful Woman.

ON THE ENTRY INTO JERUSALEM

O. 16 (K. 10)

Title: Εἰς τὰ βάϊα

Manuscripts and editions: The manuscripts vary in the prooimion used; in fact, Prooimion II occurs only in the Δ group and in the *Triodion*. P includes the whole kontakion, with this exception, and so does A. Other manuscripts include only some of the strophes.

> Pitra edited this kontakion, *A.S.*, I, ix.
> Tomadakis, III, 33, 177–205.
> *Fr. ed.*, IV, 13–53.

Tone: ἦχος πλάγιος β′

Acrostic: Εἰς τὰ βάϊα 'Ρωμανοῦ

Refrain: '' Εὐλογημένος εἶ ὁ ἐρχόμενος τὸν 'Αδὰμ ἀνακαλέπασθαι

Biblical source and place in the liturgy: Matthew xxi.1–14, and Luke xix.28–48, tell of the entry into Jerusalem. The former is the main source for the first part, but Luke, for the mourning over Jerusalem. However, the poet does not merely relate the story.

  The kontakion was sung on Palm Sunday. The introduction to the two hymns on Lazarus (#14 and #15) tells of the procession that followed the Palm Sunday celebration and introduced Holy Week. It is the only poem on this subject in the kontakaria.

  We are told how Palm Sunday was celebrated at Jerusalem:[1] In the evening at five o'clock the people go to the Church of the Ascension on the Mount of Olives, and there they hear the reading of Matthew xxi. Then the bishop and people leave the church, singing, while children join the procession. This kind of celebration may or may not have taken place in Constantinople in Romanos' time.

Analysis of content: The first prooimion sets the stage for the antithesis of Christ seated on a throne in Heaven and on an ass on earth; the second prooimion mentions the unjust Jews and is a plea for faithful followers. Six strophes relate the story of the entry, with frequent references to Elijah, the daughter of Jairus, Lazarus, Moses, Goliath, Saul, and David interspersed with the rejoicing of the multitude and

---

1. Cabrol, *Les Origines Liturgiques* (Paris, 1906), 180, uses *Itinerarium Egeriae* as his source. See introduction to the two hymns on Lazarus, #14 and #15. It is possible that the bishop, mounted on an ass, symbolized Christ. Etheria must have heard songs that were "little kontakia."

insults for the lawless Jews. Romanos makes a point of referring to the crowd as children in the first strophe, and later he constantly refers to the lawless. Strophes 7 and 8 are full of antitheses—Christ adored by angels, and now seated on the ass; Christ in swaddling clothes, Christ on the throne. Strophes 9 and 10 focus on the point of Christ's coming to redeem Adam and all mankind, and in the following four strophes Christ is the speaker who reaffirms the weakness of the law and then pronounces His rejection of Jerusalem. In Strophe 15 Christ is in the temple, from which He casts out the money changers. This action leads to His promise, "I go to prepare a place," and to the closing prayer.

Connection with homily: There are homilies by Pseudo-Chrysostom (*P.G.*, 59, 703–8) and one attributed to Methodius (*P.G.*, 18, 384A–397B) on Palm Sunday,[2] but actually, the author of neither is known and there are no significant parallels to be noted. The *Triodion* contained Prooimion I and the first strophe of Romanos' poem.

Style of Romanos: It is typical of the poet that the story is so recast as to include direct appeals to Christ and direct answers from Christ as to the theological implications of His human and divine nature. The poet moves from a note of victory, appropriate for the Hosannah cries of Palm Sunday, to a brief narrative including references to the overcoming of Hades and the toppling of idols in Egypt. (This reference to idols can be compared with Kontakion #3, Strophe 15.) He becomes very sarcastic about the Jews who did not understand because they would not; he even has Christ remind them of the miracles He accomplished for them. The chief figures of speech follow the poverty motif—poverty willingly undertaken compared with glory in Heaven—and references to debts canceled. When the epithet of *shepherd* is used, the poet elaborates with references to "mountains, glens, and beetling crags." The human touches are evident when, in Strophe 10, the need of people for more than law is given in a series of occasions on which they felt defeat.

Meter: The metrical scheme is given in the Oxford edition, 524, XV. This scheme is rejected by the editor of *Fr. ed.*, IV, 19–25.

2. The editor of the *Fr. ed.*, IV, 15*n1*, also refers to another homily for Palm Sunday by Ps. Chrys. (*P.G.*, 61,715–720) and to sermons for the occasion by Cyril of Alexandria (*P.G.*, 77, 1049B–1072B) and one by Proclus of Constantinople (*P.G.*, 65, 772B–777A).

ON THE ENTRY INTO JERUSALEM

O. 16

Prooimion I: In Heaven on Thy throne;[1] on earth carried on an ass,

O Christ, God,

Receive the praise of the angels and the song of the children

crying out to Thee:

"Thou art the blessed One who comest to call up Adam."

Prooimion II: The unjust Jews who formerly praised Christ, God,

with palm branches,

Later arrested Him with cudgels.[2]

Let us with unwavering faith,

Always honoring Him as Benefactor, cry out to Him:

"Thou art the blessed One who comest to call up Adam."

Strophe 1: Since Thou hast conquered Hades and put to death Death,

and resurrected the world,

The children, with palm branches shout aloud to Thee,

Christ, as victor,

And today, they are crying to Thee: "Hosannah to the

Son of David."[3]

For no longer, they say, will infants be slaughtered

because of Mary's child;

But Thou alone art to be crucified for all children and elders.

No longer will the sword be in action against us,

For Thy side will be pierced with a spear.[4]

For this reason, rejoicing, we say:

"Thou art the blessed One who comest to call up Adam."

Strophe 2: Lo, our King, meek and gentle, seated upon an ass,[5]

With haste arrives to suffer and to cut suffering—

1. Ps. xi.4; lxvi.1.
2. Matt. xxvi.47; Mark xiv.43.
3. Matt. xxi.9–15; Mark xi.9.
4. John xix.34.
5. Zech. ix.9.

The Word upon the dumb, willing it that rational
  beings[6] be redeemed.
And it was possible to behold the One on the back of the ass
                    who is on the shoulders of the Cherubim,[7]
  The One who once translated Elijah in a fiery chariot,[8]
The One who is poor of His own will, but rich in His nature,[9]
  The One who is voluntarily weak, yet granting power
  To all of those who cry out to Him:
    "Thou art the blessed One who comest to call up Adam."

Strophe 3:   All Zion was shaken as Egypt once was—there it was
                              the lifeless objects,
  But here those who are living were shaken at Thy coming, Savior.
  Not that Thou art fond of causing trouble—Thou art the
    Father of peace—
But Thou, as Creator of all, dost break up all the juggler's
    tricks of the enemy
Driving him from all places, since Thou dost rule over every place.
Formerly their idols fell[10]
  Now their wise men are agitated,
  As they hear the voices of the children:
    "Thou art the blessed One who comest to call up Adam."

Strophe 4:   "Who is this man?" they said—those who were ignorant
    in their judgment,
                              for He says they did not know.
  Who was the Son of David? He who rescued
    them from corruption—[11]
  Even now they release Lazarus,[12] and they do not know

---

6. Romanos likes to play upon λόγος, the word. Christ is the word; He is seated on the ἄλογον ass; and He wills that men be λογικούς or reasonable.

7. Proclus, in his homily (*P.G.*, 65, 774B), has similar antitheses—("above borne by Cherubim, and below seated on an ass"). By this time the phrases must have been repeated often. Ps. lxxx.1; Isa. xxxvii.16.

8. II Kings ii.11; Ecclus. xlviii.9.

9. II Cor. viii.9.

10. Isa. xix.1–4. In Kontakion #3, On the Massacre of the Innocents, there is a similar reference going back to the apocryphal infancy gospels.

11. Sin produces corruption (φθορᾶς). II Pet. i.4; Rom. viii.21.

12. John xi.44. Romanos, Kontakion #15, Strophe 11. It is noteworthy that in the Lazarus poem there are references to palms and Hosanna (Strophe 14). Also the question, "Who is this man?" is used there (Strophe 12) as a point of departure for criticism of ignorance of the Jews. All of this points to the connection between the Resurrection of Lazarus and Palm Sunday. See introduction to Kontakion #15.

who raised him up!
Still their shoulders suffer from raising up the widow's son,[13]
And I suppose they were ignorant as to who rescued him from death!
Did they not come forth from the house of Jairus,
And they do not know who gave life to his daughter?[14]
They know; but they do not wish to say:
"Thou art the blessed One who comest to call up Adam."

Strophe 5:   Acting unfairly, and lawless, they welcomed ignorance;
and for this reason

they were ignorant.

The sons of deceit did not know the One whom they sought
out to kill!
It is not strange what they say; for they take first prize
in strange things!
When Moses led them out of Egypt, immediately he was
denied by them.[15]
And Christ who saved them from death, was not known!
They did not know Moses who knew the calf;
Those who were friends of Belial denied Christ.
That is why they did not wish to cry:
"Thou art the blessed One who comest to call up Adam."

Strophe 6:   The children with palm branches sang hymns to Thee,
fittingly calling Thee

Son of David, Master,

For Thou didst slay the visible reviler, Goliath.
Forming a choral dance after the victory, the women
sang, honoring him:[16]
"Saul has slain his thousands and David his tens of thousands."
That is the law; and after him, Thy grace, my Jesus,[17]
The law was Saul, envious and pursuing;
David, though pursued, sprouts forth Grace[18]
For Thou art the Lord of David;[19]
Thou art the blessed One who comest to call up Adam.

13. Luke vii.11–15.
14. Matt. ix.23–25; Mark v.38–43; Luke viii.51–55.
15. Ex. xxxii.1.
16. I Sam. xviii.6–7.
17. John i.17; Rom. vi.14.
18. Ecclus. xxiv.17; Isa. xi.1.
19. Matt. xxii.41–45; Luke xx.41–44.

Strophe 7: The sun, gleaming in his chariot, chariot of light,

was also submissive to Thee

And he submits to Thy command as Creator and God.

Now the ass pleased Thee;[20] and I do obeisance to Thy mercy.

For my sake, Thou wast once placed in the manger and

bound in swaddling clothes,

And now Thou hast mounted the ass, though Thou dost

possess a heavenly throne.

The angels encircled the manger there;[21]

Here the disciples lead the ass.

"Glory" Thou didst hear then; and now Thou dost hear

"Thou art the blessed One who comest to call up Adam."

Strophe 8: Thou hast shown Thy strength in choosing the humble,

for it was a sign of poverty

For Thee to sit on the ass; but as Glorious, Thou dost shake Zion.

The cloaks of the disciples pointed to frugality;

But the song of the children and the throng of people

was a sign of Thy strength,[22]

As they cry out, "Hosanna in the highest," that is, Save![23]

Thou who art on high, save the humbled;

Heeding the palm branches, take pity on us,

Look upon those who cry out:

"Thou art the blessed One who comest to call up Adam."

Strophe 9: Adam, when he consumed what he ought not to,

created a debt owed by us;

And up until today, those descended from him have this debt

demanded back in return for him.

It did not suffice the creditor to possess the debt;

But he imposes it on his children, asking for the ancestral debt,

And as he drags out all of them, he would empty completely the

house of the debtor.

Therefore, in so far as possible let us flee for refuge,

Since we know that we are indeed poor,

---

20. *Cf.* Kontakion #1: φάτνῃ ἐτέρφθης;
21. Luke ii.7–14.
22. These antitheses are typical of the style of Romanos. The homily of Ps. Chrys., *P.G.*, 61, 715–16, contains even more of the contrasts between royalty and poverty.
23. Matt. xxi.9; Mark xi.9–10; John xii.12–13.

And that Thou art thyself a return of what we owe.
    Thou art the blessed One who comest to call up Adam.

Strophe 10: Thou didst come to save all men, and as witness
                              there is Thy prophet, Zacharias,[24]
    He once called Thee most gentle, just, and the One who saves.
    We were weary, we were defeated, and we were
        everywhere driven away.
  We thought that we had the law as ransomer; but they enslaved us.
    Once more we thought we had the prophets; and they sent us
        away with hope.
  And so, we with our children fall at Thy knees;
    Take pity on us who have been cast down;
    Voluntarily be crucified and tear up the written decree.[25]
        Thou art the blessed One who comest to call up Adam.

Strophe 11: "O clay, moulded by my hand," the Modeler answered
CHRIST
                              those who cry out:
    "Knowing that the law was not strong enough to save you,
        I have come.
    It was not possible for the law to save you, since really it did
        not mould you;[26]
  Nor was it possible for the prophets, since they, too,
                             are of my fashioning, like you.
    It is for me alone to free you from your debt, your
        very heavy debt.
  I am to be sold in exchange for you, and I shall free you,
    I am to be crucified for you, and you will not die.
    I die, and I teach you to cry:
      'Thou art the blessed One who comest to call up Adam.'

Strophe 12: "I was not content with the angels, was I? I loved you,
CHRIST
                            the beggar; I hid my glory;
    And voluntarily I, the wealthy, became poor, because I yearn for
        you very much.
    For you I hungered and suffered thirst and hardships.

24. Zach. ix.9.
25. Col. ii.14. This same figure of speech was used in Kontakion #10 (On the Sinful Woman), Strophe 18, and in Kontakion #26 (Resurrection III), Strophe 4.
26. Rom. iii.20.

On the mountains and beetling crags and in the woody glens

I came seeking for you, the wandering[27].

I was called shepherd, in order that, charming you by my voice in
some way, I might lead you.
And, as shepherd, I wish to lay down my life for you.
In order that I may pluck you from the grasp of the wolf.[28]
I suffer all things, wishing you to cry:
'Thou art the blessed One who comest to call up Adam'."

Strophe 13: After these words of Christ, the official business was made clear;

for before He reached the city,

The hymn of the children terrified all of his enemies.[29]
Lifting up His eyes, He fixed His gaze steadily on Zion
CHRIST   And composing a dirge over it, He cried:[30] "Mourn, O Jerusalem,
Since you have found children, your sons, the teachers
of their fathers.
You act the younger of the two in evil and depravity,
And in your old age you are weary of well doing.
Better than you are those who cry out:
'Thou art the blessed One who comest to call up Adam.'

Strophe 14: "Now I enter in the city and casting you out, I shall reject you—
CHRIST

not that I hate you.

But because I discovered that you hated me and mine.
In return for what did your children contrive a cross for me?
Was it in return for the fact that for them I broke through the sea

as though it were a cloak with my staff?[31]

Do they quarry a tomb for me in return for my offering them a
cloud as shelter?[32]
Indeed, I rejoice, since I have come for their sakes;
And I am content to suffer, since I yearn over the fallen
So that those who love me say:
'Thou art the blessed One who comest to call up Adam'."

27. Matt. xviii.12; John x.11–17.
28. See the passage in the Ps. Chrys. homily (*P.G.*, 59, 707) about the good shepherd and the hunting of the wolf (quoted in *Fr. ed.*, IV, 47*n*1).
29. Matt. xxi.15–16.
30. Luke xix.41.
31. Ex. xiv.16.
32. Ps. cv.39.

Strophe 15: Thus He who sees the slow of heart, rebuking the things in their hearts,

came into the city

Along with the children—the priest of everyone in the temple,

The Son arrived in the dwelling of His Father;

And He cast out those who were buying and selling near by, saying:

CHRIST "Let nothing of all this remain, for we depart from here—

I and my Father and the Holy Spirit;[33]

For we now prepare a home for the weak,[34] the goal

Of those who faithfully cry out to me:

'Thou art the blessed One who comest to call up Adam'."

Strophe 16: O Son of God, all Holy, number us among those

who sing hymns to Thee,

And receive the prayers of Thy servants as of Thy children just now.

Take pity on those whom Thou hast fashioned, for love of whom

Thou didst sojourn here;

Grant peace to Thy churches, which are disturbed by enemies;

And grant to me, O Savior, remission of my sins.

Afford me the power to speak what Thou dost wish as Thou dost wish it.

Let not suffering make me sluggish of mind.

Teach me to cry out the beautifully wrought salutation:[35]

"Thou art the blessed One who comest to call up Adam."

33. Matt. xxi.12; Mark xi.15; Luke xix.45; John ii.14–16.
34. John xiv.2, 23.
35. καλλίεργον is rare. The editor of the *Fr. ed.*, IV, 53n1, decides on this reading but translates the line: "Donne-moi du *talent* pour crier." Sophocles gives the meaning as "beautifully wrought," and the poet may well be praying to use the beautiful salutation of the refrain. It could even be translated, "Teach me to cry in cultivated manner." The general meaning is clear. The particular poetic idea is not certain.

ON JUDAS

O. 17 (K. 16)

Title: Εἰς τὸν νιπτῆρα

Manuscripts and editions: P has the entire poem except for Prooimion II.

Δ has Prooimion II and omits Strophe 19, but includes another Strophe 19.

Pitra edited this kontakion, *A.S.*, I, xiii.

Krumbacher edits and adds critical comments, *R.u.K.*, 736–52.[1]

Cammelli includes it in the poems he edits, 251–83.

Tomadakis, II, 223–34.

Fr. ed., IV, 55–97. Notes from Pitra and Krumbacher are included.

Cammelli follows Krumbacher's text. There is a translation into French, also based on Krumbacher, which was done by R. Khawam (Paris, 1956), 55–89, "Romanos le Melode, le Christ Redemptor." It is mentioned in *Fr. ed.*, IV, 69n1.

Tone: ἦχος γ΄

Acrostic: τοῦ ταπεινοῦ Ῥωμανοῦ ποίημα

Refrain: ἵλεως, ἵλεως, ἵλεως γενοῦ ἡμῖν ὁ πάντων ἀνεχόμενος καὶ πάντας ἐκδεχόμενος

Biblical source and place in the liturgy: This kontakion is marked for Thursday of Holy Week.[2] On this day three events are celebrated: the treason of Judas, the foot washing, and the institution of the Eucharist. The foot washing incident is told in John xiii.5, and does not appear in the other Gospels. The betrayal of Judas appears in all of the Gospels,[3] as does the account of the Last Supper.[4]

Analysis of content: The emphasis in the poem is clearly on Judas and the horror of his treachery. The fact that the kontakion is marked "For the foot washing" probably indicates the occasion on which it is to be used rather than the actual subject. Certainly the references to the Eucharist are made only in passing.

Prooimion I sets the occasion as the betrayal of Judas and the foot washing, and it mentions the church in which Romanos first was deacon.

1. The analysis of the meter has been the subject of an exhaustive analysis by Krumbacher (*R.u.K.*, 695–723). He compares it with the poem on Lazarus. He decides that Kyriakos and Romanos were independent of one another and that they adapted an older heirmos. He comments that Romanos is the only poet to use the heirmos πρὸς τὸ Λάζαρον τὸν φίλον σου.
2. In the offices for this day the distribution of topics is not always the same. The French edition makes note of the differences: IV, 55n1.
3. Matt. xxvi.14–16, 47–50; Mark xiv.10–22, 43–45; Luke xxii.3, 47; John xiii.26; xviii.2.
4. Romanos certainly does not question the fact that Judas was present at the Last Supper. The Gospels indicate that he was, but Latin writers commenting on the Gospels raise a question (*Fr. ed.*, IV, 57n1).

The first two strophes introduce the horror of the idea of the treachery, along with invectives against Judas. References to the foot washing and the Last Supper alternate with invectives against Judas through Strophe 6, then the effect on the heavenly powers, figures of speech about Christ as the sea to strengthen the clay, and Christ, the vine, are combined, with references to Peter's humility as contrasted with Judas, up to Strophe 12. The central strophes, 12 through 19, center on the act of betrayal, with the pile-up of invectives in Strophe 15 as the climax.

The last three strophes, consist of a pointing up of the moral, reference to the fate of Judas, and a final prayer beginning with the thrice-Holy salutation, balancing the thrice-repeated "Have mercy" of the refrain.

Style of Romanos: Critics either admire this poem very much or not at all, depending, it seems, on whether they prefer the rhetorical style over the dramatic arrangement of narrative.

The editor of the French text states that Romanos is at his best in invective. Certainly, the accumulation of insults put into effective rhetorical groups of alliterative threes and antithetical phrases does demonstrate one of the characteristics of the style of Romanos. However, one cannot entirely agree with the statement that Romanos was a mediocre psychologist;[5] there are many passages in other kontakia in which he enters into the feelings of his dramatis personae, for example, in the kontakia On the Sinful Woman and On Mary at the Cross, arguments between Hades and Hell, the soldiers at the cross in Resurrection I, Eve's complaints about Adam, Adam's distrust of women in Nativity II. He is, one feels, not at his most attractive in the outbursts against Jews and heretics, nor is he a good theologian. He does use words effectively. The figure of Christ as the "abyss," the sea that washes "clay" or man until he is cleansed and strengthened, loses in translation but is effective. There is, as usual, very little moralizing, although this is the approach of sermons on the subject of Judas.[6] The closing strophes characteristically point up the need for all to learn from the fate of Judas.

Meter: Krumbacher devoted much space in his careful analysis of this poem, as compared with the work of Kyriakos,[7] to a study of the meter, and he was not sure that this kontakion would be attributed to Romanos, for metrical reasons. The rhythmic scheme is given in the Oxford edition, 524, XVI.

5. *Fr. ed.*, IV, 59: "mediocre théologien, mediocre psychologue."
6. Compare with: Basil of Seleucia or Pseudo-Athanasius, "On Betrayal of Judas" (*P.G.*, 28, 1048B–1054B); St. John Chrysostom, "On Betrayal of Judas" (*P.G.*, 50, 715–29) and two of his homilies on the Last Supper (*P.G.*, 49, 381–92). Three Pseudo-Chrysostom homilies are listed in *Fr. ed.*, IV, 57–58n2.
7. See note 1, above.

ON JUDAS

O. 17

Prooimion I: Judas, the lawless, while his feet were being washed [1]
            By the hands of the Master, O Christ, God,
            Like a thief secretly sharpened his tongue. [2]
        From this sort of inhumanity, deliver those
            In the home of the Virgin who sing:
                "Have mercy, have mercy, have mercy on us,
                Thou who dost bear with all men and receive all men." [3]

Prooimion II: O Father in Heaven, loving Father, Lover of men,
            Have mercy, have mercy, have mercy on us,
            Thou who dost bear with all men and receive all men.

Strophe 1:   Who on hearing this, has not grown numb, or who, beholding it,
                did not tremble? [4]
            Jesus, kissed in treachery,
            Christ, sold through jealousy,

                                    God, voluntarily seized?

            What kind of earth bore this outrage?
            What kind of sea endured the sight of the unholy deed?
        How did Heaven submit, how did the air permit,
                                    and how did creation stand it
        When He, the judge, was bargained for, sold, and betrayed.
                Have mercy, have mercy, have mercy on us,
                Thou who dost bear with all men and receive all men.

Strophe 2:   When he plotted the treachery, when he planned Thy murder,
            And the loved disciple rejected Thee,

---

1. John xiii.5.
2. Ps. lxiv.3.
3. The refrain contains a verbal antithesis in ἀνεχόμενος and ἐκδεχόμενος, which is untranslatable. The former, when used with the genitive, really means *recover from* or *hold on* and refers to Christ's patient waiting for the repentance of Judas. This theme is developed at length in the homilies mentioned in the Introduction to this kontakion.
4. Rhetorical questions like those in the homily of Ps. Chrys., *P.G.*, 59, 716:

πῶς οὐκ ἐνάρκησε;
πῶς οὐκ ἔφριξεν;

This one who was called forsook Thee, the one who was
    honored dishonored Thee,
Then Thou, O merciful and magnanimous One,
Wishing to show the murderer Thy ineffable love of man
Thou hast filled the laver, bowed Thy neck,
        and become the servant of slaves; [5]
And Thou didst take the feet of Judas to wash them, O Redeemer.
    Have mercy, have mercy, have mercy on us,
    Thou who dost bear with all men and receive all men.

Strophe 3:   With water Thou hast washed the feet of the one who was running
      to Thy betrayal,
    And Thou hast fed with mystic nourishment
    The enemy of Thy mercy and the one deprived of Thy blessing; [6]
    Thou hast lifted up the poor by Thy favors,
    Thou hast promoted to honor the piteous by gifts,
      enriched and made him blest.
He had at the tip of his tongue control of demons,
        and release from distress, [7]
    And in return for all this, he defected,
      the murderer, without compunction.
      Have mercy, have mercy, have mercy on us,
      Thou who dost bear with all men and receive all men.

Strophe 4:   Who has ever seen one whose feet were washed hurrying to kick?
    Who has ever heard of a beast who has been cherished
    Hastening to throw its rider?
    The Lord has washed and nourished him,
    The traitor has run off, he has gnashed his teeth as only the most
      savage would do.
When his manger is filled up, the vicious beast suddenly
        flees from his master,
    And actually offers his back that Satan might mount. [8]
      Have mercy, have mercy, have mercy on us,
      Thou who dost bear with all men and receive all men.

5. John xiii.4–5.
6. The word εὐλογία is especially used of the blessing connected with the Eucharist. Judas is
deprived of it because he has separated himself from Christ.
7. The Oxford and French editions agree on the punctuation, which lends itself to a translation
better than that used by Pitra. See *Fr. ed.*, IV, 74*n*1. What Judas "had on his tongue" was Christ.
8. John xiii.18: "lifted up his heel against me." *Cf.* also Isa. i.3.

Strophe 5: O lawless, heartless, implacable, pirate, traitor, swindler,[9]
> What has happened that you have rejected Him?
> What have you seen to make you so foolish? What have you
> > suffered to make you hate in this way?
> Did He not name you as His friend?[10]
> Did not He himself call you brother, even though He knew that you
> > would be a traitor?[11]
The receipt of the money in the case,[12]
> > > > > > He gave you in trust;
> And you foolishly in view of all these things suddenly
> > appeared against Him.
> > Have mercy, have mercy, have mercy on us,
> > Thou who dost bear with all men and receive all men.

Strophe 6: Peter demurred at the time when the only-begotten Son came
> Hurrying to wash his feet,
> And he said: "Lord, Lord, do not Thou wash my feet."
> The laver was on the ground and filled,
> And the Savior stood, and the Redeemer was girded[13] as a servant;
The ranks of angels looked on from on high,
> > > > and cried out with amazement,
> And the shameless fellow was not abashed, but turned against Him.
> > Have mercy, have mercy, have mercy on us,
> > Thou who dost bear with all men and receive all men.

Strophe 7: The fiery spirits stood in fear, and their invisible choirs
> Were amazed on seeing the Incomprehensible One
> Of His own will bending down and serving clay.
> Gabriel said in terror:
GABRIEL
> "Holy angels, my companions, look down and marvel.
Peter holds out his foot, and He who was born of the virgin mother
> > > takes it and washes it,

9. Paul uses an equivalent list of words for those who are wicked. II Tim. iii.2–4.
10. Matt. xii.49; John xv.15; Luke xii.4.
11. The Oxford edition adopts the reading, δεδόλωσαι, which brings out the idea of treachery rather than δεδούλωσαι, which would indicate that Judas is enslaved. However, the manuscript at Patmos uses the latter reading.
12. The word γλωσσόκομον originally meant the case for the mouthpiece of a reed of a flute, and then it came to mean any case or a moneybox. Here the poet must intend the literal meaning of γλῶσσα to remind us that the tongue betrayed Christ.
13. "Girded" does not convey the correct picture of Christ with a towel around his waist for the foot washing, but it is used in John xiii.4.

And He does not only wash Peter, but even Judas along with him
Have mercy, have mercy, have mercy on us,
Thou who dost bear with all men and receive all men.

Strophe 8: "The sea washes the brick, the Abyss washes the clay
And it does not destroy its structure,
But binds its substance and wipes clean its purpose.[14]
Behold the disposition of the One who made us.
See of what sort is the attitude of the Creator for His creatures;
They have reclined and He has stood, they are fed and He serves,
they are washed and He wipes them clean;
And the feet of clay are not cast into a mold in the hands of fire.
Have mercy, have mercy, have mercy on us,
Thou who dost bear with all men and receive all men."

Strophe 9: So spoke the angel when he saw Thee, the vine[15]
Nourishing its own branches
And extending them over all the earth, and elevating them on high;
But Peter, the chief of Thy friends,
The model for those who followed Thee, the leader of Thy servants,
On seeing Thee girdled as a servant, was troubled, and said:

PETER
"Thou wash *my* feet?
No never shall the hand which created me wash my feet!
Have mercy, have mercy, have mercy on us,
Thou who dost bear with all men and receive all men.

Strophe 10: "May sleep take me to death,[16] if I allow Thee, the Immortal,

PETER
To bend down before me, a mortal.
The enemy would laugh at me, if Thou dealest in this way with me.
Is it not enough that Thou dost consider me as Thine?
Is it not much that I am considered and called the first of Thy friends?
But art Thou to wash my feet and limbs of clay,
Thou, the Potter of the universe?

14. The metaphor here refers to Christ as the abyss, in the sense of the depths of His wisdom and goodness. Adam was formed of clay, and the image presents us with Christ actually strengthening the clay and purifying it. ἀποσμήχει (ἀποσμάω) means both to wipe off and purify.
15. John xv.1–2.
16. This recalls Peter's insistence that he would die rather than deny Christ (Matt. xxvi.35) and his subsequent sleep at Gethsemane (Matt. xxvi.40, 42, 45).

O Redeemer, dost Thou wish to wash my mortal limbs and feet?
>   Have mercy, have mercy, have mercy on us,
>   Thou who dost bear with all men and receive all men."

Strophe 11: With these words, the disciple addressed the Master,

CHRIST
>   He heard in reply: "If I do not wash your feet,
>   I shall give you no part of me, but I shall call you enemy."[17]
>   When the Creator said this,
>   Fear and disorder fell upon the disciple, so that he said:

PETER
>   "My Lord, if Thou washest me, wash not only my feet, but my whole body;[18]
>   Indeed wash me completely so that I may not be deprived
>   of Thy blessings.
>   Have mercy, have mercy, have mercy on us,
>   Thou who dost bear with all men and receive all men."

Strophe 12: O what sort of words were exchanged! Yet Judas did not
>   become a friend;
>   What sort of words and deeds,
>   And the enemy was not reconciled, the hard hearted
>   was not softened;
>   For even while he was eating what he ate,
>   And drinking what he drank without good faith, he raised his heel,
>   as is written;
> And leaving the stable he hurried to the beasts,
>   leaving behind the lambs,
>   And giving up the delightful breast, he went to a bitter teat;[19]
>   Have mercy, have mercy, have mercy on us,
>   Thou who dost bear with all men and receive all men.

Strophe 13: In vain formerly the devil drew back before the terrible Judas;
>   Lo now he recoils
>   In the presence of the one who formerly recoiled before him,
>   and Judas is wholly devil.
>   In vain was he formidable to the crowds,[20]

17. Christ really said, "Thou hast no part with me" (John xiii.8). Romanos expands this statement into a threat.
18. Ps. li.2.
19. The milk-providing breast symbolizes the Logos. Clement of Alexandria develops the idea in *Pédagogue. Fr. ed.*, IV, 83*n*3.
20. The meaning of πλήθεσιν is not clear. It must refer to the crowds who accompanied Judas when he betrayed Christ (Mark xiv.43, and Luke xxii.47). It could refer to miracles when there were

For he was seen as jealous on all occasions, and as bold
    against the Creator.
In vain, as he spoke all diseases fled,
                                    for he had at this time the illness
    Of atheism and of greed; within him was the plague.[21]
        Have mercy, have mercy, have mercy on us,
        Thou who dost bear with all men and receive all men.

Strophe 14: The traitor, raising his feet,[22] hastened with daring to the devil
        And his murderous gang
        Handing over Christ like a stranger, he became poor.[23]
        "What do you want to give me?"
        He said to those who wished to buy the blood of
            the Ever-Living One.
    Hear, O earth, and tremble; sea, hasten to flee;
                                    for murder is being arranged;
        The price of the Priceless is being discussed; the slaughter of the
            Giver of Life.
            Have mercy, have mercy, have mercy on us,
            Thou who dost bear with all men and receive all men.

Strophe 15: Now your insatiate nature has appeared; now has been made clear that
        you will never be satisfied,
        O ravenous, dissolute, implacable,
        Shameless and gluttonous, foolish and avaricious.
        "What do you want to give me?"
        You say to those who wish to buy the blood of the Ever-Living One;
    What good thing did you not have? What did you not share?
                                    What were you ever denied?
        You possessed the blessings on earth and in Heaven; yet you
            betrayed your God!
            Have mercy, have mercy, have mercy on us,
            Thou who dost bear with all men and receive all men.

---

multitudes present. Krumbacher uses as a reading φοβερός τοῖς πάθεσιν, which would mean that the passions of Judas have made him terrible.

21. πλήγη is literally *the blow* or *stroke*. It is translated freely to indicate that his illness of spirit is like a plague, which strikes the blow against Christ.

22. He raised his foot to leave, and he raised it against Christ. John xiii.18, says, "He lifted up his heel against me."

23. μέτριος means usually *reduced in number*, but Hesychius, in the fourth century, refers to its meaning of *poor*. I see no reason to question this reading in favor of μεσίτης, as used by Pitra and Krumbacher. It seems far-fetched to call Judas a *mediator*.

Strophe 16:   You carried complete wealth; you were an inexhaustible treasure
            On all sides and in every way you were wealthy;
            In your hands you had money, and in your heart you
               carried the Creator.
            What, then, happened to you, O wretch,
            That now, as a poor man, you advance to those who have nothing
               to give you?
         For what will they give you, what will they offer to you
                                          in return for the One you have sold?
            Heaven, earth, and the whole creation in exchange for *Him*?
               Have mercy, have mercy, have mercy on us,
               Thou who dost bear with all men and receive all men.

Strophe 17:   Come, fool, come to your senses; throw off your presumption,
            Abandon your daring purpose,
            Reprove your heart; and do you, foolish ones, be high minded; [24]
            For you are in no way able to estimate the value;
            Nor are they able to buy the One who now holds all in His hands.
         And if you sell and He does not will it,
                                          who would dare to seize Him?
            Who would lay hands on Him, unless He himself agreed?
               Have mercy, have mercy, have mercy on us,
               Thou who dost bear with all men and receive all men.

Strophe 18:   Elijah was poor; however, he was abundantly able to destroy with fire
            Those who moved with violence against him at one time;
            And he destroyed another commander who boldly attacked him;
            Elijah [25] was not to be overcome,
            And yet the God and Lord of Elijah is scorned by the reckless.
         O madness! Elijah was a servant
                                          of the One now being sold,
            And the traitor has not even considered as a prophet the
               Maker of prophets.
               Have mercy, have mercy, have mercy on us,
               Thou who dost bear with all men and receive all men.

24. Ps. xciv.8.
25. II Kings i.9–13. Ahaziah's fifties were consumed by fire.

Strophe 19: And so, poor fool, you were drunk with boldness and you
did not consider
That the one being sold by you was sold voluntarily,
Even though the terms of the agreement made you know who was
the One being bargained for.
You received thirty pieces of gold.[26]
Make a judgment, wretch, and decide who of the prophets
was thus sold.
The famous Joseph was the prototype of Jesus
whose price you take;[27]
And in return for it, you receive Hades with the noose for hanging.
Have mercy, have mercy, have mercy on us,
Thou who dost bear with all men and receive all men.

Strophe 20: Have mercy, have mercy, have mercy; how great is the
fall of the disciple;
And from what height has he stumbled;
What a tumble he has taken, what a crash he has made!
Formerly the devil fell;
His downward fall revealed lightning; Judas emulated him;
For when he stood out against Christ and kicked against the pricks,
his feet were crushed[28]
And he was cast down to the depths of Hades; there he
received his pay.
Have mercy, have mercy, have mercy on us,
Thou who dost bear with all men and receive all men.

Strophe 21: Then the lawless fellow came running
and treacherously kissed the Lover of man,
And deliberately destroyed
The One who voluntarily had chosen suffering, the Giver of life to all.
He was a sheep of Christ,
He became a wolf for the shepherd, like a beast which attacks.

26. Matt. xxvi.15: "Thirty pieces of *silver*." Has Romanos shifted to "thirty pieces of gold" by poetic license, or is he thinking of some translation in the Old Testament of the money exchanged for Joseph?
27. Gen. xxxvii.28.
28. In "kicking against the pricks" we have adopted an implied meaning. ἀνιάζω (ἀνιῶν) really would mean merely to be irritated or distressed by the pricks. λακτίζων would have been expected here.

Do you offer your kiss? What sort of kiss, you fool?

A kiss of betrayal.

And you are not ashamed of imitating the enemy,
  as you learn his plans.
    Have mercy, have mercy, have mercy on us,
    Thou who dost bear with all men and receive all men.

Strophe 22: Just wait a while, O all-wretched one, and you will
              see immutable justice.
    Your conscience will pass judgment on you,
    That you may know what you have done as you die
      under terrible doom.
    A tree has become for you like a public executioner,[29]
    Bringing you deserved pay; and where is your money, greedy one?
  Indeed, this very money you will give up, and you will not save
                                          yourself, as you repent too late,
    Because you have given up the wealth which you possessed,
      Christ your spiritual wealth.
        Have mercy, have mercy, have mercy on us,
        Thou who dost bear with all men and receive all men.

Strophe 23: Holy, holy, holy, God of all, thrice holy,
    Deliver Thy servants from the fall,
    And raise up Thy creature to avoid this danger;
    Then, as we learn about these things, brothers,
    And as we behold the fall of the seller, let us strengthen our own feet,
  Let us mount on the steps of the commands of the Creator,
    And let us avoid the road of Hades, as we cry out to the Redeemer,
        "Have mercy, have mercy, have mercy on us,
        Thou who dost bear with all men and receive all men."

29. The tradition that represents Judas hanging from a tree is so old in art that it is difficult to realize that the Gospel merely records that he hanged himself (Matt. xxvii.5). Acts i.18, reports that he died as the result of a fall.

ON PETER'S DENIAL

O. 18 (K. 18)

Title: Εἰς τὴν ἄρνησιν τοῦ Πέτρου

Manuscripts and editions: All of the kontakion is in P except for Prooimion III. Prooimion III and the first 22 strophes, as well as Prooimion I are in Δ.

    The poem was first edited by Pitra, *A.S.*, 108–16.

    The text was corrected by Krumbacher, *Stud.*, 114–34. As an introduction to the text he makes many valuable comments on the meter.

    Fr. ed., IV, 99–143.

Tone: ἦχος πλάγιος δ′

Acrostic: τοῦ ταπεινοῦ Ῥωμανοῦ αἶνος

Refrain: σπεῦσον, σῶσον, ἅγιε, τὴν ποίμην σου

Biblical source and place in the liturgy: The main source is Matthew xiv.28–31, xxvi.69–75;[1] Mark xiv.66–72; and John xiii.5–18, xviii.25–27. The reference to Christ, the Good Shepherd, is John x.6–10. The reference to the foot washing is John xiii.6–10.

    The hymn was used in the East on Thursday of Holy Week, although the Grotteferrata manuscripts indicate its use on Good Friday. The ceremony connected with the foot washing was variously celebrated on Thursday or Friday. On Good Friday, many churches used On Mary at the Cross (#19) as the kontakion to be sung, but On Peter's Denial could be substituted. In Jerusalem, On Judas (#17) was used on Wednesday of Holy Week, and this kontakion would logically follow. The closing strophes of #18 were used on Good Friday, according to Maas (*Chron.*, *B.Z.*, XV, 26), although he feels that we lack evidence as to the calendar of the sixth century for feast days.

Analysis of content: The first prooimion is focused on the incident of Peter's walking on the water; the second, on the incident of the maidservant; and the third, on the motif of the Good Shepherd. The refrain for all three and for the strophes centers on the prayer to the Shepherd. The first three stanzas introduce the topic by announcing

---

1. Romanos specifies in Strophe 3 his choice of Matthew as source, but he departs from this account to insert the fire in the courtyard, which Mark and Luke did mention. He uses Mark's reference to the special look the maid servant gave Peter. Also, the poet omits the Galilean accent of Peter, a detail the three Gospels included. Nor does the poet mention the oath that reinforced the second denial in Matthew.

the biblical source and reminding the listeners of the applicability of the story for all. A dialogue between Christ and Peter follows, in which Peter elaborates on the foot washing and the dinner as reasons for his not denying Christ, and Christ reminds Peter of his loss of faith when walking on the water, and then foretells the denial. Peter is given a strophe (8) for oaths underlining his refusal to deny Christ, and Strophe 9 continues the narrative. Strophes 10 through 17 give details of the denial, although constantly interrupted by the poet's antitheses to point up the frailty of Peter as compared with the Godlike mercy of Christ. Strophes 18 and 19 consist of Peter's lamentations to himself and to the other disciples, and this passage leads to the last two strophes, which remind us of Christ's forgiveness of the robbers on the cross and the closing prayer that He may "hasten and save His sheep."

Connection with homily: Krumbacher comments on the rarity of the treatment of the subject of Peter's denial among poets, although there is one anonymous hymn whose acrostic is τῆς προδοσίας ὁ θρῆνος. The services on Good Friday included the reading of the Gospels that contain the story, and there are a few homilies on the subject. St. John Chrysostom's "On the Apostle Peter and the Prophet Elijah" (*P.G.*, 50, 725–36), and Pseudo Chrysostom (*P.G.*, 59, 613–20) "On the Denial of Peter" show no significant parallels. Ephrem, in his "Fifth Homily for Holy Week," might have suggested ideas to Romanos.[2] Romanos influenced later sermons. Patriarch Eulogius began his homily for Palm Sunday with words from this kontakion, Strophe 3.

Style of Romanos: The sequence of ideas, the frequent references to the Bible, and the abundance of antitheses are all typical of Romanos. Dialogue occurs where the Gospel source used it, and elaboration of detail, such as the fire burning in the courtyard and the maidservant who looked Peter up and down with a keen glance, but there are not as many figures of speech as usual.

Meter: As Krumbacher pointed out in *Stud.*, 74–114, this metrical scheme is close to that of other kontakia. The Oxford edition gives the scheme, 525, XVII.

2. Lamy, *Sancti Ephraemi Syri Hymni et Sermones*, I, 431–39.

ON PETER'S DENIAL

O. 18

Prooimion I: Forgetful of the fearful waves[1]
       And changed by the remark of the maiden,
       Peter said, "Christ, God,
  When I was sinking in the waves, I was frightened, and with reason.
  Calling out to Thee, I have fallen, through my denial;
  But weeping, I cry to Thee:
       'Hasten, Holy One, save Thy sheep'."

Prooimion II: Another kind of deep water is here on land, the maidservant;[2]
       But as I find a pilot[3] for the future
       I flee to Thee for refuge as to a harbor.
  Lord, I shall shed my tears of intercession to you,
  And hence I shall cry out to you:
       "Hasten, Holy One, save Thy sheep."

Prooimion III: O Good Shepherd, Thou who hast placed His spirit in the flocks,
       Hasten, Holy One, save Thy sheep.[4]

Strophe 1: Let us exalt our minds, kindle our hearts; let us not
                                 quench our spirits,[5]
       But let us be uplifted in soul and hasten near by to suffer
                           with the One incapable of suffering.
  Let us lay aside all tiresome arguments
       And attach ourselves to the One on the cross.
       If it seems right, let us all go along with Peter
       To the house of Caiaphas, and with him[6]

1. Matt. xiv.28–33.
2. This strophe does not seem to be a speech of Peter, but rather it has a general significance. The temptation of which the maidservant is a symbol could be the experience of any sinner.
3. The Oxford editors adopt a correction of P, and κυρυφαῖον is used instead of κορυφαῖα, following the reading of Krumbacher. The masculine would certainly refer to a leader or chief; and it makes good sense, although the editor of the French edition (IV, 113*n*1) sees none.
4. ποίμνη refers not to one sheep but to a flock. The concern of the poet is, then, for the group of disciples, who represent the first church.
5. I Thess. v.19.
6. σὺν αὐτῷ could, I suppose, be understood as referring to Christ; but it seems better to take it with the following verb and have it refer to Peter. The punctuation of the Oxford text agrees with the latter; the editor of the *Fr. ed.*, IV, 115*n*1, prefers the former.

Let us cry to Christ the words of Peter of long ago—
"Even if He goes to the cross and enters the tomb—
We suffer with Thee, and we shall die with Thee and cry:
'Hasten, Holy One, save Thy sheep'."

Strophe 2: O lovers of Christ, it is not idly[7] that we call Peter to mind,
but in order that we may emulate
The feeling of affection of the friend, not the denial and flight
of one who was in fact cowardly.
For Peter at first was boiling over with love;
Soon, through fear it was quenched.
However, Christ, receiving his zeal, understood his misery,
For He knew his poor and weak nature,
Like stubble driven in confusion by each breeze,[8]
Always fearful at danger and crying out:
"Hasten, Holy One, save Thy sheep."[9]

Strophe 3: Do you, then, O lovers of Christ, as you hear Peter,
listen to me,
And hearken to the words of the Gospel, and pay attention to them,
For Matthew records this in the Bible,[10] he says:
After supper, Christ spoke:
CHRIST "My children, friends, disciples, on this very night
You will all[11] deny me and desert me."
And while all joined in a din of amazement, Peter cries:
PETER "Even if all deny Thee, I shall never deny Thee;
I shall be with Thee and die with Thee and cry out to Thee:
'Hasten, Holy One, save Thy sheep'."

Strophe 4:
CHRIST "What are you saying, my disciple?" Peter cried out:
PETER "Shall I deny Thee?

7. The apologetic note in οὐ μάτην and the emphasis on ἀγάπησις rather than the denial reflect the hesitance of the Church to dwell on Peter's treachery.
8. "A reed shaken in the wind," Matt. xi.7; *cf.* Job xiii.25.
9. The editor of *Fr. ed.*, IV, 115n2, comments on the application of the refrain here to general human frailty, and he quotes Ephrem's fifth sermon, *Ad Hebdomadam Sanctam*: "Fortis in ceteris in hac re ignavus et remissus fuit. Quamvis virtute accinctus viriliter se gereret, in hac tentatione debilis extitit" (Lamy, I, 433).
10. The words of Christ at the time of the Last Supper, Matt, xxvi.20–22; the protests of Peter, Matt. xxvi.33–36.
11. Christ only foretold the betrayal of *one* (Judas) and then the denial of Peter. However, the poet may be thinking of the failure of the disciples to stay awake in the Garden of Gethsemane.

Shall I leave Thee and desert Thee and not remember Thy call
    and its distinction?
Still I lay close to my heart how Thou didst wash my feet;
        And dost Thou say, 'You will deny *me*,' the Redeemer?
        Still I consider, Savior, how, holding the basin,[12]
        Thou didst approach my feet,
Thou who dost bear the earth and lift the sky
        With those hands with which I was fashioned, now dost
            wash my feet.
        And Thou dost announce that I shall deny Thee and not cry
            out to Thee,
            'Hasten, Holy One, save Thy sheep.'

Strophe 5:   "Even now, Blameless One, even now, Infinite One, I have in my mouth
PETER   The taste of Thy dinner, and how can I deny Thy bounty?
        If I, Thy initiate, become a traitor, Woe is me!
            It would be better to die then to live.[13]
            If I absolutely forget Thy teaching,
            If I do not know it, and see it, and recognize it again,
        It would be fitting for me now to go down to Hades alive,
            Let my tongue now stick in my throat,[14]
            If I shall deny Thee or cease to cry out,
                'Hasten, Holy One, save Thy sheep'."

Strophe 6:   After these words, He who created man, answered Peter:
CHRIST   "What do you say, Peter, my friend? 'I shall not deny'?
                            You will desert me, reject me.
        I only wish what you say were true; but your faith is not steadfast,
            And you do not resist temptations.
            Do you remember how you would have drowned a while back,[15]
            Had I not stretched out my hand to you?
        For you were walking on the sea, as I was;
            But suddenly you were shaken to and fro and quickly you were
                caught up in the waves,
            And then I reached you as you were crying out, saying,
                'Hasten, Holy One, save Thy sheep.'

12. John xiii.5–6. Similar antitheses occur in the kontakion on Judas (#17, Strophe 9).
13. The use of γάρ with ἤ in a similar construction is found in #20, Strophe 16, l. 5.
14. Ps. cxxxvii.6; Job xxix.10.
15. Matt. xiv.28–32.

Strophe 7: "Lo, now I say unto you that before the cock crows,
CHRIST
                                        thrice you will deny me.
          And when in your mind you are tossed about in the waves of the sea
                              and become submerged,[16] you thrice deny me,
     Then you will cry out; but this time though you weep, you will not find
          That I offer my hand as formerly;
          For, taking a reed in my hand, I am beginning to write
          Forgiveness for all the descendants of Adam;
     For my flesh which you see becomes for me as paper,
          And my dark blood, the ink in which I dip and write [17]
          As I dispense eternal life to those who cry:
               'Hasten, Holy One, save Thy sheep'."

Strophe 8: "And now, O Infinite One," answered Peter,
PETER
                                   "now that Thou hast pointed out
          How many times I shall deny Thee, I shall explain
                              my thoughts to Thee, O Savior,
     For even if Thou dost know in advance what I am going to say,[18]
          O Lover of man,
          Still, I shall make clear what is in my mind.
          In the presence of angels and mortals and in the presence of
               Thee, the Creator,
          And of those above and below, I promise
     That if it is necessary for me to die, I shall not deny Thee, O Redeemer,
          With Thee I wish to live, and without Thee I do not wish to live;
          For why should I look upon the sun and not cry out to Thee
               'Hasten, Holy One, save Thy sheep'."

Strophe 9: Peter was as zealous as a trusted friend; but the Creator was ready
          To aid him again, since He knew his tendency to slip
                              and his unstable nature.
     After saying and hearing these words, the Lord
          Was led away, of His own will, to suffer.
          When He was seized by the lawless, as He willed,
          And betrayed by Judas, as He had known,

16. Ps. xlii.7.
17. The same figure of speech is used in the kontakion On the Healing of the Leper (#8, Strophe 10, l. 7; Strophe 11, l. 6); in the one On the Sinful Woman (#10, Strophe 18, l. 3); in Lazarus I (#14, Strophe 3, l. 6); and Pentecost (#33, Strophe 6, l. 1).
18. Ecclus. xlii.19–21.

He came, then, to the house of Caiaphas.

    And Peter followed to see the end;

    And as he beheld it, he was frightened; he was terrified and

        he called out:

        "Hasten, Holy One, save Thy sheep."

Strophe 10: In the great confusion, Peter was carried along with the crowd

    And entered eagerly. Coming within the house he sees there

The fire burning, and the judge seated in the courtyard,[19]

    And Christ standing before the high priest,

    And not enduring the evil sight, he wept

    And beat his breast and said to himself:

PETER   "Thou art bound, O Christ, and Thou dost endure it manfully

        and remain steadfast,

    They spit upon His face at whose sight the Seraphim hide their eyes,[20]

    As they shudder in awe and fear and cry out,

        'Hasten, Holy One, save Thy sheep.'

Strophe 11: "Thou art cudgeled and do I live and allow it for Thee?

PETER   Thou art ill-treated, O Lover of Man,

    And does the earth behold and endure it without being split asunder

                in swallowing up[21] those who oppose Thee?[22]

Thou art mocked, and does Heaven behold it without

        being whirled about?[23]

    Are those in Heaven not grievously angry?

    Is Michael not enraged when Thou art cudgeled,

    And does he not burn and consume men on earth?

Does Gabriel endure it and not burn up those who oppose Thee?[24]

    Even if all the divine beings on high are silent,

    I shudder and weep and cry out to Thee:

        'Hasten, Holy One, save Thy sheep'."

19. As Paul Maas has pointed out (*Gram.* 257), the use of fire with an antithetical concept is characteristic of Romanos. See Introduction, p. xxxv. The editor of the *Fr. ed.*, IV, 123*n*1, translates χόρτον as *herbe* and considers the fire as a symbol of Christ and ephemeral grass as symbolic of Caiaphas. However, χόρτον also means the feeding ground of the courtyard. Mark uses αὐλή for the open courtyard (Mark xiv.54), and Mark mentions Peter warming himself by the fire, as he sat with the servants. The imagery thus has justification.

20. Isa. vi.2.

21. Ex. xv.12; Num. xvi.32.

22. The fact that κατὰ σοῦ is repeated in l. 7 does not create an objection to that reading; it even establishes a parallel structure, which adds to the rhythm.

23. Rev. vi.14.

24. Gen. xix.24. The reading κατὰ σοῦ is preferable to τοὺς τολμηρούς. See note 21, above.

Strophe 12:   After saying this, Peter became silent, and, overwhelmed by panic fear,
                    he said nothing;
                But suddenly, having done well to keep silent,
                                                    he spoke with bad effect,
            In order that Christ, the Truth, might be fulfilled,
                And every mortal become a liar.[25]
                What, then, shall we say, brothers? That Peter
                Denied Him that truth might be revealed?[26]
            Let it not be true that I should speak thus about Christ;
                But this I know that He foresees all things
                And reveals all, and He establishes in advance security for
                    all who cry:
                    "Hasten, Holy One, save Thy sheep."

Strophe 13:   For a short time, then, as we have said, Peter was quiet.
                                                            Soon he ceased
                From his anguish and sat down in the courtyard,
                                                    thoughtful and gloomy.
            One maidservant walked around the disciple
            And looked him up and down with a keen glance
            And, taking in the situation, she said to him:
MAID   "Clearly you, too, were with the Galilaean."
PETER   But Peter answered: "I do not know what you are talking about;
                I do not know the One whom people invoke as they cry:
                    'Hasten, Holy One, save Thy sheep'."

Strophe 14:   Quickly, O apostle, you let go your support,
                                                and the maiden threw you down.
                But rise up, spring up, and regain your first strength
                                                                as an athlete.
            You did not have a contest against someone stronger than you,
                Then how were you brought down by a kindly word?
                A young girl came up to you, and probably
                In a faltering voice said what she did to you;[27]

---

25. Ps. cxvi.11.

26. Cyril of Alexandria, in his Commentary on Luke (*P.G.*, 72, 928D), quoting "He went out and wept bitterly" (Luke xxii.62), adds καὶ οὐ δήπου φαμὲν ὅτι γέγονεν ἄρνησις ἵνα μὴ ψεύσηται Χριστός.

27. Like the homilist, Romanos wishes to emphasize the insignificance of Peter's adversary. St. John Chrysostom (*P.G.*, 50, 727) makes the maidservant a prostitute: κόρη --- πόρνη.

And you, terrified at her stammer, as though it were the gnashing of teeth,
 Spoke out clearly to her: "I do not know what you
  are talking about."
 Why did the maiden terrify you and why did you not cry out:
  "Hasten, Holy One, save Thy sheep"?

Strophe 15 : The apostle, noticing that the maiden was looking at the people within,
 Left the courtyard, and, stumbling against the gate, fell down there.
And another maidservant, coming up, as the Gospel reports,
 Said to those who were warming themselves:
MAID   "It is clear that this man also was
 With the Nazarene every day."
But Cephas, thoroughly terrified, answered her:
PETER   "I do not know the man; I do not know him well.
 I am ignorant of the man whom they greet as they cry out:
  'Hasten, Holy One, save Thy sheep'."

Strophe 16: You do not know the man, Peter, is that what you say?
           You do not know the man?
 Do you not rather wish to say this, that you do not know Him
            as mere man but as God?[28]
Did you not then hasten to teach the lawless
 That it is God who is crucified?
 For even if He suffered in the flesh, after He assumed flesh,
 He was born of Mary as a spiritual being,[29]
Then, dying in the flesh, it is not God who dies.
 As far as one can see, then, He is overcome; but in a way not
  to be observed
 He is at hand to no one except to those who cry out:
  "Hasten, Holy One, save Thy sheep."

Strophe 17: O Master, we sing hymns to Thee, since it is good to sing;[30]
           we praise Thee, O Lord,

28. It was, of course, important that Peter would not be made to deny the humanity of Christ nor yet His divinity. See Ps. Chrys. (*P.G.*, 59, 615) and Cyril of Alexandria (*P.G.*, 72, 928B–D) as quoted, *Fr. ed.*, IV, 130*n*1.
29. The fact that σάρκα--ἄσαρκος is old is no reason to reject that reading as the editor of the French edition suggests (*Fr. ed.*, IV, 131*n*2). The translation cannot keep the force of the antithesis in the Greek.
30. Literally, "since a psalm is a good thing." Ps. cxlvii.1.

That Thou hast suffered all things; and yet Peter, who suffered nothing,

denies Thee.

Thou wast lashed, and Peter denied Thee.

Though he endured nothing, the disciple[31]

Now that he was twice overthrown by women,

Is worsted a third time by some other men.

For after a short time, some other men came up

And accosted Peter, and he denied with oaths.

And straightway the cock convicted him and he cried out:[32]

"Hasten, Holy One, save Thy sheep."

Strophe 18:   When Peter heard the cock crow, immediately he cried out
PETER   With shrieks and lamentations: "Woe is me, woe is me,

Where am I to go, where am I to stay, where am I to appear?

What shall I say, what word can I utter, what shall I offer as an
excuse, what have I left?

What shall I do? What shall I suffer? What can I
undergo as expiation?

How shall I lament my calamity? A first time, a second time,
a third time this disaster has come upon me.

Three times the treacherous one has overthrown me, naïve me.

Invisibly was the arrow cast, visibly was I overpowered.

Where did I lose my bearings and not cry out:

'Hasten, Holy One, save Thy sheep.'

Strophe 19:   "Thou, O Lover of men, art my strength and my song,[33]
PETER

do not desert me."

These things Peter said through tears as he came to the other

disciples of the Redeemer.

He put his hands to his head,
PETER   And he cried out: "Woe is me, servants of Christ,

Now I have fulfilled the prophecy of Christ

About my threefold denial.

Lament with me and mourn with me and say to me:

'Where is your love and your zeal? Where is your faith and
your self-control?

---

31. The reading in the French edition is ἀθλητής instead of μαθητής and interprets it as a bit of irony. The Oxford edition prefers to accept the correction made by Krumbacher.
32. The subject of ἔκραζε is surely Peter and not the cock. Its cry served to remind him of Christ's words and hence *he* called out to Christ.
33. Ps. cxviii.14.

Where is your mind, Peter, when you were removed from
    anchorage, that you did not cry out:
      "Hasten, Holy One, save Thy sheep"?'"

Strophe 20: The Merciful One is touched by the tears of Peter
                         and grants him forgiveness.
    For, speaking to the robber on the cross, He makes
                         a covert allusion to Peter:

CHRIST   "Robber, beloved of me, come with me,
      Since Peter has deserted me.[34]
    Nevertheless, to him and to you and to all mortals
    I disclose my mercy, as Lover of men.
  Weeping, robber, you say, 'Remember me.'
    And Peter, lamenting, cries out: 'Do not desert me.'
  Hence to him and to you, I speak with all those who cry out:
    'Hasten, Holy One, save Thy sheep.'

Strophe 21: "No one is without sin, no one is blameless.
CHRIST   Do not consider this of small importance.
    I alone am without fault. Hence to all I dispense the 'free gift';[35]
  But someone will say probably: 'Whence does this come, O man,
    That Peter who fell was called back?'
  Now I shall show you clearly through whom
    The gift was sent to Peter.
  For the voice of an angel in speaking to the women said:
    'When you speak to all of them speak also to Peter.'[36]
  Do not fear, said the Master, but cry out:
    'Hasten, Holy One, save Thy sheep'."

Strophe 22: Come forward, man of God, and receive the Lord as He advances to you.
    Coming from the tomb as from a bridal chamber through me,
            His messenger,[37] He speaks to you:

34. Luke xxiii.43.
35. The gift of forgiveness through repentance.
36. Mark xvi.7.
37. If the poet is speaking, as is common in final strophes, the first of Strophe 22 makes sense, for then ἀγγέλου can have the double meaning of "messenger," the poet, and "angel," whose re-assuring words to the women can be applied to the neophyte. The poet wants the neophyte to remember Christ's forgiveness of Peter. In this case the difficulties of the French editor can be avoided. The general sense in a free translation would be: "Come forward and receive the message of the Lord; I convey the word of the angel: 'Speak now to Peter'; and you can then realize that Peter's failure and yours can be forgiven." The Novatian group believed that no backsliding could be forgiven.

"Speak now to Peter. Do not despair of forgiveness
But pray not to fall into temptation."
Then let no one of us be deceived into believing
That Peter's mistake was not forgiven.
For Christ came to earth wishing to grant pardon;
Because He wished to forgive, He was nailed to the cross.
And forgiving, He submitted to death for those who cry out:
"Hasten, Holy One, save Thy sheep."

Strophe 23: "Have pity, O Master," cry out to the Creator, you who are neophytes.
Since you have tasted of the fountain of sweet and good water,
Be enlightened and not merely baptized.
Now do not receive this gift without good faith
Never let God say, "Since I came
They have defiled my earth."[38]
May it not happen, Christ, that Thou shouldst say this,
But rather may it be that Thou comest quickly, in order that Thou
mayst gladly receive
With us those who everywhere cry out to Thee:
"Hasten, Holy One, save Thy sheep."

38. Jer. ii.7.

EXCURSUS: SUMMARY OF KONTAKIA ON THE PASSION AND THE RESURRECTION

Eleven of the kontakia of Romanos deal directly with the central theme of Christian faith. This does not count *Judas*, intended for Thursday of Holy Week, *Peter's Denial*, usually used on Good Friday of that week, and *Entry into Jerusalem*, which was sung on Palm Sunday to introduce Holy Week. The two hymns on Lazarus (O. 14 and 15), which preceded Palm Sunday, might be added to this list.

The eleven are:

#19 *On Mary at the Cross* was composed for Good Friday.

#20 *On the Passion of Christ* is also intended for Good Friday.

#21 *On the Crucifixion* is for "the fifth day of the fifth week of Lent" and is the kontakion used for the Great Kanon of Cosmas of Crete.

#22 *On the Victory of the Cross* has various indications in the manuscripts. The Patmos manuscript marks it for Wednesday of mid Lent; *Δ* gives it for Good Friday; and T, according to the Oxford edition, assigns it to the Sunday for the Adoration of the Cross (September 14). The French edition argues against the latter date and favors Good Friday. The Oxford edition usually adopts the readings of P.

#23 *On the Adoration at the Cross* is given in the Oxford edition for the Friday of mid Lent (fourth week of Lent). The French edition repeats this assigned date in the memoranda just preceding the hymn, but in the introductory notes a case is made for September 14 as the festival for which Romanos composed this kontakion.

Then, there are six Resurrection hymns:[1]

#24 *On the Resurrection I* for Easter Sunday.

#25 *On the Resurrection II* for Easter Sunday.

#26 *On the Resurrection III* for Easter Sunday.

#27 *On the Resurrection IV* for the third Sunday after Easter Sunday.

#28 *On the Resurrection V* for Easter Sunday.

1. The editor of the French edition numbers them differently:

Resurrection Hymns

Oxford edition	French edition, IV
#24, Resurrection I	#XLI, Resurrection II
#25, Resurrection II	#XLII, Resurrection III
#26, Resurrection III	#XLIV, Resurrection V
#27, Resurrection IV	#XLV, Resurrection VI
#28, Resurrection V	#XLIII, Resurrection IV
#29, Resurrection VI	#XL, Resurrection I

#29 *On the Resurrection VI* for Easter Sunday. This is the only kontakion that most manuscripts list for Easter Sunday. The other kontakia, though marked for Easter Sunday, are distributed throughout Holy Week.

The content and style can be summarized with some profit if one wants to understand the way in which a poet changed the emphasis and adapted to the same occasion, while at the same time his predilections are quite clear in the choice of source and the treatment of the material.

In four of the above kontakia the scene is entirely on earth:

#19 Mary follows Christ to the cross and He must convince her of the purpose of His death and resurrection.

#20 The scene is on earth in the court of Pilate where Christ is on trial and the Jews are berated.

#24 *On the Resurrection I* places the scene on earth. Pilate and the Jews and the guards are the speakers.

#29 *On the Resurrection VI* deals with the scene at the tomb: Christ, an angel, the apostles, Mary, and other women are the speakers.

The seven other kontakia introduce Hades and the Infernal Regions. This had really been done to some extent in the two hymns on *Lazarus*.

#21 *On the Crucifixion.* In this hymn the devil is the chief character. He converses with the Jews whom he has used in his plans, and he laments his losses as he talks to Death.

#22 *On the Victory of the Cross* is viewed from the infernal regions where Hades and the devil engage in a sustained dialogue, interrupted by the central theme of the Redemption. The laments of Hades and the devil continue.

#23 *On the Adoration at the Cross.* This kontakion moves from earth to Hell, to Heaven. The robber on the cross speaks to Christ; then the robber sings his song of praise, and the Cherubim greet him in Paradise; the devil returns to lament his losses in Hell.

#25 *On the Resurrection II.* This kontakion consists of an imaginary dialogue between Adam and Hades—presumably in the Infernal Regions. The poet later speaks to the soldiers who guarded the tomb.

#26 *On the Resurrection III.* The scene is in Hell, where Adam taunts Hades. Adam tells of the crucifixion and its effects on earth. Hades recognizes that he must give up the Just.

#27 *On the Resurrection IV.* After the episode of the lost coin, Hades enters and a dialogue between Christ and Hades ensues. Christ defends Himself as though in court.

#28 *On the Resurrection V.* Most of this kontakion is concerned with dialogues among Belial, Hades, and Death. The robber is introduced briefly, and then Christ, Hades, and Death. Christ binds Hades; Adam and all the Just rejoice. The devil reviews what has caused their downfall.

ON MARY AT THE CROSS

O. 19 (K. 37)

Title: Εἰς τὸ πάθος τοῦ Κυρίου καὶ εἰς τὸν θρῆνον τῆς θεοτόκου

Manuscripts and editions: This kontakion occurs complete in seven manuscripts. The readings are varied, with much evidence of contamination. Krumbacher has edited it with detailed discussion of the manuscripts.[1] He depends chiefly on P. It is noteworthy that there are two sixth strophes. The second one is probably a later edition by a reviser who wished the acrostic to have an epsilon, although Krumbacher makes it clear that τοῦ ταπινοῦ ʿΡωμανοῦ was as authentic as τοῦ ταπεινοῦ ʿΡωμανοῦ. He points up some interpolations.[2]

    This is one of the best known of the poems of Romanos. It and his kontakia on Palm Sunday are included in the *Triodion* of Holy Week.

    Pitra edited it, *A.S.*, I, xiv. Nine editions have appeared since. The ones consulted are:

Krumbacher, *Acros.*, 658–74.

Tomadakis, II, 141–72.

French edition, IV, 160–87, with an excellent introduction, 143–60.

    Several translations exist. They are listed in *Fr. ed.*, IV, 160n1. They have not been available for this study.

Tone: μέσος δ′ (P); πλάγιος δ′ (other mss.)

Acrostic: Τοῦ ταπεινοῦ ʿΡωμανοῦ

Refrain: ὁ υἱὸς καὶ θεός μου

Biblical source and place in the liturgy: This kontakion was intended for Good Friday. The simple fact of Mary's presence at the cross occurs in John xix.25. Luke (xxiii.27–31) records the laments of the group of women who came to the tomb. There is no real source for the direct conversation between Christ and Mary. The setting is real, on earth. The conversation is concerned with Adam in Hell and Christ's saving of those in Hell.

Connection with homily: There is no one sermon model. Ephrem had put into poetic form Mary's laments. (See note 7 to Strophe 2 of the kontakion.) In the tenth century Symeon Mataphrastes uses the same theme (*P.G.*, 114, 209–17). It is true that Mary

1. *Acros.*, 658–86.
2. *Acros.*, 680–81.

questions Christ about His powers and raises questions in sermons by Basil of Seleucia (*P.G.*, 32, 965–68) and Cyril of Alexandria (*P.G.*, 74, 661–64), but no real parallel exists. Romanos repeats the idea in Kontakion #4, On the Presentation in the Temple; she asks for details in #2, On the Nativity II (Adam and Eve and the Nativity), and in #5 (On the Baptism of Christ).

Connections with drama of the East and the West: One strophe from this kontakion is translated into Latin and appears in the Ambrosian Antiphonary of the British Museum; there are parallel passages in the Roman responses for Holy Week, and the first words are in the Antiphonary of Compiègne.[3]

Mme Cottas assigns the *Christos Paschon* to Gregory of Nazianz.[4] It has been established as of later date; but the important fact here is that it uses the first strophe of Romanos' kontakion. Gregory's drama, which was purely literary and liturgical, would very naturally find inspiration in the kontakion of Romanos.

Style of Romanos and analysis of content: The poem is highly dramatic and highly figurative. After the exhortation to the congregation and the statement of the theme, almost the entire kontakion is in dialogue form. In P, the names of the speakers are added in the margin,[5] and the complete balance is interesting, for Mary is given the first three strophes in which to raise her questions about the reasons for Christ's moving to an unjust death. The next three strophes give Christ's answer, with the repetition of the theological concept of a voluntary death. The second sixth strophe (a later interpolation) and the seventh are given to Mary for her review of the previous instances of power that might, she feels, be put into effect in this crisis. Christ answers with other statements of His purpose. Mary, in Strophe 10, asks for pardon in repeating her doubts, and Christ is given two strophes for His final answer. The closing prayer is typical of Romanos in its restatement of theme. Krumbacher feels that the continual carping of Mary is not poetical. However, the emphasis of the entire kontakion is on theology rather than pathos of a *mater dolorosa*. There are, indeed, bits of insight into the psychology of Mary: She remembers details of evidence of power as she recalls the wedding at Cana, the hosannas of Palm Sunday; she is resentful that the disciples do not share the pain of crucifixion in spite of their protestations of loyalty; she knows about the healing of the leper and raising of Lazarus from the dead. Her questions have, then, reality. So, also, it is natural for her to ask for details about the future. Just as Christ is hailed as human and divine in the refrain, just so, Mary is both a human mother and a vehicle for the theological elaboration on the purpose of the crucifixion.

3. The text appears in *Paléographie Musicale*, V (Solesmes, 1896), 6–15. See note 47 on general introduction.

Attention was called to this correspondence in my article, "Romanos and the Mystery Play of the East," *University of Missouri Studies* (1937), 38.

4. V. Cottas, "L'Influence du drama 'Christos Paschon' sur l'art chrétien d'orient" (Paris, 1931), 54. Her argument that the reference Romanos makes to "the theologian" proves that Romanos meant Gregory is, of course, not sound, because this is Romanos' customary reference to his Gospel source. It is the author of "Christos Paschon" who followed Romanos. See La Piana, *Le Rappresentazioni sacre*, 12.

5. *Acros.*, 681–86.

The parallel structure of the opening phrases and the prevalent antitheses are typical of Romanos. So are the plays on words and the use of similar sound in closely placed words. Such is the untranslatable Χάριν --- χεῖρον in Strophe 2, the "no one of all" as contrasted with "the one above all," Strophe 3, and the use of πάθος and βάθος in the closing prayer.

Not as many figures of speech occur in this kontakion as in others, nor as many allusions to the Old Testament. The references to manna from Heaven and the phrase "taking form as the mountain made solid like cheese" are less noticeable than the medical figure of the cross used as surgical instruments in healing. Christ the Physician is a common theme with Romanos.

Meter: The metrical analysis is given in the Oxford edition, 525, XVIII.

ON MARY AT THE CROSS

O. 19

Prooimion: Let us, then, all of us sing a hymn of praise
  For the One who died on the cross for us,
  For Mary saw Him on the cross and said,[1]
  "Even if Thou dost endure the cross, Thou art
   My son and my God."

Strophe 1: The lamb, beholding her lamb advancing to the slaughter,[2]
  Followed Him wearily with the other women, saying,
MARY   "Where dost Thou go, O my son?
Why dost Thou follow this swift path?[3]
  Is there another wedding in Cana,
  And dost Thou hasten there to turn water into wine?[4]
Shall I go with Thee, my child, or shall I wait for Thee?
  Give me word, O Word, some word, and do not pass me
   by in silence,
  O Thou who hast kept me pure,
   My son and my God.[5]

Strophe 2: "I did not think, Son, to see Thee among these people,
MARY   Nor did I believe until now that these lawless ones
  Would rage and lay hands on Thee unjustly.
For still their children cry out to Thee, 'Hosanna';[6]
  Still the road is lined with palms
  And bears witness to all of the general praise of the
   unrighteous for Thee.

1. John xix.25.
2. Isa. liii.7; Acts viii.32.
3. δρόμον τετέλεκα: This phrase is used by Paul, II, Tim. iv.7, "I have finished my course." The speed of a race suggests that Mary thinks that Christ is in too much of a hurry to go to His death. By implication we also have her say that His career, His course, has been all too brief.
4. John ii.1–11.
5. The poem χριστὸς πάσχων is later than Romanos and anonymous. It imitates this first strophe. This strophe was used in the kanon of Good Friday.
6. Kontakion #16. Matt. xxi.8–9; Mark xi.8–9; Luke xix.37–38.

Then, why has the worse counsel prevailed?
    Woe is me, would that I knew! How is
        my light extinguished![7]
    How is He nailed to the cross?
        My son and my God.

Strophe 3:   "Thou dost advance, my child, to an unjust death,
MARY   And no one suffers with Thee. Peter does not accompany Thee—
                    he who said to Thee,
            'I shall never deny Thee, even if I die.'[8]
        Thomas has left Thee—he who said: 'Let us all die with Him.'[9]
            And again the others, well-known and intimate friends,
                Destined to judge the tribes of Israel, where are they now?
        No one of all of them is here.[10] But the One above all,
            Thou, alone, O Son, art to die in return for all whom
                Thou hast gratified,[11]
                    My son and my God."

Strophe 4:   He answered these words of Mary, which she called out
                From her deep grief and cried out from great suffering.
            He who was born of her, answered her as follows:
CHRIST   "Why dost thou weep, Mother, why dost thou advance with
                these other women?
            Is it that I should not suffer, that I should not die? How, then,
                shall I save Adam?
            Is it that I should not inhabit the tomb? How then shall I restore to
                life those in Hades?
        And surely thou dost know that I am to be crucified unjustly.
            Why, then, O Mother, dost thou weep? Rather, cry aloud
                'It is gladly and willingly He suffered,
                    My son and my God.'

7. Ephrem, *Threni Mariae* "Lumen meum obscuratum est." Tom. II, 153*n*1, from *Opera omnia quae exstant graece, syriace, Latine* VI. (Vat. Rome, 1746), 574.
8. Kontakion #18. Matt. xxvi.35; Mark xiv.31.
9. John xi.16.
10. Symeon Metaphrastes (*P.G.*, 114, 216D–217A) has similar words given the Virgin: Ἀλλὰ ποῦ τῶν μαθητῶν ὁ χορός, ἵνα μοι παθαινομένη συγαλαύσωσιν;
11. It is true that complete expiation cannot be claimed until after the Crucifixion; but Mary knows of the many occasions when the power and grace of Christ have worked miracles. The word *please* is too weak. *Gratify* contains the idea of grace that satisfies a petition for help.

Strophe 5: "Banish thy grief, O Mother, banish it,

CHRIST
    For it is not fitting for thee to grieve, since thou wert called blest.[12]

    Do not by this mourning, completely conceal thy honor;

Do not descend to the level of foolish women, O all-wise Virgin;

    Thou art in the middle of my bridal chamber,[13]

    Do not, then, waste away in spirit like one standing outside.

Consider those in the bridal chamber as thy slaves,

    For everyone shall run with fear and trembling to hear thee call,

      O Holy One,

    When thou dost say: 'Where is

      My son and my God?'

Strophe 6: "Do not consider the day of suffering a bitter one—

CHRIST
    That day for which I came down from Heaven like the manna—

    Not on Mount Sinai but in thy womb;

For within it did I take solid form as David prophesied;[14]

    Consider the meaning, O Holy One, 'the mountain

      formed like cheese.'[15]

    In it I suffer and in it I save.

Then do not lament, Mother, but rather cry with joy:[16]

    'Willingly does He receive this suffering,

      My son and my God'."

Strophe 6 (2) (Interpolated):[17] In these words, the most holy mother

---

12. Luke i.28.

13. Christ as the bridegroom is a concept that occurs throughout the New Testament. See especially Matt. ix.15; Mark ii.19; Luke v.34. In Rev. xxi.9, the reference is to the church as the wife of Christ, the lamb. Eph. v.25: "even as Christ loved the church." Mary, then, in Christ's reassurance to her that she is not left out (see her words in Strophe 1) is told that she will be of central importance in the church.

14. Ps. lxviii.16: ὄρος πῖον, ὄρος τετυρωμένον. These words are not translated in the authorized English version.

15. The verb τετυρωμένον means literally "formed into cheese." It is tempting to think that the poet had in mind a word that would connect this passage with Cheese Week! The meaning seems to be, "I was fashioned in thy womb, took on solid form there; and if you think about it, O Holy One, your womb was like the mountain formed like cheese mentioned in the Psalms." Job x.10 has the same figure: "Hast thou not poured me out as milk and curdled me like cheese?" ἐτύρωσας δὲ με ἶσα τυρῷ. A note in *Fr. ed.*, IV, 167n3, explains that the Hebrews considered the embryo a result of the coagulation of blood in the womb when reached by the seminal fluid.

16. Christ does not expect her to rejoice in the suffering; but He does hope that she understands that it is voluntary and for the purpose of saving mankind. She finds this difficult.

17. This strophe is marked *spurious* in the Oxford edition (note, p. 144) because it appears in only a few mss. and because it seems to interrupt the continuity of the narrative. It is included only because of the acrostic, but ταπινοῦ does occur in other kontakia of Romanos and Krumbacher discusses this fact (*Acros.*, 655). Tomadakis considers that it was written for phonetic reasons (II, 151).

In answer to the One made flesh and miraculously
  fashioned from her,
  Cried out in her distress of spirit:

MARY "Why dost Thou say to me, my child, 'Do not go along with
    the other women'?
  For, indeed, just as they in their wombs,
  So I, in mine bore Thee and gave Thee milk at my breasts;
How is it, then, that Thou dost wish, my son, that I not
    lament for Thee
  As Thou dost hasten to submit unjustly to a death
  Which will raise up the dead,
    O my son and my God?

Strophe 7: "See, my child," she says, "I rub the tears from my eyes,
MARY   And I rub my heart still more,
  But my thinking cannot be silenced.
Why dost Thou say to me, Merciful One, 'If I do not die,[18]
                    Adam is not healed'?
  For indeed Thou hast cured many without suffering.
  Thou hast cleansed the leper and Thou didst suffer no pain but Thou
    didst will it.[19]
Having given strength to the paralytic, Thou wast not harmed;[20]
  Again, Thou didst give sight to the blind by a word,[21]
    O Righteous One,
  And Thou didst remain without harm,
    My son and my God.

Strophe 8: "Raising up the dead, Thou didst not become dead
MARY   Nor rest in a tomb, O my son and my life. Why, then,
      dost Thou say,
    'If I do not suffer, Adam is not redeemed'?[22]

18. θάνω is suspect because Mary is really objecting to suffering and some mss. prefer πάθω or πάθης. However, it is not inconceivable that Mary anticipates death as a probable outcome of the suffering of Christ.
19. Matt. viii.1–4; Mark i.40–45; Luke v.12–14; Kontakion #8.
20. Matt. ix.2–8; Mark ii.2–12; Luke v.18–26.
21. John ix.1–41.
22. Notes to the *Fr. ed.*, IV, 171n4, and also the various readings given in the Oxford edition, 145, critical apparatus point up the lack of clarity in mss. for the opening lines of this strophe. I have kept the reading of the Oxford text.

Command, O Savior, and straightway the cripple picking up
  his bed walks.[23]
  Indeed, even if Adam has been buried deep in a tomb,
  As Thou hast raised up Lazarus from the tomb with Thy voice,
   do even so with him.[24]
All things serve Thee as the Creator of all.
  Why, then, dost Thou hasten, my child? Do not
   hurry to slaughter;
  Do not court death,
   My son and my God."

Strophe 9:
CHRIST

"Thou dost not know, O Mother, thou dost not know what
  I am saying,
  Why I revealed my purpose and established the word
   which thou hearest,
  Yet in thy heart thou knowest the truth of what I am saying.
This poor Adam, whom I mentioned, was sickened,
  Not only in body but also in soul.
  Willfully he suffered; for he had not heard of me and he is in danger.
Thou knowest what I say. Then do not weep, Mother;
  But rather say this: 'Free Adam
  And pity Eve,
   My son and my God.'

Strophe 10:
CHRIST

"By profligacy and by gluttony
  Did Adam become ill and was cast into lowest Hades,
  Where he weeps in the sorrow of his spirit.
But Eve, since she taught him the lawless deed,[25]
  Mourns with him; for she became ill with him
  So that they might learn together to keep watch for the message
   of the physician.
Dost thou now understand? Art thou fully aware of what I say?
  Again, O Mother, cry: 'If Thou dost pardon Adam,
  Also pardon Eve,
   My son and my God'."

23. Matt. ix.6–7.
24. John xi.43–44.
25. ἀταξία is literally *disorder*. This deed was lawlessness, "against the arrangement with God";
it also produced, brought with it, the disorder of the universe. Rom. v.12.

Strophe 11: As she heard these words,

MARY
      The blameless lamb answered the Lamb of God: "My Lord,
        Yet again would I speak. Do not be angry with me;
  I shall tell Thee what I have in mind so that I may learn from Thee with
          certainty[26] what I wish.
      If Thou sufferest and diest, shalt Thou rise again for me?
      If Thou goest to heal Adam and Eve, shall I behold Thee again?
  For this I fear, that perhaps Thou shalt rise up to Heaven[27]
      From the tomb, and I, when I ask to see Thee,
      Shall mourn and cry out, 'Where is
        My son and my God?'"

Strophe 12: As the One who knows all things before they happen heard this,

CHRIST
      He answered Mary: "Be of good courage, Mother,
        Since thou shalt be the first to see me from the tomb.[28]
  I shall come to show thee from what suffering I redeemed Adam,
      And what suffering I endured for his sake.
      Showing the prints of nails in my hands I shall make them visible
        to my friends;
  And then, O Mother, thou shalt see Eve
      Alive as formerly, and thou shalt say with joy:
      'He has saved my ancestors, He who is
        My son and my God.'

Strophe 13: "Bear up for a short time, O Mother, and thou shalt see

CHRIST
      How, like a physician, I strip[29] and come where they lie dead
      And cure their wounds,
  Cutting their callousness and hardness with the spear;
      And I take the vinegar and use it as an astringent on the wound;

26. The meaning "wholly" in πάντως might better be translated "in every detail." It does not seem to have the common meaning "at least." The latter would not be in keeping with Mary's spirit. She simply wants to know complete details with some certainty.

27. The μήπως reflects hesitancy on the part of the Virgin in even expressing her fear. She does not question that He will be resurrected, but that He will go directly to Heaven (ἄνω) without her seeing Him on earth.

28. Kontakion #29. See introduction for the adaptation of the Gospel story used by Romanos. The *Fr. ed.,* IV, 177n2, favors an interpretation that implies a special appearance of the risen Christ to Mary.

29. An interesting reference is given by the editor of *Fr. ed.,* IV, 178n1, to suggest that doctors in the tenth century did either change their robes or actually, in some cases, strip in order to treat amputations and dislocated bones.

And when I have opened up the cut with the surgical lancet of the
    nails, I shall use my cloak as dressing,[30]
  Using my cross as remedy,[31]
    I use it, O Mother, so that thou mayest sing with understanding:[32]
    'He has redeemed suffering by suffering,
      My son and my God.'

Strophe 14: "Lay aside thy grief, Mother,
CHRIST   And advance with joy; for I now hasten to that for which I came,
      To do the will of Him who sent me;[33]
  For, from the first this was ordained for me by my Father,
      And it was not displeasing to my spirit[34]
      That I should assume human form and suffer for the fallen.
  Then, O Mother, hastening, tell all people
      That by suffering He strikes down the one who hates Adam
      And, having conquered, He comes,
      My son and my God."

Strophe 15: "I shall conquer, child, I shall conquer my suffering;
MARY   And truly I shall not mourn when I am in my chamber
              and Thou art on the cross—
      I in my house and Thou in the tomb.
  Grant that I come with Thee for it helps me to look upon Thee.
      I know the boldness of those who honored Moses;[35]
      For, as then, the blind were taking vengeance on him, so now they
        have come to slay Thee.
  Moses said to Israel
      That the time would come that they would see Life upon the tree.[36]
      Who is the Life? It is
      My son and my God."

Strophe 16: "If thou comest, then do not weep, Mother.
CHRIST   Do not again be distressed if thou seest the universe shaken,
      For such daring disturbs all Creation;

30. The editor of the *Fr. ed.*, IV, 179*n*2, uses entirely different readings for lines 6 and 7.
31. νάρθηξ is a reed, used as a splint. The νάρθηξ was also used as the doctor's case of medicine. *Remedy* is used to translate either meaning.
32. ψάλετε συνετῶς. Ps. xlvii.7: "Sing ye praises with understanding."
33. John vi.38.
34. The editor of the *Fr. ed.*, IV, 181, translates: "Et mon Esprit n'a pas refusé" which would *seem* to make ἀπήρεσε come from ἀπαρνέομαι rather than ἀπαρέσκω.
35. John iii.14; Num. xxi.8.
36. θὲς αὐτὸν ἐπὶ σημείον ("set it upon a *pole*"). Num. xxi.8.

The pole is blinded and does not open its eye until I speak.[37]
    The earth and the sea will hasten to flee.[38]

    The temple will rend its veil before such deeds of daring.[39]
The mountains will shake, tombs will be emptied.[40]
    When thou beholdest these things, if thou art terrified, as a woman
      is wont to be,
    Do not cry out to me: 'Spare me,
      My son and my God'."

Strophe 17: Son of the virgin, God of the virgin,
    And Maker of the World, Thine is the suffering, Thine, the
                                depths of wisdom.[41]
    Thou knowest what Thou art and what Thou art to become.
Willing to suffer, Thou hast deemed it of worth to save man.
    As Lamb of God, Thou hast taken away our sins;[42]
    Thou hast destroyed them through Thy death; as Savior Thou
      hast saved all.
Thou art, as a human, able to suffer, and as God, Thou
      knowest no suffering.
    Dying, Thou art saving. Thou dost grant to the holy virgin
    Fearless confidence to cry to Thee,
      "My son and my God."

37. Matt. xxvii.45; Mark xv.33; Luke xxiii.44.
38. In the Gospels it is only the earth that is shaken. Matt. xxvii.51–53; Mark xv.38; Luke xxiii.45. Compare with Ps. cxiv.3–5.
39. Mark xv.38; Luke xxiii.45; Matt. xxvii.51. The editor of the *Fr. ed.*, IV, 185*n*1, connects this with the priest's rending of his garments at Christ's seeming blasphemy (Matt. xxvi.65). The Greek seems simply to say "in opposition to those who are daring."
40. Matt. xxvii.52.
41. Rom. xi.33.
42. John i.29.

ON THE PASSION OF CHRIST

O. 20 (K. 19)

Title: Εἰς τὸ πάθος

Manuscripts and editions: The hymn is to be found only in the kontakaria at Patmos and in Italy. P and Δ are the manuscripts, and the Oxford edition depends on P. Many variations in the text seem to be arbitrary revisions that are attempts to correct the metrical scheme.

        Pitra edited this kontakion, *A.S.*, I, xvi, 116–24. Tomadakis includes it in his series, and the editor is N. Livadaras, II, #22, 173–201.

        It occurs in the French edition, IV, 202–32. The introduction makes the point that rigorous exactitude in diacritical marks would have been necessary for singers; this does not seem to have been the case with this hymn whose heirmoi fell into disuse.

Tone: ἦχος γ'

Acrostic: Εἰς τὸ πάθος ψαλμὸς ʿΡωμανοῦ

Refrain: Ἵνα χορεύῃ Ἀδάμ [or] μόνος χορεύῃ Ἀδάμ

Ephymium (added, P):   Ἀδάμ ὅτι σώζεται

Biblical source and place in the liturgy: This kontakion was intended for Good Friday. Its narrative includes the events immediately after Christ's arrest, but the main emphasis is on the actual legal procedure and the guilt of Pilate and the Jews. The material is drawn from the accounts in Matthew (xxvii), Mark (xv), and Luke (xxiii). The material is not so much concerned with a specific incident, such as the denial of Peter or even the feelings of Mary at the cross, but it is in the human setting of the courtroom, and it presents a refutation of any possible justice in the legal process by which Christ was put to death. The source of the dialogue in court is in *The Apocryphal New Testament*, *Acta Pilati*, Part I, sections I–V, "Memorials of our Lord Jesus Christ done in the time of Pontius Pilate."

Analysis of content: Both prooimia connect the crucifixion and Christ's suffering with the redemption of Adam. Frequently the refrain makes no direct sense with the last lines of the strophe. Strophes 1 and 2 express horror at the crucifixion but connect it with man's redemption. Strophes 3 through 13, the heart of the kontakion, give the scene at the court of Caiaphas with the accusations of the crowd that Christ's crime is His breaking of the Sabbath, and His answer to them that preserving the

Sabbath had never healed man nor restored him to new life. Strophe 13 introduces the flogging and Pilate's wife, and in 14 plays on the word *pillar* bring us to Strophes 15 through 17, in which Pilate "washes his hands" of all guilt. *But guilt is fixed on the Jews and their descendants.* Three strophes then present Christ and His power to quench man's thirst, and theological reiteration of the two natures of Christ by the device of references to Isaac and Jonah as archetypes. The last three strophes return to the scene of the crucifixion, the reasons for Christ's suffering, and a closing exhortation to praise Him.

Connection with homily: Two sermons of Ephrem contain similar phrases and accusations made against Christ.[1] It is also true in both the sermons of Ephrem and in the kontakion of Romanos that, although Christ does not answer Pilate, He does speak to the Jews to explain his desire to obey a higher law than mere observance of the Sabbath.[2] In Strophe 14 the rhetorical antitheses in which the One who established the foundations of the earth is stretched out on the column to be flogged may reflect Ephrem.[3] Since this hymn would directly follow the kontakion On Peter's Denial, and since that poem[4] also shows possible influence of Ephrem, the conclusion becomes more probable that the homilies of the Syrian were known to Romanos when he wrote On the Passion of Christ.

Style of Romanos: The biblical allusions, especially in the connection between Isaac, Jonah, and Christ, are typical, as are the departures from the narrative of the Gospels with insertion of dialogue to give vitality to the situation. Whether the dialogue be original or inspired by the Acta Pilati and Ephrem, it remains characteristic of Romanos. Added to these marks of identity, the condemnation of the Jews in vitriolic fashion reveals the poet. Typical antitheses pile up when he reflects on the horror of having the Creator and Redeemer and Physician condemned by Pilate, the judge who will be judged. Plays on words abound, for example, the use of ἡ πλεύρα for Eve and also for the side of Christ; the "pillar of fire" and "attached to the pillar."

Meter: The metrical scheme is given in the Oxford edition, 526, XIX.

1. Sermo V and Sermo VI, as translated by Lamy, *Sancti Ephraemi Syri Hymni et Sermones* I (Louvain, 1882), col. 429–49 and 449–523.
2. The Latin translation has the accusers say: "Moyses legem docuit qua sabbatum pie observandum est, et tu insurrexisti in Moysem solvens sabbatum et legem." Sermo V, col. 439.
3. A translation of part of the sixth sermon reveals this: "Heaven and earth are amazed as they see ... the One who stretched the sky above the earth and established the foundations of mountains ... flogged by criminals above the rock created at His nod. He embraced the column of judgment, He who supports and sustains Heaven and earth. ..."
4. Compare with On Peter's Denial (O. 18), Strophe 12, where the question is raised as to whether Peter could be forgiven.

ON THE PASSION OF CHRIST

O. 20

Prooimion I: Today the foundations of the earth were shaken;

       The sun, not bearing to behold it, was altered,[1]

   For the Giver of all life was stretched on a cross.

       Paradise has been opened up after the ancient transgression.[2]

       Adam alone exults.

Prooimion II: The tyranny of enmity[3] has been destroyed; the tears of Eve are dried

       Because of Thy suffering, O Christ, God, Lover of men.

   For through it, the dead are resurrected;

       In it, the thief finds a refuge.

       Adam alone exults.[4]

Strophe 1:   O Heaven, be struck with horror; earth be plunged into chaos;

       Do not dare, Sun, to behold

       Your master on the cross, hanging there of His own will,

   Let rocks be shattered, for the rock of life

                     is now wounded by nails;[5]

       Let the veil of the temple be rent

       Since the body of the master has been pierced with a spear

          by the lawless.[6]

   In fact, let all Creation shudder and groan at the passion of the Creator.

       Adam alone exults.

Strophe 2:[7] Thou hast taken away my nature, in order that I might assume thine;

       Thou hast revealed the Passion, in order that I now

       Shall despise passions; through Thy death, I am made to live again.

---

1. Matt. xxvii.45; Mark xv.33; Luke xxiii.44.

2. It is possible that the last phrase goes with the refrain and conveys the idea that Adam rejoices to have the original sin redeemed. This would be indicated by the punctuation in the French edition, IV, 202. If the punctuation of the Oxford edition is to be followed, then the meaning requires some such preposition as "after."

3. God declares after the original sin that He will put enmity (ἔχθραν) between Eve and the serpent. Hence, this line in Romanos probably indicates that the devil can no longer be a tyrant over the descendants of Eve.

4. The refrain makes no sense in this prooimion.

5. I Cor. x.4.

6. John xix.34.

7. In the acrostic we have an iota for the initial letter. However, ει is frequently the equivalent. *Acros.*, 652–55.

Thou wast placed in the tomb, and for this dwelling place, Thou hast
given me the gift of Paradise.
By descending to the depths, Thou hast exalted me.
In breaking down the gates of Hades,[8] Thou hast opened
for me the gates of Heaven.
Clearly Thou hast undergone all things for the sake of the fallen;
Thou hast endured all,
That Adam might exult.

Strophe 3:   The lawless have seized Thee, who dost control in Thy hand
The whole globe of the earth; now they have led Thee,
Who art not to be contained in the universe, into the
court of Caiaphas.[9]
And when those who are blind in spirit saw Thee, at once they
cried out, raving:
"The one who scorns the law of Moses is here;[10]
Whoever honors Moses and respects the law, let him show his zeal;
Let no one be slack; for the deceiver has come to suffer, as He has said,
In order that Adam might exult."

Strophe 4:   When the people cried out in this way, the priest said:
"Was it not formerly well said,[11] 'It is better
That this man alone be destroyed than that the whole race perish'?"
Who has seen an asp producing sweet honey instead of poison?
Who has observed a flame which forms dew?[12]
Who has heard of a truthful deceit like Caiaphas?
Though he does not wish to, he prophesies when he says that
Thou dost die for all, my Savior,
In order that Adam might exult.

8. Ps. cvii.16.

9. Matt. xxvi.57–58; Mark xiv.53–54; Luke xxii.54–55; John xviii.24. The kontakion On Peter's Denial treats the scene in the court of Caiaphas, but the center of interest is, of course, Peter in O. 18 (K. 18).

10. Christ is accused of blasphemy in curing the man with palsy (Matt. ix.3; Mark ii.7; Luke v.21). He is not accused in the trial before Caiaphas of scorning the law of Moses, but of proclaiming Himself the Son of God (Matt. xxvi.65; John x.33). See note 28. When Stephen is tried, false witnesses are brought in to accuse him of blasphemy, and the destruction of the customs of Moses is used as a basis for the accusations. Acts vi.11–15.

11. John xi.50. Romanos omits ὑπὲρ τοῦ λαοῦ ("for the people"). The editor of the *Fr. ed.*, IV, 209n1, comments that other ecclesiastical writers also omit this phrase, which may have been added later to John's Gospel. In John xviii.14, Caiaphas does use the phrase when he "counseled the Jews that it was expedient that one man die 'for the people.'"

12. The prevalence of this juxtaposition of fire and moisture is common in Romanos: O. 1, Strophe 13; O. 46, Strophe 21.

Strophe 10: "The Sabbath did not terrify Hades; sickness did not flee from it;

CHRIST   It did not heal the sick; no one but I do that,

     I, the Master of the Sabbath,[30] I the crucified;

For the blind man kept many Sabbaths; yet he was

                        bound fast in darkness.[31]

     Probably the paralytic honored many Sabbaths

     Throughout his former thirty-eight years;[32]

However, he was not rescued, he was not wholly cured until I came

     That Adam might exult.

Strophe 11: "You have heard the censure of people dwelling near you, saying

CHRIST   That you keep the Sabbath and still you are sick;

     For the Gentiles said: 'Where is their God?[33]

Let the One honored by them through the law drive away

     sickness from them.'[34]

     Saying things like this, your enemies

     Sneered at you, slandering you and deriding you;

But I, by saving all even on the Sabbath, have furnished glory

     That Adam might exult.

Strophe 12: "I seemed unjust in judging the repentant harlot,[35]

CHRIST   When she held my feet as masters of chastity, and showed a

     beautiful faith in me,

As she drenched with tears of love my feet which the waves

     of the sea had not wet

     And anointed with perfume the head

     Which the Forerunner had feared to touch before he

     was commanded to.[36]

He foretold the things which I now endure and suffer voluntarily

     That Adam might exult."

---

30. Matt. xii.8; Mark ii.28; Luke vi.5.

31. John ix.14.

32. John v.9–10. The sarcastic use of πολλάκις, "no doubt," "perhaps," occurs also in O. 29 (K. 20) Resurrection VI in the second strophe, where it seems to mean "most certainly."

33. Ps. lxxix.10; Joel ii.17.

34. Promises made to the faithful as a covenant included freedom from illness. Deut. vii.15.

35. The law for punishing a harlot required that she be put to death. Lev. xx.10. The story of the harlot is used by Romanos as a basis for Kontakion #10. Luke vii.36–38; Matt. xxvi.7–13; Mark xiv.3–8; John xii.7. Two scenes are really compressed into one: the anointing at Bethany, and the story of the harlot.

36. Matt. iii.14. Romanos treats this idea at length in the kontakion On the Baptism of Christ (O. 5, K. 4).

Strophe 13:   The savage people, thirsty for blood,[37] heard Jesus as He said these things
        And like a lion they roared[38] to seize the life of the lamb, Christ.
        Pilate, fulfilling their will, flogged Thee, the gentle One.[39]
    So he set to work on Thy back,
        But Thou, testing his wife,[40] showed Thy strength,
        For his wife cried out and said: "You are judging your judge,"
        That Adam might exult.

Strophe 14:   The Redeemer endured the lash; the Deliverer was in chains;
        Nude and stretched out on a pillar,[41]
        Is He who in a pillar of cloud formerly spoke to Moses and Aaron.[42]
    He who established the pillars of the earth, as David said,[43]
        is fastened to a pillar.
    He who showed the people the road in the desert,
        (For the pillar of fire appeared before them),[44] He has been
        attached to a pillar;
    The rock is on a column and the church is hewn in stone for me,[45]
        That Adam might exult.

Strophe 15:   And so, having lashed the Physician, Pilate washed his hands.[46]
        As for him, he thought that by this
        He would be held guiltless; but he was found to be responsible;
    For, having had Him flogged, he handed Him over to the cross
        and said, "I am innocent."
        Who at any time ever heard of a murderer saying
        To his knife: "Since I slay through you, I shall not
        suffer punishment?"
    Using the sword of the lawless, Pilate sacrificed the Creator,
        In order that Adam might exult.

37. It would seem simpler to have *thirsty for blood* as an adjective. No ms. authority is cited by Trypanis for the use of the adverb, αἱμοβορῶς.

38. The verb ὡρυάμαι is not given in dictionaries. Compare with the verb βυέω in Lazarus II (O. 15), and footnote 1 to Strophe 11.

39. Matt. xxvii.26; Mark xv.15; John xix.1.

40. Since Eve was created from Adam's side, she is referred to as τὴν πλευράν. The phrase is used in Ps. cxxviii.3. For Pilate's wife's warning, see Matt. xxvii.19.

41. The column or pillar on which Christ was stretched (horizontally and not upright) to be flogged is mentioned in the fourth century by Egeria (*Itinerarium Egeriae*, 37) and also by St. Jerome in one of his letters (Epistolae, 108) as at the house of Caiaphas. It is, however, supposed to be in Rome. The French edition refers to it as in the chapel of St. Zenon (IV, 221*n*2).

42. Ex. xxxiii.8–11.

43. David did not use this phrase; it does occur in Ps. lxxv.3, a song of Asaph.

44. Ex. xiii.21; Num. ix.14–22.

45. See the introduction to this kontakion for the parallel passage in Ephrem.

46. Matt. xxvii.24.

Strophe 16: "Crucify!", the murderer heard the impious cry out,[47]
      And he fulfilled their will,[48]
      Handing over, without being compelled to, the One whom
          he wished to be crucified.[49]
For having heard that he would be the enemy of Caesar,
      the coward was frightened;
      He wished to be the enemy of the Almighty[50]
      Rather than the enemy of Caesar, preferring his life to Life.
He will certainly not be blameless, since in answer to the lawless,
      he killed the Living One,
         In order that Adam might exult.

Strophe 17: Throwing the blame back on them, he killed Christ because of them,[51]
      For he found in them ministers who said:
      "His blood will be on them and their children."
For their sons, not yet born, the fathers have prepared
                    the garment of the curse;[52]
      They have added to their wound a wound for their children,
      Drawing the punishment for their sins on their descendants
         on into eternity.
But we, in taking the blood of the Savior, have found a ransom
         That Adam might exult.

Strophe 18: Earth-born man was destroyed by thirst,[53] consumed by burning heat,
      Wandering in the desert, the region without water,
      Wretched man did not find a way to quench his thirst.
Therefore, my Savior, Fountain of blessings, has caused to gush forth
        springs of life,
      As He says: "You have become thirsty through Eve[54]
      Drink, then, from my side and you will never thirst.[55]

47. John xix.6.
48. Luke xxiii.25.
49. John xix.12.
50. *Pantokrator* as an epithet for Christ is, of course, preserved in Byzantine art, notably at Daphni.
51. Matt. xxvii.24–26.
52. Romanos wishes to make clear that the Jews had brought on themselves this curse on their race over and above the words of Matt. xxvii.25. "The garment of the curse," Ps. cix.18.
53. The word has the connotations of primitive man before the Garden of Eden, and also after the curse on Adam. Adam's thirst is mentioned in the first strophe of Nativity I. See Gen. ii.5; Ezek. vi.14.
54. Again, the reference to Eve as "the side"; here, a literal translation would serve to emphasize the play on words that results when Christ's pierced side is immediately mentioned.
55. John iv.14; vii.37.

Twofold is the stream: it gives a drink and offers a bath
  to those who are foul,
    In order that Adam might exult."

Strophe 19: Let no one say that the side of Christ was merely human,
  For Christ was God and man;
    He was not divided in two; He was one from one Father;
He was the same One who suffered and did not suffer;
                    the same who died and was not lifeless;
    For He was alive in His divinity and dead in His body.
    His archetype was father Isaac on the mountain,[56]
For he was sacrificed in the ram and was brought back alive,
  as my Savior,
    That Adam might exult.

Strophe 20: Another archetype of Jesus was the prophet
  Jonah in the belly of the whale;[57]
    He was swallowed, he was not digested, just as the Lord
      in the tomb,
Jonah came forth from the monster after three days,
                    just as Christ from the tomb;
    The former saved Nineveh by his prophecy;[58]
    Christ has redeemed the earth and all creation;
He came to fulfill all the things announced to us by the prophets,
    In order that Adam might exult.

Strophe 21: Securing victory for the humble, and wearing on His shoulders
  The cross as trophy of victory,[59]
    He came forth to be crucified and to crucify the one who
      has wounded us.
Having paid all the debt which we owe, He even hastened to death.
    He made subject to the cudgel the face[60]

56. The reference is, of course, to the sacrifice of Isaac; Gen. xxii.1–15. Compare also Kontakion 41 (K. 65), Strophe 23.
57. Jonah ii.1; Matt. xii.39–40.
58. Jonah iii; Matt. xii.41; Luke xi.30.
59. The literal translation "judgment of a trophy" would not make the meaning clear. He "came forth" means first of all that He left the court of Caiaphas, and it also connotes His departure from the bosom of His Father.
60. John xix.3.

Which Cherubim dare not behold;[61] before which they
    hide their eyes;
Despising the shame,[62] He voluntarily put on the mantle of derision,[63]
    In order that Adam might exult.

Strophe 22:   They offered vinegar[64] to the fountain of sweet waters
    And they have given gall to the One[65]
    Who rains down manna[66] and causes a stream to flow
      from the rock;[67]
When beaten on the head with a reed,[68] He signed the exile
    of His enemies.
    Stretched naked on the cross, He deprived
    His enemies of life, making of them a laughingstock both for
      the living and the dead.
He was taken down from the cross, wrapped in a linen cloth,
    given over to the tomb,[69]
      In order that Adam might exult.

Strophe 23:   Sing hymns to Him, O earth-born; praise the One who suffered
    And died for you, and when in a short time
    You behold Him living, receive Him in your hearts;
For Christ is going to be resurrected from the tomb
          and He will make you new, O man,
    Make ready for Him a pure heart
    In order that your King will dwell in it, making a Heaven.
Only a short time now, and He will come to fill[70] with joy
    those who are afflicted,
      In order that Adam might exult.

61. Isa. vi.2.
62. Heb. xii.2.
63. Ps. cix.29; Matt. xxvii.28; Mark xv.17; John xix.2.
64. Matt. xxvii.34, 48; Mark xv.36; John xix.29.
65. Ps. lxix.21.
66. Ex. xvi.14–15.
67. Ex. xvii.6; Num. xx.10.
68. κάλαμος is used for the cudgel and also for the reed with which the decrees of exile are signed.
Matt. xxvii.30.
69. Matt. xxvii.59–60; Mark xv.46; Luke xxiii.53; John xix.36–42.
70. Heb. x.37.

ON THE CRUCIFIXION

O. 21 (K. 67)

Title: No title is given in manuscripts. Krumbacher calls it "Penitential Hymn" (*Acros.*, 581).

Manuscripts and editions: P contains the entire kontakion; A and P have the prooimion and the first strophe.

        It is closely connected with the Great Kanon of Andreas of Crete, where it serves as the kontakion. In fact, he paraphrased the prooimion in his own fourth ode. It appears in the *Triodion* for the Thursday of the fifth week of Easter.

        E. Mioni edits it, *Romano il Melode*, 153–61. He calls it "The Infernal Powers."

        Tomadakis, I, 17–36, calls it by the title in the acrostic.

        French edition, IV, 243–61. The same title as Mioni used.

Tone: πλάγιος β′

Acrostic: τοῦ ταπεινοῦ ʿΡωμανοῦ αἶνος

Refrain: ὁ πανταχοῦ τὰ πάντα πληρῶν

Biblical source and place in the liturgy: The source is a favorite of Romanos; namely, *The Gospel of Nicodemus* in the New Testament Apocrypha. The account of the Descent to Hell and the ensuing dialogue between Death and the Devil is probably Syrian in origin.

        The Patmos' manuscript indicates that it was to be used on the fifth day of the fifth week of Lent. It also became the kontakion for the Great Kanon of Andreas of Crete.

Analysis of content: Three introductory strophes give the setting. The devil is disturbed at the time of the crucifixion; he reviews miracles of Christ and laments. For three strophes his henchmen try to cheer him up by mentioning Cain and Abel and suggesting that Judas and Caiaphas can now be used and that he has in the past destroyed people by fire and flood. In an answering two strophes the devil expresses pleasure and announces that he will go directly to the Jews. In the following four strophes we have the exchange between the devil and the Jews; they brag about what they have accomplished, the devil reviews the past treachery of the Jews, and he compliments them on following only the letter of the law. Next, the devil goes to Death, who is distressed and not encouraged; the devil sneers at Death's loss of confidence since he lost Lazarus and others. Death, in reply, reminds the devil of the number of Christ's miracles that involved the removal of devils, but the devil says that he would be ashamed to withdraw and that Bethlehem has always opposed him. Death reminds himself and the devil that he is powerless, since, if Christ wills to die, He will do it. The Jews brag that Christ is on the cross, but Death is depressed when he hears Christ's promise to the penitent robber. The devil admits that he is undone, and the poem closes with the final prayer and its allusions to the fact that Christ's limbs were not broken and its theological emphasis that He willed His own death.

Connection with homily: Eusebius of Alexandria has two homilies (the first and the third) that deal with the plot of the rulers of the infernal regions and the Jews. The role of demons or devils in introduced by Romanos as indicating that their activity was not curbed until Christ came, although Paul suggests that it ended with Moses.[1] La Piana believes that the homily (pseudo-Eusebius) came before the apocrypha;[2] but later students suspect that Eusebius' sermons date in the sixth century and that he was really a Syrian.[3] The first of the so-called Eusebius' homilies is on the arrival of John the Baptist in Hades, and it includes expressions by the various prophets who hear with joy the news of John the Baptist, followed by the discussion between Satan and Hades of the help to come from the Jews.[4] The third sermon is entitled "On the Devil in Hades," and in it Satan complains of the successes of Christ and boasts that he will struggle alone if Hades refuses to join him. He states his plan to secure the aid of the Jews.[5] A fourth sermon deals with the entrance of Christ into Hades to free the prophets. A fifth sermon is on the same subject. The first and third sermons serve Romanos—he serves them—in the case of the kontakia on the Passion: 20, 21, 22. The theme of the harrowing of Hell became popular in the West, and Romanos includes it in some of the Resurrection kontakia.

Style of Romanos: The choice of subject is very typical, but the treatment of the dramatic confrontation of Satan and Death does not have the vigor and validity of On the Victory of the Cross (#22). In the latter, the episode of the robber is developed with more force. It is possible that Kontakion #22 was written later and that Romanos is just making a summary of his previous account. It is possible also that some stanza or lines are omitted that would have introduced the comparison of the cross and the simander, which appears suddenly in Strophe 20. The development of the idea that the Jews could help Satan by adhering to the letter rather than to the spirit of the law is rounded out with more effect; the whole attack on the Jews is typical.

Meter: The metrical scheme is given in the Oxford edition, 526, XX.

1. "Nevertheless death reigned from Adam to Moses . . .," Rom. v.14.
2. *Le Rappr.*, 84.
3. Eusebius of Alexandria probably never existed, and his homilies are possibly the work of his biographer, John the Notary. See H. G. Beck, *Kirche und theologische Literatur im byzantinischen Reich* (Munich, 1959), 400, and see F. Nau, "Notes sur diverses homélies pseudépigraphiques," *Revue de l'Orient chrétien*, 13 (1908), 433–34.
4. *P.G.*, 86, 509–26.
5. *P.G.*, 86, 384–406.

ON THE CRUCIFIXION

O. 21

Prooimion: O my soul, my soul, awake! Why do you sleep?
              The end draws near, and you will be troubled.
      Then come to your senses in order that
              Christ, God, may spare you,
                    He who is everywhere and fills all things.[1]

Strophe 1:   As he saw the surgery of Christ[2] disclosed
              And health gushing forth from Him for Adam,
      The devil suffered, was wounded;
      And as one in danger, he lamented
              And cried to his friends:
DEVIL   "What shall I do to the son of Mary?
              The man from Bethlehem is killing me
                    He who is everywhere and fills all things.

Strophe 2:   "The whole world is filled with His healings;
DEVIL   But I suffer within, especially as I hear
      That men have been cured as a free gift.
      One man put aside his leprosy;[3]
              Another recovered his eyesight;[4]
      Still another taking his bed on his
              Shoulders, danced as he cried:[5] 'He raised me,
                    He who is everywhere and fills all things.'

Strophe 3:   "Then, friends of the storm, enemies of calm,
DEVIL   What do you advise me to do to this man?
      Give consideration to my purpose;

1. Eph. iv.10. This is appropriate in that it recalls Ps. lxviii.18, with reference to "Thou hast ascended on high and Thou hast led captivity captive; Thou hast received gifts for men." Christ as fulfilling all things is the theme and refrain.
2. Christ is the surgeon in Kontakion #19, On Mary at the Cross, in the extended figure of speech in Strophe 13.
3. Matt. viii.3; Mark i.41; Luke v.12; Kontakion 8 (K. 78).
4. Matt. ix.27–30; xii.22; xx.30; Mark viii.22; x.46–52; Luke vii.21; John ix.1–8.
5. Matt. ix.2–6.

For indeed I am frustrated, I am ruined;
    I have no plan, for I am without power,
I am panic-stricken; my mind has become darkened;
    Suddenly He has amazed me,
        He who is everywhere and fills all things."

Strophe 4:   When the Deceiver said this to his own men,
DEVILS   At once he heard from them: "Belial, do not fear,
Take courage and be strong in mind;
Remember your first labors;
    Renew the victories of Paradise;
If you are again united with Cain's group,
    He will be destroyed by trickery, like Abel,
        He who is everywhere and fills all things.

Strophe 5:   "Even now there are in the world descendants of the murderer.
DEVILS   Priests, and scribes, a Judas, and a Caiaphas;
Why do you regard yourself lightly as though entirely defenseless?
Herod is your ardent friend,
    And Pilate serves you even more.
Since you find your former servants,
    Do not mourn, crying: 'He has destroyed me,
        He who is everywhere and fills all things.'

Strophe 6:   "The whole universe is full of your many exploits;
DEVILS   From generation to generation your power is reported—
How is it then that you wear yourself out with distress?
There are those whom you have washed away in floods;
    And those burned to death know you;[6]
Just as all have tasted your works,
    He, too, will enjoy them,
        He who is everywhere and fills all things."

Strophe 7:   As soon as he heard these words, the devil was pleased,
DEVIL   And rejoicing, he said to his men: "Friends,
I am delighted that you strengthened me in my plans;

6. Does he refer to the flood and Sodom and Gomorrah? The kontakion On the Man Possessed with Devils (O. 11, K. 81) uses Mark ix.17, and Luke ix.39, with references to the fact that the devil possessing the man caused him to throw himself in the fire or in water.

With the result that I advance with confidence
  And unite with the Jews,
In order that, when I have attached them to my purposes,
  I may teach them to cry out: 'Let Him be crucified,[7]
    The One who is everywhere and fills all things.'

Strophe 8:   "Behold, I see the Sanhedrin of the Jews
DEVIL   Arguing with each other without pause.
Do they, perhaps, want what I am planning?[8]
Approaching, then, I shall say: 'Courage,
  Since you anticipate my plan,
Since, then, you are very zealous,
  What do you now say that He be made to suffer,
    He who is everywhere and fills all things?'"

Strophe 9:   Night unto night showeth knowledge as tribute of darkness;[9]
        The Jews reveal their plots to Satan,
JEWS   Saying: "Put aside your anxiety,
We have accomplished what you had in mind to do;
  Have no care; rest unconcerned;
Jesus has been denied and handed over,
  He has been bound and given to Pilate,
    The One who is everywhere and fills all things."

Strophe 10: "O Jews, I have not come as one making sure you are not careless,
DEVIL   For indeed I know your zeal in matters of this kind,
I remember the first thing you accomplished,
How, after eating the manna, you denied [Him]
  And, after drinking the milk, you cheated,
You who put the calf before God in honor;[10]
  What do you wish in order that you may cause to suffer
    The One who is everywhere and fills all things?

7. Matt. xxvii.23.
8. The conference might be the one with Judas (Matt. xxvi.1–16) or the one with the Pharisees (John xi.45–53). Probably the poet is speaking in general, without regard to the sequence of events.
9. A quotation from Ps. xix.2.
10. After God "rained down bread" for the Israelites (Ex. xvi.1–5), they built a golden calf to worship (Ex. xxxii.1–7). The "land flowing with milk and honey" is mentioned when God tells Moses that the people will break His covenant (Deut. xxxi.20). Paul refers to the milk of spiritual teaching: I Cor. iii.2; Heb. v.12.

Strophe 11: "I shall speak in your defense before my henchmen,

DEVIL   Saying that you are ours in your entire purpose.

You only give lip service to hating me,[11]

And I rejoice in this pretense,

   For you catch many men in this way,

Since I am hated in words,

   While He indeed is hated in works,

      He who is everywhere and fills all things.

Strophe 12: "I see that you have regard for the letter of the law of Moses;

DEVIL   But you are not bound in these matters by the inner spirit;

Carry the law about with you on your tongue, not in your thought.

Lift up the books in your hands;

   But do not even touch them lightly with your heart.

Let Him call you and consider you, as people

   Reading the Scriptures, but not understanding them,

      He who is everywhere and fills all things."

Strophe 13: When the Deceiver confirmed the lawless with these words,

   And established their foundations in sand,[12]

He ran to jolt Death also;

DEVIL   Coming up to him he said, "Arise,

   And rejoice in what I am going to tell you:

Jesus has been denied and handed over;

   He has been bound and given to Pilate—

      He who is everywhere and fills all things."

Strophe 14: "You say this to me with a great deal of pleasure, devil,

DEATH   As for me, merely on seeing this, I was filled with distress

As I considered with fear the things to come afterwards,

For the One who was silent when being judged,

   Has me terrified in being buried.

If He has said nothing to Pilate,[13]

   He makes haste to upset the kingdom below,

      He who is everywhere and fills all things."

11. Ps. lxxviii.36.

12. Matt. vii.24–27; Luke vi.47–49. The Jews have heard the word of God and reject it; hence, "they build their house upon sand."

13. Matt. xxvii.14; Mark xv.4–5.

Strophe 15: Hearing this, the devil was filled with laughter
              And answered Death as though looking at a coward:
DEVIL   "Now I know that you are languid and wretched
              Since the [raising] of Lazarus,
                 And since being deprived of all the others,[14]
              I know that you tremble at the word, Jesus,
                 And that He considers you a useless servant,
                    He who is everywhere and fills all things."

Strophe 16: "Now you are speaking in order to shame me. As for what
DEATH   you say, O devil,
                 I know that you are more fearful and I tremble,
              For I know that you are distressed and trembling;
              For has He not driven you away from the tomb?[15]
                 Has He not driven you from the woman of Canaan?[16]
              And after that, He caused you to give up possession
                 Of the deaf-mute,[17]
                    He who is everywhere and fills all things."

Strophe 17: "I am not ignorant of what you say. I know, although it
DEVIL   is beyond reason,[18]
                 That Christ is not to be conquered, though He is in a nature
                    which is humble.[19]
              However, I do not withdraw from the contest
              For I have entered the sanded arena;
                 If I flee, I am put to shame.
              Let the neck of the Jews be strong and manly;
                 Their hearts were not pricked of old nor are they now[20]
                    By Him who is everywhere and fills all things.

14. Lazarus: John xi.1–46; Romanos #14, #15. The others: son of the widow of Nain (Luke vii.11–17); daughter of Jairus (Matt. ix.18; Mark v.22; Luke viii.41).
15. The man possessed with devils was living in tombs (Matt. viii.28; Mark v.3; Luke viii.27); Romanos, Kontakion #11 (K. 81).
16. Woman of Canaan whose daughter was healed. Matt. xv.22–28; Mark vii.24–30.
17. The devil cast out in Luke xi.14, was dumb (Matt. ix.32–33); a similar incident is in Matt. xii.22. Another such story of the devil "with a dumb and deaf spirit" is in Mark ix.14–29.
18. It makes the idea clearer to use καί as *although*. However this translation of the intensive is more common with participles or adjectives.
19. "Though" is added in the translation to make clear the poet's intention of setting in contrast the devil's realization that Christ is not to be conquered, although He appears in inferior or humble human form. I can see no justification for the translation in the *Fr. ed.*, IV, 255, "qu'abaisse la defaite."
20. The text is very corrupt; the connection with the refrain is not clear, and the word before the refrain is missing. I am adopting the conjecture of the Oxford text and translating a bit freely to

Strophe 18: "I am, then, going up to these men who dare all things,
DEVIL   And, wearing their audacity as a breastplate,
I shall range in battle against the Man from Bethlehem.
Always Bethlehem is opposed to me,
    Its children always hinder me,
For it is from there that David and his descendant
    Fled and banished me,[21]
        He who is everywhere and fills all things."

Strophe 19: As the hateful one withdrew from those who were inferior,
    Death raised his voice and spoke:
DEATH   "Just see what you are doing, ever-wily one,
And do not attach yourself to me, Death;
    For I do not associate with you in your daring.
If He gives a nod towards me, I draw near the cross;
    If He does not will it, He will not die,
        He who is everywhere and fills all things."

Strophe 20: The serpent, seeing this and seeing the fear of Death,
    Approached the Jews and found what he was seeking,
For they seized him by the hand and flattered him,
JEWS   Crying out: "Come and behold
    The One who has been disturbing you and the world.
After gross insults, after many lashings,
    He is stretched out on the wood like a simander[22]
        He who is everywhere and fills all things."

Strophe 21: "If you learn another piece of news, you have further occasion to laugh:
DEVIL   One of the robbers justly crucified with Him,
Cries out to Him: 'Remember me, Lord'."[23]

---

make sense. If οἱ refers to the Jews, it is not too violent a change to start with "their" rather than the relative pronoun. The "neck" is used instead of the heart presumably because of the implications in "the sanded arena"; and also because of the frequent use of "the stiff necked" in the Bible as referring to those who resist. The verb κατηνύησαν is used in Acts II when the disciples were pricked in their hearts; and it has relevance in Ps. lxxiii.21.

21. David was driven from *Jerusalem* after Absalom's conspiracy (II Sam. xv.13–15). When David wanted to drink from the well at Bethlehem, he was prevented (II Sam. xxiii.14–17). See Nativity I, Strophe 1. Christ, of course, was driven forth by Herod.

22. The French edition suggests that σάλπιγξ may refer to the simander whose song puts to flight the soldiers of Christ. Also, it is compared to the nails of the cross. See the references quoted, Vol. IV, note 1, 258–59.

23. Luke xxiii.42. The devil is dismayed by these same words in the kontakion On the Victory of the Cross (O. 22, K. 9), Strophe 9.

But hearing this, Death became sad,
  He turned his head and cried:
DEATH "If He chooses pupils on the cross,
   In the tomb He will establish educators![24]
    He who is everywhere and fills all things."

Strophe 22: "Then Jesus has not been injured at all from His suffering;
DEVIL   And I, more than He, have increased my groans.
  O Death, you were right in not agreeing with me;
  You will do better if you have forbearance with me,
   And take me down below and educate me;
  For I cannot endure so much shame
   Which He has brought on me through the wood,
    He who is everywhere and fills all things."

Strophe 23: O Savior of all men, especially of those who have faith,
   Because Thou wast crucified of Thy own will, and wast
    put to death voluntarily,
  The lawless say not of their will
  Were the limbs of the robbers broken;[25]
   But Thine, they did not break, in order that they might learn
  That Thou didst not come among the dead against Thy will,
   But willingly Thou didst give up Thy spirit,
    Thou who art everywhere and fillest all things.[26]

24. This bit of irony and hyperbole does not have to be attached specifically either to the saints or the prophets. The editor of *Fr. ed.*, IV, 260*n*1, raises this question.
25. John xix.32–33.
26. Matt. xxvii.50.

ON THE VICTORY OF THE CROSS

O. 22 (K. 9)

Title: κοντάκιον σταυρώσιμον

Manuscripts and editions: The first prooimion and the eighteen strophes are in A, M, P, and Δ. The second and third prooimia are in Δ. B and D have some of the first strophes.

This is one of the four kontakia that have three prooimia, and it is significant that the more Western manuscripts include the second and third.

Pitra first edited this, *A.S.*, I, viii, 53–64.

Tomadakis, IV, 297–331.

Fr. ed., IV, 282–311.[1]

Tone: ἦχος βαρύς

Acrostic: τοῦ ταπεινοῦ ῾Ρωμανοῦ

Refrain: πάλιν εἰς τὸν παράδεισον

Biblical source and place in the liturgy: The dramatic dialogue between Hades and Satan occurs in the *Acta Pilati*, Part II (or Gospel of Nicodemus).[2] The poet really continues the ideas in the dialogue of Kontakion #21, in which Satan plots the crucifixion with the Jews. It is an interesting departure on the part of the poet that he does not include the arrival of John the Baptist in Hades. The various names by which Satan is called and the combination of speakers in the Resurrection kontakia of Romanos are summarized in the comparison of his various hymns on the subject.

Duchesne[3] tells us that on Good Friday, it was customary in various places to celebrate the Adoration of the Cross in the seventh and eighth centuries. Did Romanos, then, compose this kontakion for such a celebration in the sixth century? Several manuscripts indicate its use for Wednesday of the fourth week of

---

1. The editor lists two other editions that were not available to me: *Amfilochij*, 142–43 (Prooimion I and Strophe 1); S. Eustratiadis, ᾿Απόστολος βαρναβᾶς (1934), 83–94.

2. M. R. James, *The Apocryphal New Testament*, discusses the various versions of Part II, "The Descent into Hell," 118, 95. Part II is later than Part I, which probably dates in the fourth century. Homilies attributed to Eusebius of Emesa have dialogues similar to those in *Acta Pilati*, and they may have preceded it. The dialogue is in Sections XX–XXII of Part II of *Acta Pilati*, James (Oxford, 1926), 117–19.

3. Duchesne, *Origines du culte chrétien* (Paris, 1902), 248. The editor of the French edition has a discussion of the various possibilities, including the connection it may have had with the Elevation of the Cross on September 14 (*Fr. ed.*, IV, 263–65).

Lent. Mss. A, B, D, M, and P mark it for the fourth day in the middle of the fast. T marks it for the Sabbath of worship of the cross and Δ for Good Friday.

The *Triodion* has first and fourth troparia on the third Sunday of the fast.

Analysis of content: A sprightly dialogue between Hades and Satan (the serpent) develops. Hades is in despair, and Satan tries to cheer him up by insisting that he planned the crucifixion and that it will be a gain for them. In alternating Strophes 1 through 12, Satan boasts and Hades despairs. In Strophes 11 and 12, Satan admits defeat and they lament together that they have lost control of the dead. Then the meaning of the crucifixion, its triumph over death and the release of Adam and all mankind is treated in Strophe 15. The central impact of the entire poem is on the Redemption. There is a great elaboration of the idea of the cross, the tree, the prototypes of the victory. In the next to the last strophe, Satan and Hades admit that they can no longer triumph over Adam's descendants, and the closing prayer takes all men "back into Paradise" by way of the cross.

Connection with homily: There are homilies that feature the dialogue between Satan and Hades and that follow the *Acta Pilati,* II (or even occur before the apocryphal gospel).[4]

1. *Eusebius of Alexandria:*
   In this, John the Baptist comes to Hades. (Eusebius was patriarch of Alexandria, and wrote in the sixth or seventh century.)[5] His sermon is entitled "On the Arrival of John the Baptist in Hades" (*P.G.,* 86, 509–26). Migne gives two versions of this sermon, and calls the author Eusebius of Emesa. This sermon by Eusebius contained a second part in which Hades is persuaded by Satan that Jesus is a mere man to be destroyed by the Jews.
2. A second sermon attributed to Eusebius contains passionate rhetoric against Judas. Hades is not on the scene. (*P.G.,* 86, 525–36.) This homily announces the topic for the next day.
3. A third sermon "On the Devil and Hades" (*P.G.,* 86, 384–406) is probably to be attributed to Eusebius of Alexandria and, along with the fourth sermon, provides the basis for the Latin "De Confusione Diaboli." Here Satan rejoices that Christ is in Gethsemane, as Satan announces his grievances against Christ who pardons sinners, heals the sick, and resurrects the dead. One point of similarity with Romanos' treatment is the scoffing that mentions the "insatiable Hades." Hades is sure he will win, and Satan says that he will fight alone.
4. A fourth homily, "On the Passion of our Lord" (*P.G.,* 62, 721–24), is central to the Descent to Hell. The devil stays on earth until the death of Christ and then descends to Hades, who tries to barricade the lower regions; Christ arrives and demands that Satan be given up. Hades abandons him; Christ breaks down the doors and the prophets emerge, reviewing their prophecies.

4. La Piana, *Le Rappr.,* 84, believes that the homily was earlier than the *Acta Pilati* II.
5. Beck, *K. Lit.,* 400–401.

The robber enters Paradise and finds Enoch and Elijah there. The fourth homily is also attributed to St. John Damascus.

5. Pseudo-Epiphanius has a homily "On the Tomb" ("On Joseph of Arimathea and the Descent of Our Lord to Hades") *P.G.*, 43, 440–64. The second part is very similar to the fourth homily of Eusebius and probably later. It suppresses the resistance of Satan and includes a flight of the demons. The interest centers on Adam, and Christ addresses Adam to inform him at what a price he is being rescued.

It is very unlikely that Romanos knew or used the last-mentioned homily. The spirit is quite different, and there is no evidence either that he used Eusebius of Alexandria, although some details are the same. Certainly there is not the same sequence in the kontakia as in the sermons where one is obviously supposed to follow the other.

A survey of all of the Resurrection kontakia may make comparisons simpler (see pages 191–92).

Style of Romanos: The very rapidly moving dialogue, with the frequent use of folk realism, is typical of Romanos. Hades is disgusted with Satan who "used to be a clever snake," and the boasting of the serpent is ironically effective. The exuberance of figurative ideas reaches a *reductio ad absurdum* at points. In Strophe 12, growth of "the wood" was rooted in the earth for our destruction "and although we grafted on it bitter branches we did not change its sweetness." That is consistent. However, the metaphors are thoroughly mixed in Strophe 17, where the cross is a treasure the robber stole. This statement follows immediately the idea given in Strophe 16 of a tree in whose branches robbers and harlots rest and gather sweetness, and then they use it as a sort of raft with which they swim to a calm harbor!

Pitra, *A.S.*, includes a note, translated as follows:

"There will scarcely be another theatre in the palaestra of the Melodist which in scene, actors, and apparatus is more outstanding than that unobserved drama carried out in Lent, when Orcus, Belial, and infernal ghosts and souls struggling in limbo, along with Christ triumphing through the cross, are aroused by the genius of Romanos."

Meter: The metrical scheme is given in the Oxford edition, 527, XXI.

ON THE VICTORY OF THE CROSS

O. 22

Prooimion I: No longer does the fiery sword[1] guard the gate of Eden

For the wood of the cross—marvelous fetter—suddenly

assaulted it.

The sting of death and the wrangling of Hades were nailed[2] to it;

But Thou, Savior, hast appeared, crying to those in Hades:

"Enter

Again into Paradise."

Prooimion II: O Christ, our God, as Thou hast truly nailed down

The ransom[3] of many in the form of the cross,

Redeem us; for as loving mankind, Thou hast snatched our spirits

From death by Thy precious blood.

Thou hast brought us with Thee

Again into Paradise.

Prooimion III: Heavenly and earthly beings rightly rejoice with Adam

That he is called

Again into Paradise.

Strophe 1: Pilate fixed three crosses on Golgotha,

Two for the robbers, and one for the Giver of life.

When Hades saw Him, he said to those below:

HADES   "O my priests and forces, who has fixed the nail in my heart?

A wooden spear has pierced me suddenly and I am torn apart.

I am in pain—internal pain; I have a bellyache;

My senses make my spirit quiver,[4]

And I am forced to vomit forth

---

1. Gen. iii.24.
2. The variant readings that would derive ἐνήλωτο from ἐνάλλομαι (*rush against* or *attack*) would not suit the meaning. The idea of nailing the "ordinances against us" to the cross is parallel with the figure Paul uses in Col. ii.14. The verb ἐνηλόω would seem preferable. Death is pilloried or publicly nailed to a pillar (στηλιτευθέντος) in Gregory of Nyssa's homily "On the Incarnation of the Word," *P.G.*, 25,144B.
3. Matt. xx.28.
4. The same phrases are used in Jer. iv.19: "τὴν κοιλίαν μου, τὴν κοιλίαν μου ἀλγῶ, καὶ τὰ αἰσθητήρια τῆς καρδίας μου μαιμάσσει ἡ ψυχή μου." The editor of the French edition points up a parallel passage in St. John Chrys., *P.G.*, 62, 748. *Fr. ed.*, IV, 287n2.

Adam and those descended from Adam, given to me by a tree.
    The tree leads them back
        Again into Paradise."

Strophe 2:   When he heard these things, the craftily scheming serpent
SNAKE   Ran crawling along and cried: "Hades, what is the matter?
        Why do you complain in vain? Why utter these groans?
    This wood which terrifies you,
        I fashioned up above for the Son of Mary.
    And I secretly revealed it to the Jews; it is useful for us
        For it is a cross on which I nailed Christ,
            Since I wished by the wood to destroy the second Adam.
    Then do not disturb yourself; he will not attack you.
        Continue to have what you control, of which we are masters;
        Not one will escape
            Again into Paradise."

Strophe 3:   "Away with you, come to your senses, Belial," cried Hades,
HADES   "Run and uncover your eyes, and see
        The root of the tree within my spirit;
    It has gone down into my vitals,
        So that like iron it will draw up Adam.
    Elisha once painted in advance its likeness
        When he raised up the axe from the river.[5]
        The prophet drew up the heavy axe with the light wood
    As an advance notice for you and teaching you
        That Adam is going to be led from his suffering,
        Led up
            Again into Paradise."

Strophe 4:   "Who, O Hades, suggested such an idea to you?[6]
SNAKE   From what source did you become terrified by the fear which
            was not fearful?[7]
        Are you afraid of worthless wood, dry and sterile,

5. II Kings vi.5–7. The symbolism as explained by Irenaeus (*Contra Hareses* V, 17, 4), is that the iron represents the word of God, which was lost through carelessness and found again through the οἰκονομίας of the wood. Another interpretation is given by Theodoretus: The divine nature descends on us and lifts up our human nature (*P.G.*, 80, 761A, as in *Fr. ed.*, IV, 291n1).
6. In the third homily of Eusebius of Alexandria (*P.G.*, 384–406), Hades explains that he drew his conclusion from the prophets and the miracles of Christ such as the raising of Lazarus.
7. Compare: Ps. (Greek) xiii.5: ἐδειλίασαν φόβῳ, οὗ οὐκ ἦν φόβος.

Made for the destruction
    Of evildoers and those who rejoice in bloodshed?
Pilate, persuaded by my advice, discovered this;
    Do you fear it and consider that it has power?
    In every way, is it not an aid for your salvation?
Who has deceived you? Who has persuaded you
    That he who fell by the wood of the tree would be
        raised up by wood
    And be summoned to dwell
        Again in Paradise?"

Strophe 5:   "Suddenly you have become stupid who were formerly a clever snake.[8]

HADES   All your wisdom was consumed by the cross,[9]
    And you have been caught in your own snare.[10]
Open your eyes and you will see
    That you have fallen into the pit which you dug.
For, lo, that wood which you call dry and sterile
    Is blossoming into fruit at whose taste the robber
    Has become an heir to the joys of Eden.
Beyond the wand which brought the people
    Out of Egypt, this wood has been active,
    For it leads Adam
        Again into Paradise."

Strophe 6:   "Cease, unhappy Hades, check these terrible words

SNAKE   For these words of yours reveal your thoughts.
    Do you fear the cross and the One crucified?
None of these things upsets me.
    For they start as deeds of my plan.
I shall again design this and open the tomb and lay Christ in the tomb
    So that you will have your fear repeated—
    From His tomb, as from the cross.
But I, seeing you, shall laugh;
    For when Christ is buried, I shall come to you saying:
    'Who will lead Adam
        Again into Paradise?'"

8. Gen. iii.1.
9. Ps. (Greek) cvi.27: "καὶ πᾶσα ἡ σοφία αὐτῶν κατεπόθη."
10. Ps. vii.16.

Strophe 7:	At once Hades cried out to the devil,
HADES	To the one who does not see. The blind says to the blind: "Look,
	You walk in darkness; grope your way lest you fall.

Strophe 7:

HADES

> At once Hades cried out to the devil,
> > To the one who does not see. The blind says to the blind: "Look,
> > You walk in darkness; grope your way lest you fall.
> Consider what I say, O slow of heart,
> > What you do has extinguished the sun.[11]
> This same wood in which you take pride caused everything to totter;
> > It agitated the earth; it concealed the heavens;
> > It tore up rocks near by and even the veil;[12]
> And it even raised up the dead from their tombs,
> > And the dead cry: 'Hades, catch Adam,
> > For Adam runs
> > > Again into Paradise'."

Strophe 8:

DEVIL

> "Did the tree of the Nazarene have power to terrify you?"
> > Said the devil to Hades who was undone.
> > "Have you, who have killed all, been killed by a cross?
> Did you have to fear the crucifixion of Haman?[13]
> > And that peg by which Jael nailed Sisera?[14]
> And the five crosses on which once Jesus, son of Nave[15]
> > Nailed those who were tyrants?
> > The tree in Eden has terrified you
> Excessively, since it drove out Adam
> > And does not bring him back
> > > Again into Paradise."

Strophe 9:

HADES

> "Now is the time to open your ears, Belial,
> > Now is the time to show you the power of the cross
> > And the complete sovereignty of the One being crucified,
> For to you the cross is folly;[16]
> > To all creation it is considered a throne
> On which Jesus, nailed, is as though seated;
> > He hears the robber crying to Him,
> > 'Lord, remember me in Thy kingdom,'[17]

11. Matt. xxvii.45; Mark xv.33; Luke xxiii.44.
12. Matt. xxvii.51–53; Mark xv.38; Luke xxiii.45.
13. Haman: Esther vii.10.
14. Jael murdered Sisera by driving a nail in his head (Judg. iv.21). Jael may be the symbol of the church and Sisera of earthly sin.
15. Jesus (Joshua), son of Nun. Josh.x.26. The five kings may symbolize the five senses.
16. I Cor. i.18.
17. Luke xxiii.42–43.

And He answers as though from a judge's bench:
'Today, poor fellow, thou shalt rule with me,
For with me thou shalt enter
Again into Paradise'."

Strophe 10: When he heard these things, the ever-wily serpent,
Vexed, roused up and saw the things he had just heard about;
A robber bearing witness to Christ who was being crucified.
Frightened out of his senses at these things,
He beat his breast and considered them carefully.

SNAKE   "Does He talk with a robber and not answer those who accused Him?[18]
Does He who does not consider Pilate worthy of a word[19]
Now address a murderer, saying, 'Come, live in splendor'?[20]
Why has this happened? Who has seen such
Deeds or words in the case of a robber on a cross?[21]
Through what sort of nature does He take him
Into Paradise?"

Strophe 11: Again the serpent raised his voice,
SNAKE   Crying: "Hades, my refuge, accept me,
For I submit to your orders, although I did not trust your words.[22]
I just saw the wood which terrified you
Reddened with blood and water,
And I was terrified; I do not speak of the blood, but of the water,[23]
For the former points to the death of Jesus,
But the latter to His life, for life gushed forth
From His side; for not the first
But the second Adam bore Eve,
The mother of the living,[24]
Again into Paradise."

18. Matt. xxvi.62–63; Mark xiv.60–61; Luke xxiii.9–10.
19. Matt. xxvii.14; Mark xv.5.
20. Paradise is equated with Eden, and the Hebrew word for *luxury* was used by the church fathers for Eden. Compare: Nativity Kontakion I, Strophe 1, l. 2 τὴν τρυφήν.
21. πρός with the genitive means, I presume, "in the presence of." The variant reading with the accusative would give a clearer translation, "in reply to." The refrain has shifted and the whole text is probably corrupt.
22. This departs from the *Acta Pilati*, for there Hades advises the devil to go fight alone.
23. John xix.34.
24. Gen. iii.20.

Strophe 12:   With these words, the completely villainous one

        Admitted grudgingly that he had fallen along with Hades;

        At any rate, they doubtless mourned their fall together.

DEVIL   "What," they say, "is this thing to which we have submitted?

and   Whence this wood on which we fell?

HADES   Its growth was rooted in the earth for our destruction;

        Although we grafted on it bitter trunks,

        We have not changed its sweetness.

    Woe is me, comrade. Woe is me, brother.

        As we fell together, so shall we mourn together,

        For Adam secretly goes

            Again into Paradise.

Strophe 13:   "How could we not remember the archetypes of that wood?

DEVIL   For of old they were revealed in many ways, in many forms,[25]

and   Both in the case of those who were saved and those

HADES   who were destroyed:[26]

    Noah was saved with wood,[27]

        But the whole of the disobedient world was destroyed.

    Moses was glorified by it, when he took the rod as though it

        were a sceptre,[28]

        While Egypt fell into snares through it

        And was drowned as though in deep waters.

    For what the cross has now accomplished it revealed long ago

        In a pattern. Why, then, should we not lament,

        For Adam proceeds

            Again into Paradise?"

Strophe 14:   "Wait, Hades, poor fellow," said the devil as he groaned.

DEVIL   "Be still, be patient, put your hand over your mouth,

        For I hear a voice bringing joyous information

    A cry bearing good news has come to me.

        The rustle of words as though of the leaves of the wood;[29]

---

25. Heb. i.1.
26. I Cor. i.18.
27. Gen. viii.
28. Ex. iv.1–5.
29. Paul Maas, "Frühbyzantinische Kirchenpoesie" (Kleine Texte, Bonn, 1910), 17, in the poem entitled "The Lost Paradise," Adam begs foliage to intercede for him, and ἦχος is used there of the sound (καὶ τῷ ἤχῳ σου τῶν φύλλων).

For Christ as He is about to die cried out: 'Father, forgive them';[30]

    But He afterwards distressed me as He said,

    'For the lawless ones do not know what they do.'[31]

Now we know that the Lord of glory

    Is the One suffering, and that He

    Wills that Adam be carried

        Again into Paradise.

Strophe 15: "The Lord showed Moses the wood

DEVIL   Which sweetened the water at Marah;[32]

    He did not teach him, did He, what it was, and of what it

        was the root?

He did not tell him then, for He did not wish to;

    But now He has made it clear to all.

For, lo, all things are sweetened; but we are embittered.[33]

    The wood which was cast in the ground has sprouted

    From our root; and it has become sweet,

Though it formerly brought forth thorns;[34]

    But now like the vine of Sorek,[35] it extends its shoots,

    Transplanting itself

        Again in Paradise.

Strophe 16: "Now then, Hades, mourn, and I join in unison with you in wailing.

DEVIL   Let us lament as we see the tree which we planted

    Changed into a holy trunk.

30. Luke xxiii.34.

31. I Cor. ii.8. Romanos, in this strophe, gives Satan a moment of hope that he could be forgiven and then a quick realization that he was not ignorant of Christ's true nature and hence not to be included in the redemption. This gives Satan a human appeal that is characteristic of Romanos.

32. Marah: Ex. xv.23–25. The editor of the French edition (IV, 305*n*3) adds the symbolism as given by Origen in his "Homily on Exodus," II (*P.G.*, 12, 341C–342D). The law in its literal requirements is bitter; it is sweetened by the wisdom of Christ, the cross, wood thrown into the water.

33. Isa. xiv.9: "ὁ ᾄδης κάτωθεν ἐπικράνθη."

34. The editor of the French edition comments (*Fr. ed.*, IV, 307*n*2) on the legend that the cross was carved from a shoot of the tree of life, which Seth planted on the tomb of Adam, his father. This would explain the idea in the last line of the shoots now extending into Paradise. It may echo also Ezekiel's vision of the branch of the high cedar that is to bear fruit and shelter all the birds so that the Lord has made the dry tree to flourish (Ez. xvii.22–24). More likely it is the poet's own extension of the figure of speech that expands the idea of "the wood," "the tree," "the vine."

35. Sorek: The valley of Sorek is mentioned as the home of Delilah (Judg. xvi.4). It was known for its special vines. Isaiah's song to his special vineyard (Isa. v.1–8) is a figurative allusion to the house of Israel.

Robbers, murderers, tax-gatherers, harlots,
    Rest beneath it, and make nests [36]
In its branches in order that they might gather
    The fruit of sweetness from the supposedly sterile wood.
    For they cling to the cross as the tree of life.
Leaning against it and swimming
    They are carried along with its aid and come to anchor
    As though in a calm harbor
        Again in Paradise.

Strophe 17: "Swear, then, tyrant, from henceforth crucify no one.
DEVIL   Strengthen, Tartarus, your purpose to slay no one.
    We have had experience; let us draw in our hands.[37]
What has happened may become for us
    Knowledge for the things which are to come.
Henceforth no one of us will tyrannize over the race of Adam
    For he is marked with the sign of the cross as a treasure
    And he has in a mortal vessel an inviolate pearl.[38]
On the cross the very clever thief carried it off.
    As one who had stolen, he was nailed to the cross;
    And because he was a robber,[39] he was called
        Again into Paradise."

Strophe 18: Exalted and glorious, God of fathers and youths,
    Thy voluntary shame has become our honor.
    Let us all boast in Thy cross
We shall nail our hearts upon it,
    In order that we may hang on it our instruments
And sing to Thee, Lord of the universe, from the odes of Zion.
    A ship from Tarshish [40] once furnished
    Gold to Solomon at just the right time, as it is written;

---

36. See note 34 with the reference to Ezekiel.
37. The same juxtaposition of χεῖραν and πεῖραν occurs in "The Three Children," O. 46 (K. 27), Strophe 1, l. 3. P. Maas comments on the ending, αν in the third declension. *Umarb.*, 574.
38. Compare with Romanos #43, Strophe 33. Also, II Cor. iv.7.
39. Layer on layer of meanings are provided in these few lines. The seal—sign of the cross—protects the followers of God even in the Last Judgment (Rev. vii.2–4; Rev. ix.4). The knowledge of God is a treasure, which Paul says we hold in earthen vessels (II Cor. iv.7); and Matthew compares the Kingdom of God to a pearl of great price (Matt. xiii.45–47). The robber carried off divine forgiveness that he had not earned.
40. Tarshish ships were famous as caravans for merchandise. See I Kings x.22.

Thy cross gives us untold wealth

    Daily and at time of the last judgment,[41]

    For it leads us all

        Again into Paradise.

41. "The right time" might, of course, be the specified time: "Once in three years." Probably the two layers of meaning are intentional.

ON THE ADORATION AT THE CROSS

O. 23 (K. 64)

Title: Εἰς τὴν προσκύνησιν τοῦ Τιμίου Σταυροῦ

Manuscripts and editions: P is the only manuscript used.
This kontakion is included in the edition of Tomadakis, IV, 501–39.
The French edition edits it with excellent introductory notes, IV, 313–53.

Tone: ἦχος πλάγιος β'

Acrostic: Τοῦτο τὸ ἔπος ἐστὶν 'Ρωμανοῦ

Refrain: ἐν τῷ παραδείσῳ

Biblical source and place in the liturgy: The Oxford edition assigns this kontakion to Friday in Lent. The French edition states that Romanos must have written it for the fourteenth of September, since the theme of the Adoration of the Cross suits the feast day honoring that rite, which was established in Jerusalem in the fourth century and was known as such in Constantinople in the sixth century. In the analysis of the contents that follows, the use of two themes is clear, and there would be different source material for the two parts.

Analysis of content: The prooimion and the first three strophes introduce the idea of prayer before the cross and the connection between the robber's forgiveness and Christ's redemption of Adam.

Christ speaks in two strophes, emphasizing the reason for His birth and death and commissioning the robber to replace the Cherubim as guard of Paradise. In Strophes 6 through 9 the robber sings a song of praise as he goes to Paradise, and in Strophe 10 he speaks to the Cherubim, who receive him and hand over the keys to him in Strophes 10 through 13.

A transition of four strophes presents the devil's lament that his friend deserted him. He relates the wiles he employed in arousing the Jews to persecution of the Christians. The source of this material is, of course, the *Gospel of Nicodemus, Acta Pilati*, as discussed in the introduction to Kontakion #22. The robber episode, however, was not used in #22; it occurs at the end of *Acta Pilati*, Part II, Chap. X. Here, the robber, bearing the cross, meets the archangel Michael, who suggests that he remain and see the Just enter Paradise.

The next five strophes explain persecutions through the stories of

Emperor Constantine and Saint Helena. The story of the finding of the cross through the offices of the legendary figure of Judas Kyriakos is inserted, with reference to his having attained recognition in the church and with an added detail about St. Helena's finding the nails from the cross. This section, as the French edition reasonably asserts, would not be appropriate for Good Friday, but it would suit the celebration of the cross on September fourteen.

The connection this part of the kontakion bears to the famous anonymous hymn, Ὁ ὑψωθείς, which Pitra published (*Analecta Sacra*, I, 507–14), is interesting since it reverses the emphasis by devoting only one strophe to the robber's story and granting the major attention to the discovery of the cross. It even tells of the construction of two basilicas by Constantine, but it refers to Judas merely as "a certain one of the Jews."

The editor of the French edition reasons that the poem of Romanos is the older of the two and that the poet of the anonymous hymn tried to counteract the overcredulity of Romanos in regard to the Judas legend. In any case, the anonymous hymn survived for use on September fourteen.

Connection with homily: An anonymous homily attributed to Eusebius of Alexandria, entitled "For Good Friday on the Passion of our Lord" (*P.G.*, 62, 721–24) uses the apocryphal version of *Acta Pilati*, Part II, Chap. X, as did Romanos; it elaborates on the conversation between the robber and the Just. It does not include the hymn that the robber sings in Romanos' version.

The "new song" (ᾆσμα καινόν) which the robber sings, is so prominent in the sermon of Pseudo-Chrysostom (*P.G.*, 62, 747–54) that it begins with the phrase, "Let us sing a new song, people." The rites for September fourteen include passages that recall this part of the Romanos kontakion.

Style of Romanos: The theological emphasis on the purpose of Christ's birth and death is present, as usual, but the poem pays more attention to legend, as in the narrative of Emperor Constantine and his mother, than Romanos ordinarily gives that kind of source. The dialogue between the robber and the Cherubim lacks some of the usual folk interest. The devil's lament that it is the last straw to have this friend of his, the robber, turn against him is closer to the usage of Romanos. When the narrative of the finding of the cross begins, the sentences become involved and even lack clarity. One wonders if Romanos was slightly aware of the very dubious nature of the legend.

Meter: The metrical scheme is given in the Oxford edition, 517, II.

ON THE ADORATION AT THE CROSS

O. 23

Prooimion: As we kneel before the wood of Thy precious cross,
> O Christ, God,
We beseech Thee, Lord, who wast nailed to it,
> Deliver the race of man from dangers,
Through the virgin by whose intercession Adam was recalled
> To Paradise.[1]

Strophe 1: The Most High planted in the middle of Paradise
> The thrice blessed wood, the gift of life for us,[2]
In order that, in approaching it,
> Adam might find eternal and immortal life;
But he did not strive earnestly to know this life,
> And he failed to attain it, and revealed death.
However, the robber, seeing how the plant in Eden
> Had been beautifully transplanted in Golgotha,
Recognized the life in it and said to himself:
> "This is what my father lost formerly
> In Paradise."

Strophe 2: For when he was lifted up on the cross, the condemned man
> Was justified by faith, and made his confession;
He opened the eyes of his heart[3]
> And he beheld the joys in Eden.
In the middle of Eden he beheld the blazing figure[4]
> Which he saw as the cross which he had erected.[5]

1. The refrain is similar to Kontakion #22. The announced subject and the metrical scheme resemble Nativity II.
2. Gen. ii.9; iii.22.
3. Origen spoke of the eyes of the heart as able to see and understand the supernatural. *Contra Celsum* I, 48 (*P.G.*, 11, 749B).
4. τύπος is, of course, the figure of the cross; but it is also the "type" or archetype or symbol of life.
5. The idea would seem to be that the robber had really, through his crimes, erected his own cross.

For the cross, this tree of life is commensurate with
    Each age of mortal man;
It was the same life which he saw shining on both trees;[6]
    And he groaned because Adam had lost it
        In Paradise.

Strophe 3:   As he was hanging on the cross, he was filled with both
        joy and sorrow;
    On the one hand, he beheld life on the cross and rejoiced;
But seeing Adam's sickness,
    He sympathized with him, ignoring his own suffering.
However, Christ, recognizing the thought of the one
        who confessed Him,
CHRIST   Said: "Do not grieve for Adam your forefather,
For I am a true second Adam,[7]
    And I have come voluntarily to save my Adam,
For I had given him all joy with the tree of life,
    But he, in rebelling, gained the curse for himself
        In Paradise.

Strophe 4:   "For his sake and as lover of man, I came down from on high,
CHRIST   So that as One showing pity, I might redeem his race;
And I became a curse,
    In order that I might free Adam and his descendants from the curse;
By the tree the transgression was introduced to the forefather,
    And because of it, he was cast out of Paradise as a criminal;
But he re-enters through the tree of life;
    You enter into Paradise first with him.
When you are in possession of your inheritance, call mortals and
        receive the faithful,[8]
    For today, you will enter with me, rejoicing
        In Paradise.

6. The meaning is not clear. The editor of the French edition thinks that in between Adam and Christ there was a period of law and that the tree of life is not at that age of man really spiritual. This would oppose the plant as a symbol of earthly wisdom to the tree, which is a symbol of spiritual life. It may be simply the tree in Eden and the cross (the tree).
7. I Cor. xv.45–47.
8. It really is the possession of Christ's promise that he realizes. Luke xxiii.43.

Strophe 5:   "When the first creature was shut out from Paradise,[9]

CHRIST   An order was given to the Cherubim to guard the road;

     But take my cross

         On your shoulders, and thus go into Eden with haste.

    If the sword of the Cherubim did not see you wearing the title

           rights of the inscription,[10]

        The sword of flame which stands guard would consume you.

    But, taking the inscription of my cross, robber,

      Walk up to the Cherubim,

   And they will know the symbol of life and they will give into your hands

      The power to open and to lead my friends

         Into Paradise."

Strophe 6:   Obeying these instructions, the robber fastened on his shoulders,

      As the All-merciful One had told him, the emblem of grace,

   And as he advanced, he hymned with joy

      The gift of the cross, and singing he played on the harp

        a "new song":[11]

ROBBER   "'Thou art the grafted slip of sterile souls,[12] Thou art the plow,[13]

      The very fine cultivation which purifies thought;

   Thou art the excellent root of my resurrected life;

      Thou art the rod of chastisement which struck down

        the enemy of Adam;

   Thou hast opened the doors of joy[14] which formerly

      Sin closed, the sin which Adam committed

        In Paradise.

Strophe 7:   "'Thou hast freely given the whole of life, O thrice blest wood,

ROBBER   For me and for all men who possess Thy grace

   Thou art the staff[15]

      Which guides towards life the sinners who love Thee.

---

9. Gen. iii.24.

10. τοῦ τίτλου has a double meaning, for the words inscribed on the cross are like a legal title.

11. Quoting the opening lines of Ps. xcvi.1. These lines are used in the office of Exaltation of the Cross. Ps. xxxiii.3.

12. Compare with the figure of the root and the vine in Kontakion #22, Strophe 12.

13. Ephrem, in his second sermon on Lazarus, speaks of the field of Christ as worked by the plow of the cross until all thorns are extracted. Editor of the French edition IV, 333*n*3, gives this reference.

14. The *Menaion* (Rome, 1888), 157, refers to the cross as "the door of Paradise."

15. Ps. xxiii.4: "Thy rod and Thy staff..." the staff of the shepherd; the staff of the one who is blind or lame—either is appropriate. In the *Menaion* for Vespers on September 14 it seems to refer to the staff of the shepherd: ʿΡάβδος ὁ τῆς δυνάμεως, ὑφ᾽ ἧς ποιμαινόμεθα.

Thou art shown as the winnowing fan [16] which scatters the chaff
    Skillfully on the threshing floor, to be thrown into the fire
In order that the fruit may be put in the granaries.
    Thou art the yoke, the instrument for taming the terrible Hebrews,
Thou art the divine oar of the ship which is the holy church
    In Christ; and it guides the just and the faithful
        Into Paradise.

Strophe 8: "'I have found an opportune path of confession, [17]
ROBBER   And I shall hymn Thee in praise, O wood which hast borne our life.
Thou art the title for law and order,
    The excellent guard of dwelling places and of the piety
      of the faithful.
Thou art a most holy altar, a splendid altar
    Receiving the undefiled blood of the sacrifice. [18]
Thou art the terrible spear striking the power of demons; [19]
    Thou art the pure horn which grows on the sheep of Christ.
Thou hast touched the head of Adam and put joy in it.
    And I, because I had faith in Thee am to go at once
        Into Paradise.'

Strophe 9: "I see the holy land which my ancestor possessed;
ROBBER   I have found the lands of light not swallowed up in darkness; [20]
If the outer nature is thus,
    Great are the rewards of pleasure within;
For the eye has not seen, nor the ear heard, [21]
    Nor the heart known what the Lord has made ready
For His friends, crucified with Him,
    For them I am the first to open up the road of life,
I take the symbol of the cross for my security,
    For the one who loves the seal of the cross will enter
        Into Paradise.

16. Matt. iii.12. The cross as winnower is to be found in Ps. Chrys. (*P.G.*, 62, 753) and Ps. Cesar of Nazianz (*P.G.*, 38, 1040). The latter uses the word λικμητήριον; the former uses λικμήτωρ.
17. He has confessed Christ and he has confessed his unworthiness—just barely in time to be forgiven (εὔκαιρον).
18. Heb. ix.12.
19. A similar reference occurs in the office for the Exaltation of the Cross: "Σταυρὸς ἀγγέλων ἡ δόξα, καὶ τῶν δαιμόνων τὸ τραῦμα." *Menaion*, Vespers for September 14.
20. The robber, out in space, beholds the universe and sees that it is not subject to darkness.
21. I Cor. ii.9.

Strophe 10: "I do not fear the flaming sword which acts as guard,
ROBBER   For I hold upright the seal of the cross and I take courage."
Saying this, he approached Paradise
       And presented himself to the Cherubim
And cried out: "O most trusted guard, safest of keeper of keys,
       O holy one of four shapes, many-eyed Cherubim,
I have come to show to you the seal of Christ.
       I was sent by Him today from the land of Israel;
Examine for yourselves the inscription and hand over to me
       The ancient abode of my father which he controlled as he rejoiced
              In Paradise.

Strophe 11: "Receive the sure seal and the divine inscription,
ROBBER   The signature of a king, of God the All-Merciful One."
Saying this, he followed out eagerly
       The commands of Christ, the King.
The Cherubim receiving it recognized the letters
       Shining out with the grace of the purple of blood.[22]
They[23] delighted in how beautifully it was inscribed,
       And as they took it, immediately they found the wise words,
And they recognized the power in them as they applied to the robber:
       "Today you will be with me rejoicing
              In Paradise."

Strophe 12: "Come, robber, take the rights of your father,"
CHERUBIM   Answered the Cherubim: "We recognize the divine pronouncement
Of the great King.
       Lo, the accoutrements[24] of Paradise, I now place in your hands;
Receive, then, the allotted abode of your fatherland of old.
       Take again your ancestral property; it is incorruptible;
For the cross has canceled out the confiscation—
       The cross which you bear as you come now presenting
              yourself to us.
In it are united your supplication to Christ
       And the decision which gave you untroubled inheritance
              In Paradise.

22. Purple ink was used in signing royal documents.
23. The Greek is usually singular, a collective noun, but since we speak of the Cherubim in the plural, this was done in the translation.
24. The word in Greek would literally mean *tools* or *household utensils*. It maintains the figure of speech, which is comparing the return of Paradise to the legal repossession of property.

Strophe 13: "Since you are now in possession of the keys, we gladly withdraw;

CHERUBIM   For Paradise was not assigned to us as masters;

For the inheritance of Paradise

     Was to be enjoyed at the command of God by the first man

         from the beginning;

It was confiscated by ordinance and he was exiled

         to mortal corruption,[25]

And then we were made guardians of what he had possessed.

For we, along with the Seraphim, have other domains,

     Considerable ones, most hallowed and sacred.

You have revealed to us the restoration of Adam;

         Receive, then, your rights which Adam formerly possessed

             In Paradise."

Strophe 14: Obeying these words, the robber took over Paradise,

         And holding the shield, he became keener

Than the flaming sword

         Against the devil who saw the robber amid the joys of Paradise;

DEVIL   And lamenting, he said: "A terrible thing has happened to me;

         A robber has been exonerated, and has opened up Paradise

At the time when I was trying secretly to steal Peter.[26]

         I, the thief; a robber has now defrauded me.

While I was laughing in my madness at my pupil, the

             betrayer of Christ,

         I am laughed at by him as he hurries, through his faith,

             Into Paradise.

Strophe 15: "Cunningly and ingeniously I withstood the apostles;

DEVIL   I made ready my weapons against them as against an enemy;

But I was despoiled of my friend,

         At the very time when I wanted to give the robber

            other fellow ministers;

If I had seen Judas receiving Paradise,

         Would I have suffered pain about him to the same extent?

He was not mine, but a disciple of Christ;

         But the robber was mine; he had become a faithful pupil;

---

25. Gen. iii.19.

26. The manuscript gave ζητῶν. Trypanis corrected the participle and uses ζητῶ for metrical reasons.

And leaving me, he ran to Jesus and hated me;
And what is worse, because of the cross, he has become
keeper of the keys
In Paradise.

Strophe 16: "Now I shall prepare a fiercer war;
DEVIL   I shall close off the road into Paradise,
In order that I may show the keeper of the keys
That it is in vain that he has put faith in having the keys in Eden."
Saying this, he ran in a frenzy; and first of all he roused
The Hebrews to be horrified at the proclamation of faith;
And the kings, impostors, and tyrants of the earth
He spurred on with violence against the cross of life.
He instigated persecutions against Christ and His followers,
Imagining that he would check the dead from entering
Into Paradise.

Strophe 17: In shedding the blood of the meek, the all-wicked one was worsted.
When he pursued the apostles as well as the martyrs,
He lamented in his shame
As he saw the endurance of the champions of Christ.
But for a considerable number of years, he troubled them
by working with
Tyrants and rulers, kings, and legal decrees,
At times secretly and again openly;
But he never left a battle without defeat.
He observed the virtue of saints, and he mourned the road
Of those who because of their victory ran to the trusted robber
In Paradise.

Strophe 18: For He who governs all the centuries with goodness
In His all-wise will, He the Merciful One, raised
up Emperor Constantine
From the race of Abraham and David, a man of faith.[27]
He followed the example of his ancestor and revealed his
Certain kinship and stopped the war on the church.
Taking three hundred and eighteen trusted hoplites,
Abraham won a difficult war;[28]

27. This must be in a general sense; that is, Emperor Constantine is in the line of men of faith.
28. Gen. xiv.14–16.

And with just such a number,[29] the faithful and brave king
    Put down the atheistic heresies[30] which did not allow advancing
        Into Paradise.

Strophe 19: Great are the works of Christ and indescribable,
    Not disclosed to the faithless and the unworthy,
But to the worthy and just.
    Just such a thing once happened to Helen, the mother
      of the Emperor,
For she set her heart upon finding the wood of our life,
    And this friend of God was indeed worthy of it; it had been
      hidden for a time.
And she went with haste[31] where Christ was crucified,
    At once leaving the palace halls;
She put to one side the inconvenience and the suffering of travel,
    For she yearned to find the lamp[32] which guides
      Into Paradise.

Strophe 20: He who receives all men observed her zeal,
    Since from the first to the eleventh hour[33]
He does not hesitate to go forth
    And invite the elect and the chosen to [eternal] life,
Just as not long ago he sought for Paul and found and called
    Him and displayed him as his herald and apostle.
Thus He at one time decided that Judas[34] was of the elect;
    He found the cross, and was happily called by a new name
For formerly he had the name of the traitor, but he changed it,
    Since he was not shown to be a traitor; but he arrived
      In Paradise.

29. The Fathers of Nicaea equaled in number the followers of Abraham, according to a common tradition.
30. Arianism, Paulianism, Novatianism might be in the poet's mind. *Fr. ed.,* IV, 347*n*3.
31. Not too much haste, for she stopped at Cyprus for the winter (*Fr. ed.,* IV, 347*n*4).
32. See Resurrection IV (O. 27), Strophe 4, in which the same comparison is used.
33. Matt. xx.1–7.
34. The reference is to a legend about Judas Quiriacus or Cyriacus who revealed to the Empress Helena where the cross was hidden. He was later martyred, and in some accounts he had been made bishop of Jerusalem. The account of the discovery of the cross, "De inventione crucis dominicae," is in *Acta Sanctorum,* May, Vol. I. St. Ambrose, "De obitu Theodosii" tells of Helen's discovery. A thorough discussion of the various sources of a very suspect legend is given in the French edition, IV, 314–21. Leclerq, *Dictionnaire Archéologie Chrétienne et de liturgie,* III, 3131–39, gives evidence of the decrees that expressed mistrust in the legend.

Strophe 21: Now the Lord accepted the faith of the woman of God,
　　　　Lifting up his servant, zealous and most trustworthy,
　　Formerly a Jew,
　　　　After that, an excellent shepherd of the Christian people,
　　For he was named and bore the name of Kyriakos, the saint
　　　　Who kept up his courage and sought out the cross.
　　He sought to find out what was the nature of Christ;
　　　　But death proved to him at this very time to be life.
　　As formerly in the tomb, death withdrew in the presence of Christ,
　　　　Just so death withdrew when he saw by the bed, the life which leads
　　　　　　Into Paradise.

Strophe 22: However, in order that the gift of grace might be complete,
　　　　Christ, our King, uncovered the nails
　　Which the holy woman found;
　　　　And they were inserted like pearls with the cross.
　　Making the nails in a bridle [35] she fulfilled
　　　　The prophecy of the prophet Zacharias as he said:
　　"In that day there will be a holy [symbol] on the bridle." [36]
　　　　For the eternal victory of those who have had faith in Him.
　　She has given the cross to future generations for the security of life
　　　　For those who have confidence in it, enter with glory
　　　　　　Into Paradise.

Strophe 23: Under the shadow of the cross, let us exult with joy.
　　　　Sinners, let us live soberly, Paradise is opened up;
　　The robber is the guard
　　　　Of Paradise. Christ chose him on the cross.
　　Let us not close up what is not closed; the friend of
　　　　Christ is established,
　　　　The very sympathetic and friendly robber is host to newcomers.
　　Let us honor the cross, guardian of our life,
　　　　For it is the defender of our life in Heaven;

---

35. The word σαλλιβάριον is an unusual word. *Soph. dict.* spells it with one λ and quotes Theophanes.

36. The Greek words, Zech. xiv.20, are:

"ἐν τῇ ἡμέρᾳ ἐκείνῃ ἔστα τὸ ἐπὶ τὸν χαλινὸν τοῦ ἵππου ἅγιον τῷ κυρίῳ παντοκρατόρι."

Romanos abstracts from the inscription, "Holiness unto the Lord," the word ἅγιον and uses it as a sacred thing or holy symbol.

It defends all men from the wicked one and from his assault.
    Those who have this seal have confidence in entering
        Into Paradise.

Strophe 24: Thou hast become the son of Mary, O Son of God, our Savior,
    And Thou hast been nailed to the cross, though Thou
      art God incarnate,
In order that Thou might save those in affliction;
    And take pity on sinners, since Thou art powerful and good;
Grant slumber to all those who put their hope in Thee;
    They hope to serve Thee zealously in psalms and prayers.[37]
With the robber we cry out to Thee as though we were on the cross,
    "Remember us in Thy kingdom."
Consider all of us worthy of Thy choir of saints, O Christ,
    Since we have taken the seal of Thy cross for unity [38]
      In Paradise.

37. The infinitive δουλεύειν is loosely constructed. It might depend on παράσχου as a part of the prayer; it might go with hope (ἐλπιζουσι).
38. Unity with Christ and unity of all Christians.

ON THE RESURRECTION I

O. 24 (K. 72)

Title: Εἰς τὴν τριήμερον ἀνάστασιν τοῦ κυρίου καὶ σωτῆρος ἡμῶν Ἰησου Χριστοῦ

Manuscripts and editions: P has the only complete kontakion. M has the prooimion and one
strophe.
> Cammelli, R.M., 370–87.
> French edition, IV, 424–51.

Tone: ἦχος α΄

Acrostic: Τοῦ ταπεινοῦ Ῥωμανοῦ αἶνος

Refrain: Ἀνέστη ὁ κύριος

Biblical source and place in the liturgy: The main source is Matthew xxvii.51–54, 62–66.
> It is intended for Easter Sunday. See the Introduction, on the matter
of Easter dramatic presentations, East and West.
> In the middle of the sixth century, Dorothea, who founded a monastery,
wrote some instructions for the celebrations for the day. In Number XXII, the
abbot speaks of psalms and specifies that attention be paid not only to the melody,
but to the spirit of such words as the following: Ἀναστάσεως ἡμέρα καρποφο-
ρήσωμεν ἡμᾶς αὐτούς. The idea of a sacrifice of our own lives on the day of
resurrection is attributed by Pétridès to Gregory of Nazianz.[1] Liturgical books
do not contain this psalm, but the reference points up the rhythmic singing of
troparia in connection with special services, such as those on Easter.
> The refrain of this kontakion has in essence passed over into the language
of the church today when the greeting on Easter is Χρίστος ἀνέστη, "Christ
has risen."

Analysis of content: The prooimion sets the tone of rejoicing with "The Lord is risen," and
the first two strophes make clear that guards watch the tomb of the One who
despoiled Hades. Strophes 3 through 11 are direct dialogue between the lawless
and Pilate. For four strophes the lawless express satisfaction that He who was
supposed to be so powerful is dead, but they know they must be wary. They
ask Pilate for guards but assure him that they are not really worried even if
the entombed Christ promised that He would arise. Pilate answers in four strophes

---

1. "Notes d'hymnographie byzantine," *B.Z.*, XIII (1904), 424–29.

in which he assures the lawless that setting guards is very silly, because Christ is safely buried. If, however, this precaution serves any purpose they may have some guards; just go away and let him alone. The poet then asks Pilate if he himself is not a bit bothered.

The next dialogue is between the lawless and the guards. In Strophes 11 and 12 the guards are told that they will be rewarded for staying awake; in fact, they will get twice as much as Judas, but if they are careless, the money will be wasted. Strophes 13 and 14 present the antithesis of having soldiers occupying the tomb and an army guarding the King. The guards now are shaken; some weep, some rejoice, as they realize the tomb may be robbed. One soldier speaks in two strophes and says that he will go inside just to search the tomb, since he remembers what happened when Christ was on the cross. He puts a question to the rest: "Who is on the stone?" The others tell him to go back to sleep, but when day dawns in Strophe 18, they face the fact that Christ is gone. A series of allusions to the Son of Light precede the closing prayer, which refers also to Mary, to Adam and Eve, and to all mortals who should glorify the risen Lord.

Style of Romanos: It is clearly organized in the kind of drama that elaborates the biblical version; its literary appeal is strong. The lawless are both cautious and cowardly, yet grandiose in their appeal to Pilate as the upholder of the law. They are positive that Christ could not rise again, but they state that precautions should be taken to prevent false rumors. They bribe the soldiers, but warn them to earn the money. Pilate's crisp common sense and his desire to get rid of them are as convincing as his cynical warning that the guards might be led astray again. These are the creative touches Romanos adds to the biblical allusions and antitheses that proclaim again and again the greatness of the power of the divine Christ in the extremities of human degradation. Romanos uses fewer figures of speech than usual. The editor of the French edition comments on the great number of colloquialisms.[2]

Meter: The metrical scheme is given in the Oxford edition, 521, X.

2. *Fr. ed.,* IV, 427n1.

ON THE RESURRECTION I

O. 24

Prooimion: Death was swallowed up in victory [1]
　　　　At Thy resurrection from the dead, O Christ.
　　Hence, glorying in Thy passion,
　　　　And always celebrating it, we rejoice.
　　　　With jubilation let us cry out:
　　　　　　"The Lord is risen." [1]

Strophe 1: Once the host of lawless people handed over
　　　　Life to the tomb, God to death,
　　　　And the One who despoiled Hades to Hades;
　　With the result that a mortal made mortals immortal,
　　　　And One who was dead, at a word, raised up the dead.
　　They placed guards at the tomb of the One who rules all at His nod.
　　　　O the folly of you lawless ones!
　　　　If He is dead, have no fear. If He is alive, pray to Him
　　　　　　and cry with us:
　　　　　　　　"The Lord is risen."

Strophe 2: When, after the crucifixion, the God of Joseph,
　　　　Who once saved Joseph from the well,
　　　　Was laid in the tomb by Joseph, [2]
　　As far as one could see, He was being guarded as one dead;
　　　　But what one could not see was the way He filled the guards
　　　　　　with deadly fear.
　　There was a stone against the tomb; and the interior of the tomb
　　　　was of rock. [3]
　　　　The guards became stones

---

1. Isa. xxv.8; I Cor. xv.54. The prooimion and Strophe 1 were part of a series added to the *Pentekostarion*; they were really troparia read with Gospels of Resurrection in the Sunday morning service (*Fr. ed.*, IV, 430n1).
2. Matt. xxvii.59–60; Mark xv.46; Luke xxiii.53.
3. I Cor. x.4: the spiritual rock is, of course, Christ.

When they beheld the angel[4] seated on the stone, saying
    to the women:
        "The Lord is risen."

Strophe 3:   The judges were affected by the evil
        Counsels of the lawless. They said:
THE   "Lo, He who shook the earth lies in the ground:
LAWLESS   He who was discussed by everyone and hailed by everyone,
        He at whose deeds the whole earth wondered, is dead.
    Let us then be wary, for the final outcome may become worse
        than the first.[5]
    Let us watch lest His disciples
    Hide His body, and then with falsehood cry out to all:
        'The Lord is risen.'

Strophe 4:   "We shall, then, ask Pilate for a guard,
THE   And he will have men to watch over Him;
LAWLESS   For this Jesus is to be feared, living and dead.
    In His life He broke the law of the Sabbath;
        But if now He is risen from the dead, every law is broken.
    He lies there as one dead; yet there is hope. He is bound, yet He is
        expected to live;
    For all His disciples say:
    'After three days we shall look upon the Master and say:
        "The Lord is risen".'

Strophe 5:   "We, and foreigners, too, O Pilate,
THE   Are clearly guided by you.
LAWLESS   Therefore we who are yours flee to you for refuge.
    Through you let the justice of the nation be established.
        We ask that He who is dead may not break the law of God."
    Why do you act foolishly, lawless ones? Pilate is put in charge
        of the law;
    But how much greater is Christ than Pilate!
    He both establishes law and dispenses grace to those who cry out:
        "The Lord is risen."

4. Matt. xxviii.2–6.
5. Matt. xii.45; xxvii.64.

Strophe 6: "This is the word He spoke to His disciples:
THE
　　　　　　'After three days I shall rise again,[6]
LAWLESS
　　　　　　For even if I am dead, I shall trample on death.'
We are not afraid that this will happen,
　　　　　But we think that He will be stolen away by some of the disciples.
Of course He will not rise again, let us recognize that and understand it.
　　　　　The breath of life, once gone, does not turn back again[7]
　　　　　Unless God speaks. If He is God, then let us say:
　　　　　　　'The Lord is risen'."

Strophe 7:　Pilate heard and answered them:
PILATE
　　　　　　"Your words are really funny; for who would steal
　　　　　　A dead body? What is the gain in a corpse?
The one who loves a friend loves him to the tomb;
　　　　　After the tomb, his affection is spent in vain.
This dead body lies there motionless. What difference does the one
　　　　　　　lying there make to you?
　　　　　Once buried, leave the corpse,
　　　　　For it will not be stolen, nor will He rise up for those who cry out:
　　　　　　　'The Lord is risen.'

Strophe 8:　"Scourged by me, crucified by you,[8]
PILATE
　　　　　　Placed in the tomb by Joseph,
　　　　　　He is clearly dead, undeniably a mortal.
Just as He died with all beholding Him,
　　　　　Just so let Him rise from the tomb with all beholding Him.
You say that they will steal Him away and claim that He is risen.
　　　　　Are they not, then, blind?
　　　　　If we do behold these things and believe them, then let us say:
　　　　　　　'The Lord is risen.'

Strophe 9:　"Everyone who talks like that seems to me to rave,
PILATE
　　　　　　Saying that He will be stolen away, or that He will rise again.
　　　　　　The one is false, and the other is inconceivable.
However, if it will serve any purpose,
　　　　　Take guards to guard the tomb.

6. Matt. xvi.21; xvii.23; xx.19; Mark viii.31; ix.31; x.34; Luke ix.22; xviii.33.
7. Wisd. of Sol. xvi.14.
8. Pilate reminds the Jews that they are responsible for the crucifixion.

But see to it that the guards are not again led astray so that they say:
    'In truth, this One was the son of God.'
    Just as once at the cross, so now at the tomb they will cry out:
        'The Lord is risen'."

Strophe 10: So spoke Pilate to them:
PILATE
    "You have the guard, go on your way,
    And do whatever you have agreed upon."
Pilate, wash your soul,
    As you once washed your hands, and say: "I am innocent."[9]
Or did the dream of your wife perhaps disturb you?
    What then will you do if you hear
    Angels in Heaven and men on earth after the
        resurrection crying out:
        "The Lord is risen"?

Strophe 11: The lawless ones then say to the soldiers:
THE
LAWLESS
    "Do not give in to drowsiness,
    But wait patiently, staying awake;
Be sure to keep awake for a little while, and work until weary,
    So that finally Jesus will be judged truly dead.
If you do that, you will carry out the will of Pilate;
    And your labor will have a reward.
    There will be renown for us, for no one after the corruption
        of the body can say clearly:
        'The Lord is risen.'

Strophe 12: "Do not think that this command
THE
LAWLESS
    Is without profit to you, for after your labor
    We shall strive hard to provide for you.
Thirty pieces of silver were given to Judas.
    Take, now, double those thirty pieces.[10]
This is what we contend: alive or dead He is the cause of trouble.
    Then do not let us go to this trouble for nothing,
    So that we no longer have our money and still we have
        against us Christ and those who cry:
        'The Lord is risen'."

9. This entire strophe uses Matt. xxvii.
10. No mention of this occurs in the Gospels. The poet adds this bit of realism.

Strophe 13:   Encouraged by the senseless plan of the lawless,
                    The soldiers occupied the tomb,
                    And an army guarded the King.
                Outside of the tomb were soldiers;
                    Within was war between Christ and Death.
                As the former gained strength, the latter lost strength;
                    The one overpowered those below; the latter cried out
                    To those below. . . . Let us cry:[11]
                        "The Lord is risen."

Strophe 14:   So while Death was being overpowered,
                    And while [Hades] was stirring up a [hubbub][12]
                    The guards said: "Now what is the trouble?"
                The [first] watch of the night: those within were quiet;
                    The second watch: they were at rest; but on the third watch,
                        they were shaken.
                They mourn and rejoice at the same time; they weep and they cry
                    To one another, "Woe, alas!"
                    Then, rejoicing, they say to one another: "It is right,
                        The Lord is risen."

Strophe 15:   The earth was shaken by great fear,
                    And the stone was rolled away from the tomb.
ONE   "Is not this man who now raises up Adam
SOLDIER   And is resurrected, is not He the same one
                    Whom formerly we guarded on the cross when all were frightened?
                Then He burst rocks apart; now He has moved this stone.
                    Furthermore, He is the same One
                    Who has rent the veil and opened the tomb while we were sleeping.
                        The Lord is risen.

11. The editor of the French edition terms this the call of Death to his cohorts; the Oxford edition, the words of the poet. I adopted the latter interpretation.
12. In the midst of loose constructions and lacunae, at times I have used conjectures in the Oxford edition, and at times, those in the French edition:
Line 2: I used ᾅδου and θορύβους.
Line 3: I used ἡ ταραχή and ended the question there.
Line 4: I adopted the idea of the first watch, rather than the first night (*Fr. ed.*, IV, 445n1).
Line 8: The εὖ is placed with the refrain. It seems to have both the meaning, "They say correctly," and also, the sense of "Joy," "It is well."

Strophe 16: "Let us arise now, friends, and search
ONE   The tomb and see; for it is possible
SOLDIER   That the stone was moved by an earthquake.[13]
                   If the body lies within, we shall keep still;
                       But if the dead has vanished, we shall weep with those below;
                   For Death was just now lamenting, and Hades was weeping,
                       All the time we were disputing.
                       Some saying: 'Woe is me,' and some crying: 'It is well,'
                           and some voices exclaiming:
                               'The Lord is risen.'

Strophe 17: "Lo, no one is within; but who is on the stone?
ONE   Whom do I see, or seem to see, or imagine
SOLDIER   That I see? Perhaps night misleads me?"
GUARDS   "Friend, the night does mislead you; lie down with us and sleep.
                   It is a spirit which deceives you; be quiet and go to sleep.
                   Rather now we shall be on our guard, and we shall pay attention to this:
                       That no one catch us asleep
                       And coming here steal Him away; for then who will be able
                           to put out of countenance those who cry:
                               'The Lord is risen'?

Strophe 18: "The night passed at last—if truly it did pass—[14]
GUARDS   And what you said first, my friend, was true:
                   He who was once dead now became visible.
                   He rolled the rock from within the tomb.[15]
                       He frightened us with His words, for He is to be feared.
                   He brings light, He sends light, He is light. Truly He is the
                       son of Light,
                       And He is the servant of light;
                       These are the [shining] [16] words which He cried to the women

13. In the account of Matthew (xxviii.2) the angel rolled away the stone and the earth quaked "because the angel of the Lord descended from Heaven." The poet wants the soldiers to see for themselves that the Lord is risen.
14. The soldiers are confused as to whether the light comes from the angel or from the rising sun.
15. Christ or the angel? The editor of the French edition suggests that line 5 might be another guard speaking. It seems more likely that the light from within the tomb [Christ] and the light from the angel are both cause for confusion of the guards.
16. *Shining* is a pure conjecture, assuming a reading like τίνα φωτός on the grounds that the poet likes a play on the word such as *light*, or we could have φωτεινὰ ἦν. Paul likes to speak of the "light of the Gospel" (II Cor. iv.4). He does not use it with *words*, however.

when He said:
  'The Lord is risen'."

Strophe 19: For others a snare,[17] for us gain;
          For the lawless shame, for us glory;
          For them a scourge, for us life.
      Because, in truth, the Lord is risen.
          Even if those who guard the tomb took money[18]
      So that they would willingly keep silent, the stones themselves
              will cry out[19]
          That without the aid of human hands
          This stone cut from the mountain[20] has risen—just as once from
              the womb of the Virgin, so now from the tomb
                  The Lord is risen.

Strophe 20: Thou, O Savior, didst come forth unbegotten
          From the Virgin's womb, leaving her virginity unsullied;
          Just so now Thou hast abolished Death in death.
      Thou hast left in the tomb the fine linen of Joseph,
          But Thou hast raised from the tomb the ancestor of Joseph;[21]
      For Adam came following Thee; Eve came after Thee,
          Eve serves Mary,
          But all the earth is prostrate before Thee as it sings the
              song of victory:
                  "The Lord is risen."

17. Adopting λάκκος, the conjecture suggested by Maas.
18. Matt. xxviii.12–15.
19. Luke xix.40.
20. Dan. ii.34–45. Again the poet uses the symbol of strength for Christ, and at the same time plays on the word *stone*.
21. References to Joseph the patriarch and to Joseph of Arimathea.

ON THE RESURRECTION II

O. 25 (K. 73)

Title: ἕτερον κοντάκιον ἀναστάσιμον

Manuscripts and editions: The kontakion exists only in the Patmos manuscript, P.
It is edited by Tomadakis, III, 7–41, and it is given in the French edition, IV, 458–83, where it is called Resurrection III.

Tone: ἦχος πλάγιος β′

Acrostic: τοῦ ταπεινοῦ Ῥωμανοῦ αἶνος

Refrain: Ἀνέστη ὁ κύριος

Biblical source and place in the liturgy: The kontakion is marked for Easter Sunday.

The story of the soldiers at the tomb and the angel uses as its source Matthew xxviii. The first section, which centers on the conversation of Hades, has some relation to the apocryphal Gospel of Nicodemus, although it is not directly quoted. The prophets are called up; the source for this passage is the Old Testament and the general idea of the Descent to Hell.

Analysis of content: The prooimion states the topic of the resurrection and the place as a tomb. Actually, the first strophe is a statement by the poet that he is going to talk first to Hades and then to the soldiers at the tomb in order to prove [?] to the incredulous that the resurrection took place. Strophe 2 then introduces his conversation with Hades, who speaks for six strophes. Hades complains of the way he is unjustly mocked for a mistake anyone would have made if they had seen Christ buried and put in the tomb. He elaborates on his sufferings.

Strophe 9 is central. Christ comes forth from the tomb and tells the prophets to follow him. Christ's command leads into one strophe naming some of the prophets and their prophecies. The poem returns to Hades and his lamentations for Strophes 11 and 12, and next a transitional strophe introducing the soldiers and their evidence. In Strophes 14 through 18 the soldiers tell their questioner that their flight speaks for itself, and they insist that no one can accurately report what happened at the tomb. In Strophes 18 and 19, the conversation between the women at the tomb and the angel is reported, and the soldiers state that they gave false testimony for gold. A final prayer ends the kontakion.

Style of Romanos: The poem is typical of Romanos in its general organization and in the use of dialogue. Hades is not as convincing as he is in his conversation with Satan, in On the Triumph of the Cross (#22), nor are the guards as realistically portrayed as in Resurrection I (#24). The author's purpose is entirely one of argument to prove a theological point, and the artistry of the work suffers from this avowed emphasis. However, the complaints of Hades, in his hurt pride at being mocked for a natural mistake, and the alibis of the guards do reflect some of the human interest that indicates the power of Romanos to enter into a situation.

It is odd, really, that he does so little with the procession of prophets. This aspect of the Descent to Hell was, of course, very much elaborated in the medieval drama of the West. Probably the poet wanted to keep to his central emphasis on evidence in order to convince those without faith; prophets emerging from Hades would not directly support his point. There are fewer figures of speech than usual. The one on the bitter taste has parallels in St. John Chrysostom's liturgy for Easter morning (see note to Strophe 6).

Meter: The Oxford edition points up the similarity in metrical scheme between this rather unusual grouping of units and the plan for the kontakion on Elijah. The scheme is given in the Oxford edition, 527, XXII.

ON THE RESURRECTION II

O. 25

Prooimion: I adore Thy cross, O Christ, God,
> And I shall glorify Thy tomb, O Immortal One,
> And in celebrating the festival of Thy resurrection, I cry to Thee:
> "The Lord is risen."

Strophe 1:   No one, my Savior, knew clearly Thy road
> > to Hades, except Hades
> For he was able from what he saw and what he suffered
> > to learn of Thy power.
> So, I wish first to ask him what happened,
> > And then, after that, I shall ask the guards at Thy tomb
> > > who stole Thy body.
> For even though I know exactly how Thou wert resurrected,
> > O Eternal One,
> > > since I learned it from Thy friends
> Still, even from those who hate Thee I am eager to secure faith
> > in the words of those who cry:
> "The Lord is risen."

Strophe 2:   For the one who loves magnifies the one whom he loves,
> and the one who hates tells the truth even when he does not wish to.
> As it is written: Salvation is from our enemies[1]
> > and from those who hate us.

ADAM   "Tell me, then, first of all, Hades, eternal enemy of my race,
> How did you hold in the tomb the One who loved my race?
> > Who did you consider He was?
> In any event, had you considered Him like all men on earth,
> > O wretch, forever miserable,
> You have lost those whom you did possess, and Him whom you
> said you would hold,
> > For truly you did not find Him,
> The Lord is risen."

1. Presumably the poet has turned around the scriptural passage that states that salvation delivers us from the enemy. The Old Testament usually says, "God delivers from our enemies." (Luke i.71. Compare Ps. xviii.48, and cxxxvi.24.)

Strophe 3:
HADES

"Do you desire to learn from me, O man, how my murderer
                                                        descended against me?
        I have been annihilated, and I do not have the strength
            to bellow against you,
                                                    for I am still dumbfounded.
    O man, as was customary, I was watching Him at the time,
            In that very moment, as I was observing, I saw Him move
                                                    His mortal remains as He lay there;
    And in a short time, leaping up with vigor, He arises,
                                                    and the hands which I bound
        He places around my throat, and all the people I had swallowed
                                                    I disgorge as they cry:
            'The Lord is risen.'

Strophe 4:
HADES

"But why do I mourn for the dead of whom I am despoiled?
                                    I mourn for myself and the way I am mocked.
        The one thing was not enough shame for me;
                                                    but I must be jeered at.
    Those who have escaped me call me greedy and a glutton,
            And with such words they irritate me, saying,
                                                    'Why do you open up your large gullet?
    Why do you thrust in your mouth any old thing in any old way,
                                                    O greedy and insatiable one?
        Why do you rush for food, causing distress to your stomach?
                                                    For lo, having emptied you,
            The Lord is risen.'

Strophe 5:
HADES

"But if they wish an answer, I am able to reply:
                                                    'Who would not have been led astray
        Seeing Him wrapped in the linen shroud and
                                                    placed in the tomb?[2]
    Who would have been so dumb as not to know that He was dead,
            When He was anointed with unguent of myrrh and aloe
                                                    and brought to me?[3]
    Again, who would have said that He was not dead when they saw
                                                    the stone where He was lying?

2. Mark xv.46.
3. John xix.39.

264

Who would have imagined such a thing, or who would ever have
hoped to hear them say about Him,
"The Lord is risen"?'

Strophe 6: "None of the things they say about me are against me,
HADES   for He voluntarily came against me;
At first I suffered; and finally I do not know
what I suffered.
The sweet flower became for me euphorbia[4]
And all my throat was irritated by the taste, and I
disgorged those whom I had held.
No one had imagined or accomplished such a thing against me
as He did;
I ruled over kings and was in control of prophets
and of those who cry out:
'The Lord is risen.'

Strophe 7: "Lo, I, the master, am in chains, and I am a slave
HADES   who ruled a short time ago;
I, the terrible, am caught in terror, and I am
a laughingstock to all.
I am entirely naked for He has taken from me all my possessions;
He gave a command and suddenly all surrounded Him,
as bees, a honeycomb.[5]
And then, having securely bound me, He told them to mock me,
and to strike my head,
And to bend my back, and crush my heart and cry,
'The Lord is risen.'

Strophe 8: "It was night when I endured these things, but by dawn
HADES   I beheld something else;
As the fiery assembly rushed in to greet
and escort Him,
While fears from without and battles within held me,[6]
I did not have the courage to look one way or the other,
since all threatened me.

4. Euphorbia is bitter; medicinally it is used as a purgative. The editor of the French edition notes
the frequent play on the words meaning *bitter* in On the Victory of the Cross, Strophe 15; Resur-
rection IV, Strophe 4, and even in the Byzantine ritual for Easter morning (*Fr. ed.*, IV, 465n2).
5. Ps. cxviii.12.
6. II Cor. vii.5.

And so, hiding my face between my knees,

                                         I cried out, weeping,

    'Thou who hast broken down my gates and crushed the bars,

                              move on, since I cry,[7]

      "The Lord is risen".'"

Strophe 9:   But He, smiling at these words, said to those behind Him,

CHRIST   "Follow me,"

    And to those in front He said: "Precede me, since it is for this

                            that you have come."

Suddenly, silence and fear prevailed over the whole Creation,

    For the Lord of Creation came forth from the tomb.

Before Him were all the prophets repeating what they had foretold

                        and making known to all

That "This is the One who voluntarily came down to earth,

                   and of His will departs from it.

    The Lord is risen."

Strophe 10:   In a loud voice Sophronias[8] cried to Adam: "He is here

    Whom you awaited up to the day of resurrection,

                        as I prophesied to you."[9]

After him, Nahum[10] announced the good news to the poor, saying,

    "From the earth He has arisen, breathing on your face,

                      He who frees from oppression."

And Zacharias[11] with joy cries out, "Thou hast come, our God,

                          with Thy saints."

And David[12] sang a song of good omen, "How like a mighty one,

                      roused out of sleep

    The Lord is risen."

Strophe 11:   "While they slapped my face with prophecies, psalms, and hymns,

HADES   Women arose and prophesied, dancing in triumph over me;[13]

And the first of them was the sister of Moses,

7. Ps. cvii.16; Isa. xlv.2. The phrase is in common currency, reflecting the frequent references to *Acta Pilati*, II (xxi).
8. Zeph. iii.8.
9. Isa. lxi.1.
10. Nahum in the English translation is quite different; the Greek Nah. ii.2, reads: ἀνέβη ἐμφυσῶν εἰς πρόσωπόν σου, ἐξαιρούμενος ἐκ θλίψεως––
11. Zach. xiv.5.
12. Ps. lxxviii.65 (really by Asaph, not David).
13. Ex. xv.20–21 (Miriam, sister of Aaron).

Leaping and shaking in her hands a drum

which she had just brought;

And coming across my domain like another Red Sea,

she joyfully beat the drum:

'Let us praise our God, for He has been gloriously glorified,

having demolished Hades,[14]

The Lord is risen.'

Strophe 12: "Ah, of what evils was that one night the mother,

HADES   and of what horrors was one dawn the father!

The one produced them, the other outstripped them in

putting a name to my suffering.

They call the Resurrection the day of my fall;

They make a high festival of the time of my destruction.

Woe is me, woe is me, what I have suffered!"

These things Hades said to me as he answered me;

and he did not persuade me by words;

But he was revealed by facts—after he was shown

as naked and destitute,

The Lord is risen.[15]

Strophe 13: After this kind of talk for quite a time, when I found

the guards of the tomb,

I was moved to hasten to question them,

to finish up what I had said before.

Let no one of my friends consider that I am talking foolishly,

Or saying something out of season; I considered it necessary

to do what I ought to do.[16]

"Tell me, then, you most unreasonable soldiers,

what was it that happened?

Who rolled away the stone and carried off the dead,

and said after that,

'The Lord is risen'?"

14. *Fr. ed.,* IV, 470n1. There is a parallel reference quoted from a letter of St. Jerome (Lettre xxii, 41, ed. J. Labourt, I, Paris, 1949, 159) to Eustachius, "On Virginity," in which Mary is to come with a chorus of virgins, singing of the glory of the defeat of Pharaoh.
15. These constructions are very irregular; the text is faulty.
16. This transitional strophe is rhetorically important in clarifying the poet's purpose, as a preacher, to assemble all the evidence. Of course, he pretends to be unconvinced in order to make his witnesses more credible.

Strophe 14:   But when they heard this, the men who formerly guarded

                                                                        the tomb of the Immortal

                   Answered, not conversing loudly with me,

                                                                        but explaining in flight:

GUARDS   "What do you see us doing, man, living in peace or fleeing?

                   From this, then, know that we were absolutely dumbfounded;

                                                                        it is not that we stole,

                   For not a one of us allowed drowsiness in his eyes,

                                                                        nor terror in his spirit; [17]

                   But all were awake; all were constantly on guard,

                                                                        and we do not know how

                   The Lord is risen."

Strophe 15:   Now what you say, guards of the tomb

                                                                        is not acceptable to me;

                   And I am not persuaded that you were entirely ignorant

                                                                        of the resurrection of Christ;

                   For you do everything in every way with safety in mind;

                   How could you not know what happened to the one guarded?

                                                                        Knowing this, then, explain.

GUARDS   "No one is able to report to you accurately what you wish,"

                                                                        the guards said to me.

                   "No one of these in the tomb, not even the incorporeal one

                                                                        who said in the tomb:

                   'The Lord is risen.'

Strophe 16:   "Whatever we know, this we reveal to you;
GUARDS   for if we were to keep silent now,

                   The stones would cry out and refute our hardness [18]

                                                                        and our blindness;

                   For we do not know that very hour of the resurrection;

                   But we know what we have endured since that hour;

                                                                        just hold on and listen.

                   As we were watching over the tomb and taking care

                        lest something happen,

                                                                        suddenly we perceive

17. Ps. cxxxii.4.
18. Luke xix.40.

268

Fiery hands which take away the stone from the tomb,
                                    and a voice cries out this:
        'The Lord is risen.'

Strophe 17: "By him the stone was rolled away, and all our force was weakened
GUARDS   And nothing was left for us by way of aid, no word, no thought,
    For we were all dead men, we who guarded the dead,[19]
        And all our wisdom was consumed suddenly[20]
                            as what we beheld was accomplished.
    For the shape like fire of the one who rolled the stone
                                was manifest to us,
        And on earth he showed spirit, as though angry
                            at those who did not cry,
        'The Lord is risen.'

Strophe 18: "What you wish to learn in order that you may marvel is this:
GUARDS   he was approachable by the women,
        And to us wretched men he was not approachable,
                                that fiery one.
    He conversed with them; he threatened death to us.
        Them he strengthened; and humbled us with fear,
                            and overtaking us, he buried us.
    To the women he was gay; with us he became as one
                            rather haughty.[21]

    And he mortified us, but he nerved them
                                to cry: 'Fear not,
        The Lord is risen.'

Strophe 19: "When the women stood still,
GUARDS   and wisely looked in the vault,
        The incorporeal one spoke to them:
                            'The One whom you seek is risen.
    But if you do not believe and consider me as a phantom,
        Follow me and behold the place
                            where the Lord was lying.'
    And when they went within, at that time we fled,
                                and said this:

19. Matt. xxviii.3–4.
20. Ps. cvii.27.
21. Matt. xxviii.4–6.

If the servant has come and has shaken up the earth[22]

what, then, happens now that

The Lord is risen?

Strophe 20: "Do not now, man, enlist yourself
GUARDS

among those fools,

And believe us when we falsely say that Christ

was stolen away and did not arise;

It is gold which persuaded us to conceal the truth,[23]

Gold which turns all the things they wish as they wish,

for those who boast of it.

That is exactly why we were bought off, and taking the profit,

we filled everyone full

Of the rumor of the theft, for we were paid

not to say that in truth

'The Lord is risen'."

Strophe 21: So Hades first said these things to me,

and such are the words the guards

Added besides, as a seal to those words which the insatiable

one had babbled.

But I from the two reaped the harvest which I desired,

From the couple of liars I reaped the truth;

and for this indeed I rejoiced.

It is what Samson said as a riddle for such times;

I now understand:

From Hades who eats, and from the strong army

has come forth a sweet pronouncement:[24]

"The Lord is risen."

Strophe 22: Thou art without beginning and without end,

Creator, and God of truth,

Who hast caused death to Death and hast made man

immortal,

22. The servant must refer to the angel, and the idea is that he has caused some disturbance; then, of course, Christ's resurrection will cause much more.
23. Matt. xxviii.15.
24. Judg. xiv.14: "Out of the eater came forth meat, and out of the strong came forth sweetness": the riddle of Samson. The poet compares the product of the bees in the carcass of the dead lion to the resurrection, which brings forth Christ from the confines of greedy Hades.

In the last hour, when Thou dost come to resurrect me,
    For Thou wilt come, my Savior, not as now from the tomb,
                                    but from the firmament;
  Then, seeing Thee, I rise up,[25] O Lover of men,
                             for loving Thee, I possess Thee.
    Do not then condemn me, I pray, so that I may say,
                  "Not for my punishment, but to redeem me
      The Lord is risen."

25. If we accept the conjecture made in the Oxford edition for this lacuna as ἐνεργῶ, "I become active or alive," the meaning would seem to be: "If when I behold Thee, I rise up, O Lover of Man, then . . ."; this interpretation makes more sense than the supposition of the editor of the French edition in the note, IV, 483.

ON THE RESURRECTION III

O. 26 (K. 75)

Title: ἕτερον κοντάκιον ἀναστάσιμα

Manuscripts and editions: The complete kontakion is given only in the Patmos manuscript. The editors of the Oxford edition question the authenticity of the last stanza, since it doubles the upsilon in the acrostic; it is then considered another form of Strophe 10. In the absence of a closing prayer, Romanos may be giving two strophes to Adam as presenting the reactions of all mankind to the Resurrection.

It is edited by Tomadakis, IV, 207–30, and it is included in the French edition, IV, 550–63.

Tone: ἦχος πλάγιος δ'

Acrostic: 'Ωδὴ 'Ρωμανοῦ(υ)

Refrain: διὰ τῆς ἀναστάσεως

Biblical source and place in the liturgy: The manuscript indicates that it was written for Easter Sunday. The apocryphal account of the Descent to Hell is the general source, as indeed it is for most of the Resurrection kontakia; but in this poem Hades is also Satan as he carries on a dialogue with Adam who, of course, represents all mankind.

Analysis of content: The topic of the Resurrection and the two speakers, Adam and Hades, are introduced in the prooimion. Each speaker is then given a strophe in the ensuing dialogue until the end, where Adam speaks through two strophes. In the first four strophes Adam foretells the coming of Christ to set him free and Hades brags of his invincible power. It is curious that, in Strophe 4, Hades says he has been given orders to keep the race of Adam in his power. This implies that it was God who gave the command at the time of Adam's disobedience. Strophes 5 and 6 are central, in that they include details of Christ's suffering as told by Adam and a brief account of the Resurrection and its effect on all of creation. In the dialogue, Hades laments and Adam continues to gloat in alternate strophes. There is no closing prayer. In the last few strophes, the use of "O Death where is your victory" reflects I Cor. xvi.54–56, just as in Resurrection, IV, Strophe 7. Here it becomes an effective part of the refrain.

Style of Romanos: This kontakion is not at all typical of Romanos' style. It is much shorter than others, and, although it is in dialogue form, it presents practically no touch of dramatic realism and no special originality. The references to the Old Testament are reduced to almost nothing, and the poem gives only a brief account of Christ's victory and the redemption of mankind through the Resurrection, which brought the defeat of the nether powers.

Meter: The meter is simple. The scheme is given in the Oxford edition, 528, XXIII.

ON THE RESURRECTION III

O. 26

Prooimion: "By Thy Passion, our Savior, we are set free from passions."
Adam cried out to Thee, and Hades was overwhelmed
Because of the Resurrection.

Strophe 1: As the earth gladly accepts the rain from Heaven,
Just so, Adam who was held captive in Hades, awaited[1]
The Savior of the world, and Giver of life,
ADAM And said to Hades: "Why are you conceited?
Wait for me; wait a short time, and you will soon see
Your power destroyed and mine exalted;
Now you hold in bondage me and my race,
After a while you will see that I am freed from you,
For Christ will come for me,[2] and you will tremble;
And He will bring to an end your tyranny
Through the Resurrection."

Strophe 2: "No one has ever possessed such abundance of power of this sort;
HADES For I am king of all," said Hades to Adam.
"For what other person will control me and rise superior to me?
Who will take my kingdom from me?
Abraham, and Isaac, and Jacob, and Joseph,
And all the prophets I hold in my power;
And you I first possessed as chief of all of them.[3]
How, then, can you say that someone will come and trample on me?
Would this person, then, be superior to all these others,
So that He will deliver you, as you say,
Through the Resurrection?"

Strophe 3: Adam heard Hades boasting in this way,
And at once, the first created of mortals said to him:

1. Job xxix.23.
2. The δι ἐμὲ means both "because of me" and "for me."
3. Adam is first, in point of time, and chief because his sin condemned the rest.

ADAM   "Hear my words, and do not in vain exalt yourself,
    For I whom you possess you cannot dominate;
I was thrown out from the joy of Paradise because of you,
    Treacherous one, and I was sent down to you a short time ago;[4]
You are my guard; but you do not have the power to destroy me;
    For I have a King who will wipe out your power;
I serve under Him . . .[5]
    So that He may raise me up to Heaven
        Through the Resurrection."

Strophe 4:   "No one is going to come forward to tear up your sentence;[6]
HADES   The One whom you call your ally, I rule over as king,
For I shall seize Him as I do all men;
    For there is no one anywhere greater than I am.
Do not, then, make a mistake, Adam; why do you struggle in vain?
    I hold you in the tomb, and I rule over your race.
The One whom you think you have as protector
    You will now see crucified and swallowed down by me.
How, then, can you say that He will free you from me?
    I have been given orders to hold your race in my power
        Because of the Resurrection."[7]

Strophe 5:   "Just as He will be made a second Adam, and my Savior because of me,
ADAM   He would not for my sake beg off from wounds.
He will undergo my punishment for me,
    Since he wears flesh, like me.
They will pierce the side[8] of Him whom the Cherubim do not behold,
    And water will gush forth and quench my burning heat.
You think that you will hold Him as a man;
    You will devour Him as a mortal; but you will disgorge Him as God
After three days; for you will not be able to endure
    The torture which He will inflict on you
        Through the Resurrection."

4. The word νῦν must suggest that Adam now feels his term with Hades has not been long, in view of his impending release.

5. This lacuna is not filled in the Oxford edition. The editor of French edition (IV, 554n1) suggests βοηθῷ ἀνθρώπων, "defender of men."

6. The debt or the sentence of condemnation is canceled by the cross. Romanos uses this figure of Paul (Col. ii.14) in Kontakion #16, Strophe 10, and Kontakion #10, Strophe 18.

7. God sent Adam to Hades. Christ will redeem him, but Hades does not believe there will be any resurrection. The refrain is not clearly connected with the strophe.

8. John xix.34.

Strophe 6:   Let us learn, then, my brothers, what the Lord does.

           For when He had tasted the vinegar and gall[9] on the cross,

CHRIST   He said: "This is the end of my sufferings,"

           And bowing His head, He gave up His spirit.[10]

      The sun and moon and stars of Heaven

           Were not able to endure this gross insult and hid their brilliance.[11]

      Little hills and mountains took thought of flight,

           And even the veil of the temple was torn in twain;[12]

      But the first-created man cried out from the abyss,

ADAM   "O my God, deliver me from Hades

              Through the Resurrection."

Strophe 7:   But Christ, Life, came to reveal death as sleep;[13]

           Hades received Christ like each of the earth-born.

      He devoured the heavenly bread like bait,

           He was wounded by the hook of divinity.

      And Hades, lamenting, cried out:

HADES   "I am pierced in the stomach; I do not digest the One

           whom I devoured;

      What I have devoured gave me strange eating!

           Not one of those whom I have eaten hitherto has troubled me.

      Perhaps He is the One whom Adam had announced to me

           Saying, 'When He comes, He will chastise you

              Through the Resurrection'."

Strophe 8:   "Now you will recall my words, which I said to you a long time ago,

ADAM   'My King is stronger than you.'

      But you considered these words a dream.

           Experience will teach you His force.

      For it is not only I, but all my descendants,

           And all men that you will lose; you will be deprived of all.

      The Christ whom you saw hanging on the cross,

           He will himself enchain you, and joyfully I shall reply:

---

9. Matt. xxvii.34; John xix.29.
10. John xix.30.
11. Joel ii.10; Luke xxiii.44–45.
12. Matt. xxvii.51; Mark xv.38; Luke xxiii.45. The τέμπλον in a Greek church separates the altar from the nave; the Temple at Jerusalem contained a "Holy of Holies," which received light through the veil that separated it from the next room.
13. Compare Lazarus II (#15), Strophe 4, and note.

'Where, O Death is your victory, and where your power?[14]
    God has destroyed your strength
        Through the Resurrection'."

Strophe 9:   "Just so, on the third day, the whale disgorged Jonas.[15]
HADES   Now I disgorge Christ and all of those who are Christ's;
Because of the race of Adam I am being chastised."
       Uttering these laments, Hades cried out with groans.
"I did not believe Adam when he told me these things in advance;
       But I boasted and loudly proclaimed: 'No one rules over me.'
For formerly I was lord of all;
       But now I have lost all men, and taunting me, they say:
'Where O Death is your victory? or where is your power?
       God has destroyed your strength
         Through the Resurrection'."

Strophe 10:   "In His coming, Christ has humbled your proud strength;
ADAM   In assuming my whole natural form, He has put you to flight.
I am now bought by His precious blood;
       He who knows no corruption has freed me from corruption.
Wherever you may turn, you see on all sides
       Tombs which are emptied, and you,[16] shameless one, naked.
Where are your bolts and bars, strong one?
       My Jesus has come down and shivered to atoms all your possessions.
Where, O Death is your victory, or where is your power?
       God has destroyed your strength
         Through the Resurrection.

Strophe 11:   "He has lifted me to the Heavens; you He has put to flight;
ADAM   For the rest of time I share the throne, I am no longer
         subject to you.
He took my body that He might make it new;
       He will make it immortal and cause it to share His throne.
I shall reign with Him, for I have been resurrected with Him.[17]

14. I Cor. xv.55; Hos. xiii.14.
15. Jon. ii.10; Matt. xii.40.
16. ἄσχημον necessarily understands σε and applies to Hades.
17. Eph. ii.6.

No longer are you my master; but I rule over you.
My pledge of surety is now on high,
  But you are trampled on below by those who cry,
'Where, O Death, is your victory, or where your strength?
  God has destroyed your strength
    Through the Resurrection'."

ON THE RESURRECTION IV

O. 27 (K. 79)

Title: Εἰς τὴν ἀνάστασιν τοῦ κυρίου καὶ εἰς τὰς δέκα δραχμάς

Manuscripts and editions: This kontakion is found only in P.
French edition, IV, 565–601.

Tone: ἦχος αʹ

Acrostic: Τοῦτο ταπεινοῦ ʽΡωμανοῦ

Refrain: ἡ ζωὴ καὶ ἀνάστασις

Biblical source and place in the liturgy: The story of the woman and the lost coins comes from
Luke xv.8–10.[1]

> The source for The Harrowing of Hell is *Acta Pilati*.[4]
> The kontakion is marked for the third Sunday after Easter.[2]

Analysis of content: The prooimion addresses those who have been baptized and brings in
the motif, "Death, where is thy victory?" This was used effectively by the poet
in Resurrection III (#26). The refrain is significantly similar to that of Lazarus I
(#14), which introduced the Easter cycle after Palm Sunday.

The story of the woman and the lost coins is used in the first four strophes
as an introduction to an explanation of the nature of Christ. Hades enters in
Strophe 5, and in Strophe 6 Christ calls on Adam and all the patriarchs to rise
up.[3] Strophes 7 through 17, the center of the kontakion, consist of a dialogue
between Christ and Hades,[4] in which Hades in three strophes says that his kingdom

---

1. The title given in the lemma reads: "Kontakion on the Resurrection of the Lord and the Ten
Drachma."
2. The first Sunday after Easter is given over to On Doubting Thomas (Kontakion #30), and
the second Sunday to the Women at the Tomb (Kontakion #29, On the Resurrection VI).
3. It seems to me that the editor of the French edition is right in using as an argument for the
absence of a lacuna between Strophes 5 and 6 the organization of the hymn and the close connection
between those two strophes (*Fr. ed.*, IV, 571).
4. *Acta Pilati*, Part II, xxii, Tischendorf, ed. (Lipsiae, 1853), 307. The frequent use Romanos
makes of the *Acta Pilati*, which is of Syrian origin, points up again the fact that Ephrem is a source
of inspiration for his kontakia. However, the uses made of the dialogues between the Devil
and Hades in connection with the Harrowing of Hell are different in many ways from the tradition.
In The Crucifixion (#21), The Victory of the Cross (#22), and Resurrection III (#26), Satan and/or

is being unjustly entered, that it is not fair that he is bound. He calls on his minions to bar the gates. He ends each of his three strophes with comments on the divine and the human Christ. Christ, in Strophe 11, defends Himself as though in court, and in Strophe 12 He explains the reasons for Adam's fall. In the next four strophes He states that He is glad to be examined because He will be shown to be faultless; hence, Hades must release all men and destroy his records against them.[5] In Strophe 17 all the dead rise up, and an angel rolls away the stone from the tomb. The poet then asks why the angel is needed, and Christ explains His power.[6] The poet asks how he can be sure that the machinery that opens the tombs will work for him, and Christ promises eternal life.

Connection with homily: The preliminary strophes find parallels in a Pseudo-Chrysostom homily, *P.G.*, 61, 781. The relevant passage is quoted in *Fr. ed.*, IV, 573. It is probable that there was a common source for homily and kontakion.

Style of Romanos: Very typically, the theological emphasis on the two natures of Christ pervades the first strophes on the woman and the coins and also the major strophes on the Harrowing of Hell. The dialogue between Christ and Hades is given realistic touches in the setting of a trial. To be sure, Christ is made necessarily certain, and Hades is given no more arguments than are necessary to bring out the two natures of Christ.

The figures of speech centering on Christ as the light are used effectively in the first strophes; rather unusual is the one that presents Christ as a lamp on a lampstand, thus recalling the cross. The symbolism of the ten coins seems far-fetched, but it would suit the medieval taste for an allegorical sense underlying the literal story. The use of gall, vinegar, and the spear as weapons against Hades occurs also in other kontakia. There are not as many references to the Old Testament as usual. The comparison of Christ in the tomb with Jonah in the whale was familiar at that time.

Meter: The metrical scheme is given in the Oxford edition, 528, XXIV.

Hades admit their defeat. In the present hymn, as in Resurrection II (#25), Christ calls up the prophets and Hades laments. The addition of the legal procedure when Christ defends himself before Hades is unusual.

5. The case is really a parody on the treatment Christ had received on earth, for He was cudgeled before He was tried; He was deserted by friends; His judge was also His accuser. The demon claims that there has been an abuse of power. Interesting articles are cited on the rights of demons in *Fr. ed.*, IV, 567–68.

It is important to observe that the poet interchanges or consolidates the roles of Hades and Satan. The second half of the dialogue is chiefly addressed to Satan, who deals with sinners on earth and in Hell.

6. The poet likes to insert some question unexpectedly, before the final prayer. In this way he can work in theological answers to questions the preacher must have had to answer. Such is this insertion about the need of an angel.

ON THE RESURRECTION IV

O. 27

Prooimion: Let those of us united[1] with Christ through baptism
          And risen with Him sing praises and cry out:
     "Where, O Death, is thy victory, and Hades, where is thy sting?"[2]
          For the Lord is risen,
               The Life and Resurrection."[3]

Strophe 1:   As we hear the parable of Christ
                              which Luke narrates in his Gospels,[4]
          Let us not consider it of secondary importance;
                              but let us examine it in faith.
     The woman and the drachma: Who are they,
                         and what is the nature of the coin she lost?
          She sought for it diligently, lighting a lamp and sweeping
          Her whole house; and when she had found it,
                              she called in her neighbors, saying:
     "Come, rejoice with me, for I have found what I lost."[5]
          Now we long for Christ, saying,
          "Lord, illumine our spirits
          So that light is established,
               The Life and Resurrection."

Strophe 2:   The number of the coins is clear to all, for there were ten—
          Ten in all which the Lord who made the universe possessed.

1. The conjectural reading for the beginning of the prooimion is οἱ [κολλη]θέντες in the Oxford edition, and οἱ [συνταφ]έντες in the French edition. The latter seems more likely, since Paul uses the word in Rom. vi.4, and Col. ii.12. In the former the "buried with him by baptism into death; that like as Christ was raised up from the dead . . . even so we should also walk in newness of life" becomes very appropriate to the Resurrection Kontakion.
2. I Cor. xv.54–55. Romanos uses this in Resurrection III (#26) and in Lazarus I (#14).
3. John xi.25.
4. Luke xv.8–9.
5. The Oxford text uses the plural [ἅσ]περ, with the ten drachma in mind, but in Luke the woman had "ten drachmas," but she says: "I have found *the* drachma ἣν ἀπώλεσα."

The woman is, they say, the virtue and wisdom of the Creator,
  Or she is Christ, the wisdom and power of God.[6]
  There are ten coins, prime causes, resources, powers, and thrones,
And dominions, angels, archangels,
  Cherubim and Seraphim,
  And the first created man whom He destroyed and sought for,
  And whom He found when fallen, He—
    The Life and Resurrection.

Strophe 3:   Overcome by love, He came into the world
                                      to seek His creature who had wandered.
  Without beginning, and Ineffable, Son of God and our God,
Wisely and with divine providence, as a God, He makes the search.
    He is made flesh from His mother whom He cleansed (as though
      swept clean) and sanctified;
    And He offers[7] His body as a lamp to the fire and oil
Of His divinity which illumines all.
    For fire and clay always make light.
    Thus from His divinity and Incarnation, Christ
    Shed the light of the Lamp—
      The Life and Resurrection.

Strophe 4:   Then He ascended the cross, as a lamp in a lampstand,[8]
                                      and from there He saw
    Adam, the first created man sitting in gloom and darkness;
  And He who is inseparable from His home, hastens
                                      to journey far in the flesh to Adam,
    He who was not separated from the bosom of His Father,
                                      still brings to pass all events.
    He took with Him the gall and the vinegar,
                                      the nails and the spear
In order that, with the spear and the nails, He might
    immediately overcome Death
    And Hades, when Hades came in contact with the bitter gall
    And vinegar which He has drunk, He,
      The Life and Resurrection.

6. I Cor. i.24. This symbolism is used by Cyril of Alexandria (*P.G.*, 72, 800B–801A). Other references are given in *Fr. ed.*, IV, 579*n*3.
7. The reading προσφέρει is adopted rather than προφέρει. His body, like a lamp, contains the fire and oil.
8. Matt. v.15; Luke viii.16; xi.33.

284

Strophe 5: After the crucifixion, when the King first arrived below in Hades
His light shone in the darkness and illumined it below,[9]
For the darkness was not able to check Christ;
He had ample strength in darkness.
For, just as Jonah was in the belly of his tomb,
So He was carried into the tomb and yet in the grave He was alive,[10]
For His divinity was not separated from the flesh.
Thus, Hades on beholding His awesome miracle,
HADES   Cried out, "Come, Death, let us behold
What sort of light He has kindled, He,
The Life and Resurrection.

Strophe 6: "Quickly," he said, "let us take courage,
HADES   for this is the body of a man carried in the tomb;
Let us guard with bolts the one who comes,
and let us give him over to putrefaction."
And immediately as he said this, he ran quickly
and laid hold on the body;
But Jesus Christ, as though arising from sleep,[11]
Enchains him and forcibly puts him down as
He cries out to those in Hades:
CHRIST   "Rise up, all, and trample on Hades.
Adam and Eve come into my presence;
Do not be afraid as though liable for past debts,
For I have delivered all, I,
The Life and Resurrection.

Strophe 7: "Shamelessly strike the face of Hades, ye mortals,
CHRIST   and trample on his neck;
Come to them crying: 'Hades and Death are destroyed.'
For you I have come, for I am the life and resurrection of all;
So, all with joy recite psalms and songs:
'Where is thy victory, O dishonored Hades?
Where, O Death is thy sting?'[12]

9. John i.5. Whether $δύ[ναται]$ is to be supplied in line 3, although it adds syllables to the line (Oxford ed. conjecture), or whether $οὐδ[έν]$ is used, as in *Fr. ed.*, IV, 582n1, the general meaning is the same. In Kontakion #28 (Resurrection V), there is a reference to light in the darkness of Hell.
10. Job xxi.32.
11. Ps. lxxviii.65.
12. See note 2. Compare Hos. xiii.14.

You lie powerless, Death, condemned to death,
    And you, Hades, skillfully bound down,
    You who were ruling have been enslaved as you behold
That He is at hand,
      The Life and Resurrection."

Strophe 8:   In answer to this, the hated Hades, along with Death,
                           and bound with him,
    Even as he lay there cried out; and as master he gave
      order to his men:
HADES   "Run now, since you see that I suffer injustice,
    Do you quickly close the bronze gates and guard them. [13]
    Put up the iron bars on the gates and permit no one
Of those assembled to come forth from the tomb,
    For I wish to contend with the one
    Who comes against me. Make fast and secure
    Those who cry out: 'He has come,
      The Life and Resurrection.'

Strophe 9:   "What kind of injustice am I undergoing,
HADES   since until now I have been king of men?
    Tell me then, O man, who you are, and how you have come here?
For it is clear that you are a man; I see a human body;
    But everyone descended from the race of Adam is my possession.
    Why, then, do you, who come from all men overpower me
                 as though you came on behalf of all men? [14]
For every man is subject to me whether he lived
    A long or short time on earth.
    How, then, have you become more than human
    And a redeemer of men,
      The Life and Resurrection?

Strophe 10:   "Let me who have been treated unjustly state a case against you,
HADES   for I see that the son of man
    Has accomplished the deeds of God and not of man,
                 though he appears human.

---

13. *Acta Pilati,* xxi (Tischendorf, ed.), 306.

14. That is to say, Christ is a man ἐκ πάντων, and He has divine power for all men ὑπὲρ ἀπάντων.

I see the wound in your side and the prints of nails;
> But I see your power and the undefiled light flashing forth;
> If, then, you are man, you are subject to Death and Hades;
But if, becoming man—a thing to be seen,
> You have become God—a thing to be discerned in you,
> Then now interpret for me that we may see how, if
> > you appear as man,
> You have become
> > The Life and Resurrection."

Strophe 11: Now when Christ heard him shouting these things,
> > > > at once He spoke to him:

CHRIST
> > "I plead my case and am judged; for I do not wish
> > > > to do you wrong in any way.
> For even if you are unjust and shameless and worthy of condemnation,
> > I have indeed become man, as you see; but I am
> > Faultless, the Word of God, and Creator of all men
> > > > > and God, the Ruler of all.
> But even if I am God, I do not judge as a despot,
> > But, along with you, I shall plead my case as far as Adam is concerned.
> > I was born of his nature,[15] and I shall conquer you
> > > and overthrow you
> > From the kingdom which you possess. I am
> > > The Life and Resurrection.

Strophe 12: "Adam had the complete joy of eternal life;

CHRIST
> > > > > but he was especially[16] deceived.
> > I, the Creator of all things, am become life which really exists;[17]
> But you, Hades, did not exist in the beginning, nor did the
> > > reality of Death.[18]
> > The suffering of terrible sin engendered him and you.
> > And so Adam, through a trick of the Deceiver, became enslaved to sin,

---

15. In Strophe 28 of Kontakion #28, a similar line reads "as the earthborn Adam. . . ." Here τοῦτο must mean "I became *this kind of thing*" and refer to Adam as the representative of human nature.

16. ἐν πρώτοις probably has the double significance of time, "from the first," and also its usual idiomatic meaning of "especially."

17. ἐνυπόστατος means "I took on the nature" or "I have in me" the kind of life that brings immortality.

18. James i.15; Rom. vii.5. Death and Hades actually had no existence other than that created by Adam's sin. ὑπόστασις does not seem to have its usual doctrinal significance.

And he became subject to you and a prisoner
    For you and bitter Death.
    For this reason you are without any actual existence [19]
        and easily captured.
    How, then, will you prevail over
        The Life and Resurrection?

Strophe 13:   "Exalted by folly, you control the descendants of Adam

CHRIST   as partners in sin,
        And you imprison them as though they still owe an ancestral debt.
    But every descendant of Adam, born in sin, was liable to me.
        He was born of corruption, and of union with husband, and
            intercourse;
        But I am free from all that, from sin, and from intercourse,[20]
    For even if I became man, as I willed it,
        A virgin womb brought me forth blameless;
        And, for the sake of all men, I have given my blood
        To the One who engendered me,
            The Life and Resurrection.

Strophe 14:   "Examine me, readily do I allow it,[21] and see that you will find

CHRIST   no unjust word or deed.
        For I have not done wrong in any action, nor have I uttered
                                                anything deceitful in word.[22]
    Therefore I speak. 'Who of you will accuse me of sin?'[23]
        For among all the dead now I am shown to be free
            in every respect,[24]
        And of all sensual mortals I am the one who is
            unacquainted with sin.
                                                How, then, Hades, did you dare
    To restrain the faultless as guilty?
        Examine me carefully,
        For I wish to know the truth, that I have even now
        Refuted you justly, I,
            The Life and Resurrection.

19. ἀνυπόστατοι: meaning without any visible, real, or actual existence. They are mere abstractions.
20. Prov. xx.9.
21. A use of ῥᾴως with the idea of *I am ready to be examined*, rather than "examine easily."
22. Ps. xvii.3; Isa. liii.9; Ps. xxxii.2; I Pet. ii.22.
23. John viii.46.
24. Ps. lxxxviii.5.

Strophe 15: "And so you are shamelessly angry, for it is a just trial

CHRIST   and you will have been completely thrown out,

       You lawless leaders[25] of the realm of darkness,

                                for transgressing what is just;

   For if you have found in me any remnant of sin,

       Then use against me, O unjust one, all of your punishments;

       But if you have found nothing, restore quickly whatever

         record[26] you keep.

  Since, in this case, you happen to have been exerting all your strength

       Against the faultless Christ,

       Make ready for restitution of those whom you seized in advance,

       Those whom I have raised up, I,

         The Life and Resurrection.

Strophe 16: "Only in order that you may not be ignorant about what you

CHRIST   are facing, Hades:

                               not only will you give back

       Those whom you took, but also I have raised up those

                     whom I take with me as I leave here,

   For indeed, as you know, if for the rest of time,

                   men are conveyed to you, they will arise,

       Since at the sound of the trumpet I shall raise them

         up all together[27]

       Because you have had the daring to lay hold on the blameless

         Son of the King."

  As Christ said this, Hades was overcome.[28]

       The gatekeepers threw away their keys

       And fled as they saw Christ

       Crush and break their bolts, He,

         The Life and Resurrection.

Strophe 17: Suddenly the bodies of the dead became animated;

       they were resurrected,

                        and they trampled on Hades,

---

25. ἄδικος means unjust, lawless, without reverence for God. No one English word carries the full meaning. The poet enjoys repeating the root word: δικαία, ἄδικοι, δίκαιον, ἄδικε with slightly different meanings each time.

26. The poet repeatedly uses Paul's figure of speech from Col. ii.14. *Cf.* On the Entry into Jerusalem, Kontakion #16, Strophe 11; On the Sinful Woman, #10, Strophe 18; On the Resurrection III, #26, Strophe 4. It refers to sentence of condemnation against Adam and the Mosaic law.

27. I Cor. xv.52; I Thess. iv.16.

28. Literally, *submerged.*

Crying out, "O unjust one, where is thy victory

and Death, where is thy sting?"[29]

Suddenly all of the tombs were opened of themselves[30]

And all of the dead were released from them and formed a chorus;

And an angel coming down rolled the stone from the tomb

of the Savior.[31]

"O Lord, Master, Thou hast opened the tombs

At a command, not needing anyone.

How is it then that Thou hast need of someone

To roll away the stone from Thy tomb? Thou,

The Life and Resurrection."

Strophe 18: "Now in order that no one may be led astray, I shall answer you

CHRIST   and explain the question set by you.

The stone was not wholly a hindrance to my way out of the tomb,

Since everything obeys and is subject to me as God,

For even if I become flesh, I am still Lord and Creator of all,

And at my command not long ago sea and land came forth;

The Jordan was turned back;[32]

Springs of water gushed from the rocks[33]

For people in the desert; and the sun withdrew

When they crucified me,[34]

The Life and Resurrection."

Strophe 19: O Thou who at the mere nod of command opened up all the tombs

and released the dead,

And never had need of an angel to roll away Thy stone,

Now, teach me a clever scheme; for I fear that this symbol,[35]

And sign for mortals, the opening up of this stone from the tomb

Will not work in the graves as formerly,

When in this hour, the gates of Hades were pulled up

from their foundations.

29. Hos. xiii.14; I Cor. xv.55.
30. Matt. xxvii.52–53.
31. Matt. xxviii.2.
32. Ps. cxiv.3.
33. Ex. xvii.1–7; Num. xx.2–13; I Cor. x.4.
34. Luke xxiii.44–45.
35. The angel at the tomb of Christ opens His tomb while He at the gates of Hell opens tombs of the dead.

Then, there appeared in shining raiment
An angel who sang a paean of victory,
Saying that there has been resurrected
    The Life and Resurrection.

Strophe 20: In return for these things, O Redeemer, what do we have to offer
                                    except a doxology?[36]

        Therefore, spare, O Christ, as God,
    Those who believe in Thy cross, tomb, and resurrection.
        Grant to us forgiveness of sins,
        And whenever the awakening common to all comes,
    Consider us worthy to see Thy face
        And to hear Thy voice with confidence.

CHRIST   "Along with my saints, inherit
            My kingdom with joy."

        Then grant to our spirits, O Thou full of mercy,
        A spirit of peace that we may glorify
            The Life and Resurrection.

36. A song of praise expected of the Christian who honors God.

ON THE RESURRECTION V

O. 28 (K. 74)

Title: κοντάκιον ἀναστάσιμον

Manuscripts and editions: The manuscript used is P. The Oxford edition indicates that Strophes 24 through 28 are of dubious authenticity, for they could be a revision of #27 (K. 79), Strophes 5 through 13.

The kontakion is included in the French edition with a discussion of this possible rearrangement of #27. *Fr. ed.,* IV, 486–541.

Tomadakis edits it, III, 43–107.

Tone: ἦχος πλάγιος β′

Acrostic: τοῦ ταπεινοῦ ʿΡωμανοῦ αἶνος εἰς τὸ πάθος

Refrain: ὁ λύσας τοῦ βελίαρ τὰ βέλη, τοῦ ῞Αιδου τὸ νῖκος καὶ θανάτου τὸ κέντρον

Biblical source and place in the liturgy: The manuscript indicates that it is for Easter Sunday.

As the analysis of content will reveal, the source of the section on the Descent to Hell is again the Gospel of Nicodemus. Most of the kontakion is strictly theological, and one could go so far as to say that its other source is edicts of Justinian.

Analysis of content: The prooimion announces the theme of the Resurrection, and the refrain names the three speakers: Belial, Hades, and Death. Actually, it is difficult at times to be sure just who is speaking. Hades and Death are evidently the same, and the various names for the devil are given by each strophe in the translation.

The first ten strophes are strictly theological, with the emphasis on the fact that the seeming divergence between the divine and human natures of Christ is resolved in His essential unity; the first four strophes of this group are theoretical, then Judas and the Jews are assailed for five strophes. Strophe 10 defines the effect of the crucifixion.

Strophes 11 and 12 serve to introduce the robber, but only incidentally, because he states a theological point of importance. Strophes 13 through 16 are an attack on various heresies and close this section of the kontakion.

The devil and Hades carry on a dialogue that is very like that of the other Resurrection kontakia. First, they blame one another, then they lament together (Strophes 17 through 21). Strophe 22 states that Christ is the giver of life; it seems to me that this was probably the next to the last strophe originally and that a closing prayer made this a 23-strophe hymn with a reasonable organization of ideas.

As the poem stands, Strophe 23 introduces the legend of the punishment of Satan because he refused to kneel before Adam. Five strophes follow, and these are quite weak reflections of the taunting Hades and Death undergo and Christ's declaration that He will not be tyrannical. The idea of a trial, which Romanos had used in #27, is not well developed here. The last five strophes contain laments by the infernal powers about the tree. They are weak echoes of #22.

The Oxford edition questions Strophes 24 through 28. If the present Strophe 23, beginning with *sigma*, were replaced by the closing prayer, which also begins with *sigma*, it is tempting to conjecture that the acrostic could read τοῦ ταπεινοῦ ʽΡωμανοῦ αἶνος, and we could then omit Strophes 23 through 32 and have a more reasonable poem.

In the introduction to Resurrection VI, #29, which follows, is a summary of the main emphasis in each of the Resurrection kontakia. It reveals that the use of the same material was inevitable. Usually, however, Romanos keeps to a more unified kontakion in the order of strophes than the 33 of #28 would provide without the omission of the last group.

Style of Romanos: Even if the above deletion is at all conceivable, this is not a poem in which Romanos is at his best. It is typical in the theological emphases, with their repetitive insistence on slogans that can be traced to edicts of Justinian. Paul Maas, in *Chron.*, 13, 16, refers us to the edicts of 533 and 551. The kontakion is typical also in the violent condemnation of the Jews. The dialogue is nontypical in its weakness; the lack of imaginative imagery and the paucity of subtle but natural references to the Old Testament are also indications of the fact that the poet has perhaps exhausted creative ideas on this subject.

Meter: The metrical scheme is given in the Oxford edition, 529, XXV.

ON THE RESURRECTION V

O. 28

Prooimion: We have found eternal life in Thy voluntary death,
> O All-powerful One, only God of the universe;
For in Thy holy Resurrection, Merciful One, Thou hast
> recalled all men,
> O Thou who hast destroyed the weapons of Belial,
> > > the victory of Hades,
> and the sting of Death.[1]

Strophe 1: The mystery of Thy plan of salvation,[2] O our Savior,
> > > is ineffable, incomprehensible,[3]
> Since Thou hast remained of the same substance with the Father
> and with us; but in order that we may understand clearly,
Thou art one from both, not mingled together,[4]
Thou hast remained what Thou art and become what Thou wast not,[5]
> Since Thou hast assumed flesh from a pure virgin,
> > > for us and like us, except without sin.[6]
And being God in truth, and man not just in appearance,[7]
> Thou art one and the same who hast received suffering in
> the plan of salvation,
> In order to give freedom from suffering to all men,
> O Thou who hast destroyed the weapons of Belial,
> > > the victory of Hades,
> and the sting of Death.

Strophe 2: Thou who hast by Thy command created all things, Thou hast
> appeared on earth
> > > while remaining inseparable from the Father,

1. *Acta Pilati*, Part II, xxi; Hos. xiii.14; I Cor. xv.55.
2. Justinian, *Confession of Faith*, in 551: τὸ τῆς θείας οἰκονομίας μυστήριον (*Chron. Pasc.*, I, 662).
3. Justinian, *ibid.*, 641: ἀρρήτως, ἀφράστως, ἀκαταλήπτως, ἀϊδίως.
4. Some of the Apollinarists argued this point. The Monophysites who were followers of Eutychus did not agree.
5. Justinian, *ibid.*, 652: εἷς γὰρ ἐξ ἀμφοῖν ὁ Χρίστος.
6. Justinian, *ibid.*, 640: μείνας ὅπερ ἦν οὐ μετέβαλεν ὅπερ γέγονε. Heb. iv.15.
7. Justinian, *ibid.*, 657: μίαν φύσιν καὶ φαντασίαν εἰσάγοντες. See note 4.

For Thy divinity has not had a beginning,
and Thou hast not been made in any time,
But with the Father Thou dost continue before
and without beginning;
For Thou art not a created being, but a creative force,
Word always coeternal, of the same nature as the One
who engendered Thee,
Thus, Thou art of one substance with the Father and the Spirit,
Proclaimed by the faithful as indivisible in the Trinity,[8]
Even if Thou hast to be crucified in the flesh,
O Thou who hast destroyed the weapons of Belial,
the victory of Hades,
and the sting of Death.

Strophe 3:   Thou who art in Thy divinity Son of the Father without beginning,
Thou hast become
man of Thy own will;
Thou hast not changed the divine substance in taking
from Thy mother the form of a slave;
Thou art proclaimed by all the one only-begotten Son;
As incomprehensible Word, Thou art uncreated
But Thou art created in the flesh and seen
in the form of a slave for the race of mortals.[9]
On high Thou art invisible; but below seen by all;[10]
Thou hast accepted suffering of the body for our sakes,
O Thou who hast destroyed the weapons of Belial,
the victory of Hades,
and the sting of Death.

Strophe 4:   We know the same Christ, one Son,
God and man at the same time,
Immortal in His nature which is before time,
submitting to death in the flesh;[11]
For everything which is of matter submits to the laws of mortals,

8. This seems to be directed against Arianism.
9. Justinian, *ibid.*, 652: ἔκτισεν ἐπὶ τοῦ τὴν μορφὴν τοῦ δούλου λαβόντος. Also, Phil. ii.6–7.
10. Justinian, *ibid.*, 641: καὶ ἀόρατος ὢν ἐν τοῖς ἑαυτοῦ ὁρατὸς γέγονεν ἐν τοῖς πὰρ ἡμῖν.
11. Justinian, edict of 533, Mar. 26 (I, 1, 7): οὐ γὰρ ἄλλον τὸν θεὸν λόγον καὶ ἄλλον τὸν Χριστὸν ἐπιστάμεθα, ἀλλ᾽ ἕνα καὶ τὸν αὐτόν.

Which is to say it endures outrages and bodily pain,
    Mocking, and finally even blows;
                but the uncreated is without suffering.
Thus if you have faith, O man, you will never go wrong:
    The Word, born of God the Father, was crucified in the flesh;
    For never is the unity of the natures to be divided,[12]
    O Thou who hast destroyed the weapons of Belial,
                the victory of Hades,
    and the sting of Death.

Strophe 5:   Not recognizing Thee as the Creator of the universe, understanding
      only the created,
              Judas accomplished a treacherous deed[13]
    And this fellow who had an avaricious nature
           sold the splendid treasure to the lawless;
    But he did not obscure the divine will.
For partaking of Thy body at the Last Supper
    He straightway handed Thee over to death;
         but he did not deceive Thee who knowest secrets.[14]
And though he was accused, he was not ashamed to carry out his plan,
    But rather, inclining towards murder, he called the
      rebels to action;
    And so, by a treacherous kiss, Thou wast handed over to suffering,[15]
    O Thou who hast destroyed the weapons of Belial,
                the victory of Hades,
    and the sting of Death.

Strophe 6:   The inhuman mob of criminals, acting without reverence,
             perpetrated wicked acts of daring,
    And in smiting His undefiled face,[16]
        they immediately fell short of their traditional honor,
    Not understanding at all the words of the prophets.

12. Justinian, *Confessions of Faith* (*Chron. Pasc.*, I, 655): δύο φύσεων ἕνωσιν λέγομεν καὶ μίαν ὑπόστασιν. Romanos usually avoids φύσις for the human nature of Christ. Maas, *Chron.*, 18, comments on faulty constructions in this strophe and surmises that there was a revision later than Romanos.
13. Matt. xxvi.14–15; Mark xiv.10–11; Luke xxii.3–6. Romanos' kontakion on Judas, #17.
14. Justinian, *ibid.*, 675: ἐκεῖνος γὰρ νομίσας λανθάνειν τὸν τὰ κρυπτὰ τῶν ἀνθρώπων γινώσκοντα.
15. Matt. xxvi.48–49; Luke xxii.48; Mark xiv.44–45.
16. Matt. xxvi.67–68; John xviii.22.

"O wicked and stupid hardness of heart!"
So said Isaiah once, denouncing their unforgivable acts
In his pronouncement: "The Lamb will come to the slaughter.
He will not open His mouth in His humility;
And so, putting an end to condemnation, He will offer mercy."[17]
He who has destroyed the weapons of Belial,

                the victory of Hades,

    and the sting of Death.

Strophe 7: But even more than this did the lawless with their venomous purpose

                plot to carry out wicked deeds;
They were dispersed;[18] but they were not pricked at heart,

           these men who many times received many favors:
Formerly in the desert they acquired delicacies.[19]
Considering that they honored the law by their deeds
They handed over to be crucified in the flesh

              the One who fulfilled their law.[20]
They dared to call a blasphemer[21] the One who brought the
   dawn of grace,
And to say the One who raised from the dead was liable for death
Because He patiently reproached the passion of their frenzy,
He who has destroyed the weapons of Belial,

              the victory of Hades,

    and the sting of Death.

Strophe 8: When Joshua, son of Nun, made war against hostile people,[22]

            O Judaea, you marched with him,
Thinking that as you vainly poured out blood,

         you would have a chance to destroy

---

17. Isa. liii.7–8.
18. Ps. xxxv.15.
19. τρύφησον is used for Christ's words to the robber, On the Victory of the Cross, Kontakion #22, Strophe 10, with the meaning of "enter Eden" or Paradise. This was true in Nativity I, Strophe 1. The quail given the Israelites, Ex. xvi.13, in the desert was considered a delicacy (Wisd. of Sol. xvi.2). It was even called "food for angels" (*ibid.*, 20).
20. Matt. v.17.
21. Matt. xxvi.65–66; Mark xiv.64.
22. Romanos writes Ἰησοῦ τοῦ Ναυῆ. Joshua is frequently called Jesus, and it suits the poet's purpose to bring out the parallel with Jesus in the next sentence. Trypanis, in the Oxford edition, must have a reason for the substitution of Ἐναπίων (foreigners) for the manuscript reading of ἐναντίων, but since the latter makes good sense, I have adopted it. Jos. vi.21–22; viii.24–28; x.28–40; xi.10–14.

The strong walls of many rulers, even to level ground.[23]
Jesus has come, the fruit of the Virgin,
     Having appeared to men in the flesh
                     and He brings the gift of life to the dead.
And now, you, entirely without gratitude, hand over your benefactor
     To Pilate, thinking Him worthy of being crucified;
     But He will be crucified of His own will to save mortals,
     He who has destroyed the weapons of Belial,
                     the victory of Hades,
    and the sting of Death.

Strophe 9:   The mob of the lawless thought they were keeping divine law,
                     and condemned the Maker of law;
     For they cried out to Pilate: "Crucify
                 the One who has always broken the Sabbath,[24]
     And who has turned from the commands of Moses."
O shameless and inhuman deed!
     They are not ashamed to hand over to the cross
                 the One whom prophets clearly foretold;
But He, the magnanimous, enduring the folly of the faithless,
     Is to die in the flesh in order to redeem the world
     As He signs forgiveness to the fallen first-created.
     He who has destroyed the weapons of Belial,
                     the victory of Hades,
    and the sting of Death.

Strophe 10: When, then, they crucified Him in the flesh and nailed to the cross
                     the One who formed heaven and earth,
     The sun beholding it was darkened, the sky hid its eyes,
     The air appeared as though it were night,
A gash caused by fear suddenly split the rocks;
     The mysterious veil in the midst of the temple was rent.
And the faithless people, seeing this, felt no remorse;
     But they brought forth their stupid words, as they cried:
     "If He is the Son of God, He will free Himself."
     He who has destroyed the weapons of Belial,
                     the victory of Hades,
    and the sting of Death.

23. Isa. xxv.2.
24. Matt. xxvii.22–23; Mark xv.13–14; Luke xxiii.21; John xix.6, 15.

Strophe 11: Seeing the Lover of man lifted up on the cross,[25] the criminal then
who was nailed to the left of Him,
(Yes, He Himself joined with evildoers!)
blasphemed Christ and repeated the words of the others;
But immediately he saw himself accused
By the one on the right[26] who spoke to him in this way:
"You are blaspheming and you dare to mock
the Judge who is crucified, *you*, the condemned;
But you suffer punishment justly, as I do for my deeds;[27]
But He suffers voluntarily in order that He may destroy passions
And relieve the suffering of Adam[28] who suffers for his transgression."
O Thou who hast destroyed the weapons of Belial,
the victory of Hades,
and the sting of Death.

Strophe 12: When he had struck at the roots of the matter[29] in this last statement,
the former robber
worded a valuable phrase
When he recognized that the One who voluntarily chose suffering
in His divinity was unharmed,[30]
He said to Him: "I beg You not to leave me!
Since You publish the deed of the earthborn
Do not remember my wicked deeds
which I perpetrated in my past life,
But just as now Thou dost suffer with me, be seen as compassionate then,
And remember me in Thy kingdom, as Thou art merciful;[31]
For Thou diest for this to show mercy to sinners,
O Thou who hast destroyed the weapons of Belial,
the victory of Hades,
and the sting of Death."

25. John viii.28; xii.32.
26. The editor of *Fr. ed.*, IV, 514*n*1, calls attention to the fact that the detail about the robber's hanging at the right of Christ comes from *Acta Pilati*, Part II, in the Latin and Coptic versions, as given in Tischendorf, *Evangelia Apocrypha* (Leipzig, 1876), 246–47.
27. Luke xxiii.39–41.
28. Adam is not mentioned by name, but the singular τὸν must refer to him, and the use of the name avoids ambiguity.
29. Ῥιζωθεὶς is an unusual word, and it needs some amplification to make the probable meaning clear. Hence, I added "of the matter." The poet seems to indicate that the theological dogma that follows is the basis or *root* of all faith.
30. Justinian, *ibid.*, 638, 3: ἀπαθὴς ὁ αὐτὸς θεότητι.
31. Luke xxiii.42.

Strophe 13: O terrible, slanderous hardness of heart! O opinion of the faithless

who think what is opposite to the Scriptures;

For they hide the truth, inventing various paths;

Not recognizing one Son, the Christ.

Some wish to divide the divine essence

And call a mere mortal

the One who appeared in the world in the flesh for us.[32]

But He has been recognized as God, remaining immortal in nature,

Even though He appeared as a mortal,

since He took the form of a slave,[33]

For He willed to be crucified in order that He

might destroy corruption,

He who has destroyed the weapons of Belial,

the victory of Hades,

and the sting of Death.

Strophe 14: In the world great is the mystery of Thy advent,[34]

which the followers of Arius blaspheme,

Since they betray Thee who art consubstantial with the Father,

calling Thee "made" and "created,"

Putting an improper sense to the words of the Scripture;[35]

Take thought of this—O terrible hard-heartedness—,

If you call the Creator created,

and if you babble of God made by God,

You also make gods of the angels who are of immaterial substance;

But a time exists when they were not.[36]

Only the Word of the Father is beyond all time,

He who has destroyed the weapons of Belial,

the victory of Hades,

and the sting of Death.

32. Romanos is, as usual, insistent that Christ is not mere man. Compare Lazarus I, #14, Strophe 7; and Passion, #20, Strophe 19. Also, in the Presentation at the Temple, #4, the two natures are strongly emphasized; the mystery of the union of the divine and human is expressed in the Epiphany, #6, Strophes 9 and 10. The kontakia telling of miracles also underline the point.
33. Phil. ii.6–8.
34. I Tim. iii.16.
35. See Prov. viii.22. The French edition refers to a collection of such texts. Epiphanius, *Heresies*, 69, 72–79 (*P.G.*, 42, 221–233).
36. Arian statement: ἦν ποτε ὅτε οὐκ ἦν.

Strophe 15: Read carefully [37] the account of the Resurrection, know from it,

> how the risen Christ appeared to Mary [38]

CHRIST   And said, "Do not touch me, woman,

> do not draw near the flesh which suffered on the cross;

For I have not yet taken it up to Heaven;

But hasten now, and tell my disciples

That I am now going to my Father and yours—

Your Father through grace, and mine through nature, [39]

For He does not exist in time as I have not;

But now I am honored with my Father and the Spirit,

I who have destroyed the weapons of Belial,

> the victory of Hades,

and the sting of Death."

Strophe 16: Nerved by the words of Paul, [40] those who think bitterly [41]

> and interpret mischievously

Point out that Christ took on flesh from Heaven

> and not from His mother;

"For of such a kind," says Paul, "is a heavenly being,

Such, indeed, are all celestial ones." [42]

But know, lover of evil, what sort of beings the Just have become.

Abraham, O heretic, Abraham, our ancestor, how does he seem to you—

He who was born of Tera and did not come from those on high?

Paul calls celestial those whom the Creator sanctified,

He who has destroyed the weapons of Belial,

> the victory of Hades,

and the sting of Death.

Strophe 17: When Thou didst illumine the world by Thy Resurrection, and didst arise in Thine own power,

> Thou who hast brought life to all by Thy divinity,

37. The verb means literally "unroll the scroll," but this more picturesque meaning would not make the sense clear.
38. John xx.14–17.
39. The Arians claimed that Christ was Son of God but only κατὰ χάριν (by grace of adoption) and not κατὰ φύσιν (by nature).
40. I Cor., especially xv.45: "The first man Adam was made a living soul; the last Adam was made a quickening spirit." The Monophysites who followed Eutychius may be the heretics intended in this attack.
41. He must mean that they merely plan evil, but also that their reasoning is faulty. The idea of bitterness is a favorite with Romanos.
42. I Cor. xv.48.

Then the beginner of evil, the Serpent, lamented to Death, crying,

THE
SERPENT
(DEVIL)

"Now we are worsted, for in seizing one, we are deprived of many;
I took Him to be a mere man,
I did not know, wretched me,
since He concealed His eternal nature,
In order that He might war against me in return for what He endured
from me.
What good was it for me to prepare the vinegar mixed with gall
And to move Pilate [43] to have Him die on the cross?
He who has destroyed the weapons of Belial,
the victory of Hades.
and the sting of Death."

Strophe 18:

DEATH

"It is because of you that I submit to all these things, since you
are the cause of this defeat which has come on us,"
Said Death to the wily Serpent. "Because of you I have
lost my kingdom;
I said from the beginning, 'Do not carry off Christ';
For I knew clearly the power in Him:
There was the child of Jairus
which He snatched from me by His voice alone; [44]
And again, He dragged Lazarus from my chains; [45]
[If] He has done deeds such as this to unfortunate me,
How many more will He do through the flesh which He has
assumed without change?
He who has destroyed the weapons of Belial,
the victory of Hades,
and the sting of Death."

Strophe 19:

THE ENEMY
(DEVIL)

"But it is to me that the son of Mary has done more terrible things,"
said the Enemy to Hades,
"Since as many as I have humbled and consigned to bitter illness
These He has restored to health by His command.
When I saw the man born blind, [46] I laughed,

---

43. There is a lacuna in the manuscript (–άτον); it can be filled out to read (πιλ) άτον.
44. Matt. ix.18; Mark v.22–23; Luke viii.41.
45. John xi.1–46. Romanos, Kontakia #14 and #15.
46. Matt. xi.5; xii.22; Luke vii.21. Adam is represented as blind in Romanos' Kontakion #6, Strophe 2, and the blind man becomes here a symbol of fallen man.

But the blind man came to Him and He at once gave him vision
    by His command.
But I supposed that if I killed Him,
    Henceforth I would hold prisoners those whom I formerly flogged;[47]
    And, wretch that I am, I did not know that He would end my power,
He who has destroyed the weapons of Belial,

                the victory of Hades,

    and the sting of Death."

Strophe 20: "O snake, evil counselor, three-headed dragon,[48] what have you done?
HADES   For I heard you, and I am myself worsted,"
(DEATH)   Hades answered the wily one. "Let us both bitterly lament,
    Since in His descent He has attacked my stomach,
So that I vomit forth those whom I formerly devoured.
    But now lament with me for we are despoiled of our common glory.
For Adam has been set free from my former chains,
    And the prophet cries out, 'Where, O Death, is your victory?'[49]
    And Eve, too, rejoices that He has saved her,
He who has destroyed the weapons of Belial,

                the victory of Hades,

    and the sting of Death."

Strophe 21: "When Christ was put to death, as I took Him below, He joined
DEATH   the other cadavers,

                but I have not understood what happened to me;
    For now I am in a state of shame,

                and I furnish a laughingstock for mortals;
    Then how does it help me to accuse you, my fellow-sufferer?
Since I am completely worsted, why am I tormented in vain?
    But grant that we know we are completely overcome;
For the tree of knowledge brought death into the world;

47. "Flogging" is his word for the infirmities of mankind; for example, Christ refers to the issue of blood suffered by the woman who was freed from her plague, and the Greek words used are: ἴσθι ὑγιὴς ἀπὸ τῆς μάστιγός σου (μάστιξ), literally, *a whip*, Mark v.34. Romanos, in his kontakion on her health, does not use that phrase (#12, Strophe 19).
48. The homilists refer to the three heads, and it may well be, as the editor of the French edition suggests (IV, 525n2), that this tradition reflects Cerberus. Dante gives Lucifer three faces, and the symbolism of the trinity may even be transferred to the devil.
49. Hos. xiii.14; I Cor. xv.54. This is obviously a favorite quotation for Romanos.

The tree of death is seen by all as the Resurrection.
He is preparing to empty my storehouse,[50]
He who has destroyed the weapons of Belial,

                              the victory of Hades,

      and the sting of Death."

Strophe 22: Death said this in accusing the Deceiver

                      of the things he had brought to pass in life;

For both of them the honored tree planted

                      in the earth had brought defeat;

It was revealed as the tree of life for men,

Where the fruit of good things[51] was nailed down,

    In order that in dying it might bring to flower the Resurrection

                  for mortals in the meadows of earth.[52]

It is He who is Son of God according to His nature, and of David

    in the flesh,[53]

He who remained with the Father and issued from Mary

For the salvation of all and for the despair of the faithless,

He who has destroyed the weapons of Belial,

                          the victory of Hades,

      and the sting of Death.

Strophe 23: The wily one, the hostile Serpent lamented with groans

              what he had undergone from the beginning through Adam:

SERPENT   Saying, "When God created man from the earth,[54] indeed

(DEVIL)   He ordered us,

All of us, as One who knows the future and is Lord,

Saying, 'Come, all powers together now

    Kneel before the one in my image whom I have created.'[55]

---

50. ταμιεῖον is a receptacle for treasure. It is also used in Proverbs to mean "inner parts" (Prov. xx.27, 30; xxvi.25) and probably carries the two levels of meaning, so that Death is saying that he is being robbed in his inner sanctuary where the treasure of dead bodies is stored.

51. "The good things" must be the fruits of Christ, the tree of life; hence the joys of eternal life.

52. John xii.24.

53. Rom. i.3–4.

54. Gen. i.27.

55. The idea of Satan refusing to bow down to Adam is an old one. Many references are given in the French edition, IV, 528–29n1. The most interesting is the *Koran*: "And when we said to the angels, 'Prostrate yourselves,' they did it, except for Satan who refused and was puffed up. He was among the infidels." Trans. from Fr.: *Mohammed Hamidullah* (Paris, 1959), 9.

And at that time I fled, since I did not wish this;
    I was not willing to kneel before a created being,
    And I did not know, wretched me, that He would save the mortal,
    He who has destroyed the weapons of Belial,
                            the victory of Hades,
        and the sting of Death."

Strophe 24: Hades, continuing with these words, cried out in fear,
HADES   "Death, come here, and let us observe
    How the light is shining in darkness,
                        and has illumined all our kingdom below,[56]
    And it has raised up the descendants of Adam from the tombs.[57]
Come with me and let us guard Him;
    He has come to destroy us; let us hasten to contend with Him."
Saying this, then, the evil Hades runs
    And tried to seize Him from His suffering flesh[58]
    For he seemed mere man; but He is God and Word,
    He who has destroyed the weapons of Belial,
                            the victory of Hades,
        and the sting of Death.

Strophe 25: Jesus Christ arose then, as from a sleep;[59]
                        He violently bound the hands of Hades,
CHRIST   Crying to those in Hades, "Rise up,
                            and mock Hades, crying out to him,
    And saying, 'Where is your victory?'[60]
As for him, I shall hand him over to chains in Tartarus,
    Since I have freed Adam entirely
                        from the debts for which he was liable.
And treading on his neck, cry out, 'Now Hades is consumed
    Along with Death, and he has cast down his power.'

56. Isa. ix.2. *Acta Pilati*, xxii, Latin A. (Tischendorf, ed.), 378, "tam tanti luminis claritatem, dum Christum repente in suis sedibus viderunt." Also, 379.
57. Actually, in the following strophe Christ tells the dead to rise up. Romanos constantly uses poetic license in chronology. Hades really did not yet know that Christ had come to destroy him. Matt. xxvii.52.
58. The poet means that Christ was still in the form in which He suffered on the cross.
59. Ps. lxxviii.65.
60. This is not the reading given in the Oxford edition. The faulty manuscript is given by conjecture as ποῦ[ἡμῶν τὸ ἀδ]ίκημα. The sense does not fit. They *know* where their injuries are. The conjecture in the edition of Tomadakis III, #30 is "Ἅιδη σου, "Ἅιδη, τὸ νίκημα, and this taunt is used many times by Romanos and is in the refrain. See note 49.

For it is for you that I appeared on earth and became man,
I who have destroyed the weapons of Belial,

the victory of Hades,

and the sting of Death."

Strophe 26:   Then all, with songs and psalms cry out:

"Hades is now without power!"[61]
And you, O Death, trod underfoot at the same time, you

now have useless power,
For every one of the earthborn in escaping will enslave you.
Then Hades answered as he cried loudly,
Like a master immediately giving orders

to his servants, saying to them:
HADES   "Now you behold me for the moment suffering unjust daring deeds.
Run now, as you have power, close the bronze gates,
For the Son of Mary wishes to pass sentence upon me,[62]
He who has destroyed the weapons of Belial,

the victory of Hades,

and the sting of Death."

Strophe 27:   Saying this, the miserable Hades immediately answered

the Savior, and cried to Him,
HADES   "I was formerly the lord of all men,

and I was master of the race of Adam;
Tell me, then, who are you, O man?[63]
And how have you now arrived here?
For it is clear that you are a man,

for I see in you a human body;
Now everyone from the race of men is my possession;
Why, then, do you use force against me, having come for
the sake of all?
But, Thou art the Resurrection and the Life of the dead,
Thou who hast destroyed the weapons of Belial,

the victory of Hades,

and the sting of Death."

61. There is a lacuna here that the Oxford edition leaves unfilled. The general meaning seems clear.
62. Actually, Christ did not say this. Compare with Romanos' Kontakion #27, On the Resurrection IV, Strophe 8.
63. The series of questions in *Acta Pilati*, XXII, are reduced to the one that will emphasize the human and divine in Christ. Strophe 28 is full of this idea.

Strophe 28:　When he asked Christ these things, the Lord cried out

and said to Hades:

CHRIST　　　　　"I act as a judge and bring you to trial,

for I do not ever wish to play the tyrant;[64]

But you are shameless, you are worthy of condemnation;

However, as you see, I have become man,

I am the Word, without sin, All-powerful God,

Creator of the universe.

For even if I am seen as visible to you, I do not pass judgment as Lord;

But as the earthborn Adam, I now declare judgment against you

And after I have won, I shall drive you from your former tyranny,

I who have destroyed the weapons of Belial,

the victory of Hades,

and the sting of Death."

Strophe 29:　"Cease these crafty words, O wicked, lawless, treacherous one,"

DEVIL　　　　　　　　　　　　　　said the hostile one to Hades,

(ENEMY)　　　　　"Do not play the tyrant any more, wretch,

for you have learned His intention,

Just as He has done terrible things to us from the beginning.

Why, then, do you struggle to blaspheme Him?

For you are not able to endure the ideas which He made

clear to all:

For the cross of the Savior has appeared as destruction for us,

Indeed, planting with it was rooted in Creation;

Its trunk was ingraft[65] and, through it, He saves all men,

He who has destroyed the weapons of Belial,

the victory of Hades,

and the sting of Death.

Strophe 30:　"So, you see, that same wood which the Lord formerly showed Moses,[66]

DEVIL　　　　　　　　　　　　　　has flowered in opposition to us.

If this is known to all men,

our plan is clearly overthrown,

For all who run towards it rejoice;

64. Again, compare with #27, Strophe 11: "I do not judge as a despot."
65. Compare with #22, On the Victory of the Cross, Strophes 5 and 12.
66. Ex. xv.23–25. Compare with Romanos, Kontakion #22, On the Victory of the Cross, Strophe 15, where the figure is more completely developed.

If only I had not been taken captive by Him;
    Nor with my brutal words
                            urged on Judas to betray Him,
And Pilate to pass sentence and deliver Him to the cross,
    And, in brief, to lord it over Christ, the King.
    For He has deprived me of everything and has taken away my power,
    He who has destroyed the weapons of Belial,
                          the victory of Hades,
    and the sting of Death."

Strophe 31: "I wish that you knew, Hades, my ally, that He endured all
BELIAL   because He wished to save the race of mortals.
(DEVIL)   Because of men, He has been seen as a man
                     and of His own will took on flesh,
    In order that, as God, He might save Adam with Eve."
Belial, lamenting, said these things to Hades,
    "If only I had not worked to kill Christ
               He would not ever have conquered us;
    But we made great haste to seize Him as though He were a mortal
    And to barricade ourselves with the gates, and secure ourselves
      with the bars,[67]
    And now He has captured our thoughts,
    He who has destroyed the weapons of Belial,
               the victory of Hades,
    and the sting of Death.

Strophe 32: "Let us consider what we have just passed through because
BELIAL   of our ignorance:
                   how there were standing at the tomb
    Some beings, fiery in appearance,
                  and invested with white robes,
    And from their lips they sent forth flashes as of lightning.[68]
And then they rolled away the awesome stone,
    And at once, they made all the guards at the tomb appear
      as though dead;

---

67. The source is, of course, *Acta Pilati*, XXI–XXII; the accusation against Christ is similar to that in Kontakion #27, On the Resurrection IV, Strophes 13–16.
68. Matt. xxviii.1–6; Mark xvi.4–6; Luke xxiv.2–6. Compare the account here with the poet's treatment of the women at the tomb in Kontakion #29, On the Resurrection VI.

And the women came and saw them lying as though dead,
　　And they saw two who were guarding the tomb on the stone;
　　And the guards said to them: 'He is risen from the tomb,
　　He who has destroyed the weapons of Belial,
　　　　　　　　　　　　　　　　　　　　the victory of Hades,

　　and the sting of Death'."

Strophe 33: We who are stamped with the seal of Thy wood,[69] O Master, exalt
　　　　　　　　　　　　　　　　Thy Incarnation for the sake of men,
　　We know Thee both as mortal and immortal, as God and
　　　man, one Son;
　　For even if Thou didst suffer in the flesh in Thy plan of salvation,
However, Thou dost remain indivisible in the Trinity.
　　Strengthen Thy church, O Savior, in this faith;
As the only Merciful One, confirm and save Thy people,
　　In order that we may all kneel in obeisance to the Resurrection;
　　For Thou dost dispense to all light, life, and knowledge,
　　Thou who hast destroyed the weapons of Belial,
　　　　　　　　　　　　　　　　　　　　the victory of Hades,

　　and the sting of Death.

69. The use of the "seal" of the cross occurs also in Kontakion #22, On the Victory of the Cross, Strophe 17, and the reference to "the wood" is consistent with the idea in note 66.

ON THE RESURRECTION VI

O. 29 (K. 20)

Title: Εἰς τὴν τριήμερον καὶ ζωοποιὸν καὶ ὑπέρλαμπρον ἀνάστασιν τοῦ κυρίου καὶ θεοῦ καὶ σωτῆρος ἡμῶν Ἰησοῦ Χριστοῦ

Manuscripts and editions: This kontakion exists in almost all of the manuscripts: A B J M P T Δ. It does not appear in D G K or S. Furthermore, it is the only hymn for Easter Sunday in all of the manuscripts except P. Short forms of other kontakia on the Resurrection occur in various kontakaria. Six hymns on the Resurrection are by Romanos. They are distributed throughout Holy Week. See the summary, pages 191–92.

Pitra edited this hymn, *A.S.*, I, xvii, 124–40. He makes valuable comments that are usually repeated in the notes to the French edition.

French edition: IV, 378–421.

Tomadakis, IV, 375–413.

Tone: ἦχος πλάγιος δ′

Acrostic: Τοῦ ταπεινοῦ Ῥωμανοῦ [ὁ] ψαλμός

Refrain: ὁ τοῖς πεσοῦσι παρέχων ἀνάστασιν

Analysis of content of the kontakion and comparison with biblical source: Romanos uses chiefly the account of the Resurrection in John. Since, however, he makes various changes and adaptations in an attempt to avoid seeming discrepancies with the other Gospels, it is well to examine exactly what is in John, xx, and compare it with Romanos.

1. Mary Magdalene goes to the tomb early on the first day of the week. It is dark; she sees the stone rolled away.

(Romanos, in Strophe 3 has Mary Magdalene go when it is dark; she sees the stone rolled away, *but* she is with a group of women.)

2. She runs to the disciples and tells them that "they have taken away the body."

(Romanos has her run to tell the disciples, *but* she expresses faith that Christ has risen.)

3, 4. Peter and John run to the tomb, and John outruns Peter.

5. John looks into the tomb but does not enter.

6, 7. Peter enters and sees the grave clothes lying empty.

8. John enters.

9. As yet, they do not know that Christ must rise.

10. They leave.

(Romanos, in Strophes 4 and 5, has Peter and John run to the tomb, and John waits for Peter so that Peter could be honored. Evidence from Christ's words to Peter is quoted here, but in advance of the occasion for their utterance. Peter and John wonder why Christ has not appeared to them, and they decide that they have been too presumptuous. Mary tells them not to lose heart, that it was part of the divine plan that women see Christ first. Strophe 6.)

11, 12, 13. Mary remains by the tomb, weeping; she looks in and sees two angels by the empty tomb. They ask why she weeps.

(Romanos, in Strophes 7 and 8, has Mary seeking to reassure herself as she remembers Christ's power. Christ appears to her and asks why she weeps.)

14, 15, 16. Christ appears to Mary and repeats the question the angels had asked; she mistakes Him for the gardener; Jesus calls her by name, and she then recognizes Him.

(Mary, in Strophe 9, mistakes Christ for the gardener, and in Strophe 10 she recognizes Him.)

17. Jesus warns Mary not to touch Him, since He has not yet ascended. He tells her to go report to the disciples what she has learned.

(Christ, in Strophes 11 and 12, warns Mary not to touch Him, and tells her to announce the good news.)

The dependence on the account in the Gospel of John ends here.

In Strophe 13 Mary tells the other women what she has experienced, and in Strophes 14, 15, and 16, the women state their desire to share the wonderful experience she has had. In Strophe 17 they glorify the tomb, and then, when they see the angel they are frightened in Strophe 18 and reassured in Strophe 19. In Strophe 20 the angel reminds them of Christ's victory over Hades, and in 21 they are reassured, not just by the angel's words but by the fact that he would not have remained seated, had the Lord been there. In Strophe 22, the women tell the disciples, who question Mary in Strophe 23, and this passage introduces the closing prayer.

The Gospels of Matthew, Mark, and Luke mention the other women and in those Gospels they are charged with telling the disciples of Christ's resurrection. The effect of the vision on the women differs in these three Gospels.

In Romanos' attempt to consolidate the evidence and make it more consistent, he leaves some questionable discrepancies. Peter and John are told by Mary, and yet the women tell the disciples. (Matthew has Christ appear to the apostles on the road to Emmaus; Mary Magdalene tells them, in Mark; they refuse to believe the women, in Luke, and Peter himself goes to the tomb to verify their story.)

Connection with homily and the style of Romanos: Romanos is not the only writer who tried to resolve the discrepancies in the accounts. In 515, Severus of Antioch devoted a sermon (*P.G.*, 46, 628C–652C) to this purpose, and there are two Syriac versions of his interpretation.[1] He may have drawn his material from a sermon by Eusebius of Cesarea "On Discrepancies in the Gospels,"[2] or perhaps from Hesychius of Jerusalem, who wrote in the early fifth century about the difficulties of interpretation.[3] These early preachers and authors grant that each writer had his own peculiar vantage point, and they try to prove that all the Gospels point to the same truth. Romanos certainly does not follow any one of the conclusions of the homilists in detail. Rather, he avoids many details, keeps the narrative simple, and makes the motives humanly understandable. For example, the women wish to share an exciting experience; Mary has a simple reason for believing that Christ has risen by observing that the angel is seated. By using John's version that has Mary go and bring the other women, he avoids complications. By having Peter honored before John he uses a device, rather common with him, of inserting passages from the Gospel that were not yet known. It is not really inconsistent, in Romanos' version, for Mary to be despondent right after she has reassured the disciples. Her need to convince herself is a very human one. Historical sequence does not concern the poet as much as an emphasis on the revelation of Christ as God and man.

More liturgical echoes occur in this kontakion than is usual.[4] In Strophe 7 Mary quotes "Holy, Holy, Holy." "Truly Christ has arisen" is repeated by Romanos in Prooimion II and in Strophe 21, reflecting the salutation of Easter Week. The baptism of Christ is referred to in Strophe 7, and the baptismal font may be alluded to in Strophe 17 where the tomb is compared with the immaculate womb, and the mystic significance of being born again may thus be emphasized.[5] "Lift up your hearts" echoes the *Sursum corda* (Strophe 22); and Strophe 24, in the closing prayer shows a parallel between "My Father, holy, and full of mercy, may Thy name always be holy" with the beginning of the *Pater noster*. Pitra points up parallels with liturgical drama, the celebration of the Eucharist being a natural occasion for the recall of the narrative of the Resurrection.[6]

Meter: The metrical scheme is given in the Oxford edition, 529, XXIV.

1. *Fr. ed.*, IV, 358*n*1 refers to M. A. Kugener, "Une homilie de Severe d'Antioche attribuée à Gregoire de Nysse et à Hesychius de Jerusalem," *Revue de l'Orient chrétien*, III (1898), 431–51.
2. Fragments only exist. *P.G.*, 22, 879–1006.
3. *P.G.*, 93, 1433A.
4. This is documented in the French edition, IV, 369–70.
5. *Fr. ed.*, 408*n*2.
6. *Fr. ed.*, 370.

ON THE RESURRECTION VI

O. 29

Prooimion I: Even if Thou didst descend into the tomb, O Immortal One,
                   Still Thou hast overthrown the power of Hades
                   And Thou hast arisen as victor, Christ, God;
               To the women bearing incense Thou hast said, "Hail,"[1]
                   And on Thy apostles Thou hast bestowed peace,[2]
                       Thou who dost offer resurrection to the fallen.

Prooimion II: When the women arrived at Thy tomb,
                    And did not find Thy undefiled body,
                    Weeping, they said through their tears:[3]
                "Could He have been stolen, He who affected the cure of the woman
                    with the issue of blood?[4]
                Would He not have arisen, He who, even before His Passion,
                                                    foretold His Resurrection?[5]
                    Truly, Christ is arisen,
                        He who offers resurrection to the fallen."

Strophe 1: To the Sun before sun who had then sunk in the tomb[6]
                 The young women bearing incense hastened towards the dawn,
                 As though seeking day, and saying to one another,
WOMEN   "O friends, come let us anoint with spices
                 The body, life-bringing and buried,
                 The flesh which resurrects the fallen Adam
                                             which lies here in the tomb.

1. Matt. xxviii.9.
2. John xx.19.
3. In the Gospel accounts, only Mary wept; the other women were perplexed. (Luke xxiv.4).
4. Matt. ix.20–22; Mark v.25–34; Luke viii.43–48; and the Kontakion #12 of Romanos.
5. After Peter's declaration of Christ's identity, He announced His Passion and Resurrection (Matt. xvi.21); again, after the casting out of devils in Galilee, He foretold His betrayal and Resurrection (Matt. xvii.22–23); and again on His way to Jerusalem (Matt. xx.17–19). There was a fourth allusion to His death and Resurrection in the comparison between the destruction of the temple and that of His body (John ii.19–21).
6. Ps. lxxii.17. The comparison between Christ in the tomb and the setting sun occurs in the offices of Saturday of Holy Week (*Fr. ed.*, IV, 383n1).

Let us go, let us hasten like the Magi,
    And let us kneel down and bring with us
The spices as gifts—not to Him in swaddling clothes
    But to Him wrapped in a shroud;
And let us weep and cry out: 'O Master, arise,
        Thou who dost offer resurrection to the fallen'."

Strophe 2:   When the holy women were saying these things to each other,
        They considered another idea, which is full of wisdom,
WOMEN   And they said to one another: "Women, why are we self-deceived?
For surely[7] the Lord is not in the tomb!
    Up until now, would it have held in subjection
    One who controls the breath of living beings?
                Would He still be a buried corpse?
Unbelievable! This idea does not bear examination!
    Therefore let us then take careful thought, and act as follows:
Let Mary leave and go see the tomb
    And let us act in conformity with what she says,
For most certainly, as He foretold, the Immortal One has arisen,
        He who offers resurrection to the fallen."

Strophe 3:   The wise women, having made arrangements according to this plan,
        No doubt sent forward Mary Magdalene
        To the tomb, as the Theologian[8] says.
It was dark, but love lighted the way for her;
        And so she saw the great stone rolled away
        From the entrance of the tomb,
                and she returned and said:
MARY   "Disciples, learn what I saw,
        And do not keep secret what you understand.
The stone no longer covers the tomb.
        Would they have taken away my Lord?
For the guards are not there; they have fled. Would He not have risen,
        He who offers resurrection to the fallen?"

7. Perhaps the construction requires that we understand the verb "to be deceived," which was just used. This would make the complete sentence: "You are entirely deceived if you say that the Lord is in the tomb."
8. The Theologian is John, and the reference is to his Gospel: John xx.1.

Strophe 4: When Cephas and the son of Zebedee heard this,
                    Immediately they ran as though in a race with one another;[9]
                    And John was first, before Peter;
              However, on his arrival, he did not go within the sepulchre;
                    But he waited for the leader
                    So that like a lamb he would follow the shepherd,
                                             and it was truly fitting this way,
CHRIST   For to Peter, He said: "Peter, do you love me?"[10]
                    And, "Then tend my sheep, at your pleasure."
              And to Peter He promised: "Blessed Simon,
                    I shall give you the keys of the kingdom."[11]
              For Peter He had formerly subdued the waves on which
                    Peter was walking.[12]
                    He who offers resurrection to the fallen.

Strophe 5: But, as I was just saying, Peter and the son of Zebedee
                    Came up to the tomb, after what Mary had said,[13]
                    And they entered into it; but they did not find the Lord;
              So that, terrified by this, the holy ones said,
DISCIPLES   "For what reason would He not have appeared to us?
                    Can it be that He considered our liberty too great?
                                             for we have been very daring
              For we ought to have stayed outside[14]
                    And looked around at the things in the tomb;
              For this tomb is really not a tomb,
                    But, in truth, it is the dwelling of God,
              For He was in it, and He dwelt in it of His will,
                    He who offers resurrection to the fallen.

Strophe 6: "Has our liberty then turned into boldness,
DISCIPLES   And our courage been considered rather presumptuous?
                    It is for this reason perhaps that He is not seen by the unworthy?"

---

9. John xx.3–5.
10. John xxi.15–17.
11. Matt. xvi.19. Clearly, the poet is not bothered by placing side by side remarks made to Peter at different times, regardless of the chronology.
12. Matt. xiv.28–32. Compare, also, the references to this incident in Romanos' On Peter's Denial, Kontakion #18, Prooimion and Strophe 2.
13. Luke xxiv.12; John xx.3–7.
14. The idea is that it is sacrilegious to enter the "house of God," "the temple," "the tomb," "the throne."

As the true friends of the Creator talked like this to one another,
    Mary who followed them said:
MARY   "Initiates of the Lord, and you who truly love Him warmly,
                          do not assume this;

But just wait, do not lose heart;
    For what has happened was the divine plan,
In order that women, who were the first to fall,
    Might be the first to see the resurrected One.[15]
He wishes the greeting 'Hail' to be a sign of grace to us who mourn,[16]
    He who offers resurrection to the fallen."

Strophe 7:   Mary, when she had fully reassured herself in this way,
    Remained at the tomb after the holy women had gone away,
    For she truly believed that the body had been raised up;
And so she cried out, not with words but with tears,
MARY   "Woe is me, my Jesus, where have they taken you?
    How didst Thou endure, Immortal One, to be lifted up
                      by dishonored hands?

'Holy, Holy, Holy' cry
    The six-winged ones with many eyes;[17]
And their shoulders can scarcely carry Thee,
    Yet did the hands of deceivers lift Thee up?
The Forerunner in baptizing Thee cried out: 'Do Thou baptize me,[18]
    Thou who offerest resurrection to the fallen.'

Strophe 8:   "Lo, Thou who dost renew all things art dead for three days,
MARY   Thou who didst raise up Lazarus on the fourth day[19]
    And showed him moving, though bound in grave clothes;
Thou dost lie in the tomb; and how I wish that I knew where
    Thou art buried,
    So that, like the harlot,[20] I might bathe with tears
Not only Thy feet, but truly Thy whole body,
                      and even Thy sepulchre,

15. The same idea is put forward in a homily on the Resurrection by Severus, *P.G.*, 46, 632D. It is quoted in *Fr. ed.*, IV, 391n3.
16. Matt. xxviii.9.
17. Isa. vi.2–3; Rev. iv.8.
18. Matt. iii.14. See also Romanos' Epiphany Kontakion #5, Strophe 5, and *passim*.
19. John xi.43–44, and Romanos' Kontakia #14 and #15.
20. Luke vii.38. Compare Romanos' Kontakion On the Sinful Woman, #10.

Saying, 'Master, just as Thou didst raise up
  The son of the widow, raise up Thyself,[21]
Thou who didst give life to the daughter of Jairus,[22]
  Why dost Thou still remain in the tomb?
Arise, stand up, and be revealed to those who seek Thee,
  Thou who dost offer resurrection to the fallen'."

Strophe 9: Conquered by her weeping, and touched by her suffering,
  He who sees all, beholding Mary Magdalene,
    At once was moved to pity, and was revealed, as He said to
      the young woman,
CHRIST "Woman, why do you weep? Whom do you wish within the tomb?"[23]
  Then Mary turned and said:
MARY "I weep because they have taken away my Lord from the tomb,
      and I do not know where He lies;
Is not this entirely your work?
  For unless I am mistaken, you are the gardener;
In any case, if you have taken away the body, tell me,
  And I shall take my Redeemer;
He is my Teacher, and Lord,
  He who offers resurrection to the fallen."

Strophe 10: He who searches the hearts and reins and watches over them,[24]
    Knowing that Mary would recognize His voice,
    Like a shepherd, called His crying lamb,
CHRIST Saying, "Mary." She at once recognized Him and spoke:[25]
MARY   "Surely my wonderful shepherd calls me,
      In order that henceforth He may number me among the
          nine and ninety lambs;[26]
For I see behind Him who calls me
    The bodies of the saints, the ranks of the Just,
And so, I do not say, 'Who art Thou who callest me?'
    For I know clearly who He is who calls me;[27]

21. Luke vii.11–15.
22. Matt. ix.25; Mark v.41–42; Luke viii.54–55.
23. John xx.14–15.
24. Ps. vii.9; Jer. xi.20; xx.12.
25. John xx.16.
26. Matt. xviii.12–14; Luke xv.3–6.
27. εἰ is probably not in the manuscripts (*Fr. ed.,* IV, 397*n*3).

It is my Teacher and my Lord,
    He who offers resurrection to the fallen."

Strophe 11: Carried away by the warmth of her affection, and by her fervent love,
    The maiden hastened and wished to seize Him,
    The One who fills all creation without being confined by boundaries;
But the Creator did not find fault with her eagerness;
    He lifted her to the divine when He said,
CHRIST   "Do not touch me; or do you consider me merely human?[28]
                                        I am God, do not touch me.
O holy woman, lift up your eyes
    And consider the heavenly spheres;
Seek me there, for I ascend
    To my Father, whom I have not left;
For I share His throne, and with Him I am without time and beginning,
    I who offer resurrection to the fallen.

Strophe 12: "Let your tongue, woman, publish these things for the rest of time
CHRIST   And let it explain them to the sons of the kingdom
    And to those who eagerly await resurrection of me, the Living.
Hasten, Mary, and gather together my disciples[28]
    I use you as a trumpet with a powerful voice;
    Sound forth peace to the fearful ears
                                        of my concealed friends:
Arouse them all as from a sleep,
    In order that they may come to greet me and light torches.[29]
Say, 'The bridegroom has arisen from the tomb,
    And nothing has been left in the tomb;[30]
O apostles, banish deadness, since He is arisen,
    He who offers resurrection to the fallen'."

Strophe 13: When she clearly understood all the words of the Word,
    The maiden turned and spoke to her companions:
MARY   "Wonderful are the things, women, which I have seen
    and will describe.

28. John xx.17.
29. Liturgical practice probably included a procession with candles on Easter morning. John of Damascus in his kanon for Easter morning includes in the fifth ode the words: "προσέλθωμεν—λαμπαδηφόροι—Πάσχα θεοῦ τὸ σωτήριον (*Pentekostarion*). See *Fr. ed.*, IV, 401, 1.
30. He has raised up all humanity with Him.

Let no one consider my words as idle talk;[31]
　　For I have not had a dream, but I have been inspired;
　　I am filled with a divine conversation with Christ.

　　　　　　　　　　　　　　　　　　　Learn how and when.
When the men with Peter left me,
　　I stood weeping near the tomb,
For I thought that the divine body of the Immortal
　　Had been taken from the tomb.
But immediately, taking pity on my tears, He appeared to me,
　　He who offers resurrection to the fallen.

Strophe 14:　"Suddenly sorrow has been changed to joy,

MARY　　　　　And all has become joyous and a cause for rejoicing;
　　　　　　I do not hesitate to say, 'I have been glorified as Moses,'[32]
For I have seen, I have seen—not on the mountain but in the tomb,
　　Not [concealed] by a cloud,[33] but by flesh,
　　The Lord of the Immortals and of the clouds,

　　　　　　　　　　　　　　Lord of old, now and forever;
And He said, 'Mary, hasten and tell
　　Those who love me that I have arisen;
Take me on your tongue, like a branch of the olive[34]
　　To the descendants of Noah;[35] announce the good news,
Pointing out to them that death is destroyed and that He has arisen,
　　He who offers resurrection to the fallen'."

Strophe 15:　When they heard this, the group of reverent young women
　　　　　　Answered Mary Magdalene with one accord:

WOMEN　　　"It is the truth which you speak and we all agree with you;
We do not disbelieve you; but we are amazed at one thing alone,
　　That He was in the tomb up until now,
　　And that the Life was numbered among the dead,

　　　　　　　　　　　　　　and was held for three days;

31. Luke xxiv.11.
32. When Moses came down from Mount Sinai, his face shone (Ex. xxxiv.29, 35). He was bringing the words of the Lord to the people. Mary has seen Christ and is announcing His Resurrection. The poet doubtless intends the Old Law and the New Law to be put in juxtaposition.
33. Moses was not allowed to see all of the Lord (Ex. xxxiii.18–23).
34. Gen. viii.11.
35. The dove is usually used as a symbol of Mary, the mother of Jesus. Romanos stretches the symbolism to include Mary Magdalene.

For it was to be expected and we hoped that He would come out
    From the earth, and so we said:
'Formerly He delivered His servant from the whale;[36]
    How can He be conquered by death?
If He collected his due from the wild beast, He will rise from the tomb,
    He who offers resurrection to the fallen.'

Strophe 16: "Do not think, holy one, that your tale is halting;

WOMEN   You have spoken to us directly, and nothing was faltering
        in your remarks.
    Your speech was sincere and your manner was appropriate;
However, Mary, we wish to share with you,[37]
    So that not just one among us fares luxuriously
    While all the rest remain dead without a taste of that life
                        and excluded from it.
Let there be many voices along with yours
    To put a seal upon your testimony.
Let us all go to the tomb,
    And confirm the vision;
Let it be shared, friend, this glory which He offered you,
    He who offers resurrection to the fallen."

Strophe 17: Speaking thus, the group of God-inspired women
    Left the city along with the narrator,
    And, seeing the tomb, cried out from a distance:

WOMEN   "Behold the place, or rather the immaculate womb,
    Behold the spot which bore the King,
    Behold what contained the One whom the Heavens do not contain,
                        but the saints do contain.[38]
Praise to you, a hymn to you, holy tomb,
    Small yet very large; poor yet rich;
Treasury of life, holder of peace,
    Symbol of joy, sepulchre of Christ;
Monument of one man; but glory of the world, since voluntarily
    He offers resurrection to the fallen."

36. Jonah ii.
37. I Cor. xii.25–27.
38. Most of the comparisons in this strophe were in common usage: The tomb is compared to a womb; the tomb is a treasury. The series of "come see" has specific parallels to homily, as is indicated in the introduction to this kontakion.

Strophe 18:   After having sung hymns of praise to the tomb of the Giver of life,

They turned and saw the one seated upon the stone,[39]

And from fright they drew back;[40]

And feeling awe, they turned aside their faces,

And with fear they said this:

WOMEN   "What is this figure, whose shape is this?

Who is this whom we behold?

An angel? A man? Has he come from on high?

Or has he just arisen into our presence from below?[41]

He is fire; he sends forth light; his glance is like lightning;[42] he shines.

Let us flee, maidens, lest we be consumed.

O divine, heavenly shower, descend on those who thirst for Thee,[43]

Thou who offerest resurrection to the fallen.

Strophe 19:   "The words of Thy divine mouth, like drops of moisture[44]

WOMEN   Will now refresh us, O grace of the afflicted,

Life of all, so that we may not die from terror."

This I imagine, was the prayer[44] of the God-loving women.

So that the one seated on the stone[44] was touched,

ANGEL   And he said to the holy women: "Do not *you* be afraid;

but the men who guard the tomb

Will tremble, cower in fear, and be deadened

From fear of me, in order that they may learn

That He is Lord of the angels,

He whom they now guard but whom they do not control,

For the Lord is risen, and they do not know how He has roused Himself,

He who offers resurrection to the fallen.

Strophe 20:   "Henceforth be immortal, women; do not be subject to death.

ANGEL   You seek to behold the Creator of angels,

Then why do you fear the sight of one angel?

39. Matt. xxviii.2; Mark xvi.5.

40. Luke xxiv.5. Literally, they "turned their faces down"; but "looked down" connotes a false idea of shame rather than awe.

41. In Romanos' Annunciation Kontakion, #36, Mary asks Gabriel: πόθεν εἶ; ἄνωθεν ἦλθες ἢ κάτωθεν; Satan, it seems, could appear as an angel. II Cor. xi.14.

42. Matt. xxviii.3; Luke xxiv.4.

43. Isa. lv.1. Romanos has used elsewhere the juxtaposition of heat or fire and cooling moisture. See Introduction, note 85.

44. The liturgy for Easter Sunday may well be suggested in "drops of moisture" (the gift of the Holy Spirit), "the prayer" (ἐλιτάνευον), which means both that "they prayed" and also "they advanced in a procession," and the angel may be the equivalent of the priest who says, in Strophe 21, l. 3, "He has arisen indeed" (Luke xxiv.34).

I am the servant of the One who inhabited the tomb;
    I have the rank and the nature of a slave.
    As I have been commanded, I am here to announce to you,
                     'The Lord is risen;
He has broken the bronze doors of Hades,[45]
    And He has crushed his iron bars.
And He has brought prophecy to fulfillment,
    And exalted the horn of the saints.'[46]
Come, see, young women, where the Immortal was lying,[47]
    He who offers resurrection to the fallen."

Strophe 21: Taking a commendable courage from the voice of the angel,
    The women wisely answered as follows:
WOMEN   "Truly the Lord is risen, as you say;[48]
You have proved to us by your words and by your attitude
    That the Merciful One has risen;
    For if He had not raised up and departed from the tomb,
                 you yourself would not be seated.
For when would a soldier of the king
    Be seated and conversing if the king were present?
Indeed if such things are not in order on earth,
    Certainly they are not done on high
Where there is the invisible throne, and the Ineffable One is seated,
    He who offers resurrection to the fallen."

Strophe 22: The women, with mingled joy and fear, rejoicing and sorrow,[49]
    Turned away from the tomb, as the Bible teaches,
    To meet the apostles; and they said:
WOMEN   "Why are you disheartened? Why do you hide your faces?
    Lift up your hearts, Christ is risen;
    Form choruses and say along with us:
                 'The Lord is risen.'
He has shone forth, He who was created before the dawn;[50]
    Do not be downcast, but take courage;

45. Ps. cvii.16, and *Acta Pilati*, Part II, xxiii.
46. An expression from the O.T. that Romanos uses often to mean "increase the power." Ps. cxii.9; cxlviii.14; Luke i.69.
47. Matt. xxviii.6.
48. See note 44. Luke xxiv.34.
49. Matt. xxviii.8; Luke xxiv.9–10.
50. Ps. cx.3. εἰς τὸν αἰῶνα τοῦ αἰῶνας. Compare the refrain of Nativity I.

Spring has appeared; come to bloom, ye branches,
    Producing fruit and not misery.[51]
Let us all clap our hands and say: 'He has returned to life,
    He who offers resurrection to the fallen'."

Strophe 23: When the men heard this and were rejoicing in the words,
    They were immediately astonished and said to the women:[52]

MEN   "What is this, women, do you understand what you say?

WOMEN   An angel spoke?" "Yes," they said, "he both spoke and showed us:
    In fact, the God of the angels, and the Creator
    Was seen by Mary and said, 'Tell my people,[53]

                  The Lord is risen.'

Come, then, like rams, like sheep,
    Let us all of the flock, skip as we say:[54]
'Our shepherd, come, gather together those of us
    Who were scattered through fear.[55]
Thou hast tread upon Death; come near those who love Thee,
    Thou who dost offer resurrection to the fallen'."

Strophe 24: O Savior, let my dead spirit be raised up with Thee.
    Let not grief destroy my spirit; and hereafter may it not forget
    The songs which sanctify it.
Yes, Merciful One, I beg Thee not to scorn me,
    Though I am covered with many faults;
    For in impiety and sin my mother conceived me.[56]
My Father, holy and full of compassion,
    May Thy name always be holy

51. The branches are the followers of Christ. The verb ἀνθήσατε has really been translated twice as "come to bloom" and "producing." The literal meaning would be: "branches, flower into fruit, not misery." The allusion, of course, is to Christ's statement that He is the vine and that those who abide in Him bear fruit (John xv.5).

52. Mark xvi.8 (astonished); Matt. xxviii.8 (rejoicing). These emotions are applied to the women, not the disciples. The latter were incredulous (Luke xxiv.11; Mark xvi.13).

53. John xx.17.

54. Ps. cxiv.4–6; Wisd. of Sol. xix.9.

55. Zach. xiii.7; Matt. xxvi.31; Mark xiv.27. Christ had announced at the Last Supper that the disciples would leave Him. Here the poet suggests that now they will be called together to spread the Gospel.

56. Ps. li.5.

In my mouth and spirit,[57]
    In my voice and my song.
Grant to me grace as I herald Thy hymns, since Thou hast power,
    Thou who dost offer resurrection to the fallen.

57. The literal translation is *reins*. Although the word is commonly used in the Bible as meaning "the seat of the feelings," it does not convey any special significance to most readers.

ON DOUBTING THOMAS

O. 30 (K. 21)

Title: Εἰς τὴν ψηλάφησιν τοῦ ἁγίου ἀποστόλου Θωμᾶ (B) Εἰς τὸν Θωμᾶν (P)

Manuscripts and editions: The following manuscripts contain the strophes: A, P, and Δ. Prooimion I is in all manuscripts. A omits II and III, as does P. B, M, and T contain the first prooimion and some of the strophes.

> Pitra has edited the poem in *A.S.*, I, xviii. It occurs also in Tomadakis, III, 111–43.

> As in The Victory of the Cross (#22, K. 9), the Western manuscripts contain the second and third prooimia.

Tone: ἦχος πλάγιος δ′

Acrostic: Τοῦ ταπεινοῦ Ῥωμανοῦ

Refrain: "Κύριος ὑπάρχεις καὶ θεὸς ἡμῶν."

Biblical source and place in the liturgy: The kontakion is marked for "The New Sunday," "The Sunday after Easter." The presence of three prooimia indicates that new uses were found for the poem, especially in the West.[1] It is also noteworthy that several manuscripts include only part of the kontakion. It evidently fell into disuse as time went on.

> In spite of the acrostic and the meaning, there is a second Strophe 16 in P and Δ, and a third one in A, pointing to a probable change in ritual for different localities.

> The story of the doubts of Thomas occurs in John xx.24–30. The poet names his source, but departs from it, with the addition of many details.

Analysis of content: The first prooimion states the incident that provided the subject of the poem. The first three strophes express wonder that Thomas was not destroyed at touching the "side of fire," and state the result of Thomas' doubt in the faith of many. The next three strophes give the incident itself. When the disciples tell Thomas that Christ has appeared, Romanos has Thomas accuse them of not announcing an event of such importance to the whole world. He also refuses to believe that Christ would have appeared to the others without asking for him. In the next three strophes, Christ appears, Thomas wonders how he can justify his

---

1. It is entirely possible that only the first prooimion is genuine and that the second and third belong to other hymns (*Tom.*, III, 122–23).

doubts, admits he was jealous of the others, but still insists that one who did not see Christ could not believe in His Resurrection. Strophes 10 through 12 contain the dialogue between Christ and Peter. Christ asks Thomas about his doubts, and he assures Christ that it is only the disciples he doubted, for they had once fled in time of trouble! Christ reminds him that he was a part of the group who left Him alone, and He takes occasion to summarize His crucifixion, burial, and resurrection for the good of ungrateful men like Thomas. Then, after expressing wonder over Christ's forbearance and humility, Thomas begs forgiveness and prays to be accepted in the inner circle. Two strophes present the words of Christ, reassuring Thomas that he will not be consumed by fire, and Thomas' proclamation of faith and his promise to tell the world of the events of Christ's death and resurrection. Christ is then able to state the function of Thomas' doubts in aiding the faith of those who could not see Him. The closing prayer, as usual, asks for forgiveness of the poet himself.

Style of Romanos: The psychology of Thomas, as seen in his excuses, is fully credible. He was jealous of the others, he expected that Christ would notice his absence, he insisted that he could not be blamed for not believing the other disciples because they had not been trustworthy in the past. These insights of the poet must have made the whole incident vivid to the early Christians. Some of the figures of speech are not clear and some are mixed metaphors; for example, in Strophe 3 Thomas is a pen writing an article of faith. From the pen, water gushes forth and is used to refresh various people. When Thomas wishes to be free of the load of doubt and guilt, the metaphor of the hay does not quite seem clear. There are allusions to the Old Testament and to miracles of the New Testament, which are woven in skillfully. The kontakion does not contain an excessive number of restatements of the theology connected with Christ's death and resurrection; its chief charm lies in the touches of human nature in the dialogue.

Meter: The metrical scheme is given in the Oxford edition, 522, XII.

ON DOUBTING THOMAS

O. 30

Prooimion I: Thomas examined with meddlesome hand
 Thy life-giving side, O Christ, God,
 For when the doors were closed, Thou didst enter,
 And along with the rest of the disciples, he cried:
 "Thou art our Lord and God."[1]

Prooimion II: The doubt of Thomas was arranged as positive faith,
 O Savior, in accordance with Thy will,
 In order that no one would ever doubt the Resurrection.
 Only to him didst Thou reveal Thyself—
 Both the print of the nails, and the prick of the spear.
 So that he confessed Thee, saying:
 "Thou art our Lord and God."

Prooimion III: Without faith in Thy resurrection from the dead,
 And examining Thy sacred side,
 Thomas Didymus said in faith:
THOMAS "Sympathize with me, Master, as I boldly feel around,
 And, O Lover of man, accept me as never doubting
 But crying out in faith,
 'Thou art our Lord and God'."

Strophe 1: Who protected the hand of the disciple which was not melted
 At the time when he approached the fiery side of the Lord?
 Who gave it daring and strength to probe
 The flaming bone? Certainly the side was examined.
 If the side had not furnished abundant power,
 How could a right hand of clay have touched
 Sufferings which had shaken Heaven and earth?[2]
 It was grace itself which was given to Thomas
 To touch and to cry out,
 "Thou art our Lord and God."

1. John xx.26–28. In John xx.19, when Christ appeared, the doors were shut.
2. Matt. xxvii.51; Mark xv.33; Luke xxiii.44–45.

Strophe 2: Truly the bramble which endured fire was burned but not consumed.[3]
　　From the hand of Thomas I have faith in the story of Moses.
For, though his hand was perishable and thorny, it was not burned[4]
　　When it touched the side which was like burning flame.
Formerly fire came to the bramble bush,
　　But now, the thorny one hastened to the fire;
　　And God, Himself, was seen to guard both.
Hence I have faith; and hence I shall praise
　　God, Himself, and man, as I cry,
　　　　"Thou art our Lord and God."

Strophe 3: For truly the boundary line of faith was subscribed for me
　　By the hand of Thomas; for when he touched Christ
He became like the pen of a fast-writing scribe[5]
　　Which writes for the faithful. From it gushes forth faith.
From it, the robber drank and became sober again;[6]
　　From it the disciples watered their hearts;
　　From it, Thomas drained the knowledge which he sought,
For he drank first and then offered drink
　　To many who had a little doubt. He persuaded them to say,
　　　　"Thou art our Lord and God."

Strophe 4: What happened? How and for what possible reason did the
　　　　apostle lack faith?
　　Let us ask, if it seems right, let us ask the son of Zebedee;
For John clearly recorded the words of Didymus
　　In the Bible, in his Gospel.
The wise man reports: After the Resurrection of Christ,
　　The other disciples said to Thomas:
DISCIPLES　　"O friend, we have seen the Lord here."
But Thomas at once said to them:
THOMAS　　"Those who have seen Christ do not conceal it, but they cry out:
　　　　'Thou art our Lord and God.'

3. λόγοις is to be understood with τοῖς and would refer to the account of the angel of the Lord, speaking to Moses from the burning bush. Ex. iii.3–5. The emphasis on the divine and human Christ is made again. John the Baptist also feared to touch the fire of Christ (Kontakion #5, Strophe 12).
4. βατώδης is usually used as an adjective in classical Greek. Obviously, here the poet wants the metaphor of Thomas as the thorny one.
5. Ps. xliv.2: "ἡ γλῶσσα μου κάλαμος γραμματέως ὀξυγράφου".
6. Luke xxiii.42.

330

Strophe 5:
THOMAS

"Announce to all the people what you have seen and heard.
     Do not, disciples, conceal the light under a bushel.[7]
What you say in darkness, proclaim aloud in the light.
     With confidence take a stand openly.
Right now you are in a concealed place and you take courage;
     You say fine things when the doors are closed;[8]
     You cry out in a loud voice,[9] 'We have seen the Creator';
Let it be clear to all; let all Creation learn of it;
     Let mortals be taught to cry out to the Risen One,
        'Thou art our Lord and God.'

Strophe 6:
THOMAS

"How can I have trust in you when you utter incredible words?
     For if the Redeemer had come, He would have asked for me,
        a member of His household;
If the day had shone, it would not seem past the right time;[10]
     If indeed the Shepherd had appeared, He would have called his sheep;
Formerly He asked: 'Where did you bury Lazarus?'[11]
     Now He did not say, 'Where have you sent Thomas?'[12]
     Would He have deceived the one who wished to die with Him?
I remain incredulous until I see;
     Whenever I see and touch, I shall say,
        'Thou art our Lord and God'."

Strophe 7:

While Thomas was still saying these things to his friends,
     The Savior came near—He who is the courage of those in fear,[13]

---

7. Matt. v.15; Luke xi.33.

8. "When the doors were closed." Actually, the disciples had not said this to Thomas (Strophe 1). Here, in Strophe 5, Thomas accuses the disciples of being courageous when the door is closed, then in Strophe 7 Romanos reports that Christ entered when the doors were closed, and in Strophe 9 Thomas claims ignorance that Christ had appeared in this way. Actually, Thomas was with the others when Christ appeared to all of them the second time, according to John xx.26. Romanos departs from the Gospel in having Thomas use as an excuse for his lack of faith the fact that he did not know how Christ had appeared. The closed door is both a proof of the divine power and a repeated symbol of Christ's birth from the "closed door of the Virgin's womb." See Strophe 9.

9. Understanding φωνῇ with γεγωνυία.

10. This is a bit obscure. The day connotes the expected day, and it also is a symbol for Christ. The idea seems to be that it is past the time when Christ would have been expected to appear after His resurrection.

11. John xi.34.

12. The reading of manuscripts M and P is ἐπορεύθη, and the translation becomes simpler, "Where has Thomas gone?" than the correction, made for metrical reasons, to ἀφήκατε.

13. Prov. xiv.26; Isa. xxxv.4; Heb. xi.34.

The pure confidence of those in flight and in a state of cowardice.

       He appeared in the midst of the disciples when the

           doors were closed.[14]

But when Thomas saw Him, he lowered his head;

THOMAS   And he said to himself: "What am I going to do?

       How now can I defend myself to those whom I formerly distrusted?

What shall I say to Peter and to the others?

       Those whom I reproached a while back—How shall I appease

           them and cry,

               'Thou art our Lord and God'?

Strophe 8:   "Would that I had exercised control and kept quiet when there was the

THOMAS   discussion about Jesus.[15]

       But the sight of those who were rejoicing roused me to speak;

I was irritated by the words of those who cried with joy,

       'We have clearly seen alive the One who died voluntarily.'

When I saw Peter who had denied Him rejoicing,[16]

       And again when I saw those who fled with Peter rejoicing,[17]

       I was jealous, for I wanted to join the rejoicing with them.

In my zeal, I said what I openly proclaimed.

       Do not blame me, my Jesus, may I be received favorably as I cry:

           'Thou art my Lord and my God.'

Strophe 9:   "The words of my companions were for me night and deep shadow,

THOMAS   For they did not touch my spirit nor bring to light

The lamp of the miracle[18] which I now behold beyond all hope,

       For I see Christ again though the doors were closed.

If I had hastened to understand that He had come in this way,

       I should not have lost faith, for I was able to contemplate

14. John xx.26. See note 8.

15. *Tom.* adopts the reading Ἰοῦ (Δ) and translates, "Lo, I remained silent." κρίνεσθαι seems to mean here "while Jesus was being judged by the disciples." In this case, we have to consider the discussion which *explained* the risen Christ, and not his trial. The "Keep silent" phrase recalls, of course, Christ at His trial (Matt. xxvi.63; Mark xiv.61). *Tom.* IV, 135, note to Strophe 8, states that the silence does not go back to the first brief exchange between Thomas and the disciples but looks ahead to the words in Strophes 4 and 5. Certainly, Thomas adds that he was roused to speak by the rejoicing of the others, and that remark would refer to the first dialogue.

16. Matt. xxvi.74; Mark xiv.68–71; John xviii.27; Luke xxii.57. χαρίεις for χαρίεντας.

17. Matt. xxvi.56; Mark xiv.50.

18. Christ is the Light of the world (John viii.12). The *miraculous* light shines in the transfiguration (Matt. xvii.2) and again at Paul's conversion (Acts ix.3; Acts xxii.6). Here we have by metonymy the "lamp of the miracle."

His appearance and His departure from Mary;[19]
I merely said that I was assured of it.
    But if one did not see Him, how would it be possible to say,
        'Thou art our Lord and God'?"

Strophe 10: So Didymus, speaking to himself, spoke also to our God.
        Christ, testing his nerves,[20] when He beheld Thomas,
    Who was broken-hearted, took pity on him, as once He pitied
CHRIST   The tax collector,[21] and He said: "Place your hand here;
    Why do you hesitate? Tell me, man of little faith,
        What is there of my experiences which seemed incredible?
        Was it the crucifixion, the death, or the resurrection itself?
    At what point do you raise a question with me?
        As you see me whom you longed to see, lo, cry out,
            'Thou art our Lord and God.'

Strophe 11: "Sleeping a short sleep in the tomb, after three days I arose.[22]
CHRIST   I lay in the tomb for you and those like you;
    And you, in place of gratitude, gave me lack of faith.
        For I heard what you said to your brothers."
    Thomas was terrified at this and answered:
THOMAS   "Do not blame me, Savior, for I always trust Thee;
        But I find it hard to trust Peter and the others,
    For I know that, though they were not deceived,
        Still in a time of trouble they were afraid to say to Thee,[23]
            'Thou art our Lord and God'."

Strophe 12: When the One who sees all things, saw that Thomas wished
        To cast aside the accusation of lack of faith, He answered him:
CHRIST   "You, too, were with them in that time to which you referred;[24]
        For everyone left me to suffer alone.

19. See note 8.
20. God tests the "reins," the hearts of men throughout the Old Testament. Jer. xi.20; Ps.vii.9.
21. Luke xviii.13.
22. Matt. xxvii.63; Mark viii.31.
23. The reference is to the failure of all the disciples to stay awake in Gethsemane (Matt. xxvi.40–45; Mark xiv.37–41; Luke xxii.45); and of course Peter is mentioned especially because of his threefold denial (Matt. xxvi.69; Mark xiv.68; Luke xxii.57). Romanos in his kontakion On Mary at the Cross, #19, Strophe 3, complains about the desertion of Peter and Thomas and all the others.
24. See note 23.

It was a hard time, Didymus, do not utter reproaches.
    About it, it was written: 'I shall strike the shepherd,
    And the flock of the shepherd will be scattered abroad.'[25]
Understand what I say; do what you say.
    Do you wish to touch me? Touch me and say,
        'Thou art our Lord and God'."

Strophe 13:   O the marvel! the forbearance! the immeasurable meekness!
    The Untouched is felt; the Master is held by a servant,
And He reveals His wounds to one of His inner circle.
    Seeing these wounds, the whole Creation was shaken at the time.[26]
Thomas, when he was considered worthy of such gifts,
    Lifted up a prayer to the One who deemed him worthy,
THOMAS   Saying, "Bear my rashness with patience,
Have pity on my unworthiness and lighten the burden[27]
    Of my lack of faith, so that I may sing and cry,
        'Thou art our Lord and God.'

Strophe 14:   "Remain gentle in order that I may luxuriate in Thee, Lord,
THOMAS   Fully confirm me as Thine; Thou didst raise up those
            who were outsiders,
Then, support me as Thy own, and show me Thy wounds
    That I may drain and drink them as though they were springs.
Do not consume me, Savior, for Thou art fire in Thy essence;
    But, according to Thy will, Thou didst become human;
    So, I beg Thee keep hidden how great Thou art;
Receive me, my Savior, like the woman with the issue of blood.[28]
    I do not grasp the hem of Thy garment; but I touch Thee, saying,
        'Thou art our Lord and God'."

Strophe 15:   "Once and for all, my good disciple, be faithful and not unfaithful.
CHRIST   Do not fear, for I shall not burn you. I guard those living in me.

25. Matt. xxvi.31; Zach. xiii.7.
26. Matt. xxvii.51.
27. The exact figure of speech is not clear. Thomas wishes to get rid of a load of doubt; he considers it as so much fodder. The poet undoubtedly liked the sounds of χόρτου and φόρτου; the former is used of hay or any fodder, and the verb φεῖσαι could mean either spare in the sense of "turn away from," "forbear," or "use sparingly." Hence, the poet could be saying "turn away from the old fodder of my doubt," or he might mean "use this stuff sparingly, for I want to get rid of it." Both levels of meaning are present in the Greek, but not in the translation.
28. Matt. ix.20.

334

I taught the furnace of Babylon how to do this; [29]
    How much more do I now do this and teach it.
Are you more perishable than the sinner, the harlot—[30]
    She who anointed my head with myrrh,
    And wiped my holy feet with her hair?
Come, then, my friend, do not anoint me with myrrh;
    But be fragrant with faith as you cry to me,
        'Thou art our Lord and God'."

Strophe 16: "Yes, Lover of men, I shall perfume Thee, not as the
THOMAS   harlot did formerly;
    I shall not approach the perfume merchant, saying,
        'Give me myrrh';
I shall offer faith to Thee who hast more than myrrh,
    Thou hast, as grace, the side which I grasp and from which I profit.
O Christ, I shall extol Thy faithful condescension:
    How Thou didst become man in order that Thou mightst save
    From the vanity of idols the man whom Thou didst create;
And then, O Savior, how Thou didst give Thyself over to be lashed,
    And by Thy suffering redeemed me as I cry,
        'Thou art our Lord and God'."

Strophe 17: "Hear, then, and understand clearly: you have become the ally
CHRIST   of the wise;
    I was recognized by men as the wisdom of the Father.[31]
Blessed are you in your faith. Still more do I bless
    Those who come to me merely on hearing of me.
You yourself in touching me just now recognized my glory;
    But they worship me from the sound of words.
    Great is the insight of those who believe on me in this way.
I am beheld by you, my disciple,
    And by those holy servants who cry:
        'Thou art our Lord and God'."

Strophe 18: As I am supported by Thy grace in spirit and body, save me, Most High,
    So that, touching Thy side, I may receive Thy grace,

29. Dan. iii.26–30.
30. Luke vii.37–38.
31. He is called "The Word of God" (Rev. xix.13). Paul calls Christ "the wisdom of God" (I Cor. i.24).

And taking Thy body and Thy blood, that I may be redeemed
  from my sins,
  In order that I may find pardon for my transgressions.
Thomas, touching Thee, knew Thy glory;
  But I am afraid, for I know Thy commands;
  And I know my deeds. My conscience troubles me.
Pardon, my Savior, pardon, Merciful One,
  That by words and deeds I may ceaselessly cry to Thee,
    "Thou art our Lord and God."

ON THE MISSION OF THE APOSTLES

O. 31 (K. 25)

Title: Τῶν ἁγίων Ἀποστόλων or Τῶν ἁγίων καὶ κορυφαίων τῶν ἀποστόλων πέτρου καὶ παύλου (*AP*)

Manuscripts and editions: Δ contains both prooimia and the entire kontakia.

Prooimion I and a few strophes are in B, M, and T. Prooimion II and the kontakia are in A, D, and P; M and T contain an extra strophe for Strophe 13, and 20 is different in various manuscripts.

Pitra has edited it in *A.S.*, I, xxii, 169–78. Christ uses his text in *Anth. Christ.*, 131–40.

Tomadakis, IV, 12–36.

Tone: ἦχος β'

Acrostic: τοῦ ταπεινοῦ Ῥωμανοῦ ὁ ψαλμός

Refrain: Ὁ μόνος γινώσκων τὰ ἐγκάρδια

Biblical source and place in the liturgy: Trypanis indicates that it is for June 30. Pitra places it on June 29 or 30.

The biblical account of the sending out of the apostles is in each Gospel: Matthew xxviii.19; Mark xvi.15–17; Luke xxiv.44–49; and John xx.23. The exact words of Christ's commission to them are repeated several times in the poem.

Analysis of content: Prooimion I is a simple dedication to Christ and the apostles whom He strengthened, and Prooimion II picks up the emphasis on their being fishermen and prays for the strengthening of the church. The first three strophes are introductory and the poet uses them to promise to do what he preaches as the apostles did. Strophes 4 through 14 present Christ on the mountain after His resurrection, repeatedly telling the apostles to go forth and preach repentance and baptism. He addresses, in turn, Peter, Andrew, John, Matthew, Philip, and Thomas. In each case the poet relates the special stories about the Apostle; in some cases these had been given special kontakia (as in the case of Peter and Thomas) that explain the emphasis for that disciple. In the last two strophes of this section, He addresses them all. The next six strophes present a dialogue between Christ and the apostles, in which they doubt their ability and are told that they will surpass the Greeks and should remember the fate of Judas. The last three strophes summarize their importance to the world and Christ's church and also summarize the doctrinal importance of Christ's unity with God and the Holy Spirit, followed by a repetition of Christ's commands and the commitment of the apostles to obey them.

The strophe that is included in A, D, P, and Δ for Strophe 13 is to Bartholomew; a translation of it follows:

"Bartholomew, along with them, do you herald me to the world, as you clearly
    know me to be risen from the dead,
And you, too, James, the son of Alphaeus, and Judas, not the Iscariot,
And Simon, become the zealot, because of your faith in me.
My eleven chosen ones, aside from the one separated from your group,★
I now send out to the ends of the earth to turn aside and save the
    world from destruction,
        I who alone know what is in the heart."

Style of Romanos: Building on the few words of Christ as He commissions the apostles to go out and preach the Gospel to all the earth, the poet manages to work in a dialogue between Christ and the apostles and some rather effective touches in the directions He gives the individual disciples. The latter contain allusions to other kontakia the congregations would have heard at other times of the year. The reminders to Peter and Thomas of their past failings and the suggestion that Thomas will now have his longed-for chance to refute the Jews—these bits are quite typical of Romanos. He also is able to work in the theological points he wishes to emphasize when he has Christ warn Philip not to say that he has known the *Son* but not the *Father*. Again, at the end, the essential unity of Christ with God and the Holy Spirit is the topic for one of the closing strophes. Figures of speech center on agriculture and the sea; they are not always quite clear, but the one that puts side by side the apostles who dealt in the sea with their new "gushing forth of words like the sea foam on the beach" is a happy idea, impossible of translation, since it is included in the one verb. The chance to strike at Greek rhetoricians by comparing their work with the speech of the apostles is not so violent as in On Pentecost, but it is still typical. The organization follows the usual pattern of a few introductory strophes making clear the topic, a few stating the story, and then direct dialogue for the heart of the kontakion.

Meter: The metrical scheme is given in the Oxford edition, 523, XIV.

★ This is not consistent with Strophe 20, l. 4.

ON THE MISSION OF THE APOSTLES

O.31

Prooimion I: O Lord, Thy heralds, secure and inspired,

        And the choicest of them, Thy disciples,

          Thou didst claim for the refreshment and enjoyment of Thy blessings;

     Thou didst approve their sufferings and death

                         As beyond all burnt offerings,

       Thou who alone dost know what is in the heart.

Prooimion II: Thou who hast given fishermen wisdom beyond that of orators,[1]

        And hast sent them forth over all the earth,

          By Thy ineffable wisdom, O Christ, God,

     Through them strengthen Thy church,

        And send Thy blessing on the faithful,

       Thou who alone dost know what is in the heart.[2]

Strophe 1:   Make my tongue clear, my Savior, open wide my mouth,

                         and fill it; prick my heart

     In order that I may obey what I preach[3] and be the first to do what

        I may teach;

     For He says that the one who does everything which he teaches is great;[4]

     But if I do not do what I preach, then I shall be considered

        as sounding brass,[5]

          O Thou who alone dost know what is in the heart.

Strophe 2:   So once Thy disciples carried out Thy commands above all;

                         they taught just what they did.

     In full power, together, they attained the teaching for Christian life.[6]

---

1. The second prooimion is the only one given by Christ, *Anth. Gr.*, 131. Pitra, *Hymn.*, I, uses the first line of Prooimion II, and then uses all of Prooimion I, with a note saying that τοὺς ἀσφαλεῖς and the first strophe appear *passim* on January 16 and June 30.

2. τὰ ἐγκαρδία might better be translated "concerns of the heart."

3. Literally, "follow what I say," "practise what I preach." I Cor. ix.27. Paul's "lest when I have preached to others, I myself should be a castaway" is, in essence, what we use as a slogan, "Practice what you preach."

4. Matt. v.19.

5. I Cor. xiii.1.

6. πολιτεία literally means citizenship; it certainly applies here to life in the Christian community. It is used by Paul, Eph. ii.12, in relation to rights of Israel.

The one who sees this teaching and strives after it, is great.

It means[7] to be deprived of all material things in life, and to consider

heavenly matters at all times,

To take the cross upon one's shoulders,[8] and to revel[9]

in dying, as Thou didst command,

O Thou who alone dost know what is in the heart.

Strophe 3: Great is the number[10] of the virtuous, the list of all the apostles

grows long, and it perfumed the earth.

They are the branches of Christ's vine,

the field of the One on high.[11]

They were fishermen before Christ, and they are fishermen after Christ.

Those who formerly dealt with sea water, now utter sweet eloquence;[12]

Those who captured fish a while ago, now are fishers of men, as He said,

He who alone knows what is in the heart.

Strophe 4: The Leader gathered together the lambs whom fear had scattered[13]

at the time of the crucifixion after the resurrection,

And standing on the mountain top,

He sang a sweet song, giving courage to the flock,

A bit as though speaking with hints for timid men, He said:

CHRIST "Be of good courage, I alone have conquered the world,[14]

I alone have scattered the wolves,

no one was with me; I was the one, the only one,

Who alone knows what is in the heart.

7. The phrase *it means* is supplied to make the apposition of the series of infinitives clear.

8. Matt. x.38; xvi.24; Mark viii.34; x.21; Luke ix.23.

9. Heb. xii.2.

10. The exact construction of τοσαυτῇ is not clear. The noun ὕλη does not appear in the translation, but the idea is clear. The poet is thinking of the faithful and virtuous, the apostles, as the *material* with which Christ had to work; and he wants to emphasize the abundance of evidence they gave of working out Christ's plans. Perhaps, a literal translation would read: "The material of the virtuous to such a great abundance, the list of the virtues of the apostles. . . ." Pitra translates it by *copia*, "great is the abundance." He uses πιστοὶ in line 2 rather than κομῶν.

11. The word καλλιέργου is not clear and is omitted from the translation. It could be masculine and refer to Christ as the One who does beautiful work, or it could be neuter and refer to a beautifully worked field in Heaven to correspond to the field on earth that is to be worked by the apostles. Pitra comments that it is rare.

12. "Utter sweet words" cannot convey the continued figure of speech that the Greek verb ἐρευγόμενα conveys. It means to splash out as foam of the sea, or metaphorically, to spit out words. So, formerly the apostles dealt with sea water, and now they splash out words like foam of the sea.

13. Matt. xxvi.31; Mark xiv.27; Zach. xiii.7.

14. John xvi.33.

Strophe 5:   "So, go forth to all nations, sowing the seed of repentance on the earth

CHRIST   and watering it with doctrinal teachings;[15]

Peter, look to me as to how you educate;

remembering your own fall,[16] sympathize with all;

Mindful of the maiden who caused your fall, do not be harsh;

If conceit attacks you, hear the sound of the cock's crow,

And remember the tears with whose streams I washed you,[17]

I who alone know what is in the heart.

Strophe 6:   "Peter, do you love me? Feed my flock,[18]

CHRIST   and love those whom I love, sympathizing with sinners.

Heed my mercy to you, since I received you

who had thrice denied me.

You have a thief as gatekeeper of Paradise to give you courage.[19]

Send him those whom you wish. Because of you, Adam turned to me

Saying, 'O Creator grant to me the robber as gatekeeper,

and Cephas as keeper of keys.

Thou who alone dost know what is in the heart.'

Strophe 7:   "Be strong in me; and you, too, Andrew;[20] just as you were the first

CHRIST   to find me, you were found by me; so find the one who has wandered;

Do not forget your first skill;

from it I shall educate you for this new art.

Formerly, naked into the deep sea, now naked into life;[21]

Formerly, hunting with a fishing-rod, now taught to fish with the cross;

Formerly you used a worm as bait; now I order you to hunt

with my flesh.

I alone know what is in the heart.

Strophe 8:   "Now, John, accept Thy work. Now let all men learn

CHRIST   that it was not in vain that I formerly had you lean on my breast.[22]

---

15. Matt. xxviii.19. This is the source of the hymn's oft-repeated message.

16. Matt. xxvi.69; Mark xiv.66; Luke xxii.57; John xviii.17. See also Romanos' Kontakion #18.

17. Matt. xxvi.75; Mark xiv.72; Luke xxii.62.

18. John xxi.15.

19. Luke xxiii.43. *Acta Pilati*, XXVI; Romanos' Resurrection Kontakion #23, especially Strophe 13.

20. Matt. iv.18; John i.40.

21. Andrew appears half-naked in the lower right of the icon from Novgorod of the "Blessed Virgin of the Veil." See frontispiece.

22. John xiii.23.

Make furrows for my spring

whose waters your love has drained.[23]

With your tongue as with a hoe, dig for me a passageway.

Indeed I shall come when you wish it, and offering drink shall
    moisten your seed.

Cast your words out like kernels,[24] and I shall increase and fill
    out your crops.

I who alone know what is in the heart.

Strophe 9:   "So, too, James, do not neglect your work as herald,

CHRIST   and remember Zebedee whom you formerly preferred to me;

For you know how you sent away your father in a boat,[25]

and loved me, the Creator.

Together with my fellow servants, carry out my will.

Do not fear treachery; I have put to naught their plots.

When they pierce you with swords,

think who has pierced my side with a spear,[26]

I, the only one who knows what is in the heart.

Strophe 10:   "Come, Philip, along with the others; herald me as you now

CHRIST   see and hear me; do not separate me from my Father.

Do not say, 'I saw the Son;

but I did not see his Father at all.'[27]

For I showed you Him in me and me in Him.

I did not come apart from Him; what He wills, I bring to pass; what I
    will, He brings to pass.

We are in the same spirit. I send you forth as herald of Him
    Who alone knows what is in the heart.

Strophe 11:   "Thomas, through your present faith, abandon the former words of

CHRIST   faithlessness; and herald the One whom you touched.[28]

The time has come for which you always longed,

time to attack the Hebrew people.

23. Pitra translates "ebibit"; but the form is certainly aorist and not future.
24. A reference to John xii.24.
25. Matt. iv.21–22; Mark i.19; Luke v.10. James left his father, in each of the Gospel accounts.
This passage reflects Christ's words in Matt. x.37.
26. John xix.34.
27. John xiv.8–9. This gives Romanos a chance to emphasize his theological point about Christ's
not being separate from the Father.
28. John xx.27. Romanos' Kontakion On Thomas, #31, treats the incident in detail.

You have clear evidence of the resurrection;
You saw the prints of the nails,

                      and you saw the marks of the spear.
There is no excuse left; for I took away all pretext for doubt.
          I who alone know what is in the heart.

Strophe 12: "Matthew, remain as tax collector,[29] and collect from the
CHRIST   enemy of Adam as you once collected from travelers.
Do not hold back until you have taken away
                        every last penny from him;
Sit down guarding the road which leads to Hades,
And if you find the destroyer who traffics off my people,
Oppose him and exact toll, and despoil him, as I tell you,
         I who alone know what is in the heart.

Strophe 13: "I send forth one word for all so that I may not weary you
CHRIST   in teaching you one by one. Once and for all I say to my saints:
'Go forth into all the world;
                    teach races and kingdoms;
For all things have been given me by my Father,
Things on earth and in Heaven[30] over which I was in charge before
        I assumed flesh.
And now I have become King of all, and I have you as my sacred senate.
         I who alone know what is in the heart.'

Strophe 14: "Then go forth to all nations, sowing the seed of repentance
CHRIST   on the earth, water it with doctrinal teachings."
The disciples, when they heard these things,
              looked at one another and shook their heads.
DISCIPLES   "From what source will we have the voice and tongue to speak
        to all nations?[31]
For we are illiterate and uneducated, weak fishermen, as Thou has said,
        Thou alone dost know what is in the heart."

29. Matt. ix.9; Mark ii.14; Luke v.27.
30. Matt. xxviii.18; John iii.31; viii.23; Rev. i.5.
31. Moses, too, told the Lord that he was slow of speech and tongue (Ex. iv.10). The disciples refer to their inability to speak other languages, and the gift of tongues, which Christ promises in Strophe 16, was received (Acts ii.7–13). Romanos' Kontakion On Pentecost, #34, becomes a sequel to this one.

Strophe 15: "Now do not be disturbed in your hearts, nor let the enemy

CHRIST   disturb your spirits; do not reason like children;

But become wise as serpents;[32]

                         for on your behalf I have been exalted as serpent.

Do not, doubting yourselves, abandon your work as heralds.

I do not wish to conquer by force; but I prevail over the weak.

I do not rejoice in those who Platonize; but I have loved the foolish

         of the world.[33]

            I who alone know what is in the heart.

Strophe 16: "Truly I shall give you power,[34] the power which prevents many

CHRIST   from falling; and I shall make your tongue skilled.

The people will drive away Demosthenes;

                   and Athenians will be worsted by Galileans.

Cephas, as he tells of me will put an end to written records,

Immoderate speeches and myths;

                  he will eclipse the speech of Maranatha;[35]

Nazareth will shake Corinth;

                you are the ones to speak and I obey,

            I who alone know what is in the heart.

Strophe 17: "All men will cudgel you with insults, and throw you in prison;

CHRIST   and binding you cruelly, they will give you over to the rulers;

But I shall not leave you orphans,

                  for I am with you even unto the end.[36]

Whenever you stand trial, you will see me in your midst.[37]

You will be bound, and I am bound with you;

                endure all things with me and for my sake.

You extend my will, as I fight for you,

            I who alone know what is in the heart."

Strophe 18: When they heard the words of the wise Teacher,

                      the wise disciples answered:

32. Matt. x.16.
33. I Cor. i.20; James ii.5; Matt. v.3, 5.
34. Acts i.8.
35. The word means "Our Lord cometh"; it is used by Paul in I Cor. xvi.22, where it is placed with *anathema* and means "accursed, the Lord cometh."
36. Matt. xxviii.20.
37. Matt. x.19; xviii.20.

344

DISCIPLES   "Thou dost tell us all these terrible things,

                                things full of fear and death;

But, if we are united with Thee, we think we shall avoid them;

Even now dost Thou give us over to more terrible things, our Savior?

Thou hast called us to rest,[38] and lo! Thou dost anoint us for struggle,

        Thou who alone dost know what is in the heart."

Strophe 19:   "Your fate[39] calls you to the contest, the law of love

CHRIST   asks of you that you show the act of friendship;

Suffer for me as friends,

               as I indeed suffered for my friends, though I did not have to.

No necessity was found which called me to death;

Nevertheless, I accepted it and underwent the cross as a debtor.

Voluntarily I, guiltless, paid off your ancestral debt,[40]

        I who alone know what is in the heart.

Strophe 20:   "Go forth, then, to all the world, and cast the seed

CHRIST   of repentance in the ground and water it with doctrinal teachings.

See to it that no one who repents remains outside your net.

For I rejoice in those who are converted,[41] as you know.

Would that the one who betrayed me had turned back to me

           after the sale.

But I have wiped out his sins and united him with you,

        I who alone know what is in the heart.

Strophe 21:   "Hate grief and cowardice, for cowardice sends many men

CHRIST   to death as Judas made clear.

Know how despair throttled the traitor with a rope for hanging.[42]

However, the snare of the devil was in this case all in vain,

38. Matt. xi.28.

39. The Greek word ψῆφος means, of course, the pebble that casts the vote or determines the fate of a person.

40. The idea of the "ancestral debt" occurs throughout the Resurrection Kontakia, especially in Nos. 22, 23, 26, and 27, Strophes 6 and 15. Often Romanos speaks of nailing the accusations against sinful Adam to the cross, as Paul does, Col. ii.14.

41. The literal meaning of the verb is stronger, for it means "turned around and came back"; but this does not fit the general rhythm nor yet modern terminology.

42. Matt. xxvii.5. The manuscript P writes σχοινίῳ, and the dative makes for a clearer translation than σχοινίον, which Trypanis uses.

And he will get small vengeance; for instead of Iscariot I provide you
     with the Cilician;[43]
Instead of the treacherous one, the man of excellence; instead of
     the traitor, Paul.
        I who alone know what is in the heart.

Strophe 22: "My friends and brothers, initiates, for I call you initiates,
CHRIST   no longer servants, but sons and co-heirs with me,[44]
You are lights of the universe and bright beams of my sun,
Faithful guardians of my treasures,
Mediators of the gifts which I gave to Adam when he was guided back,
Columns of my church whom I brought up from the sea,
        I who alone know what is in the heart.

Strophe 23: "So herald me to the world as you make clear what I am;
CHRIST   and henceforth hate parables and enigmas.
Say that, being God and ineffable,
                I took on the form of a servant.[45]
Show how I voluntarily took on the wounds of the flesh.
Being God, though not dying,
                I came to death in the body;
And entombed as one condemned, I came forth from Hades as Lord,
        I who alone know what is in the heart.

Strophe 24: "Save the world on these terms, baptizing in the name of the Father,
CHRIST   and the Son, and of the Holy Ghost."[46]
Strengthened by these words,
                the apostles said to the Creator:
DISCIPLES "Thou art God before all time and without end.[47]
We shall herald Thee as one Lord, along with the Father and Holy Spirit,
Just as Thou hast commanded.
                Become with us and above us
     The one who alone knows what is in the heart."

43. The country of Paul. Acts xxi.39; xxii.3.
44. Rom. viii.17.
45. Phil. ii.7.
46. Matt. xxviii.19.
47. Rom. i.20. The refrain of Nativity I brings out the poet's insistence that, just as God is eternal, so Christ is before all time. In his Epiphany Kontakion, #6, Strophe 1, Romanos uses the phrase τὸ πρός πρωΐ πρωΐ, which echoes Ps. xlv.6.

ON THE ASCENSION

O. 32 (K. 22)

Title: Εἰς τὴν ἀνάληψιν τοῦ κυρίου καὶ θεοῦ καὶ σωτῆρος ἡμῶν Ἰησοῦ Χριστοῦ

Manuscripts and editions: The second prooimion occurs only in Δ. The rest of the strophes appear in A, B, M, P, and T.

Pitra edited it, *A.S.*, I, xix.

Tomadakis has edited it, IV, 40–79.

Tone: ἦχος πλάγιος β′

Acrostic: τοῦ ταπεινοῦ Ῥωμανοῦ

Refrain: "Οὐ χωρίζομαι ὑμῶν ἐγώ εἰμι μεθ' ὑμῶν καὶ οὐδεὶς καθ' ὑμῶν."

Biblical source and place in the liturgy: Luke xxiv.50–53; Acts i.9–13; John xvi. The hymn is marked for Resurrection Sunday, κυριακῇ τῆς Ἀναλήψεως.

Analysis of content: The first prooimion announces the Ascension as the subject and reaffirms the lack of change in the nature of Christ; and the second prooimion mentions the Mount of Olives and thus brings in the refrain, which is effective in its reassurance: "I am not separated from you. . . ." After the first strophe, which urges all to be inspired by the event of the Ascension, Christ in two strophes blesses the apostles. They, in Strophes 4 through 7, show their grief because of His leaving. They even remind Him of what they have given up to follow Him. Then Christ speaks for three strophes and urges them to rejoice, for He goes to prepare a mansion especially for them, and He assures them that this is no mere bodily ascension. Then He signals the angels, and the command, "Lift up the gates," rings out. Two strophes of narrative describe the cloud's forming a chariot to convey Christ on high. Now, speakers are heard from Heaven; the angels are given direct speech, in which they restate the fact that Christ never lost His divinity. The dialogue shifts to the apostles, who reassure each other of the value of what the angels reveal; the angels speak again, assuring them that Christ will return. For two strophes the apostles review the life of Christ and speak of their determination to battle the heretics. The kontakion closes with a hymn of praise to Olivet and a prayer.

Connection with homily: There is a spurious homily by Athanasius (*P.G.*, 28, 1099C) that is parallel to Strophe 11, 3–9, in that it, too, explains the difference between this ascension and that of Enoch and Elijah. The cloud and the angels also appear in the sermon, which is probably by Basil of Seleucia.

In a homily by St. John Chrysostom, the angels become heralds to Mary. The parallels with this kontakion are between Strophe 15, 6–12, and *P.G.*, 60, 30C.

Style of Romanos: This kontakion contains not only dialogue, but also dialogue on several levels. The angels talk to the apostles, and they, in turn, speak with Christ. Christ addresses the angels and also reassures the apostles. Theology is included, of course, with some emphasis on the fact that this is a divine Christ who ascends to Heaven, quite different from the ascensions of Elijah and Enoch. The human insights are chiefly evident in the speech of the disciples to Christ, in which they remind Him of their sacrifices for Him and of the extent of their love for Him. His promise that He goes to prepare a special place for them in Heaven is a touch that lends reality to the biblical text. Also, the apostles, in reminding themselves of the role of angels in all of the events of Christ's life, provide themselves with a basis for believing the wonderful sight they have just witnessed. The cloud that serves as chariot and the elaborate imagery of Strophes 10 through 12 add to the triumphant command to "Lift up the gates and open wide the doors." The refrain, which is based on "If God be for you, who can be against you," is handled with special aptness as Christ assures the apostles that He is not really separated from them and that therefore no one can prevail against them.

Meter: The metrical scheme is given in the Oxford edition, 518, III.

ON THE ASCENSION

O. 32

Prooimion I: Having fulfilled for us God's plan of redemption,[1]
        And having united the affairs of earth with those of Heaven,[2]
        Thou wert taken up in glory, Christ, God,
    In no way separated but remaining without difference,
                    and announcing to those who love Thee:
        "I am with you, and no one is against you."[3]

Prooimion II: On the Mount of Olives, after Thou hadst consecrated the disciples,[4]
        Thou wert taken up to Heaven, Lord,
    Committing to them the ministry[5] and proclaiming to them:
        "I am not separated from you; I am with you, and no one
        is against you."[6]

Strophe 1:   Leaving behind on earth, the things of earth,
        Yielding up to the earth things of ashes,
        Come, let us return to our senses, and lift our eyes
                    and our thoughts on high;[7]
    Let us mortals expand our vision and our sensibilities
        Up to the heavenly gates.
    Let us consider that we are on the Mount of Olives,[8]
        And that we are gazing at the Redeemer
        Who is carried upon a cloud.[9]
    For the Lord went straight up to Heaven from here;
        And there the bountiful Giver, bestowed gifts

1. The whole plan of death, resurrection, and ascension is God's dispensation or οἰκονομία: the real theme of this poem.
2. I Tim. iii.16.
3. The poet no doubt intends us to have in mind Rom. viii.31: "If God be for us, who can be against us?" Matt. xxviii.20; Hag. i.13.
4. Luke xxiv.51.
5. John xiv.26; Acts i.8; Luke xxiv.49.
6. John xiv.18; Rom. viii.31; Matt. xxviii.20.
7. Phil. iv.8.
8. Matt. xxiv.3; Mark xiii.3; Luke xxi.37; John viii.1; Acts i.12.
9. Rev. i.7.

On the apostles, flattering them as a father,
    And having guided them like sons and talked to them, he proclaimed:
      "I am not separated from you; I am with you,
      and no one is against you."

Strophe 2: He who descended to earth, as He alone knew how,
    Rising up from it (again as He knew how),
    He took the ones whom He loved, and gathering them together,
He led them to a high mountain
    In order that, when they had their minds and sensibilities
      on the height,
They might forget all lowly things.
    And so, when they were led up to the Mount of Olives,
    They formed a circle around the Benefactor,
As Luke, one of the initiates, narrates in full.[10]
    The Lord, raising His hands like wings—
Just as the eagle covers the nest of young birds which she warms—[11]
CHRIST   Spoke to the nestlings: "I have sheltered you

                            from all evil[12]

    Since I loved you and you loved me.
      I am not separated from you; I am with you,
      and no one is against you.

Strophe 3: "O my disciples, on high over you,
CHRIST   As God and maker of the whole world,
    I stretch out my hands, hands which the lawless stretched,
                  bound, and nailed down.[13]
Do you, then, place your heads under my hands;
    Understand and know, friends, what I am bringing to pass.
For just as though baptizing you, I place my hands on you now,[14]

10. Luke xxiv.50–53.
11. Deut. xxxii.11.
12. John xvii.12.
13. The Gospel account of the crucifixion does not include this detail. The prints of the nails are mentioned (John xx.25), and Romanos uses them, of course, in his kontakion on Thomas #30. The nails are mentioned in his hymn On the Passion, #20, and in #21 On the Crucifixion, the poet mentions His being "stretched out like a simander" (Strophe 20). Christ is said to be "nailed to the cross," #22, Strophe 9, and there are frequent figurative references to our hearts, our sins, the condemnation of Adam being nailed to the cross.
14. The hand of God for blessing is a commonplace in the Bible. The kontakion On Baptism, #53, has references to the ritual of baptism, and in Kontakion #5, Romanos represents John the Baptist as asking Christ why He inclines His head beneath his hand (Strophe 6), and again in Strophe 12 he states his fear of being burned if he holds the head of Christ.

And blessing you, I send you forth
Enlightened and made wise.
On your heads, praise and beauty,
On your spirits, a shining glory, as is written.[15]
For I pour out on you from my own spirit,[16] and you will be
accepted by me,
Instructed and chosen, trusted members of the inner circle.
I am not separated from you; I am with you,
and no one is against you."

Strophe 4:   When the Savior said these things to the apostles,
It produced great and considerable grief.
Soon they were lamenting; and as they groaned deeply,
they said to the Teacher:

APOSTLES   "You are dismissing us, O Merciful One, you remove yourself to a
distance from those who love you,
And you spoke to us as one setting out on a journey.
These words indicate a departure from here,
And for that reason we are in great distress
Since we long to be with you.
We seek for Thy face for it brings joy to our spirits.
We are hurt, we stand in need of the very precious sight of Thee.
No one except Thee is God. Do not separate Thyself from those
who love Thee;
But remain close by with us and say to us:
'I am not separated from you; I am with you,
and no one is against you.'

Strophe 5:   "We have left behind us all livelihood,
APOSTLES   And we fled from it as though it were violence.
In order that we might gain Thee, we have become strangers
and sojourners on the earth.[17]
Peter was the first of us to become Thy friend,[18]
He was estranged from all his former friends.

15. Acts ii.17–18.
16. Acts x.45; Isa. xxxii.15.
17. Heb. xi.13; Eph. ii.19.
18. The calling of the disciples: See especially Matt. iv.18–21; ix.9; xix.9, 27; Luke xiv.26–33.

Then Andrew, his kinsman, when he found you,
    Straightway abandoned things of this world
    And took Thy cross upon his shoulders.[19]
Dost Thou wish to abandon such a condition, Master,
    Dost Thou hasten to run away from us as though forgetful of us?
Let it not happen, O King, lest those who hate us laugh at us,
    And lest they say to us: 'Where is the One who said,
        "I am not separated from you; I am with you,
        and no one is against you".'

Strophe 6:   "O Redeemer, art Thou disregarding and failing to consider
APOSTLES   The love of the sons of Zebedee?
        Dost Thou remember, O Lover of men, how they heard Thy divine
                                    word and did not misunderstand?
    They did not say in their hearts: 'Who is this man who has called us?'
        But they chose Thee in preference to their fathers.
    Again, Matthew considered the tax collector's
        Way of providing means as poverty[20]
        When he longed for Thy wealth.
    Indeed, Thomas Didymus also despised property;
        And all of us said together: 'We love Thee before all.'[21]
    Do not leave us alone; but having fulfilled all things,
                                    take us in Thy arms,
        Encircle us and say to us:
            'I am not separated from you. I am with you,
            and no one is against you'."

Strophe 7:   When the Savior heard the apostles,
        And saw the grief of those who loved Him,
        Then, like a father, He came to their aid,
                                    and pitied them, and said:
CHRIST   "Do not mourn, my friends, it is not time for tears,
        Nor is this a day of lamentation,
    But it is a time of grace, for I ascend
        To my Father;[22] I lift up my wings,
        And I come to rest in my tent;

19. Matt. x.38; xvi.24; Mark viii.34; Luke ix.23.
20. Literally, "as lack of means."
21. John xi.16.
22. John xx.17.

352

For I created the firmament of Heaven as a tent—
  A tent not to circumscribe but to encircle me.
As Isaiah puts it: 'God established Heaven as a vaulted arch
  And dwells in it as a tent.'[23] He says to those who are His:
    'I am not separated from you; I am with you,
    and no one is against you.'

Strophe 8:   "Be gay and radiant, then,
CHRIST   And as you assume a joyous appearance,
             Sing a new song; for indeed everything which will happen,
                                              happens for your sake.
  For your sake I came; and I came for all
    In order that I might be pleasing to you and that you
      might accept me.
  Again, it is for you that I ascend to Heaven
    In order that I may prepare a place[24]
    Where I am bound to be with you.
  For above in my Father's house are many mansions;
    Some, the Fathers possess,[25] others, the spirits of the Just,
  And still others, the prophets; no one now knows your mansion;
    So, I prepare it for you and I shall receive you,
      I am not separated from you; I am with you,
      and no one is against you.

Strophe 9:   "Now, upright ones, arise, remain steadfast,[26]
CHRIST   And with blameless eye consider
             This Ascension. Seeing it, you will know that it is
                                      of the body and not of divinity;
  For the body which you see, will arrive on high;
    But every part of the world is full of my divinity.
  Just as the part of me which is visible is raised on high,
    The invisible part will be raised with it,
    For it was united with the visible.
  I am, then, One who is invisible and still visible;
    I am One whom you see; but truly I am not changed,

23. Isa. xl.22.
24. John xiv.2–4.
25. This usually means in Romanos' kontakia the O.T. Fathers, rather than the Fathers of the church.
26. I Cor. xv.58.

353

As Scripture says,[27] I am immortal, and at the same time
    I am above you and still in your midst.
        I am not separated from you; I am with you,
        and no one is against you."

Strophe 10: When Christ said these things to His friends,
    He then gives a nod to the archangels
    So that they may prepare for His sacred footsteps a way up
                        which was not traversed.
And then, as ordered, the first line of angels
    Announced to all the leaders on high:
ANGELS   "Lift up the gates and open wide the doors,
    The heavenly and glorious doors,
    For the Lord of glory draws near.[28]
Clouds, strengthen your backs for Him to mount;
    Air, prepare for Him to travel through you;
Heavens, be opened up; Heavens, the heavens of Heavens, receive Him,
    Since He comes to you, He who says,
        'I am not separated from you; I am with you,
        and no one is against you'."

Strophe 11: At once those on high, obeying,
    And opening up all the high places,
    The thrones, dominions, along with principalities and powers,[29]
                        ran to the encounter
And quickly spreading out the cloud like a chariot,[30]
    They sent it to the Mount of Olives.
And when it descended it took to its bosom
    The One who guides the clouds
    And makes them heavy with rain.
Taking Him up, it bore Him, or rather was borne,
    For He who is being carried, bore the cloud which carried Him,
Just as formerly in the case of Mary whom
             He guarded while dwelling in her; for the Scripture

27. Mal. iii.6; Num. xxiii.19.
28. Ps. xxiv.7–9; *Acta Pilati*, II, xxiii (Latin B) uses these phrases for the triumphal entry of Christ into Hell (Tischendorf, ed.), 406.
29. Col. i.16; Eph. i.21.
30. Elijah, of course, ascended in a chariot of fire (II Kings ii.11); Christ is taken up in a cloud (Acts i.9). The poet has the cloud assume the shape of a chariot.

Summoned this cloud in advance.[31] He said to His friends:
"I am not separated from you; I am with you,
and no one is against you."

Strophe 12: Not one of the apostles was remiss, but together
They paid careful attention to what came to pass;
For all fixed their gaze on high watching the Ascension.
Immediately the cloud putting its back beneath Him[32]
Became a chariot for the foot of the blameless One;
The sky was cleft like a cloak,
And the son of Mary ascended
As fiery bands of singers preceded
ANGELS   Crying: "Come, Lord, for Thy throne is ready;[33]
Mount, rise up on the wings of the winds,[34]
And hasten to the Father's embrace, for clearly Thy throne
is always the same.
Thou dost occupy it and Thou dost not leave it, even if
Thou dost cry to those below:
'I am not separated from you; I am with you,
and no one is against you'."

Strophe 13: When the faithful saw what had taken place,
Singing psalms much in the manner of David,[35] they said:
APOSTLES   "Truly He has ascended; as God, in the sound of the shouting;
as Lord, in the voice of the trumpet."
While they were singing together and looking on high
A band of angels came to them
In the way in which the Book of Acts teaches:[36]
While the Creator was ascending,
And the holy ones were gazing at Him,
Two angels, as men, shining in their raiment, stood near,
ANGELS   Saying: "Why do you stand there? At whom are you gazing?
What do you wish to behold? For lo! God is seated upon His throne.

31. Isa. xix.1, speaks of the Lord as riding on a cloud. The poet wants to draw an analogy between Christ's being borne by Mary and still bearing her, just as the cloud bears Him aloft and is still supported by Him. προκαλέω seems to mean "names this cloud in advance."
32. Acts i.9.
33. Ps. xciii.2.
34. Ps. xviii.11.
35. Ps. xlvii.6.
36. Acts i.10.

He who ruled us as King, He who cried out to you:
'I am not separated from you; I am with you,
and no one is against you.'

Strophe 14:   "Do not, then, be disturbed, O men of Galilee,[37]

ANGELS   For just as Jesus Christ was taken up,
So, too, He will return, just as you observed Him arriving on high.
For clearly He was taken up and He was not translated.
For Christ's Ascension was not like that of Enoch,
the earliest [example].
For the latter, Enoch, lived in the midst of men on earth,
And he was not considered worthy of Heaven,[38]
But he was put into the tabernacles of the just.
Elijah, seated upon a fiery chariot, ascended,[39]
And he did not arrive in Heaven, as is written,
But as though in the direction of Heaven. The God of Enoch,
and the God of Elijah,[40]

Ascending into the heavens declared to you:
'I am not separated from you; I am with you,
and no one is against you'."

Strophe 15:   When the disciples of the Redeemer
Heard these words, they said to one another:

APOSTLES   "Truly faithful witnesses of the ascension of Christ are these men,
like heavenly beings.
For if they had not seen Him in Heaven on High,
They would not have come down to announce it to us.
He controls the angels and through angels He makes known
What accomplished God's plan of redemption for man.
He was born of the Virgin,
And the angels told of His birth.
He was raised up from the dead, and again angels announced it;
He ascended into Heaven, and He revealed to us
His divine and radiant Ascension
Through good angels. He told us:
'I am not separated from you; I am with you,
and no one is against you.'

37. Acts i.11.
38. Heb. xi.5.
39. II Kings ii.11
40. Enoch and Elijah are in Paradise, in the account of *Acta Pilati*, XXV (James, ed.), 140.

Strophe 16: "Let us, then, be strengthened against the heretics;

APOSTLES   Let us prepare for the noise of battle against the false accusers,

      Let us work hard and struggle continuously against them

                                until we cast them out.

Let us speak openly to the sons of perdition:

      'Where is the man whom the soldiers guarded and over whom

           your seals kept watch?[41]

Where has He been stolen away? Where has He been raised up?

      Who stole Him? Who raised Him up?

      Was He stolen from the tomb? How from the firmament of Heaven

Did He send a message to us and say to us: "Do not fear;

      They shall not overcome you, for I say to you,

           I am not separated from you; I am with you,

           and no one is against you"?'"

Strophe 17: When the disciples thought of the Redeemer in this way,

      And of the Ascension of Christ,

      Then they descended from the mountain rejoicing and exulting;

And when they came down, as the Scripture teaches,[42]

      Bowing down, they did obeisance to God on high,

And full of praise, they let their voices ring out to the mountain,

      As though shouting in honor of Olivet,

      Since it was deemed worthy of so much.

APOSTLES   They said: "You have surpassed Mount Sinai; for it became the

           speaker's platform for Moses' words,[43]

      But you, for the words of Christ.

The former was the law; but the grace is in Thee,

      The same grace which created Moses and said to us:

           'I am not separated from you; I am with you,

           and no one is against you.'

Strophe 18: "From now on Thou art above Lebanon,[44]

APOSTLES   Tabor and Hermon[45] art inferior to Thee,

      Since the Lover of man did not do on them what

41. Compare with Romanos' Kontakion #24, Resurrection I, Strophe 17.
42. Luke xxiv.52–53.
43. A play on words here. βήματα means literally "the footsteps of Moses," but the connotation certainly implies the rostrum from which Moses set forth the tablets of the law. Ex. xxiv.12–18.
44. Lebanon, famous for its cedars, its pure water, and its beauty. Ps. lxxii.16.
45. Mount Tabor and Mount Hermon, Ps. lxxxix.12.

He has brought to pass on you."
When they had finished speaking, the disciples of the Creator
    Put an end to their words,
And, raising their eyes and their hands,
    They made supplication to the King
    Of Heavenly Beings and those on earth, saying:

APOSTLES "Thou who art without sin, grant peace to us,[46]
    And through us to Thy world, to the ambassadors of Thy mother,
For the enemy does not endure seeing the fine things which have
      happened to us.
    Drive him away from us, Thou who dost say:
      'I am not separated from you; I am with you,
      and no one is against you'."

46. Isa. xxvi.12; John xiv.27.

358

ON PENTECOST

O. 33 (K. 23)

Title: Εἰς τὴν ἁγίαν Πεντηκοστήν

Manuscripts and editions: The prooimion and the first strophe occur in G. The prooimion and the first nine strophes occur in P; T puts Strophe 14 before 9; Δ gives the whole kontakion, as do A and M.
  The only edition other than this is in Pitra, *A.S.*, I, xx.

Tone: ἦχος πλάγιος δ′

Acrostic: Τοῦ ταπεινοῦ Ῥωμανοῦ

Refrain: Τὸ πανάγιον πνεῦμα

Biblical source and place in the liturgy: The manuscript and the contents make it clear that this kontakion was written for the Sunday designated as Pentecost.
  The biblical source is Acts ii.1–15.
  The shortened form in G and P would point to an abandonment of this kontakion for widespread use—even at Patmos.

Analysis of content: The prooimion announces the subject, and the first strophe presents the setting for the worship on Pentecost Sunday. Strophes 2 and 3 emphasize the facts that Christ never left earth, and that He is everywhere. They continue with the disciples' return from the Mount of Olives to the upper room. Strophes 4 and 5 tell us of their prayers with Peter as leader, and then of Christ's command to the Holy Spirit (Strophe 6). Strophe 7 repeats that Christ is everywhere. The story of the coming of wind and fire occurs in Strophes 8 and 9, with Peter's exhortations in Strophes 10, 11, and 12. The disciples are urged not to try to explain these wonders, just to marvel at them.
  The next three strophes tell of the speaking in tongues and the wonder of people who hear them. Strophes 16 and 17 express the poet's admiration of oratory of the erstwhile fishermen and his scorn of Greek rhetoricians and philosophers. The closing strophes praise the disciples for preaching the cross of Christ to win people to His teachings.

Connection with homily: No homily contains passages that parallel this kontakion.

Style of Romanos: Vivid the poem certainly is. Human bits of psychology have been added to the account in the Gospels. The winds blow fiercely, and the disciples beg Christ to check the storm and send the Holy Spirit. The elaboration of the story concerning the different tongues they could speak well is effective, and the conversation given to the people who wonder at their new ability is convincing. However, the figures of speech get decidedly out of hand in the last strophes where the poet shifts from the reed that would write their words to the figures of fishhooks and webs; another quick shift poses a hunting comparison, with Christ's flesh on the cross as bait. On the other hand, the naïve simplicity of the figure by which the prayers are signed, sealed, and sent on high is charming. In an excess of zeal, Romanos discounts all of the classic rhetoricians and philosophers. Did he really know their works—or did he use the rhetorical device of discrediting them solely to praise the disciples? The effectiveness of his design would be enhanced if the sound of the names and the rhymes in the verbs could be reproduced in translation.

Meter: The metrical scheme is given in the Oxford edition, 530, XXVII.

ON PENTECOST

O. 33

Prooimion: When the Holy Ghost descended, He confined [1] the tongues,
                            separated the nations;

          Inasmuch as He distributed the tongues of fire,
                        He summoned all to unity; [2]

          And we praise in unison,
            The All-Holy Spirit.

Strophe 1:   O Jesus, grant to Thy servants speedy and constant consolation
          In time of neglect of our spirits.
    Do not separate Thyself from our spirits in time of affliction;
          Do not be far from our minds in the midst of outward pomp, [3]
                      but always show Thyself to us.
    O Thou who art everywhere, draw near to us, draw near.
          Just as Thou art everywhere with Thy apostles, [4]
  Just so, take thought for us who love Thee
          So that we who are brought together may hymn and praise Thee,
            The All-Holy Spirit.

Strophe 2:   O Savior, Thou wert not separated from Thy disciples
                    when Thou didst journey to Heaven.
          Indeed Thou art the first to contain what is above and what is below,
    Because, O Infinite One, no place is apart from Thee;
          And even if there be such a place, it is destroyed, and disappears
                          as Sodom did. [5]
    For Thou hast established the universe, fulfilling all things.
          The apostles possessed Thee in their hearts;

1. The meaning would seem to be clearer if a "which" is understood, but no such reading is suggested in the ms. tradition. "He confined the tongues *which* separated the nations" would lead logically to the unity mentioned in line 2.
2. Acts ii.1–8.
3. Is Romanos referring to special emphasis on "pomp" in Constantinople, which steadily increased its ceremonies? Does he refer to a special "time of affliction," or is he making a more general prayer?
4. This connects directly with Kontakion #32 On the Ascension with the refrain in which Christ promises the disciples that He will be with them always.
5. Gen. xviii.20; xix.25.

Hence, when Thou didst formerly ascend from the Mount of Olives,[4]
    They returned home rejoicing, playing and singing praise
        To the All-Holy Spirit.

Strophe 3:   The eleven disciples returned with joy

                        from the Mount of Olives.
        Luke, who records sacred things,
     Writes that they returned to Jerusalem,
       Mounted to the upper room, sat down,[6]

                        and remained there—[7]
    Peter and the rest of the disciples.
       Cephas who was their chief spoke to them:
PETER   "Lovers of the kingdom, let us lift up our hearts
       To the One who made us a promise in these words: 'I shall send you,
         The All-Holy Spirit'."[8]

Strophe 4:   Peter, speaking like this to the apostles,

                        roused them to prayer,
       And standing in their midst, he spoke as follows:
PETER   "On bended knee let us beg and pray
       That we shall make this chamber a church,

                    for so it is and has become.
    Let us be eager to cry unto God,
      'Send us Thy good spirit
    So that it may lead all of us to correct knowledge[9]
       Which Thou hast prepared for those who worship and praise
         The All-Holy Spirit'."

Strophe 5:   When they heard this, those who had been called with him

                        gathered together
       As lambs in the presence of the shepherd, charmed by his speech;
    And silently they specified what they desired,
       And they held up to the Pantokrator the prayers

                      which pressed for these things:

6. Luke xxiv.33–53; Acts i.1–5; 12–14.
7. Acts i.15; ii.14–40.
8. Matt. iii.11; John xiv.26.
9. The Holy Ghost as teacher, John xiv.26.

DISCIPLES   "To the Lord of angels and the King,
                 To the Ruler of men and the Maker of the world,
             To the One who holds sway with His nod over those in
                      Heaven and earth
                 Thy friends and servants cry to Thee: 'Quickly send us
                      The All-Holy Spirit'."

Strophe 6:   Immediately after completing their prayers,
                                              they wrote their names under them,
                 And sealing them in faith, they sent them on high—[10]
             Prayers which the Master recognized and He said:
CHRIST   "Comforter, descend as Thou dost wish, of Thy own initiative,
                                       and without being summoned,
             The disciples expect Thee; they are the ones
                 Whom I gather together for Thee and the Father,
             The ones whom I educated when I said: 'Teach the nations,[11]
                 Extolling the Father, and worshiping the Son, and praising
                      The All-Holy Spirit'."

Strophe 7:   God heard their wants and His Comforter
                 Descended on those who were praying,
             The Ineffable One was not removed from one place to the other,
                 Nor was there alteration, nor accommodation,
                                       nor did He endure diminution,
             For He was above, and below, and everywhere;
                 For the divine nature is ineffable and not to be touched;
             It is not seen by the eyes, but it is apprehended through faith;
                 It is not grasped in the hands; but it is felt in hearts of faith—
                      The All-Holy Spirit.

Strophe 8:   When the divine Pentecost was complete, the eleven chosen ones
                                              set up a din.

                 As they persevered in their prayers;
             And as the passage read from Acts says,[12]

10. The leper writes his prayer in Kontakion #8, Strophe 9, and then in Strophe 11 we are told that it is written on the paper of his soul. Christ mentions receiving a letter from Mary and Martha summoning Him to the aid of Lazarus (#14, Strophe 3), but this was not, of course, a prayer.
11. Matt. xxviii.19–20.
12. Acts ii.1–4.

When the sound of the powerful wind of the spirit suddenly
came resounding from Heaven,
The whole chamber was filled with fire.
Indeed it amazed the beloved disciples rather too much.
When they saw the dwelling tossed like a boat, they cried:
"O Master, check the storm and send
The All-Holy Spirit."

Strophe 9: When the disciples recognized that the whole upper room
was shaken as by an earthquake from the wind,
They all lowered their eyes in fear;
And lo! Another trembling still more to be shuddered at,
And one upon another marvel brought a second trembling
in addition to the first fear,
For fiery tongues touched them anew
And began to appear on the heads of the chosen group.
Indeed the fiery tongues did not burn their hair but lighted
up their hearts
And sent them forth cleansed and purified—
The All-Holy Spirit.

Strophe 10: Peter seeing all the things which were happening,
PETER
cried out: "Brothers,
Let us hold in reverence what we see, and let us not examine it.
Does anyone say what it is that has been done?
For what has been accomplished transcends belief
and defies thought.
Spirit and fire are united—a true miracle,
Air and flame are joined together—awesome sight!
Along with winds, torches; along with dew, sparks of fire.[13]
Who has seen, who has heard of this? Who is able to speak of what
is produced by
The All-Holy Spirit?

Strophe 11: "Do you, then, dearly beloved, stand and simply observe the fire
PETER
Which the One who is in Heaven has sent from on high;

13. The combination of refreshing dew and fire is a favorite antithesis of Romanos.

Do not fear, for the coals do not burn;
    Do not be amazed that the fire does not burn;[14]
                          but as prudent men remember
How long ago the fire received kindly the three children,[15]
    How their bodies were not burned, nor their hair,
How the furnace revealed the three as four,
    For it gave back those whom it received with interest, since it feared
        The All-Holy Spirit.

Strophe 12: "Then, brothers, let the One descended upon us cast out
PETER   fear from our minds,
    And make a show of love to the Ascended One.
Since He loved those whom He called,
    Since all the things which He prophesied, He has fulfilled,
                    and since He has done as He said,
Why, then, should we be afraid of a flame which does not burn?
    Let us consider the fire as roses, which indeed it is.
It has been placed upon our heads like flowers,
    And on our heads it has formed a crown, an ornament,
        and illumined us,
            This All-Holy Spirit."

Strophe 13: When Cephas said these things to the apostles,
                          he was quiet with them,
    And, with them received the Holy Spirit.
Afterwards, he left, as is written,
    And use was made of the two miracles of fire and wind,
                          as forerunners;
For he knew that the miracle ran ahead of the wind,
    And the flame preceded the enlightening
In order to inform in advance, as though sounding a trumpet
        to the world,
    Because it descends on earth as it knows how to do and as it wills—
        This All-Holy Spirit.

Strophe 14: Great and marvelous were all the things which happened,
                      and they stirred the hearts of all,

14. John the Baptist, in Kontakion #15, Strophe 6, and Thomas in Kontakion #30 feared touching fire.
15. Dan. iii.26.

For suddenly all were filled with the Spirit.
They conversed with those who heard them as they listened,
With Romans, not as though they were foreigners; with Parthians,
and, I think, with Medes as though natives;
With the Elamites, they appeared to be speaking clearly and sweetly;
With the Arabians they were at once intelligible,
With Asians and with Phrygians, their speech was clear and distinct;
Indeed, they spoke with all races, as it gave them power,
This All-Holy Spirit.

Strophe 15: But when the people, present from all places, saw them
speaking in tongues

PEOPLE   They shrank back, saying: "What does this mean?
The apostles are Galileans;[16]
How is it that we now see them as though they were
fellow-countrymen of all races?
When did Peter Cephas look upon Egypt?
When did Andrew dwell in Mesopotamia?
How did the sons of Zebedee possibly see Pamphylia?
How shall we make these things known? How shall we speak?
It was entirely at the will of
The All-Holy Spirit."

Strophe 16: Now, those who were formerly fishermen have become Sophists;
now they are clear orators
Who once stood on the banks of the lakes;
Those who formerly mended their fishing nets
Now unravel the webs of the orators and make them easy,
in simpler words;
For they say one word instead of many,
They proclaim one God, not one of many;
They worship the One God as one, the incomprehensible Father,
The Son of the same nature, undivided, and similar to them—
The All-Holy Spirit.

Strophe 17: Then was it not granted to them to excel all
through the tongues which they speak?
Indeed why do those who act foolishly strive for victory?

16. Acts ii.7–13.

Why do the Greeks snort and chatter?
>   Why do they make a show of Aratus, the thrice-accursed?
>>   Why are they led into error by Plato?
>   Why do they love Demosthenes, the weak?
>> Why do they not see that Homer is a flitting dream?
Why do they keep talking about Pythagoras who justly is to be muzzled?
>   Why, in fact, do they not run and have faith in those to
>>   whom has appeared
>>>   The All-Holy Spirit?

Strophe 18: Brothers, we shall hymn with praise the tongues of the disciples,
>>   because, not with elegant speech,
>   But in divine power they have revived all men.
Because they took up His cross as a reed,
>   So that they might again use words as fishing lines
>>   and fish for the world
Since they had speech as a sharp fishhook,
>   Since the flesh of the Master of all
Has become for them a bait, it has not sought to kill
>   But it attracts to life those who worship and praise
>>   The All-Holy Spirit.

ON THE SECOND COMING

O. 34 (K. 7)

Title: Τῆς Δευτέρας παρουσίας

Manuscripts and editions: The manuscripts are not complete. T has the first six strophes; and A, B, D, M, P had Strophes 13 to the end. Δ has the entire kontakion, except that C is deficient.

>   The poem was edited with considerable commentary on the meter by Krumbacher in *Stud.* 163–83.

>   Pitra edited it in *A.S.*, I, vi.

>   Wehofer edited it in *Sitz-ber. Akad. Wien*, CLIV (1907), 5, 108–20.

>   Cammelli, *Romano il Melode*, 215 ff.

>   Soyter edits it from the manuscript of Maas, *Byzantinische Dichtung* (Heidelberg, 1930), 14–20, 60–62.

Tone: ἦχος α'

Acrostic: Τοῦ ταπεινοῦ ʽΡωμανοῦ τὸ ἔπος

Refrain: κριτὰ δικαιότατε

Biblical source and place in the liturgy: It is marked for the Sunday of carnival week.

>   The chief biblical source is Revelation xx.12. Matthew xxiv tells of the signs of Christ's coming and warns of the Second Coming. References in Strophe 3 to the Ascension are to Acts i.9–11, and the prophecy about the Jews reflects John xix.37, while the appearance of the righteous is taken from Matthew xiii.43. In Strophe 4, the allusion to John the Forerunner comes from Matthew iii.1, and Malachi iv.4, 5. Elijah is mentioned in Matthew xvii.10–13 as well as elsewhere in the Gospels when Christ asks what people call Him. Elijah and Enoch are identified as the prophets referred to in Revelation xi.3. Revelation and Daniel's prophecy in ix.27, are the basis for Strophe 6. The coming of Antichrist is mentioned in II Thess. ii.3, and in Daniel, ix.27; this is the basis for the numbers in Strophe 13. In Strophe 16 the description of the righteous at the right hand of God comes from Matthew xxiv.22. The sounding of the trumpet is mentioned in I Cor. xv.53, and in I Thess. iv.16. The fact that all one's deeds are laid bare is mentioned in Heb. iv.13. The justice of the last judgment is affirmed in Rom. ii.12, and I Peter i.17. The outer darkness is mentioned in Matthew viii.12. Other

common phrases for fruits of repentance have their biblical sources. The over-all sources are the above passages from Daniel, Revelation, and Matthew.

Analysis of content: The prooimion announces the subject, and the first three strophes give the setting and the reaction of the poet at the thought of Hell's fire. The next three strophes introduce Elijah, the prophecies of Daniel, and references to Enoch. Then three strophes equate Antichrist with the devil, three more give the general suffering on earth under Antichrist, and this leads to Strophes 13 through 16, with the climax of desolation on earth and the end of all religious worship. These passages prepare for the coming of Christ, which is described as it will be in Heaven and on earth, and for the judgment of both the righteous and the wicked. Strophes 20 and 21 place the righteous on the right hand of God, with the assurance that both the joy and the suffering will be eternal. Strophe 22 describes the lamentations of those who deserve punishment, and the poet exhorts all to repentance in order to avoid these evils. The kontakion ends with a personal prayer that he, too, may be spared eternal punishment.

Wehofer, in the study that has been quoted, comments on the careful organization of materials in Romanos. The opening of the prooimion and the first strophe are balanced by material in the closing prayer. The poet takes up six questions in logical sequence; namely, What do we mean by the Second Coming? Who gives us assurance of it? When is it to take place? Why? Who will be involved? What will be the practical results?

Connection with homily: Sources for the concepts of Antichrist go beyond the mention of him in I John ii.18, 22; iv.3; and II John 7.

He was considered as a man by most of the early church Fathers. Important possible sources for Romanos' concepts of Antichrist are the following: In the fourth century, Ephrem considered that the fall of the Roman Empire was caused by Antichrist, and Jerome, in his commentary on Daniel, interprets details of Daniel's vision. Cyril of Jerusalem, in *Catech.* xv.4, and Chrysostom in his commentary on II Thess., represent Antichrist as sitting in the temple and as gaining control of the Empire.

Interesting parallels are pointed out by T. W. Wehofer, "Untersuchungen zum Lied des Romanos auf die Wiederkunft des Herrn," *Sitzungsber. d. phil.- hist. Kl.* (Wien, 1907), 20–108. Strophe by strophe he points out similarities between Romanos and Ephrem, as he emphasizes the more lyrical aspects of Romanos. The sixteenth strophe of Romanos contains passages that are very close to Ephrem's writings. In both authors we have ranks of angels and arch-angels, rivers of fire running ahead to proclaim the glory of Christ, Cherubim who hide their faces in awe of the Almighty One. The case for this use of Ephrem as source from the use of the original title to the closing prayer is conclusive. Gustav Soyter, *Byzantinische Dichtung* (Heidelberg, 1930), Kommentar, 61–62, refers to Ps.-Hippolyt., Philippus Solitarius, as well as Ephrem as sources.

The legend that Antichrist by a trick imitated the virgin birth was common in the Middle Ages, but its source is not to be specifically proven.

We know that French verse contains thirteenth-century versions of the Antichrist legends. E. Walberg published two of them, and he refers to a special source, the Abbot Adson of Montier-en-Der who composed *Epistola ad Gerbergam reginam de ortu et tempore Antichristi* in about 950. Page 106 of this account brings forward the information that Antichrist was born like other men and not, as some say, from a virgin. E. Walberg, *Deux Versions inédites de la légende de L'Antichrist en vers français du xiii*e* siècle* (Oxford Press, 1928), xviii*n*2.

Style of Romanos: Two typical approaches of Romanos are illustrated in this kontakion. In the first place, he has used a variety of sources and woven them into his account of the Second Coming. Then, too, he has let himself go in his descriptions of the horrors of Hell's fire and in his vituperative account of the actions of Antichrist. Figurative language and dramatic touches are, however, at a minimum. The organization is characteristic, since groups of three strophes work up to the actual scene of the Last Judgment and the closing strophes of exhortation and prayer. The poet does not repeatedly emphasize the divine-human Christ as in other kontakia, but the whole theme is one in which that dogma is implicit.

Meter: The metrical scheme is used also in #4 and #57. Krumbacher discusses its relation to #18 and #4. It is given in the Oxford edition, 518, IV.

ON THE SECOND COMING

O. 34

Prooimion: O God, when Thou dost come on earth with glory,
      All the universe trembles.
A river of fire flows in front of the judgment seat,
      Books are opened up and secrets are made public.[1]
At that time, rescue me from the inextinguishable fire,
      And deem me worthy to stand at Thy right hand,[2]
          O most just Judge.

Strophe 1: O Lord, good beyond measure, when I bear in mind Thy
        fearful judgment seat,
      And the day of judgment,
      I shudder and am terrified as I am convicted

                            by my conscience.
When Thou dost intend to sit on Thy throne

                      and hold a close examination,
      Then no one will be quite able to deny his sins,
      Since truth will convict him and terror restrain him.
Loud will be the roar of Gehenna's fire,

                   and sinners will gnash their teeth,
      Therefore, before the end, have pity on me and spare me,
          O most just Judge.

Strophe 2: When the Lord first came and appeared before men,
      He was not separated from the Father,
      He was not unobserved by those on high, the powers and rulers
                    and ranks of angels.
Indeed, He who made man became man, as He willed it,
      And He was taken up to the Father who had not given Him up.
      My Savior, Thy mystery is inexplicable,
For in no way didst Thou go from Thy Father,
               indeed Thou didst show forth the Father;

1. Rev. xx.12.
2. Matt. xxv.33.

Thou art inseparable from Him, and Thou dost fulfill all things,
O most just Judge.

Strophe 3: Hymned by the angels, the Lord ascended with glory
As His disciples watched.[3]
Just so, with angels running ahead, will He return
in full sight, as is written.
When heavenly and earthly bodies, along with infernal beings,
Will sing praises and bow before the crucified Christ,
Clearly they will confess that He is God and Creator;[4]
Then the Jews with lamentations will see Him whom they pierced;
The Just will be radiant as they cry: "Glory to Thee,
Most just Judge."

Strophe 4: John was the forerunner of the former arrival of our God,
As he announced repentance for all.[5]
Elijah, the just, will be the forerunner
of the second coming.
Malachi,[6] the prophet, foretold this when he said:
"Elijah, the Thesbite,
Will be sent before the day of the coming of the Lord."
And Matthew writes,[7] my Savior, how Thou didst teach
About John, saying: "This is he, if you are willing to receive him—
Elijah who is going to come to announce me
As most just Judge."

Strophe 5: John, the theologian, also handed down important secrets,
and clearly taught
And made clear
In his Apocalypse that Elijah would come.
Also he revealed that Enoch,[8] the blessed, would come with him,
Saying, "I shall send two prophets into the world,
They will put on sackcloth and proclaim me to all."

3. Romanos, Kontakion #32; Acts i.9–13.
4. Phil. ii.10–12.
5. Romanos, Kontakion #5; Matt. iii; Mark i; Luke i.17.
6. Mal. iv.5.
7. Matt. xvii.11–13.
8. Rev. xi.3. Jude refers to Enoch as prophesying the Judgment Day (Jude 14, 15). Elijah is mentioned by Christ in connection with John the Baptist, Matt. xi.14; Luke i.17. The two witnesses, clad in sackcloth, are not given names, but they are mentioned in Rev. xi.3.

He foretold that they would precede Thy second coming
　　By one thousand and two hundred and sixty days,[9]
　　　　O most just Judge.

Strophe 6:　Daniel,[10] the God-inspired, clearly indicated beforehand things to come,
　　　　If we examine him accurately.
　　　　He says, "I shall make a covenant for seven days,"
　　　　　　　　　　and straightway he added:
"The vaunted worship service shall be increased
　　　　　　　　　　up to one half of seven days."
　　　　And he interprets it that two of the saints will herald
　　　　The second coming in three years and one half.
The wicked Antichrist will prevail for another such period,
　　　　Causing terrible fear to those who await Thee,
　　　　　　O most just Judge.

Strophe 7:　Antichrist will find the root a bitter one
　　　　　　　　　from which he will be fashioned.
　　　　This terrible and all-wicked one wishes
　　　　To imitate the incarnation of Christ,
　　　　　　　　　　and he hates the truth.
He will assume a bodily instrument worthy of his wickedness.
　　　　Through tricks, he will be born of an impure woman,
　　　　And he will deceive the lawless, as though born of a virgin.
The wicked deceiver will perform marvels through tricks;
　　　　And the lawless will be pleased and they will deny Thee,
　　　　　　O most just Judge.

Strophe 8:　In order that the abominable, accursed devil may appear
　　　　As one who is opposed to good,
　　　　A son of perdition, exalted to be worshiped as God

---

9. Rev. xi. 3.
10. Daniel's vision of the four beasts and of God's kingdom is given in Chap. vii, and the equivalents in Revelation are interesting. The big horn and the little horn are usually given political meaning in reference to the Roman Empire. The persecution is to last three and one-half years (Rev. xiii.5), as Gabriel tells Daniel (ix.22–27). He tells him that after three score and two weeks destruction of the sanctuary in Jerusalem will take place, and then the people will have one week for repentance, but sacrifices and worship will cease. The people were given seventy weeks to make an end of sins and find reconciliation (Dan. ix.24). The translation of τῆς λατρείας τὸ καύχημα is literally "the boast of the worship service," and the idea is that the use of the sanctuary for worship had been a source of pride, but it is to be cut off.

374

By those deceived by his tricks (indeed he will be received

    By those who do not accept the love of the true Christ,

    But rather have faith in the deceit of the wily one),[11]

The savage serpent will utter words against the Most High,

    And he will oppose those who await

        The most just Judge.

Strophe 9:   Then the lawless one will build a temple and lead astray

    The proper assembly of Hebrews and others.

    The tyrant will perform false miracles and signs.

He will change from one shape to another, fly away into the air,

    And, ready to do anything, he will assume the form of

      angels or demons

    For those who hasten to obey his commands.

Great and immeasurable will be the tribulation for men;

    By it will Thy servants be tested,

      O most just Judge.

Strophe 10: There will be great hunger, and the earth will deny its fruits;

    And there will not be any rains at all,

    Suddenly all growth will die away,

                and pastures will dry up.

Men will flee from place to place,

            and they will mourn without ceasing.

    The persecution against the saints will prevail

    On desert mountains, and hills, and in caves.

Men will become exiles, in fear of the tyrant,

             retiring before the serpent,

    And crying, "Look upon Thy servants and save them,

      O most just Judge."

11. II Thess. ii.3. This is no place for a summary of the literature about Antichrist. Only John calls the adversary of Christ "Antichrist." In his Epistles, I.ii.18, 22, and iv.3, are the sources of Romanos' identification. Paul, in II Thess. ii.9, refers to the one "whose coming is after the working of Satan." I Tim. iv.1, refers to "later times when some shall depart from the faith, giving heed to seducing spirits."

    Antichrist has been variously interpreted by later theologians as referring to an evil principle, or perhaps specifically to Nero and Diocletian, or still later to the Papacy.

    Medieval accounts of magicians who fly through the air and perform magical shows are numerous. The legends about Antichrist are numerous. In the thirteenth century, St. Thomas Aquinas refers to Magian philosophers who perform miracles that parody those of Christ.

    Important as a source for Romanos' treatment of Antichrist as a man are the various homilies of the period. See the Introduction.

Strophe 11: Through many wiles, the completely wicked one will come

as a humble person,

    As our good shepherd,
    For he will imitate His voice and turn the flocks

from the fold.

And many men will listen to him, and tricked,

will go away,

    And he will take away from them

the seal of the Savior,

    And he will mark them with his own seal of perdition.
Those who know his deceit, will hate and despise
    His voice and love only Thee,
        O most just Judge.

Strophe 12: The all-wicked trickster then hisses,

and is terribly angry,

    And like a savage serpent,
    Attacks all men as an enemy,

especially the saints.

The merciless one hurls his special secret poison

against all men,

    He will cause fear, and create displays and crashes of thunder
      in the air,
    Which bring about fear and terror to men.
Everything on land and sea will be moved,

sacred objects will be carried away.

    Hence the Just cry out: "Show Thyself,
        O most just Judge."

Strophe 13: Just so, those who await Christ and are persecuted

will die,

    Yet, psalms and hymns will cease;
    There will be no liturgy, no sanctus,

no offering, nor incense.

For three and one-half years, the sacrifices will be carried away,[12]

as it is written.

    Earthquakes, and deaths, and every affliction

will prevail in the world.

    Children will be left incomplete in the wombs of the mother.

12. Dan. ix.27.

Indeed the mother will die before the child;

in the fields, the remains;

No one appears to bury them, but Thou dost sustain all,
O most just Judge.

Strophe 14: No one city, nor desert will be strong enough

to save the exiles;

Grief oppresses the ends of the earth.
All men in the day pray in sorrow that

night may come,

And when night has come, they pray that they may

see the day again.

Those who are alive, weeping, consider blessed those in tombs.
A father, meeting his child, embraces him,
And the two will die, locked in an embrace; those who stand will fall.
Blessed will be the one who endured and loved Thee,
O most just Judge.

Strophe 15: Who has strength to tell[13] of the unspeakable tribulation

which the hardened sinner will reveal

At the time when offenses are paid in full.
As is written, the Master for His chosen ones

will curtail

The days of tribulation, sparing His own, since He

is merciful.[14]

And then, He will come from on high, flashing forth with glory
Like the sun in the clouds, as God incarnate.
In the same way as the Holy and Immaculate One who rules all ascended,
The angels tremble before Him and cry out: "Glory to Thee,
O most just Judge."

Strophe 16: Holy Bridegroom, our Savior, in order that Thou mightst reveal

Thy incomparable power,

Ranks of angels and archangels run ahead of Thee,
Singing hymns before Thy throne,

O Lord;

13. This translation adopts the reading of the Patmos manuscript, which Trypanis marks as possibly correct. It makes more sense than any of the other suggested readings.
14. Matt. xxiv.22.

And they become a river of fire burning over the earth,

and cleansing it,
As the river filled with fearful fire runs ahead of Thee.
Cherubim and Seraphim with fear conduct the worship service,[15]
And they sing the doxology as they sing without ceasing
the thrice-holy hymn,
They hide their faces, as they cry out: "Glory to Thee,
O most just Judge."

Strophe 17:   All the tombs are shaken, and they are opened up,

when the trumpet sounds,[16]
And the dead will rise up,
All the living will suddenly be lifted up,

and all will be at an end.
They will behold that ineffable beauty of the Bridegroom, and
they tremble,
Both the races and the tribes of sinners and of righteous;
For truly the coming of Christ is fearful.
Suddenly the great Heaven will separate, and the earth will be changed,
And all the races will confess Thee,
The most just Judge.

Strophe 18:   Still later, the righteous will behold

the face of the Lord,
And they will be in the bridal chamber,
In freedom kneeling before the Most High,

they will stand near the angels.
Each righteous man, rejoicing, will conduct his own trial,
When his deeds have been bared and exposed to view[17]
In the presence of the Judge and King.
Whoever will show a firm faith along with his acts
Will cry out in pride, "Grant us Thy grace,
O most just Judge."

Strophe 19:   Then the wily one, in chains, is brought before the judgment seat

by the angels

15. Isa. vi.2.
16. I Cor. xv.52; I Thess. iv.16.
17. Heb. iv.13. The verb used is very colorful, though impossible of exact translation. τετραχη-
λισμένα is a wrestling term that means to bend back the victim's neck and thus bare it to view.

Together with all his servants;
And those who were obedient to him and denied Christ
are brought along with him.[18]
The enemy and his devils will be cast
into everlasting fire.
The impious will be assigned to the lot of the devil,
And with him endure eternal punishments.
Whoever of his own will sinned in the law will be judged in the law;[19]
For Thy judgment is just and no respecter of persons,
O most just Judge.

Strophe 20: When we, both sinners and righteous before the judgment seat
of Christ
Undergo a just examination,
Then the righteous will stand to the right,
like gleaming light;
And the sinners will take the left,
with mourning and lamentation;
For no chance for defense will be given them,
Since all the deeds done by each have been discussed.
For the first appearance was the guardian of safety;
But the second coming is one of judgment about which Thou hast
warned all men,
O most just Judge.

Strophe 21: All men will then be incorruptible and immortal
after their resurrection,
For all mortal things will have passed away.
No longer will there be fear, since change
and death do not occur.
The government will be eternal, endless and without change.
Those who had been justly cast into outer darkness[20]
Will be set apart, weeping, in eternal punishment;
But the righteous as they again possess Thy incorruptible kingdom,
Will have endless joy as they sing praise to
The most just Judge.

18. Rom. ii.12.
19. I Peter i.17.
20. Matt. viii.12.

Strophe 22: How great and of what kind is the mourning of the condemned
in the hour of judgment
(And indeed I have been set down as chief of the condemned).
When they see the Judge seated, fearful and exalted
on His throne,
And when they behold the lines of the righteous and the saints
shining in joy
And the sinners in dejection and eternal punishment,
They will cry out and show vain penitence.
Would that in the world we might show the fruit of repentance[21]
And find the grace of mercy and forgiveness,
O most just Judge.

Strophe 23: This is the character of Judgment Day; but let us avoid
eternal punishment;
Let us despise temporal things,
And think on those things which are eternal,
that we may find mercy.[22]
Let us not think that if we have sinned we are entirely cast aside,
For indeed we shall cure the wound of sin quickly
By the remedy of repentance, if we are really willing.
And now let us all pray to the Savior, crying,
"Grant slumber
To Thy servants, Lord, that we may find rest,
O most just Judge."

Strophe 24: All-holy Savior of the world, since Thou hast appeared
and raised up the nature
Which was lying in the midst of transgressions,
Invisibly reveal Thyself to me, as Merciful,
O Forbearing One,
Raise me up, I pray, as I lie in much sin,
So that I do not have to guard what I say and advise others;[23]
But I beseech Thee, grant me time for repentance,
And through the intercessions of the Virgin, Mother of God, spare me,[24]
And do not tear me from Thy sight,
O most just Judge.

21. Matt. iii.8. 22. II Cor. iv.18. 23. Ps. li.13.
24. The closing prayer is a typical part of the style of Romanos. See the Introduction. It is significant that "the mother of God" is supposed to intercede, although the poet has been clear that the judgment of the Most Just Judge is final (see the end of Strophe 19).